ABOUT THE AUTHORS

SLASH lives in Los Angeles, California, with his wife, Perla, and their two sons, London and Cash.

Former *Rolling Stone* staff writer ANTHONY BOZZA is the author of three *New York Times* bestsellers, including *Whatever You Say I Am: The Life and Times of Eminem* and *Tommyland*, the autobiography of Mötley Crüe drummer Tommy Lee. He lives in New York City.

SLASH

DEY ST.
AN IMPRINT OF
WILLIAM MORROW *PUBLISHERS*

SLASH

Slash with Anthony Bozza

DEY ST.
AN IMPRINT OF
WILLIAM MORROW *PUBLISHERS*

A hardcover edition of this book was published in 2007 by HarperEntertainment, an imprint of HarperCollins Publishers.

FIRST HARPER PAPERBACK PUBLISHED 2008.

Designed by James L. Iacobelli

Library of Congress Cataloging-in-Publication Data has been applied for.

ISBN 978-0-06-135143-3

23 24 25 26 27 LBC 31 30 29 28 27

To my loving family, for all their support through the good times and the bad

And to Guns N' Roses fans everywhere, old and new; without their undying loyalty and limitless patience, none of this would matter

Introduction

HAVING CONSIDERED ALL THINGS

viii

STOKED

xii

TWENTY-INCH-HIGH HOOLIGANS

012

HOW TO PLAY ROCK-AND-ROLL GUITAR

028

EDUCATION HIGH

048

LEAST LIKELY TO SUCCEED

072

YOU LEARN TO LIVE LIKE AN ANIMAL

100

APPETITE FOR DYSFUNCTION

136

OFF TO THE RACES

192

DON'T TRY THIS AT HOME

242

HUMPTY DUMPTY

294

CHOOSE YOUR ILLUSION

326

BREAKDOWN

382

COMING UP FOR AIR

416

IF MEMORY SERVES

454

PHOTOGRAPHY CREDITS

461

Having Considered All Things

I t felt like a baseball bat to my chest, but swung from the inside. Clear blue spots twinkled in the corners of my vision. It was abrupt, bloodless, silent violence. Nothing was visibly broken, nothing radically changed to the naked eye, but the pain made my world stand still. I kept playing; I finished the song. The audience didn't know that my heart had done a somersault just before the solo. My body had delivered its karmic retribution; reminding me, onstage, of how many times I'd intentionally served it up a chemical loop-de-loop.

The jolt quickly became a dull ache that felt good. I felt more alive than I had a moment before, because I *was* more alive. The machine in my heart had reminded me of just how precious this life is. Its timing was impeccable: with a full arena in front of me, while I played my guitar, I got the message loud and clear. I got it a few times that night. And I got it a few more times onstage after that. I didn't know when it was coming, and, as arresting as they were, I don't regret those moments of alienated clarity.

A doctor installed a defibrillator in my heart when I was thirty-five. Fifteen years of overdrinking and drug abuse had swollen that organ to one stop short of exploding. When I was finally hospitalized, they told me I had six days to six weeks to live. It's been six years since then and this piece of machinery has saved my life more than twice. I've enjoyed a convenient side effect that the doctor failed to mention: when my indulgences have caused my heart to beat too dangerously slow, my defibrillator has popped off, keeping death from my door for one more day. It also shocks my heart into submission when it beats fast enough to court cardiac arrest.

It's a good thing I got it adjusted before the first Velvet Revolver tour. I did that one sober for the most part; sober enough that the excitement of playing with a band I believed in to fans who believed in us moved me to my core. I hadn't been that inspired in years. I ran all over the stage; I basked in our collective energy. My heart raced with excitement hard enough that

it would have triggered that secret machine inside me each and every night, without a doubt. I didn't need them by then, but I had welcomed those reminders when they happened a few years earlier. I saw them for what they were. Those strange moments out of time that encapsulated a life's worth of hard-won wisdom.

SLASH

Slash's parents loved photography. This one looks like one of his dad's.

Stoked

I was born on July 23, 1965, in Hampstead, England, and raised in Stoke-on-Trent, the town where Lemmy Kilmister of Motörhead was born twenty years before me. It was the year rock and roll as we know it became greater than the sum of its parts; the year a few isolated bands changed pop music forever. The Beatles released *Rubber Soul* that year and the Stones released *Rolling Stones No. 2*, the best of their collections of blues covers. There was a creative revolution afoot that has never been equaled and I'm proud to be a by-product of it.

My mom is an African American and my dad is English and white. They met in Paris in the sixties, fell in love, and had me. Their brand of interracial intercontinental communion wasn't the norm; and neither was their boundless creativity. I thank them for being who they are. They exposed me to environments so rich and colorful and unique that what I experienced even while very young made a permanent impression on me. My parents treated me as an equal as soon as I could stand. And they taught me, on the fly, how to deal with whatever came my way in the only type of life I've ever known.

Tony Hudson and his sons, 1972. Slash looks exactly like his son London here.

My mom, Ola, was seventeen and my dad, Anthony ("Tony"), was twenty when they met. He was born a painter, and like painters historically do, he left his stuffy hometown to find himself in Paris. My mom was precocious and exuberant, young and beautiful; she'd left Los Angeles to see the world and make connections in fashion. When their journeys intersected they fell in love, then got married in England. And then I came along and they set about creating their life together.

My mom's career as a costume designer started around 1966, and over the course of it, her clients included Flip Wilson, Ringo Starr, and John Lennon. She also worked for the Pointer Sisters, Helen Reddy, Linda Ronstadt, and James Taylor. Sylvester was one of her clients, too. He is no longer with us, but he was once a disco artist who was like the gay Sly Stone. He had a great voice and he was a supergood person in my eyes; he gave me a black-and-white rat that I named Mickey. Mickey was a badass. He never flinched when I fed rats to my snakes. He survived a fall from my bedroom window after he was tossed out by my younger brother, and was no worse for the wear when he showed up at our back door three days later. Mickey also survived the accidental removal of a section of his tail when the inner chassis of our sofa bed cut it off, as well as close to a year without food or water. We left him behind by mistake in an apartment that we used as

storage space, and when we eventually popped in to pick up some boxes, Mickey came up to me congenially as if I'd been gone only a day, as if to say, "Hey! Where you been?"

Mickey was one of my more memorable pets. There have been many, from my mountain lion, Curtis, to the hundreds of snakes I've raised. Basically I am a self-taught zookeeper and I definitely relate to the animals I've lived with better than to most of the humans I've known. Those animals and I share a point of view that most people forget: at the end of the day life is about survival. Once that lesson is learned, earning the trust of an animal that might eat you in the wild is a defining and rewarding experience.

———◆•×•◆———

SOON AFTER I WAS BORN, MY MOTHER returned to L.A. to expand her business and to lay the financial foundation our family was built upon. My dad raised me in England at his parents', Charles and Sybil Hudson's, home for four years—and it wasn't easy on him. I was a pretty intuitive kid, but I could not discern the depth of the tension there. My dad and his dad, Charles, from what I understand, had less than the best relationship. Tony was the middle of three sons, and he was every bit the middle child upstart. His younger brother, Ian, and his older brother, David, were much more in step with the family's values. My dad went to art school; he was everything his father wasn't. Tony *was* the sixties; and he stood up for his beliefs as wholeheartedly as his father condemned them. My grandfather Charles was a fireman from Stoke, a community that had somehow skated through history unchanged. Most residents of Stoke never leave; many, like my grandparents, had never ventured the hundred or so miles south to London. Tony's unyielding vision of attending art school and making a living through painting was something Charles could not stomach. Their clash of opinion fueled constant arguments and often led to violent exchanges; Tony claims that Charles beat him senseless on a regular basis for most of his youth.

My grandfather was as consummately representative of 1950s Britain as his son was of the sixties. Charles wanted to see everything in its right place while Tony wanted to rearrange and repaint it all. I imagine that my grandfather was properly appalled when his son returned from Paris in love

with a carefree black American. I wonder what he said when Tony told him that he intended to be married and raise their newborn child under their roof until he and my mom got their affairs in order. All things considered, I'm touched by how much diplomacy was displayed by the parties involved.

<center>◆ ✦✕✦ ◆</center>

MY DAD TOOK ME TO LONDON AS SOON as I could handle the train ride. I was maybe two or three, but instinctively I knew how far away it was from Stoke's unending miles of brown brick row houses and quaint families because my dad was into a bit of a bohemian scene. We'd crash on couches and not come back for days. There were Lava lamps and black lights, and the electric excitement of the open booths and artists along Portobello Road. My dad never considered himself a Beat, but he had absorbed that kind of lifestyle through osmosis. It was as if he had handpicked the highlights of that type of life: a love of adventure, hitting the road with nothing but the clothes on your back, finding shelter in apartments full of interesting people. My parents taught me a lot, but I learned their greatest lesson early—nothing else is quite like life on the road.

I remember the good things about England. I was the center of my grandparents' attention. I went to school. I was in plays: *The Twelve Days of Christmas*; I was the lead in *The Little Drummer Boy*. I drew all the time. And once a week I watched *The Avengers* and *The Thunderbirds*. Television in late sixties England was extremely limited and reflected the post–World War II, Churchill view of the world of my grandparents' generation. There were only three channels back then, and aside from the two hours a week that any of them played those two programs, all three played only the news. It's no wonder that my parents' generation threw themselves headfirst into the cultural shift that was afoot.

Once Tony and I joined Ola in Los Angeles, he never spoke to his parents again. They disappeared from my life quickly and I often missed them growing up. My mother encouraged my father to stay in touch but it made no difference; he had no interest. I didn't see my English relatives again until Guns N' Roses became well known. When we played Wembley Stadium in 1992, the Hudson clan came out in force: backstage before the

show I witnessed one of my uncles, my cousin, and my grandfather, on his very first trip to London from Stoke, down every drop of liquor in our dressing room. Consumed in full, our booze rider in those days would have killed anyone but us.

———◦•✕•◦———

MY FIRST MEMORY OF LOS ANGELES IS the Doors' "Light My Fire" blasting from my parents' turntable, every day, all day long. In the late sixties and early seventies L.A. was *the* place to be, especially for young Brits involved in the arts or music: there was ample creative work compared to the still-stodgy system in England and the weather was nothing but paradise compared to London's rain and fog. Besides, deserting England for Yankee shores was the best way to flip off the system and your upbringing—and my dad was more than happy to do so.

My mother continued her work as a fashion designer while my father parlayed his natural artistic talent into graphic design. My mom had connections in the music industry so her husband was soon designing album covers. We lived off Laurel Canyon Boulevard in a very sixties community up at the top of Lookout Mountain Road. That area of Los Angeles has always been a creative haven because of the bohemian nature of the landscape. The houses are set right into the mountainside among lush foliage. They are bungalows with guesthouses and any odd number of structures that allow for very organic, communal living. There was a very cozy enclave of artists and musicians living up there when I was young: Joni Mitchell lived a few houses down from us. Jim Morrison lived behind the Canyon Store at that time, as did a young Glen Frey, who was just putting together the Eagles. It was the kind of atmosphere where everyone was connected: my mom designed Joni's clothes while my dad designed her album covers. David Geffen was a close friend of ours, too, and I remember him well. He signed Guns N' Roses years later, though when he did he didn't know who I was—and I didn't tell him. He called Ola at Christmas in 1987 and asked her how I was doing. "You should know how he's doing," she said, "you just put his band's record out."

———◦•✕•◦———

we moved south to an apartment on Doheny. I changed schools, and that is when I discovered just how differently the average kid lived. I never had a traditional "kid" room full of toys and primary colors. Our homes were never painted in common neutral tones. The essence of pot and incense usually hung in the air. The vibe was always bright, but the color scheme was always dark. It was fine with me, because I was never concerned with connecting with kids my age. I preferred the company of adults because my parents' friends are still some of the most colorful characters I've ever known.

I listened to the radio 24/7, usually KHJ on the AM dial. I slept with it on. I did my schoolwork and got good grades, although my teacher said I had a short attention span and daydreamed all the time. The truth is, my passion was art. I loved the French Postimpressionist painter Henri Rousseau and, like him, I drew jungle scenes full of my favorite animals. My obsession with snakes started very early. The first time my mother took me to Big Sur, California, to visit a friend and camp up there, I was six years old and I spent hours in the woods catching snakes. I'd dig under every bush and tree until I'd filled an unused aquarium. Then I'd let them go.

That wasn't the only excitement I experienced on that outing: my mom and her friend were similarly wild, carefree young women, who enjoyed racing my mom's Volkswagen Bug along the twisting cliffside roads. I remember speeding along in the passenger seat scared stiff, looking out my window at the rocks and ocean that lay below, just inches past my door.

Slash used to be convinced that he was a dinosaur; then he entered his Mowgli phase.

The sight of a guitar still turns me on.

MY PARENTS' RECORD COLLECTION WAS flawless. They listened to everything from Beethoven to Led Zeppelin and I continued to find undiscovered gems in their library well into my teens. I knew every artist of the day because my parents took me to concerts constantly, and since my mom took me to work with her often as well. At a very early age I was exposed to the inner workings of entertainment: I saw the inside of many recording studios and rehearsal spaces, as well as TV and film sets. I saw many of Joni Mitchell's recording and rehearsal sessions; I also saw Flip Wilson (a comic who was huge then but whom time has forgotten) record his TV show. I saw Australian pop singer Helen Reddy rehearse and perform, and was there when Linda Ronstadt played the Troubador. Mom also took me along when she outfitted Bill Cosby for his stand-up gigs and made his wife a few one-off pieces; I remember going with her to see the Pointer Sisters. All of that was over the course of her career, but when we lived at that apartment on Doheny, her business was really taking off: Carly Simon came over to the house, soul singer Minne Ripperton as well. I met Stevie Wonder and Diana Ross. My mom tells me that I met John Lennon, too, but unfortunately I don't remember that at all. I do remember meeting Ringo Starr: my mom designed the very Parliament-Funkadelic outfit that Ringo wore on the cover of his 1974 album, *Goodnight Vienna*. It was high-waisted and metallic gray with a white star in the middle of the chest.

Every backstage or soundstage scene that I saw with my mother worked some kind of strange magic on me. I had no idea what was going on, but I was fascinated by the machinations of performance back then and I still am now. A stage full of instruments awaiting a band is exciting to me. The sight of a guitar still turns me on. There is an unstated wonder in both of them: they hold the ability to transcend reality given the right set of players.

Slash and his brother, Albionn, at the La Brea Tar Pits.

MY BROTHER, ALBION, WAS BORN IN December 1972. That changed the dynamic of my family a bit; suddenly there was a new personality among us. It was cool to have a little brother, and I was glad to be one of his caretakers: I loved it when my parents would ask me to look after him.

But it wasn't too long after that that I began to notice a greater change in our family. My parents weren't the same when they were together and too often they were apart. Things started to get bad I think once we moved into the apartment on Doheny Drive and my mom's business began to really succeed. Our address was 710 North Doheny, by the way, which is now a vacant lot where Christmas trees are sold in December. I should also men-

tion that our next-door neighbor in that building was the original, self-proclaimed Black Elvis, who can be booked for parties in Las Vegas—if anyone's interested.

Now that I'm older I can see some of the obvious issues that ate away at my parents' relationship. My father never liked how close my mother was to her mother. It bruised his pride when his mother-in-law helped us financially, and he was never fond of her involvement in the family. His drinking didn't help things: my dad used to like to drink—a lot. He was a stereotypically bad drinker: he was never violent, because my dad is much too smart and complicated to ever express himself through brute violence, but he had a bad temper under the influence. When he was drunk, he'd act out by making inappropriate comments at the expense of those in his presence. Needless to say, he burned many bridges that way.

I was only eight, but I should have known that something was really wrong. My parents never treated each other with anything but respect, but in the months before they split up, they completely avoided each other. My mom was out most nights and my dad spent those nights in the kitchen, somber and alone, drinking red wine and listening to the piano compositions of Erik Satie. When my mom was home, my dad and I went out on long walks.

He walked everywhere, in England and Los Angeles. In pre–Charles Manson L.A.—before the Manson clan murdered Sharon Tate and her friends—we also used to hitchhike everywhere. L.A. was innocent before that; those murders signified the end of the utopian ideals of the sixties Flower Power era.

My childhood memories of Tony are cinematic; all of them afternoons spent looking up at him, walking by his side. It was on one of those walks that we ended up at Fatburger, where he told me that he and Mom were separating. I was devastated; the only stability I'd known was done. I didn't ask questions, I just stared at my hamburger. When my mom sat me down to explain the situation later that night, she pointed out the practical benefits: I'd have two houses to live in. I thought about that for a while, and it made sense in a way but it sounded like a lie; I nodded while she spoke but I stopped listening.

My parents' separation was amicable yet awkward because they didn't divorce until years later. They often lived within walking distance of each

other and socialized in the same circle of friends. When they split up, my little brother was just two years old, so for obvious reasons they agreed that he should be in his mother's care, but left me the option of living with either one of them so I chose to live with my mother. Ola supported us as best as she could, traveling constantly to wherever her work took her. Out of necessity, my brother and I were shuffled between my mom's house and my grandmother's home. My parents' house had always been busy, interesting, and unconventional—but it had always been stable. Once their bond was broken, though, constant transition became the norm for me.

The separation was very hard on my father and I didn't see him for quite a while. It was hard on all of us; it finally became reality to me once I saw my mother in the company of another man. That man was David Bowie.

———◆◆◆◆◆———

IN 1975, MY MOTHER STARTED WORKING closely with David Bowie while he was recording *Station to Station*; she had been designing clothes for him since *Young Americans*. So when he signed on to star in the film *The Man Who Fell to Earth* my mom was hired to do the costumes for the film, which shot in New Mexico. Along the way, she and Bowie embarked on a semi-intense affair. Looking back on it now, it might not have been that big of a deal, but at the time, it was like watching an alien land in your backyard.

After my parents split up, my mom, my brother, and I moved into a house on Rangely Drive. It was a very cool house: the walls of the living room were sky blue and emblazoned with clouds. There was a piano, and my mom's record collection took up an entire wall. It was inviting and cozy. Bowie came by often, with his wife, Angie, and their son, Zowie, in tow. The seventies were unique: it seemed entirely natural for Bowie to bring his wife and son to the home of his lover so that we might all hang out. At the time my mother practiced the same form of transcendental meditation that David did. They chanted before the shrine she maintained in the bedroom.

I accepted David once I got to know him because he's smart, funny, and intensely creative. My experience of him offstage enriched my experience of him onstage. I went to see him with my mom at the L.A. Forum in 1975,

and, as I have been so many times since, the moment he came out onstage, in character, I was captivated. His entire concert was the essence of performance. I saw the familiar elements of a man I'd gotten to know exaggerated to the extreme. He had reduced rock stardom to its roots: being a rock star is the intersection of who you are and who you want to be.

Twenty-Inch-High
Hooligans

No one expects the rug to be yanked out from under them; life-changing events usually don't announce themselves. While instinct and intuition can help provide some warning signs, they can do little to prepare you for the feeling of rootlessness that follows when fate flips your world upside down. Anger, confusion, sadness, and frustration are shaken up together inside you like a snow globe. It takes years for the emotional dust to settle as you do your best just to see through the storm.

My parents' separation was the picture of an agreeable split. There were no fights or ugly behavior, no lawyers and no courts. Yet it still took me years to come to terms with the hurt. I lost a piece of who I was and had to redefine myself on my own terms. I learned a lot, but those lessons didn't help me later on when the only other family I'd known disintegrated. I saw the signs that time, when Guns N' Roses started to come apart at the seams. But even though I did the leaving that time, the same blizzard of feelings lay in wait for me, it was every bit as hard to find my way back to my path again.

When my parents got separated, I was transformed by the sudden change. Inside I was still a good kid, but on the outside I became a problem child. Expressing my emotions is still one of my weaknesses, and what I felt then defied words, so I followed my natural inclinations—I acted out drastically and became a bit of a disciplinary problem at school.

At home, my parents' promise of a two-abode existence that wouldn't change a thing hadn't come to pass. I hardly saw my dad for the first year or so that they were apart, and when I did, it was intense and weird. As I mentioned, the divorce hit him hard and watching him adjust was difficult for me; for a while he couldn't work at all. He lived meagerly and hung out among his artist friends. When I visited with him, I was along for the ride as he and his friends hung out, drank a lot of red wine, and discussed art and literature, the conversation typically turning to Picasso, my dad's favorite artist. Dad and I would go on adventures, too, either to the library or the art museum, where we'd sit together and draw.

My mother was home less than ever; she worked constantly, traveling often to support my brother and me. We spent a lot of time with my grandmother Ola Sr., who was always our saving grace when Mom couldn't make ends meet. We also spent time with my aunt and cousins who lived in greater South Central L.A. Their house was boisterous, filled with the energy of a lot of kids. Our visits there brought some regularity to our idea of family. But all things considered, I had a lot of time on my hands and I took advantage of it.

Once I was twelve, I grew up fast. I had sex, I drank, I smoked cigarettes, I did drugs, I stole, I got kicked out of school, and on a few occasions I would have gone to jail if I hadn't been underage. I was acting out, making my life as intense and unstable as I felt inside. A trait that has always defined me really came into its own in this period: the intensity with which I pursue my interests. My primary passion, by the time I was twelve, had shifted from drawing to bicycle motocross.

In 1977, BMX racing was the newest extreme sport to follow the surf-

ing and skateboarding craze of the late sixties. It already had a few bona fide stars, such as Stu Thompson and Scott Breithaupt; a few magazines, such as *Bicycle Motocross Action* and *American Freestyler*, and more semi-pro and pro competitions were popping up constantly. My grandmother bought me a Webco and I was hooked. I started winning races and was listed in a couple of the magazines as an up-and-coming rider in the thirteen to fourteen age category. I loved it; I was ready to go pro once I'd landed a sponsor, but something was missing. My feelings weren't clear enough to me to vocalize just what BMX didn't satisfy inside me. I'd know it when I found it a few years later.

After school, I hung out at bike shops and became part of a team riding for a store called Spokes and Stuff, where I began to collect a bunch of much older friends—some of the other older guys worked at Schwinn in Santa Monica. Ten or so of us would ride around Hollywood every night and all of us but two—they were brothers—came from disturbed or broken domestic situations of some kind. We found solace in one another's company: our time spent together was the only regular companionship any of us could count on.

We would meet up every afternoon in Hollywood and ride everywhere from Culver City to the La Brea Tar Pits, treating the streets as our bike park. We'd jump off every sloped surface we could find, and whether it was midnight or the middle of rush hour, we always disrespected the pedestrians' right of way. We were just scrappy kids on twenty-inch-high bikes, but multiplied by ten, in a pack, whizzing down the sidewalk at top speed, we were a force to be reckoned with. We'd jump onto a bus bench, sometimes while some poor stranger was sitting there, we'd hop fire hydrants, and we'd compete constantly to outdo one another. We were disillusioned teenagers trying to navigate difficult times in our lives, and we did so by bunny-hopping all over the sidewalks of L.A.

We'd ride this dirt track out in the Valley, by the youth center in Reseda. It was about fifteen miles away from Hollywood, which is an ambitious goal on a BMX bike. We used to hitch rides on bumpers over Laurel Canyon Boulevard to cut down on our travel time. It's nothing I'd advise, but we treated passing cars like seats on a ski chairlift: we'd wait on

the shoulder, then one by one we'd grab a car and ride it up the hill. Balancing a bike, even one with a low center of gravity, while holding on to a car driving thirty or forty miles an hour is thrilling but tricky on flat ground; attempting it on a series of tight uphill S curves like Laurel Canyon is something else. I'm still not sure how none of us were ever run over. It surprises me more to remember that I did that ride, both up and down hill, without brakes more often than not. In my mind, being the youngest meant that I had something to prove to my friends every time we rode: judging by the looks on their faces after some of my stunts, I succeeded. They might have been only teenagers but my friends weren't easily impressed.

To tell you the truth, we were a gnarly little gang. One of them was Danny McCracken. He was sixteen; a strong, heavy, silent type, he was already a guy everyone instinctively knew not to fuck with. One night Danny and I stole a bike with bent forks and while he deliberately bunny-hopped it to break the forks and make us all laugh, he fell over the handlebars and slashed his wrist wide open. I saw it coming and watched it as if in slow-motion as blood started squirting everywhere.

"Ahhh!" Danny shouted. Even in pain, Danny's voice was oddly soft-spoken considering his size—kind of like Mike Tyson's.

"Holy shit!"

"Fuck!"

"Danny's fucked up!"

Danny lived just around the corner, so two of us held our hands over his wrist as blood kept squirting out between our fingers as we walked him home.

We got to his porch and rang the bell. His mom came to the door and we showed her Danny's wrist. She looked at us unfazed, in disbelief.

"What the *fuck* do you want me to do about it?" she said, and slammed the door.

We didn't know what to do; by this time Danny's face was pale. We didn't even know where the nearest hospital was. We walked him back down the street, blood still spurting all over us, and flagged down the first car we saw.

I stuck my head in the window. "Hey, my friend is bleeding to death,

can you take him to the hospital?" I said hysterically. "He's gonna die!" Luckily the lady driving was a nurse.

She put Danny in the front seat and we followed her car on our bikes. When he got to the emergency room, Danny didn't have to wait; blood was pumping out of his wrist like a victim in a horror movie so they admitted him immediately, as the mob of people in the waiting room looked on, pissed. The doctors stitched up his wrist but that wasn't the end of it: when he was released into the waiting room where we were waiting for him, he somehow popped one of his newly sewn stitches, sending a stream of blood skyward that left a trail across the ceiling, which freaked out and disgusted everyone in range. Needless to say, he was readmitted; his second round of sutures did the trick.

<hr>

THE ONLY STABLE ONES IN OUR GANG were John and Mike, who we called the Cowabunga Brothers. They were stable for these reasons: they were from the Valley, where the typical American suburban life thrived, their parents were intact, they had sisters, and all of them lived together in a nice quaint house. But they weren't the only pair of brothers: there were also Jeff and Chris Griffin; Jeff worked at Schwinn and Chris was his younger brother. Jeff was the most adult of our crew; he was eighteen and he had a job that he took seriously. These two weren't as functional as the Cowabungas, because Chris tried desperately to be like his older brother and failed miserably. Those two had a hot sister named Tracey, who had dyed her hair black in response to the fact that her entire family was naturally blond. Tracey had this whole little Goth style going before Goth was even a scene.

And there was Jonathan Watts, who was the biggest head case among us. He was just insane; he would do anything, regardless of the bodily harm or potential incarceration that might befall him. I was only twelve, but even so, I knew enough about music and people to find it a bit odd that Jonathan *and* his dad were dedicated Jethro Tull fans. I mean, they *worshipped* Jethro Tull. I'm sorry to say that Jonathan is no longer with us; he died tragically of an overdose after he'd spent years as both a raging alcoholic and then a flag-waver for Alcoholics Anonymous. I lost touch with

him way back, but I saw him again at an AA meeting that I was ordered to attend (we'll get to all of that in just a little bit), after I was arrested one night in the late eighties. I couldn't believe it; I walked into this meeting and was listening to all of these people speak and, after a while, realized that the guy leading the meeting, the one who was as gung ho about sobriety as Lieutenant Bill Kilgore, Robert Duval's character in *Apocalypse Now*, had been about surfing, was none other than Jonathan Watts. Time is such a powerful catalyst for change; you never know how kindred souls will end up—or where they might see each other again.

Back then, those guys and I spent many an evening at Laurel Elementary School, making very creative use of their playground. It was a hangout for every Hollywood kid with a bike, a skateboard, some booze to drink, or some weed to smoke. The playground had two levels connected by long concrete ramps; it begged to be abused by skaters and bikers. We took full advantage of it by deconstructing the playground's picnic tables to make them into jumps that linked the two levels. I'm not proud of our chronic destruction of public property, but riding down those two ramps and launching over the fence on my bike was a thrill that was well worth it. As delinquent as it was, it also drew creative types, many kids in Hollywood who went on to do great things hung out there. I remember Mike Balzary, better known as Flea, hanging out, playing his trumpet and graffiti artists putting up murals all the time. It wasn't the right forum, but everyone there took pride in the scene we created. Unfortunately, the students and teachers of that school were left paying the bill and cleaning up the aftermath every morning.

The principal unwisely decided to take matters into his own hands by lying in wait to confront us one night. It didn't go over well; we kept taunting him, he got too worked up, and my friends and I got into it with him. It got out of hand so quickly that a passerby called the cops. Nothing scatters a pack of kids like the sound of a siren, so most of those present escaped. Unfortunately, I wasn't one of them. Another kid and I were the only two who were caught; we were handcuffed to the handrail in the front of the school, right on the street, on display for all to see. We were like two hog-tied animals, going nowhere and none too happy about it. We refused to cooperate: we cracked wise, we gave them fake names, we did everything

Slash jumping out at the track on his Cook Bros. bike.

short of oinking at them and calling them pigs. They kept asking and did their best to scare us, but we refused to reveal our names and addresses, and since twelve-year-olds don't carry ID, they were forced to let us go.

<div align="center">※</div>

PUBERTY KICKED IN FOR ME AROUND thirteen, while I attended Bancroft Junior High in Hollywood. Whatever I was feeling about my family breaking up took a backseat to the intense surging of hormones. Sitting through a whole day of school seemed pointless, so I started to cut. I began smoking pot regularly and riding my bike intensely. I found it hard to control myself; I just wanted to do whatever I wanted to do at a moment's notice. One night while my friends and I were scheming about how to break into Spokes and Stuff— the same bike store where we hung out—for what reason I can't remember, I noticed a kid spying on us through the window of an apartment across the alley.

"What are you lookin' at?" I yelled. "Don't look at me!" Then I threw a brick through the kid's window.

His parents called the cops, of course, and the duo that responded to the call chased my friends and me all over town for the rest of the night. We biked for our lives all over Hollywood and West Hollywood; we turned down one-way streets into on-coming traffic, we cut through alleys and through parks. They were as tenacious as Jimmy "Popeye" Doyle, Gene Hackman's character in *The French Connection*; every time we turned a corner, they were there. Eventually we fled into the Hollywood Hills and hid in an out-of-the-way canyon like a pack of Wild West outlaws. And just the way it goes down in a cowboy movie, when we thought it was safe to leave the hideout and head back to the ranch, we were headed off at the pass by the same two deputies.

I assume it was because I was the smallest that they decided to chase me when my friends and I split up. I rode hard, all over the neighborhood, unable to shake them, until I finally sought refuge in an underground parking garage. I flew down a few levels, weaving between parked cars, hid in a dark corner, and lay on the ground, hoping they wouldn't catch me. They had run down there on foot and by the time they got to my

level I think they were over it. They vigilantly searched between the cars with their flashlights; about hundred feet away from me they turned back. I got lucky. This battle between my friends and the LAPD continued for the rest of the summer and it certainly wasn't a constructive use of my time, but in my mind, at that point, that's what I considered fun.

I was pretty good at keeping my affairs to myself even back then, but when I slipped up, my mother and grandmother were very forgiving. I was home as little as possible by the middle of junior high. In the summer of 1978, I had no idea that my grandmother was moving into a unit in a monstrous new complex that occupied an entire block between Kings Road and Santa Monica Boulevard, although I knew the building well because I'd been riding my bike through it since it was a construction site. My friends and I would get high and race one another through the hallways and down the stairwells, slamming doors in one another's faces, jumping onto banisters, and leaving creatively shaped skid marks on the freshly painted walls. We were in the midst of doing so when I came screaming around a corner and nearly bowled over my mother and grandmother, who were carrying armloads of Ola Sr.'s belongings into her new apartment. I'll never forget the look on my grandmother's face; it was somewhere between shock and horror. I collected myself and shot a look over my shoulder, where I saw the last of my friends take a hard turn out of sight. I had one leg on the ground, one on a pedal, still thinking that I might get away.

"Saul?" Ola Sr. said, in her too-sweet, high-pitched grandmother voice. "Is that *you*?"

"Yes Grandma," I said. "It's me. How are you doing? My friends and I were just coming by to visit."

That shit didn't fly at all with my mom, but Ola Sr. was so glad to see me that Ola Jr. let me get away with it. In fact, it all worked out so well in the end that a few weeks later I moved into that very apartment, and that's when my junior varsity exploits in Hollywood really began to take off. But we'll get to all of that in just a little bit.

———◆※◆———

I'M NOT GOING TO OVERANALYZE WHAT became my other new interest—kleptomania—aside from saying that I

Tearing up the bike track out by the Youth Center in Reseda.

was a pissed-off early adolescent. I stole what I thought I needed but couldn't afford. I stole what I thought might make me happy; and sometimes I stole just to steal.

I stole a lot of books, because I've always loved to read; I stole a ton of cassettes, because I've always loved music. Cassettes, for those too young to have known them, had their disadvantages: the sound quality wore down, they got tangled in tape machines, and they melted in direct sunlight. But they were a breeze to lift. They are like a thinner pack of cigarettes, so an ambitious shoplifter could stuff a bands' entire catalog in their clothes and walk away unnoticed.

At my worst, I'd steal as much as my clothes could hide, then dump my payload in the bushes and go steal more, sometimes at the same store. One afternoon I stole a few snakes from the Aquarium Stock Company, a pet store that I used to hang out in so much that once they got used to my presence I don't think they'd ever considered that I'd steal from them. They weren't complete suckers; I was there out of a true love for the animals they stocked—I just didn't respect the store enough not to take a few home with me. I'd snatch snakes by wrapping them around my wrists and then putting my jacket on, making sure that they were nestled high enough on my forearm. One day I really went to town and took a load of them, which I stashed somewhere outside while I returned to the store to steal books that would teach me how to care for the rare snakes I'd just stolen.

On another occasion I lifted a Jackson's chameleon, which isn't exactly a subtle steal: they are the horned chameleons that measure about ten inches and feed on flies; they are as big as small iguanas and have those strange, protruding, pyramid-like eyes. I had a lot of balls when I was a kid—I just walked right out of the store with it, and it was a very expensive, exotic member of the pet store jungle. As I walked home with the little guy, I couldn't come up with a story that would adequately explain his presence in my room to my mom. I decided that my only option was to let him live outside, on the vine-covered chain-link fence at the back of our yard, by our garbage cans. I'd stolen a book on Jackson's chameleons, so I knew that they love to eat flies, and I couldn't think of a better place for Old Jack to find flies than by the fence behind our garbage

cans—because there were plenty to be had. It was an adventure finding him every day because he was so skilled at fading into his environment, as chameleons are known to do. It always took me some time to locate him and I loved the challenge. This arrangement lasted for about five months; after a while, he got better and better at hiding among the vines, until the day I just couldn't find him at all. I went out there each afternoon for two months, but it was no use. I have no idea what happened to Old Jack, but considering the myriad possibilities that might have befallen him I hope that it ended well.

I'm very lucky not to have been caught for the majority of my shoplifting exploits, because they were pretty extensive. It got this stupid: on a dare, I lifted an inflated rubber raft from a sporting goods store. It took some planning but I pulled it off, and somehow I *didn't get caught.*

It's no big deal; I'll reveal my "methods," such as they were: the raft was hung on a wall near the back door of the store, near the hallway that ran right into the back alleyway. Once I managed to get that back door open without arousing suspicion, pulling the raft off the wall was easy. And once the raft was off the wall and on the floor, hidden from general view by some display of camping gear or whatever, I just waited for the right moment to carry it outside and walk it around the corner to where my friends were waiting for me. I didn't even keep that raft. Once I'd proved that I'd pulled that dare off I dumped it one block away on someone's front lawn.

I'm not proud of it, but all things considered, when I was ten miles from home with no money and my bike got a flat, I'm glad that it was easy for me to steal an inner tube from Toys "R" Us. Otherwise, I might have been out there hitching home into God only knows what kind of situations. Still, like anyone who repeatedly tempts fate, I must admit that however often you convince yourself that your actions are necessary when you know that they're not quite right, they will catch up to you in the end.

In my case, in as much as we're talking about shoplifting, in the end, I got nabbed at Tower Records on Sunset Boulevard, which was my parents' favorite record shop. I remember that day all too clearly: it was one

of those moments when I'd known something was wrong but embarked on the adventure anyway. I was fifteen, I think, and I remember thinking, as I parked my BMX bike outside, that I should be careful in this store in the future. That revelation didn't help me in the short term: I greedily stuffed cassettes in my jacket, down my pants, and glutted my clothing so much that I thought I should probably buy a few albums just to throw the cashiers off. I believe I walked up to the counter with Cheap Trick's *Dream Police* and Led Zeppelin's *Houses of the Holy*, and after I was rung up, I was home free in my mind.

I was outside, straddling my bike, ready to jam when a hand clamped down hard on my shoulder. I denied everything but I was busted; they brought me up to the room above the store where they'd been watching me steal through the one-way window and they showed me the footage. They called my mom; I gave up all of the tapes in my pants and they arranged them on a table for her to see when she got there. I got away with a lot as a kid, but getting busted for shoplifting cassettes at the store my parents had frequented for so many years was an offense that meant more within the confines of our family than it did within the letter of the law. I'll never forget Ola's expression when she came up to that office above the store and found me sitting there with everything I'd stolen laid out before me. She didn't say much, and she didn't have to; it was clear to me that she was over thinking that I could do no wrong.

In the end, Tower didn't press charges because all of the merchandise was recovered. They let me go on the condition that I would never set foot in their store again, most likely because some manager there recognized that my mom was a well-liked regular.

Of course, when I was hired at the very same store six years later in the video division, during every shift for the first six months, I was convinced that someone was going to remember that I'd been caught stealing and have me fired. I figured that any day now, someone would figure out that I had blatantly lied on my application form and presumed what I knew to be true: that what I did manage to lift until I was caught was worth more than a few months' paychecks.

———— ❖◆❖◆❖ ————

usually we had weed, which was always a crowd pleaser.

ALL OF THOSE PERMUTATIONS WERE going to work themselves out over the next eight years of my life, but only once I'd found a stable family of my own design.

In the vacuum that my family's dissolution left in its wake, I made my own world. I'm lucky enough that, despite my age, during a period of testing my boundaries, I made one friend who has never been far from me, even when we've been worlds apart. He is still one of my closest confidants, which, after thirty years, says a fuck of a lot.

His name is Marc Canter; his family owns the famous L.A. institution Canter's Deli on North Fairfax. The Canter family moved from New Jersey and opened the restaurant in the 1940s and it's been a hub for show-business types ever since, because of the food and the fact that it's open twenty-four hours. It's only a half mile from the Sunset Strip, and in the sixties it became a haven for musicians and has remained so ever since. In the eighties, bands like Guns had many a late-night meal there. The Kibbitz Room, which is their bar and live music venue next door has hosted too many great nights of music to name. The Canters have been wonderful to me; they've employed me, they've sheltered me, and I can't thank them enough.

I met Marc at Third Street Elementary School, but we didn't really become friends until I almost stole his mini bike in fifth grade.

Our friendship was solidified from the start. He and I hung out in Hancock Park, which was next to the affluent neighborhood where he lived. We used to go down to the ruins of the Pan Pacific Theater, which is where the Grove shopping center is today. The Pan Pacific was an

amazing relic; it had been a glamorous 1940s movie palace, with an arched ceiling and huge screen that showed news reels and defined a generation's worth of cinematic culture. In my day, it was still beautiful: the green Art Deco arches were still intact, though the rest was reduced to rubble. Next to the lot was a public library and a park with a basketball court and a pool. Like Laurel Elementary, it was a meeting point for kids aged twelve to eighteen, who, for one reason or another, found their way out at night.

My friends and I were the young ones on the scene; there were chicks so far out of our league that we couldn't even count the ways—though we did anyway. There were flunkies and dropouts, many of whom lived in the ruins of the theater and subsisted on the food they stole from the farmers' market that took place next door twice a week. Marc and I were fascinated; we gained acceptance among them because usually we had weed, which was always a crowd pleaser. Meeting Marc triggered a change in me; he was my first best friend—he was someone who understood me when I felt no one else did. Neither of us have had lives that one might call normal, but I'm proud to say that we're just as close as we were then. That is my definition of family. A friend still knows you as well as they used to even if you haven't seen them in years. A true friend is there when you need him; they're not around just on holidays and weekends.

I found that out firsthand a few years later. When I barely had money to eat, I didn't care, so long as I had money to promote Guns N' Roses. And when I didn't have money to print flyers or even buy myself guitar strings, Marc Canter was there for me. He'd front me the cash to take care of whatever needed to be done. I paid him back once I was able, once Guns got signed, but I never forgot that Canter was there for me when I was down and out.

How to Play Rock-and-Roll Guitar

Slash rocking with Tidus Sloan, June 1982.

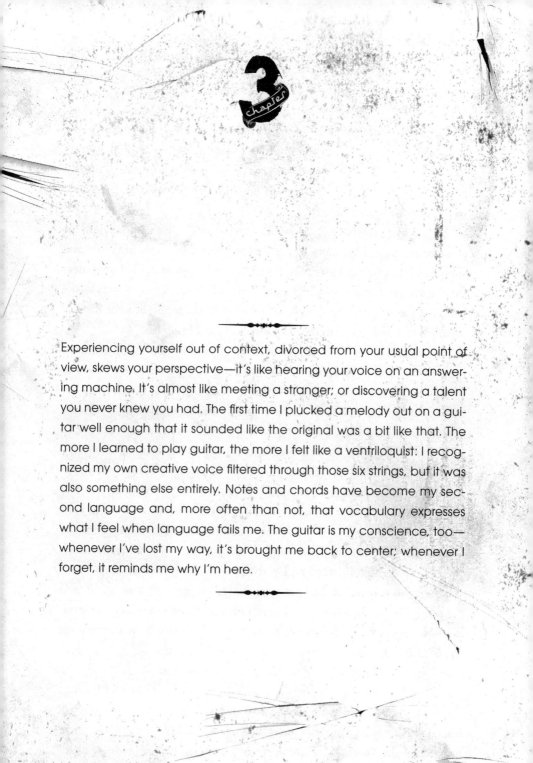

3
chapter

Experiencing yourself out of context, divorced from your usual point of view, skews your perspective—it's like hearing your voice on an answering machine. It's almost like meeting a stranger; or discovering a talent you never knew you had. The first time I plucked a melody out on a guitar well enough that it sounded like the original was a bit like that. The more I learned to play guitar, the more I felt like a ventriloquist: I recognized my own creative voice filtered through those six strings, but it was also something else entirely. Notes and chords have become my second language and, more often than not, that vocabulary expresses what I feel when language fails me. The guitar is my conscience, too—whenever I've lost my way, it's brought me back to center; whenever I forget, it reminds me why I'm here.

I owe it all to Steven Adler—he did it. He is the reason that I play guitar. We met one night at the Laurel Elementary playground when we were thirteen. As I remember it, he was skateboarding miserably. After a particularly hard fall, I rode over on my bike and helped him up and we were instantly inseparable.

Steven had grown up in the Valley with his mom, his stepdad, and his two brothers until his mom couldn't take his bad behavior anymore and shipped him off to live with his grandparents in Hollywood. He lasted there for the remainder of junior high, summers included, before he was bused back to his mom to attend high school. Steven is special; he's the kind of misfit that only a grandmother can love, but can't live with.

Steven and I met the summer before eighth grade and hung out until high school, since I had just moved into my grandmother's new condo in Hollywood, from my mom's apartment in Hancock Park. Both of us were new to our school, Bancroft Junior High, as well as to the neighborhood. As long as I knew him, Steven never spent a full week's worth of time in school out of any given month. I got by because I did well enough in my art, music, and English classes that my grade-point average was high enough to pass. I got As in art, English, and music because those were the only subjects that interested me. Apart from those I didn't care for much else, and I cut class all the time. Since I had stolen a pad of absentee notices from the administration offices and forged my mom's signature when I needed to, in the eyes of the administration, I was there much more often than I ever was. But the only reason I actually graduated junior high at all was due to a teachers' strike during my final year. Our regular teachers were replaced by substitutes who were too easy for me to bullshit and charm. I don't want to get into it, but on more than one occasion I recall playing my teacher's favorite song on guitar for the entire class. Enough said.

To be honest, school wasn't too bad: I had a whole circle of friends, including a girlfriend (who we'll get to in just a little bit) and I partook liberally in every exercise that makes school enjoyable to stoners. Our crew met in the early morning before homeroom to snort locker room—a head-

shop brand of amyl nitrite, a chemical whose fumes expand your blood vessels and lower your blood pressure and in the process give you a brief euphoric rush. After a few hits of locker room, we'd smoke a few cigarettes and at lunchtime reconvene in the courtyard to smoke a joint. . . . We did what we could to make the school day pleasant.

When I didn't go to school, Steven and I spent the day wandering the greater Hollywood area with our heads in the clouds talking about music and hustling money. We did some offhand panhandling and odd jobs, like moving furniture for some of the random characters we'd meet. Hollywood has always been a weird place that attracts odd folks, but in the late seventies, with the strange turns culture had taken, from the letdown of the sixties revolution to the widespread use of drugs and loosened sexual mores, there were some really strange ones hanging around.

I don't remember how we met him, but there was one older guy who used to give us money for nothing. We'd just hang out and talk to him; I think he asked us to go to the store a couple of times. I definitely thought it was weird, but he wasn't threatening enough to do anything a couple of thirteen-year-olds couldn't handle. Besides, the extra pocket cash was worth it.

Steve had no inhibitions whatsoever, so he managed to acquire money on a regular basis in many ways, one of which was from Clarissa, a neighbor of mine in her mid-twenties who lived down the street. One day we saw her sitting on her porch when we passed by and Steven felt the inclination to say hi to her. They started talking and she invited us in; we hung out there for a while and then I decided to take off, but Steven said that he was going to stay there a little while longer. It turns out that he had sex with her that night *and* got money off her to boot. I have no idea how he did it, but I do know that he was with her four or five times more, and got money *every single time*. It was unbelievable to me; I was really envious.

But then again, Steven would always get involved in situations like that and they often didn't have a happy ending. In this case, he was in the middle of screwing Clarissa when her gay roommate walked in on them. She threw Steven off her and he landed hard-on first on her bedroom floor, and that was the end of that.

Steven and I got by; I stole all the music and rock magazines that we needed. There weren't too many other things that we cared to spend money

on aside from Big Gulps and cigarettes, so we were in good shape. We'd walk up and down Sunset Boulevard, then Hollywood Boulevard from Sunset to Doheny, checking out rock posters in the many head shops or ducking into whichever souvenir or music store looked exciting to us. We'd just wander, taking in the animated reality going on down there. We used to hang out at place called Piece O' Pizza for hours, playing Van Halen on the jukebox over and over. It was a ritual by then: Steven had played their first record for me a few months before. It was one of those moments where a new body of music totally overwhelmed me.

"You've got to hear this," Steven said, all wide-eyed. "It's this band Van Halen, they're awesome!" I had my doubts because Steven and I didn't always see eye to eye musically. He put the record on, and Eddie's solo that sets off "Eruption" came shredding through the speakers. "Jesus Christ," I said, "what the hell is *that*?"

it was a form of expression as satisfying and personal to me as art and drawing, but on a much deeper level.

that year, too. It was the California World Music Festival at the L.A.
Memorial Coliseum on April 8, 1979. There were 110,000 people there
and the lineup was insane: there were a ton of bands, but the headliners were
Ted Nugent, Cheap Trick, Aerosmith, and Van Halen. Without a doubt,
Van Halen crushed every other band who played that day, even Aerosmith.
I guess it wasn't hard: Aerosmith was so fucked up at the time that it was
impossible for me to differentiate one song from another in their set. I was
a fan, and the only track I recognized at all was "Seasons of Wither."

Eventually Steve and I graduated to hanging around outside the Rain-
bow and the Starwood amid the whole pre-glam metal scene. Van Halen
cut their teeth on that circuit and Mötley Crüe was about to do the same;
aside from bands like that, there were the earliest traces of L.A. punk rock
going around. There were always a ton of people outside the clubs and since
I had access to drugs, I'd sell them not just for cash, but to get us closer to
the scene. In junior high, I figured out a better method: I started making
fake IDs, which served to actually get me inside the scene.

There was so much activity in West Hollywood and Hollywood at night:
the whole homosexual scene—around a posh gay restaurant, the French
Quarter, and gay bars like the Rusty Nail, among others smashed right up
against the mostly hetero rock scene. That whole juxtaposition was bizarre
to Steven and me. There were just so many freaks everywhere and we liked
to take it all in, as strange and nonsensical as most of it was.

Steve and I got into all sorts of seemingly harmless trouble growing up.
One night my dad took us to a party thrown by a group of his artist friends
who lived in houses along a cul de sac up in Laurel Canyon. The host, my
dad's friend Alexis, made a vat of horrendously lethal punch that got ev-
eryone completely gassed. Growing up in the Valley, Steven had never seen
a scene that cool: this was a group of artistically out-there post-hippie adults,
so the combination of the crowd and the punch completely blew his mind.
He and I could hold our liquor for thirteen-year-olds, but this stuff was
way too advanced for us. I was so fried that I didn't notice Steve slip out
with the girl who lived in the guesthouse downstairs. He ended up fucking
her, which turned out to not be such a cool thing: she was married and in
her thirties. In my thirteen-year-old mind, she was a senior citizen. To me,

Steve had just fucked an old lady . . . who also happened to be someone else's old lady.

In the morning, I woke up on the floor with the taste of that punch in my mouth, feeling like an iron spike had been nailed through my head. I went home to my grandmother's to sleep it off; Steven remained behind, opting to linger in bed downstairs. I was home for about ten minutes when my dad called to let me know that Steven should fear for his life. The woman he had spent the evening with had confessed and her husband was *very* unhappy about it. The man, according to my dad, planned to "throttle" Steven, which Tony assured me was a very real threat. When I didn't seem to take him seriously, Dad told me that the guy had actually promised to kill Steven. In the end, nothing happened, so Steven got away with it but it was a clear indication of things to come. At thirteen, he had narrowed his life goals down to exactly two: fucking chicks and being in a rock band. I can't fault him for his prescience.

In his thirteen-year-old musical wisdom, which (probably due to his advanced womanizing skills) I considered superior to mine, Steven had concluded that there were only three bands that mattered in rock and roll: Kiss, Boston, and Queen. Steven paid tribute to them every day, all day, when he should have been in school. His grandmother worked in a bakery and left the house at five a.m. each day; she had no idea that Steven rarely went to class. His day consisted of playing Kiss records turned up to ten, while bashing away at a little Wal-Mart electric guitar and amp, both turned up to ten as well. I'd go over and hang out with him, and he'd be yelling at me over all the noise, "*Hey!* We should start a band, you know!?"

Steven has such an open, carefree soul that his enthusiasm is tremendously contagious. I didn't doubt his intention and drive; I was convinced immediately that it would happen. He had elected himself the guitar player, and we decided that I would play bass. When I listen to music now, after twenty-five years of playing, I can isolate all of the instruments; I can hear the key of the guitar and right away I can usually think of several ways to play the song. By the time I was thirteen, I had listened to rock and roll for years; I'd seen concerts and knew what instruments make up a rock band, but I had no idea which instrument made each sound in the music. I knew

what a guitar was, but I had no idea of the differences between a guitar and a bass and Steven's playing at the time didn't enlighten me at all.

When he and I would walk around town, we used to pass a music school on Fairfax and Santa Monica called Fairfax Music School (today it's a chiropractor's office), so I figured that was a good place to learn to play bass. So one day I stopped in, walked up to the desk, and just said, "I want to play bass." The receptionist introduced me to one of the teachers, a guy named Robert Wolin. When Robert came out to talk to me, he wasn't exactly what I expected: he was a medium-sized white guy wearing Levi's and a tucked-in plaid shirt. He had a bushy mustache, a five o'clock shadow, and unkempt shaggy brown hair—it had probably been a real haircut once, but it had gotten away from him. Needless to say, Robert didn't look like a rock star at all.

He did, however, patiently inform me that I'd need an actual bass of my own to take lessons, which was something I hadn't considered. I asked my grandmother for help and she gave me an old flamenco guitar with one nylon string on it that she had packed away in a closet. When I met Robert again at the school, he took one look at my guitar and understood that he'd better start at the very beginning, because I had no idea that what I was holding wasn't necessarily a bass. Robert put on the Stones' "Brown Sugar," picked up his guitar, and played along with the riff and the lead. And that's when I heard *the sound*. Whatever Robert was doing, that was *it*. I stared at Robert's guitar with total wonder. I started pointing at it.

"*That's* what I want to do," I told him. "*That.*"

Robert was really encouraging; he drew some chord charts for me, showed me proper fingering on his guitar, and tuned the one string I had. He also informed me that I should get the remaining five strings in the very near future. Guitar came into my life that suddenly and that innocently. There was no thought, no premeditation; it wasn't part of a grand plan outside of playing in Steven's fantasy band. Ten years later I would be, with all the perks that Steven had dreamed about: traveling the world, playing sold-out shows, and having more chicks at our disposal than we could handle . . . all thanks to that battered piece of wood my grandmother dug out of her closet.

Guitar replaced BMX as my main obsession literally overnight. It was unlike anything I'd ever done: it was a form of expression as satisfying and personal to me as art and drawing, but on a much deeper level. Being able to create the sound that had spoken to me in music ever since I can remember was more empowering than anything I'd ever known. The change was as instantaneous as turning on a light, and every bit as illuminating. I went home from music school and copied Robert's methods, putting on my favorite songs and doing my best to play along. I did what I could with one string; after a few hours I could follow the key changes and mimic the melody of a few songs in the most remedial way. Tunes like Deep Purple's "Smoke on the Water," Chicago's "25 or 6 to 4," Led Zeppelin's "Dazed and Confused," and Jimi Hendrix's "Hey Joe" can be played down the E string so I contented myself with those over and over again. Simply the understanding that I could mimic the songs on my stereo was enough to imprint the guitar on my reality forever.

I took lessons from Robert on my worn-out flamenco guitar throughout the summer before ninth grade—with all six strings in place, which, of course, he taught me how to tune. I was always amazed when he put on a record that he didn't know and learned it on the spot in a few minutes. I set about achieving that ability for myself: like every overeager beginner, I tried to jump to that level straightaway and, like every good teacher, Robert forced me to master the fundamentals. He taught me basic major, minor, and blues scales and all of the standard chord positions. He'd also sketch chord charts to my favorite songs, such as "Jumpin' Jack Flash" and "Whole Lotta Love," that I was to play as my reward once I'd done the week's exercises. Usually I'd skip straight to the reward and when I showed up at the music school the next day, it was obvious to Robert that I hadn't even touched my homework. Sometimes I liked to play as if I still had only one string. Every song I liked had a riff in it, so playing it all up and down one string was more fun until my fingers learned the proper form.

My BMX racing gear gathered dust in my closet. My friends wondered where I was at night. I saw Danny McCracken one day while I was riding back from music school, my guitar slung over my back. He asked me where I'd been and if I'd won any races lately. I told him that I was a guitar player now. He sized me up, looked at my worn-out six-string, and stared hard

right into my eyes. "Oh yeah?" He had a very confused look on his face, as if he wasn't sure what to make of what I'd told him. We sat there awkwardly in silence for a minute on our bikes then said our good-byes. It was the last time I ever saw him.

I respected my guitar teacher, Robert, but I naively and impatiently failed to see the direct line between the fundamentals he was teaching me and the Rolling Stones and Led Zeppelin songs that I wanted to play. It all came to a head soon enough, once I discovered my personal instruction manual, so to speak; it was a used book I found in a guitar store bargain bin called *How to Play Rock Guitar*. This book had all of the chord charts, tablature, and sample solos from greats like Eric Clapton, Johnny Winter, and Jimi Hendrix. It even came with a little floppy 45 that demonstrated the proper way to play what was in the book. I took that thing home and devoured it, and once I was capable of mimicking the sounds on that little record, I was soon improvising on my own, and then I was *beside myself*. Once I'd heard myself lay down patterns that sounded like rock-and-roll lead guitar it was as if I'd found the Holy Grail. That book changed my life; I still have my worn-out copy in a trunk somewhere and I've never seen another one before or since. I've looked for it plenty of times to no avail. I feel like it was the only copy left in the world and that it was there that day waiting specifically for me. That book gave me the skills I sought and once I'd begun to master them I quit music school forever.

I was now a "rock guitar player," as far as I was concerned, so out of necessity, I borrowed one hundred bucks from my grandmother and bought an electric guitar. It was a very cheap Les Paul copy made by a company called Memphis Guitars. I was attracted to the shape, because most of my favorite players played Les Pauls—it epitomized rock guitar to me. That said, I didn't know enough to even know who Les Paul was; I wasn't acquainted with his sublime jazz playing and had no idea that he had pioneered the development of electric instruments, effects, and recording techniques. I didn't know that his brand of solid body guitar would soon become my primary choice of instrument. And I had no idea at all that I'd enjoy the honor of sharing a stage with him many times, many years later. Nope, that day it was pretty basic; in my mind, that shape visually represented the sound I wanted to make.

FINDING GUITAR WAS LIKE FINDING MYSELF;
it defined me, it gave me a purpose. It was a creative outlet that allowed me
to understand myself. The turmoil of my adolescence was suddenly secondary;
playing guitar gave me focus. I didn't keep a journal; I couldn't seem to vocal-
ize my feelings in a constructive fashion, but the guitar gave me emotional
clarity. I loved to draw; that was an activity that took my mind off things, but
it wasn't enough of a vehicle for me to completely express myself. I've always
envied the artists who could express themselves through art, and only through
the guitar have I come to understand what a wonderful release it is.

Practicing for hours wherever I found myself was liberating. Playing
became a trance that soothed my soul: with my hands occupied and my
mind engaged, I found peace. Once I got into a band, I found that the
physical exertion of playing a show became my primary personal release;
when I'm playing onstage I'm more at home in my own skin than at any
other time in my life. There is a subconscious, emotional level that informs
playing, and since I'm the kind of person who carries his baggage around
internally, nothing has ever helped me tap into my feelings more.

Finding my voice through guitar at fifteen was, to me, revolutionary. It
was a leap in my evolution; I can't think of anything that made more of a
difference in my life. The only moment that came close had occurred two
years before when I first experienced the mystery of the opposite sex. Once
I'd done it, I didn't think that anything was better than sex . . . until I played
guitar. And soon after that I found out that those two pursuits couldn't
coexist peacefully in my teenage world.

My first girlfriend was named Melissa. She was a cute, kind of chubby
girl with great tits, who was one year younger than me. She was twelve
and I was thirteen when we lost our virginity to each other. That isn't
shocking by today's standards, when teens engage in very adult practices
earlier than ever, but in 1978, she and I were ahead of the curve: most of
our peers were still French kissing. We both inherently knew not to mess
with a good thing, so we stayed together, on and off, for years. The first
time we did anything was in the laundry room of her apartment building,
which was on the first floor, in the back of the building. She jerked me off;

it was a first for both of us. Eventually we moved it to the one-bedroom apartment that she shared with her mom, Carolyn. Unfortunately, the first time we did, Carolyn came home early, so I had to crawl through Melissa's bedroom window with my pants around my ankles. Luckily the bushes were forgiving.

Things got hot and heavy between us pretty quickly; when her mom wasn't home, we did it in Melissa's bed, and when she was home, we did it on the couch after Carolyn passed out on Valium, hoping she wouldn't wake up and catch us. Of course, trying to wait for Carolyn's Valium to kick in wasn't always easy. It was soon after Melissa and Carolyn moved upstairs to a two-bedroom that her mother resigned herself to what we were up to. She decided that it was better that we do it in her home than elsewhere and told us as much. According to Melissa and me, from our sexually ravenous, adolescent point of view, her mom was *the coolest*.

Caroyln smoked a ton of pot and was very open about it; she would roll us perfect joints and allowed me to stay with them, sleeping in Melissa's room, for weeks at a time. Since we got together during the summer, my mom didn't mind. Her mother didn't work; she had a very nice, much older drug-dealer boyfriend who sold coke, pot, and acid, all of which he would give to us freely, provided we enjoyed it all in-house.

Their apartment building was on Edinburgh and Willoughby, about two blocks west of Fairfax and half a block south of Santa Monica Boulevard. The location was perfect—the Laurel Elementary School that my friends and I frequented was just down the street. That's where Melissa and I met, actually. The playground was as much of a community as Melissa's block was. Her neighborhood was an interesting cultural mishmash: young gay guys, older Jewish families, Russians, Armenians, and Middle Easterners lived alongside one another. There was a quaint, *Leave It to Beaver* quality to it, with everyone smiling and waving and saying hello, but there was also a very tangible tension.

On an average night, Melissa and I would get high and listen to music with her mom, then head across the street to visit Wes and Nate, the two gay guys who lived in the only house among the apartment buildings to be found in a six-block radius. They had a huge yard, probably about an acre, and a tall oak tree with a swing hanging from it on their lot. We'd smoke

a joint with them, then proceed to the backyard, where we'd lie under the oak tree, staring at the stars.

I discovered so much contemporary music during that period, too. I mentioned that my parents played music all the time; it's my fondest memory of childhood. I listen to all of it still, from the classical composers my dad favored to the sixties and early-seventies legends they both loved. That period was rock and roll's most creative time. I'm constantly looking and rarely finding music that's better. When I think I have, a closer inspection reveals it to be just another rehash of the originators. And then I find that I'd rather just listen to the Stones or Aerosmith or whatever it's based on than listen any further.

But when I was thirteen, I wasn't satisfied with my parents' collection anymore. I sought out new sounds, and found an endless supply at Melissa's house. That is where I was first exposed to Supertramp, Journey, Styx, April Wine, Foghat, and Genesis—none of which really suited my taste. But Melissa's mom listened to a ton of Pink Floyd, which I knew from my mom, but given that Carolyn had such good pot, their music suddenly took on a whole new meaning. That apartment was paradise for a budding guitar player: getting stoned for free, discovering new tunes, and having sex with my girlfriend all night, all before I graduated junior high.

I don't think there's anything better than hearing your favorite band live.

I SPENT THE REST OF EIGHTH GRADE
and all of ninth grade touring Hollywood with Steven by day, playing
guitar in my room, and sleeping with Melissa. I stole a chunky, Panasonic
top-loading tape player at some point and carried it everywhere, soaking
up music like Ted Nugent, Cheap Trick, Queen, Cream, and Edgar and
Johnny Winter. I stole more cassettes each day, absorbing one band at a
time. I would start with a band's live album, because I believe that is the
only way to determine whether or not any band is worth your attention. If
they sounded good enough live, I'd steal their entire catalog. I also used
live records to hear their greatest hits before I embarked on stealing their
entire catalog—I was frugal. I still love live records; as a fan of rock
music—and I still feel like a fan first—I don't think there's anything bet-
ter than hearing your favorite band live. I still believe that the best repre-
sentations of my favorite bands were captured on their live albums,
whether we're talking about Aerosmith's *Live Bootleg*, the Who's *Live at
Leeds*, the Rolling Stones' *Get Your Ya Ya's Out*, or the Kinks' *Give the
People What They Want*. Much later, I was very proud when Guns N'
Roses put out *Live Era*; I think it captures some great moments.

ASIDE FROM MELISSA AND STEVEN, MY
friends were much older than I was. I had met many of them through my
bike gang and made many more along the way because I always had pot
from one source or another. My mom was a pot smoker who was very liberal
in her rearing: she preferred that I smoke pot under her supervision, rather
than experiment out in the world. With all due respect to her, she had my
best intentions in mind, but she didn't realize that not only did I smoke at
home under her watchful eye, but I also pinched a little of her weed (some-
times just the seeds) to smoke or sell when I went out. It was, without fail,
the best way to ingratiate myself and I thank her for it.

The kids in the older circles I ran in had apartments, sold drugs, threw
parties, and clearly thought nothing of entertaining minors. Aside from
the obvious benefits, such an environment also allowed me to discover bands
of the day that I would have otherwise missed. There were a bunch of surfer
and skater guys I hung out with who turned me on to Devo, the Police,

999, and a few more radio-friendly New Wave bands. Among another clique that I hung with, a lanky black guy in his twenties named Kevin turned me on to the first Cars album during one of his parties.

Kevin was the older brother of one of my bike buddies, a guy named Keith who'd nicknamed me Solomon Grundy. I looked up to Keith because he always had the hottest girls from Fairfax High School chasing him around. When I was thirteen and fourteen and really into BMX, this guy was in the scene, but so cool that he always seemed to be about one step away from ditching it altogether for more sophisticated, adult pursuits. I'm still not sure why Keith called me Solomon Grundy.

In any case, Kevin's musical taste was questionable. He was into disco, which was an interest we did not share, though I now realize that he was so inclined because it afforded him the opportunity to get as much trim as possible—so I respect him more for it now. It worked, too, because the girls in his circle and at his parties were hot and promiscuous, which was especially intriguing to me. That said, I didn't expect to like the "cool new band" Kevin was going to play for me while we smoked a joint in his room at his party that night. I changed my mind midway through the first song, and by the time the second song was over I was a lifelong fan of Elliot Easton. Elliot was the soul of the Cars, and that first record of theirs won me over. In my opinion, the Cars were one of the few impactful groups that came along when New Wave took over the airwaves.

Just before I left the party that night, I heard a snippet of music that seriously grabbed my attention. Someone had put Aerosmith's *Rocks* on the stereo and I caught only two songs, but that was enough. It had this really nasty alley cat vibe to it that I had never heard before. If lead guitar was the undiscovered voice that had resided within me, this was the record I'd waited my whole life to hear. I made sure to check out the album cover before I took off, so I'd know who it was. I remembered the name Aerosmith; four years before, in 1975, they had their only AM radio hit at the time with "Walk This Way." I ran into the *Rocks* record again a week or two later . . . but at the most inopportune moment.

I must preface this next story by saying that relationships are never easy, especially when both parties' bodies are young, inexperienced, and raging with hormones. Melissa and I really cared for each other, but we still broke

up and made up often, usually as a result of my commitment to learning to play guitar overshadowing my commitment to spending time with her. At this particular point, we were apart and I had set my sights on someone we'll call Laurie. She was a significantly older, very obviously out-of-my-league figure among my circle of friends. Laurie had incredible tits, long blond-brown hair, and wore really thin, strapped, low-cut tops. They were so sheer and loose that her chest was far too easy to see. Like me, Laurie was recently single: she'd broken up with Ricky, her very typical surfer boyfriend. I was determined to be with her; I didn't care that she was four years older than me and wouldn't give me the time of day. I knew I could do this. I kept talking to her and paying attention to her and finally got a dialogue going. She let her guard down and got to know me, and once she did, she seemed to forget that a few weeks before I was nothing but some much younger punk she didn't care to notice. Finally she invited me over to hang out one night when her mom was going out of town.

I parked my bike on her lawn and followed her upstairs to her room. It was years ahead of my comprehension of cool and groovy at the time: she had scarves over the lamps, rock posters everywhere, her own stereo, and a ton of records. We got stoned and I intended to play it cool, so I flipped through her albums looking for something to impress her. I recognized *Rocks* from Kevin's party a few weeks earlier and put it on, ignorant of the fact that it had been playing nonstop in my subconscious since the moment I heard those first two songs. Once the opening shrieks of "Back in the Saddle" filled the room, I was transfixed; I listened to the record over and over, crouched by the speakers, ignoring Laurie completely. I forgot about her altogether as well as whatever intricate plans I had for the evening. After a couple hours, she tapped me on the shoulder.

"Hey," she said.

"Hey," I said. "What's going on?"

"I guess you should go home now."

"Oh, yeah . . . Okay."

Rocks is as powerful to me today as it was then: the screaming vocals, dirty guitars, and relentless grooves are bluesy rock and roll as it is meant to be played. There was something about the raw adolescence of Aerosmith that was perfectly in tune with my inner development at the time; that

record just sounded the way I felt. After my missed opportunity with Laurie, I devoted myself to learning "Back in the Saddle." I stole the cassette and an Aerosmith songbook and replayed the song until I knew the riffs. I learned a valuable lesson in the process: music books can't teach you how to play properly. I'd sort of learned to read music, so I could tell that the notes in the songbook were not the same as those being played on the record. It made sense: I struggled for hours and still couldn't play along properly. So I ditched the books and kept at it until I'd learned to figure it out by ear; and I figured out every other song I wanted to play that way forever after.

In the process of learning every lick of "Back in the Saddle," I realized just how idiosyncratic Joe's and Brad's playing is, and how no one can ever really play like anyone else but themselves. Imitation should remain a stepping stone for a player to find his or her own voice, but it must never *become* his or her voice: no one should emulate their heroes to the point of note-for-note mimicry. Guitar is too personal of an expression for that; it should be exactly what it is—a singular extension of the player.

———————◆◆◆◆———————

BY THE TIME MY LAST JUNIOR HIGH SUMMER drew to a close, I had created a world of my own design that was as consistent as my home life was irregular, because during this period, in the wake of their separation, my mom and dad each entered into very irregular relationships. I lived with each of them for short amounts of time, but neither situation felt quite right. I ended up mostly living with my grandmother in her condo in Hollywood while my little brother lived with my mom. Of course, most of the time I slept over at Melissa's.

Following her relationship with David Bowie, my mom started dating a talented photographer we'll call "Boyfriend." They were together for about three years and eventually moved into an apartment on Cochran off Third, near La Brea, where I lived with them for a while. Boyfriend was probably ten years younger than Ola; when they met he was a star on the rise: I remember meeting Herb Ritts, Moshe Brakha, and a few other famous photographers and models at their place. My mom and Boyfriend had a

pretty tumultuous relationship, during which she regressed into his assistant and put her career aside.

Boyfriend always had a darkroom in his bathroom, and toward the end of their relationship I discovered that he was freebasing cocaine in there all night long while "working." It wasn't always all bad over there, but once freebasing suddenly popped up in Boyfriend's life, it proceeded to promptly halt his career—taking his relationship with my mom down with it. Boyfriend was tortured; he was miserable and misery loves company, so although I wasn't fond of Boyfriend at all (and he knew it), he was determined to drag me along for the ride. We'd freebase together, then go out into the neighborhood and wander into other people's garages. Usually we'd steal used furniture, old toys, and whatever odds and ends it seemed like the family had discarded. One of the items we found was a red couch that we carried all the way back to our house; we then spray-painted it black and put in the den. I can't imagine what Ola thought when she woke up the next morning. I have no idea actually, because she never mentioned it. In any case, after our adventures, Boyfriend would keep at it, basing all morning and, I suppose, all day. I'd duck into my room by 7:30 a.m., pretend to sleep for an hour, then get up, say good morning to my mother, and head off to school as if I'd just had a good night's sleep.

My mom had insisted that I live with her and Boyfriend because she disapproved of the conditions I'd been subjected to over at my dad's place. Once my dad had acclimated to their separation, he got it together to rent an apartment where his friend Miles and a group of my parents' mutual acquaintances lived. It seemed like everyone in that scene drank a lot, and my dad was dating a number of women, so my mother didn't think it was a good environment for me. My dad dated a woman named Sonny on a regular basis during that period. Life had not been kind to Sonny; she'd lost her son in a horrible accident and though she was really sweet, she was really screwed up. She and my dad spent a lot of time together drinking and fucking. So for a while there, while I lived with Mom, I saw Dad only on weekends, but when I did, he always had something interesting waiting for me: some unusual dinosaur model or something more technical, like a remote controlled airplane that you had to build from scratch.

Later on, I saw more of him once he moved into an apartment on Sunset and Gardner, in a building of studio apartments with a shared bathroom. His art buddy Steve Douglas lived just down the hall. On the first floor was a guitar store, though at the time I hadn't yet picked up the habit. My dad's art studio filled the entire room, so he'd built a loft to sleep in on the far wall and I lived there with him for a while when I was in seventh grade, just after I got kicked out of John Burroughs Junior High for stealing a load of BMX bikes—but that is a story not worth telling. In any case, for that brief period I attended Le Conte Junior High, and since my dad didn't drive, I walked the five miles to school and back each day.

I'm not quite sure what Dad or Steve did for money. Steve was an artist as well and as far as I could tell, all they did was spend their days drinking and their nights painting for their own benefit or talking about art. One of my more entertaining memories from that period involved Steve's old-fashioned medicine bag full of vintage porn that he caught me looking at one day.

His place and our place were basically shared space, so it was entirely normal for me to wander down to his studio whenever I wanted to. One day he walked in and found me looking through his treasure chest of porn. "I'll make you a deal, Saul," he said. "If you manage to steal that bag out from under my nose, you can keep it. Think you're up to it? I'm pretty quick; you'd better be good." I just smiled at him; I'd already devised a plan to make it mine before he challenged me. I lived down the hall—compared to what I was already doing out in the world in terms of theft, this wasn't much of a heist.

A couple of days later I went over to Steve's place looking for my dad and at the time they were so engaged in conversation that they didn't even notice that I'd come in. It was the perfect opportunity; I grabbed the bag, walked out, and stashed it up on the roof. Unfortunately it was a short-lived victory: my dad ordered me to give it back once Steve realized that it was gone. It's too bad; those magazines were classics.

There were periods throughout my childhood when I insisted to my parents that they weren't my parents, because I honestly believed that I'd been kidnapped. I also ran away a lot. One time when I was preparing to run away, my dad actually helped me pack my suitcase, which was a little plaid bag he'd bought me in England. He was so understanding about it

and so helpful and kind that by doing so, he convinced me to stay. That kind of subtle reverse psychology is one of the traits of his that I hope I've inherited, because I'd like to use it on my kids.

———◆·✕·◆———

I'D SAY MY BIGGEST ADVENTURE WAS the day I took off on my Big Wheel when I was six years old. At the time we lived at the top of Lookout Mountain Road and I rode it all the way down to Laurel Canyon, then all the way down Laurel Canyon to Sunset Boulevard, which, all in all, is just over two miles. I wasn't lost, I had a plan: I was going to move into a toy store, and live there for the rest of my life. I guess I've always been determined. Sure, there were many times that I wanted to get away from home as a kid, but I have no regrets about how I was raised. If it had been any bit different, if I'd been born just one minute later, or been in the wrong place at the right time or vice versa, the life that I've lived and come to love would not exist. And that is a situation that I wouldn't want to consider in the slightest.

Education
High

Slash tears it up on his BC Rich.

Chapter 4

Institutional hallways are all the same, they're just different colors. I've seen the inside of several rehab centers, some more upscale than others, but the clinical sobriety of their walls was identical. All of them were predominantly white and plastered with optimistic slogans like "It's a journey, not a destination" and "One day at a time." I found that last one ironic considering the road that Mackenzie Phillips has been down. The rooms were generic backdrops engineered to inspire hope in people from every walk of life, because, as those who have been there know, rehab is a more accurate cross section of society than jury duty. I never learned much from "group"; I didn't really make any new buddies in rehab and I didn't take advantage of multiple opportunities to make new drug connections either. After I'd spent days in bed with my body in purgatorial knots, unable to eat, speak, or think, I wasn't up for small talk. To me, the communal aspect of rehab was forced—just like high school. And just like high school, I didn't fit in. Neither institution taught me their intended lessons, but I learned something important from each of them. On my way back down their hallways toward the exit, I was confident that I left knowing exactly who I was.

I entered Fairfax High in 1979. It was an average American public high school—linoleum floors, rows of lockers, a courtyard, a few around-back spots where kids have snuck cigarettes and done drugs for years. It was painted a very institutionally neutral light gray color. There was a good spot to get high out by the football field, there was also a continuation school on the other side of campus called Walt Whitman, where all the real fuck-ups went, because they had to. That seemed like the end of the line, so although it was more interesting, even from afar, than the normal campus, I tried to stay away from that place as much as possible.

My best friend, Steven Adler, was shipped back to the Valley for high school, which was as far off as Spain in my mind. I did visit him out there a few times and it never failed to disappoint: it was flat, dry, hotter than it was at home, and exactly like a sitcom neighborhood. Everyone there seemed to cherish their identical lawns and identical lives. Even at a young age, I knew something was wrong with that place; beneath the normalcy, I could sense that those people were more fucked up than anyone in Hollywood. I felt bad for Steven, and once he was gone, I retreated further into my guitar world. I went to school, always registering as if I were there every day, but on average I'd attend my first three classes and spend the rest of my time on the bleachers playing guitar.

There was only one class that meant anything to me in high school; consequently, it's also the only one in which I earned an A. It was a music theory course that I took freshman year called Harmony, taught by a guy named Dr. Hummel. The class reduced the elements of musical composition to their roots, defining the fundamentals in mathematical terms. I learned to write time signatures, chords, and chord structures, all by analyzing the underlying logic that binds them. We never played an instrument: our teacher used a piano as a tool to illustrate the theories, but that was all; the class was purely a study of theory. While I was terrible at math, I was good at this, so it was the one class I never missed. Every time I showed up, I felt like I already knew the lessons we learned. I never consciously applied any of it to the guitar, but I can't help but think the knowledge of notation that

I picked up seeped into my mind and aided my playing somehow. There was a cast of characters in this class: among others there was Sam, the piano virtuoso, a Jewish guy with tight curly hair, and Randy, who was a long-haired, Chinese, metal guy. Randy always wore a satin Aerosmith jacket and was of the opinion that Keith Richards and Pete Townshend sucked and Eddie Van Halen was *God*. We eventually became friends and I came to enjoy our daily debates as much as I enjoyed that class, because it was made up of mostly musicians discussing nothing other than music.

Other classes, meanwhile, didn't go so well for me. There was one teacher who chose to make an example of me once when I fell asleep on my desk. I had an evening job at the time at the local movie theater, so I could have been tired; it's more likely that I was just bored out of my mind, because the class was social studies. From what I understand, the teacher stopped everything to discuss the concept of stereotype with the class. He noted my long hair and the fact that I was asleep and, illustrating the meaning of the word *stereotype*, he concluded that I was a rock musician who probably had no greater aspirations in life than playing very loud music. He then woke me up and asked me a few pointed questions.

"So I take it you're probably a musician, right?" he asked. "What do you play?"

"I play guitar," I said.

"What kind of music do you play?"

"Rock and roll, I guess."

"Is it loud?"

"Yeah, it's pretty loud."

"Notice, class, this young man is the *perfect* example of a stereotype."

I am always grumpy when I first wake up, so this was more than I was willing to take. I got up, walked to the front of the class, flipped his desk over, and left. That incident, combined with a prior weed bust, spelled the end of my career at Fairfax High.

I LEARNED MORE ABOUT MY PEER GROUP at the unofficial high school recess where freshmen to seniors from Fairfax and other high schools gathered at the end of a long dirt road at the

top of Fuller Drive, way up in the Hollywood Hills. It was called Fuller Estates; it's not there anymore—now it's just a curve on the hiking trail in Runyon Canyon. It was a teenage wasteland in the late seventies and early eighties, but before that it was much more interesting: in the 1920s, it was Errol Flynn's mansion; it occupied a few acres at the top of that wide hill overlooking L.A. Between then and when I was a kid, it fell into serious decline, and by 1979 it was a ruin of a foundation; just a big concrete slab and an empty pool. By the time I saw it, the place was a statuesque wreck with an amazing view.

the song's bombastic, apocalyptic riff just consumed my entire body.

The crumbling concrete walls were a two-level maze that was a perfect, out-of-the-way spot for stoners of all ages. It was pitch-black there at night, far away from the glare of any streetlight. But somebody always had a radio. I was on acid up there the first time I ever heard Black Sabbath. I was out of my mind, staring into the black sky above Fuller Estates, tracing trails between the stars when someone nearby blasted "Iron Man." I'm not sure that I can pinpoint how I felt; the song's bombastic, apocalyptic riff just consumed my entire body.

That place and everyone there was straight out of a seventies teen movie. In fact, it was captured perfectly in *Over the Edge*, a film starring a young Matt Dillon, about a bunch of repressed, stoned, and out-of-control Texas teenagers who were ignored by their parents to the degree that they took their whole town hostage. In the film, as I bet it was for all of the kids who hung out up at Fuller, the characters' parents had no idea as to what their kids were really up to. In its most aggressive and most realistic moments, that film was a true representation of teenage culture at the time: most kids' parents either didn't care enough to notice or naïvely thought they were doing the right thing by trusting their children and turning a blind eye.

WHEN I WAS IN HIGH SCHOOL KIDS LOOKED a few different ways. The influence of spandex seeped in, thanks to Pat Benatar and David Lee Roth, and that trend left its colorful mark: girls wore tight, low-cut, neon body suits, and some guys weren't far behind. I remember seeing Capezios when I was in junior high, but thank God, they were out by the time I was a freshman; although feathered hair was still standard for either sex. It was far too common and wasn't cool by any means.

Another huge influence was the film *American Gigolo*, starring Richard Gere, which chronicled the downfall of a stylish Beverly Hills male escort. It was the worst thing that could have happened to Hollywood teenagers because every girl who saw it strove to re-create their personal version of that world. Suddenly, girls who were thirteen, fourteen, and fifteen tried to dress as if they were twenty-five and aspired to date well-dressed, much older guys. I never dialed into their psychology, but I watched more than a few girls I knew, as early as fifteen, start wearing too much makeup, doing blow, and dating nineteen-year-olds and twentysomethings. It was fucking pathetic and straight up sad. A lot of them became casualties of the scene before they even reached legal drinking age. After all, they had a huge head start, so it caught up to them before they even got out of the gate.

I DIDN'T LOOK LIKE ANY OF THE OTHER kids in school and my interests certainly set me apart. I have worn long hair, T-shirts, jeans, and Vans or Chuck Taylors since I first had a say in the matter. Once I was in high school, all I cared about was music and playing guitar; I never abided by the trends that swayed my peers, so I was a throwback. It's always been a paradox with me; I stood out but I didn't crave or court obvious attention. All the same, I was used to not fitting in and wasn't comfortable with anything else: I had changed schools so often that I was the perennial new guy—and probably, in the minds of my peers, the freaky new guy.

It didn't help that to the naked eye, I wasn't obviously anything: upper-, middle-, or lower-class; white, black, or otherwise. As I got older, and as my

home address continued to change, I realized and understood why my mom so deeply pondered my school registration forms before checking one box or another: if I was listed as black in certain school districts I might be bused out of the zone to an inferior school when I otherwise might be enrolled in the better school down the street if I were a registered Caucasian. I never found a niche based on race in high school, and I've always been aware of my race only when it was an issue in the minds of others. I have been in many situations, back then and ever since, when I've noticed very "open-minded" individuals adjust their behavior because they were unsure of whether I was black or white. As a musician, I've always been amused that I'm both British *and* black; particularly because so many American musicians seem to aspire to be British while so many British musicans, in the sixties in particular, went to such great pains to be black. It was another way I wasn't like anyone else, but I can count on one hand the confrontations I've had that were racially motivated; they occured once I was submerged in the very white universe of eighties metal. One time at the Rainbow I got into a fight with Chris Holmes from W.A.S.P. Duff overheard Chris saying that niggers shouldn't play guitar. He didn't say it to me, but it was obviously about me. As I remember, Duff told me about it later and the next time I saw Chris I went up to confront him and he took off running. Aside from insulting me, it's one of the more ridiculous and untrue things a musician, of all people, could ever possibly say.

<hr />

I FOUND MY OWN CIRCLE OF FRIENDS in high school, people who were all pretty unique, different from the rest of the student body. My closest friends, Matt and Mark, defined that period of my life. Matt Cassel is the son of Seymour Cassel, one of the greatest character actors of the past fifty years. Seymour has been in nearly two hundred films since the sixties, most notably those made with his close friend John Cassavetes. He's been in too many films and TV shows to name; in recent years, director Wes Anderson has been his champion: he's cast Seymour in *Rushmore*, *The Royal Tenenbaums*, and *The Life Aquatic with Steve Zissou*. Seymour is a Hollywood legend; he supported indie film making before it became an institution (his philosophy was that he'd play a role

he connected with for the price of the plane ticket). He was also a figure in a hard-partying class of moviemaking royalty that included Cassavetes, Ben Gazzara, Roman Polanski, and others.

I could show up at Matt's house, sit in his room, and play guitar for hours, learning stuff off the records he had: Pat Travers's *Live*, AC/DC's newest, *Back in Black*; those albums provided hours and hours of riffs to learn. They lived right above Sunset on Kings Road, tucked behind the Riot Hyatt, next door to an A-frame house that is still there. There were porn movies being shot in that house all the time while Seymour was growing weed in the backyard of his place. The A-frame was a huge advantage to hanging at Matt's: we'd wander over there and mix it up with the porn girls. It wasn't appropriate, but they liked to get us teenage boys all fired up and frustrated by playing with each other.

Seymour had the best parties, and he had raised his kids well enough to trust them to hang out. My mom knew Seymour, but she never would have condoned the goings-on over there. At Seymour's parties there was a lot of freedom and it was full-on. His kids, Matt and Dilynn, were so smart and independent that he didn't have to worry: they'd already figured out who they were amid this crazy existence. Seymour's wife, Betty, never came out of her bedroom; it was a dark and foreboding mystery to me as to what went on upstairs. Coupled with the fact that Seymour ruled the house with a bit of an iron fist, Matt allowed only a select few of his friends, of which I was one, into their world.

One day Seymour looked at me and bestowed upon me the nickname that resonated with him more than my proper name ever did. As I was passing from one room to another in his house, at a party, looking for the next whatever it was I was after, he touched me on the shoulder, fixed me with that affable gaze of his, and said, "Hey, Slash, where ya going? Where ya going, Slash? Huh?"

Obviously it stuck. My friends who hung at Seymour's started calling me Slash back at school and soon enough that was the only name everyone knew me by. At the time, my friends and I just thought it was a cool name, but it wasn't until years later that I caught up with Seymour and he explained it properly. I was on tour during *Use Your Illusions*, and happened to be in Paris, with my mom along, when Seymour was there, too. The three of us

had lunch and he explained that the nickname embodied my sense of hustle, in every sense of the word. He was proud of the fact that I'd actually made a name for myself and that he'd been the one to give me that moniker. His reason for calling me Slash was that I never stood still for more than five minutes; he saw me as someone who was always working on his next scheme. He was right: I've always been coming or going more than I've ever stayed still. I am perpetually in motion, often saying good-bye while saying hello and Seymour summed that quality up in a word.

I met a ton of people at Seymour's—including the Stones. After they played the L.A. Coliseum they came by for an after-after party at his place. I had seen the show that night; they played "You Can't Always Get What You Want" so soulfully that I'll never forget it. I managed to shake Ronnie Wood's hand; I was fifteen and little did I know that he'd be one of my best friends later in life. In fact, my first son, London, was conceived in his house.

My other close friend, Mark Mansfield, has popped in and out of my life ever since we first met back in high school. Mark's dad, Ken, was a record producer and his stepmom was a singer—his real mom lived in Santa Barbara, where he'd often go when he got in trouble—and he was constantly in trouble. Mark's family lived in a very nice house above Sunset and Mark was a mini James Dean with a touch of Dennis Hopper. He'd try anything and he'd do anything that anyone ever dared him to do—and he'd do it with sheer enthusiasm and a smile on his face. Slowly but surely that attitude led him down a dark road: juvenile detention, rehab, and the like. Mark was the kind of guy who once called me at ten a.m. to tell me that he and a friend had just driven his friend's mom's car off the road somewhere along Mulholland. They'd stolen it out of the kid's mom's driveway since she was out of town and inevitably launched it off the shoulder, into the canyon. Luckily for them they landed it in a tree and were able to climb back up to street level. Needless to say, the next call I got from Mark was from exile at his mom's house in Santa Barbara.

◆━━◆◆◆◆━━◆

AS SOON AS I COULD STRING THREE chords together consistently and improvise a solo, I wanted to form a

band. Steven was gone, he was off in the Valley, so I struck out on my own. I had tried to start a band at the very tail end of junior high but it hadn't gone so well. I found a bass player and a drummer whose mom taught French at Fairfax High School. This was to be my first experience with a tempermental, tantrum-prone drummer; if he made one mistake, this kid would kick the entire kit over. Then we'd have to wait while he set it all back up. The bass player in that band was just awesome. His name was Albert, and we'd play Rainbow covers like "Stargazer." Unfortunately, Albert got into a bike accident on Mulholland Drive and ended up in a coma for a month or so. He was in traction; he had pins in his neck and in both of his legs and braces holding his legs apart—all of it. He came to school looking like a big captial A, and he had no aspirations of playing bass at all anymore.

My first professional gig was at Al's Bar, playing in a band with friends of my dad's. My dad was very proud of my love of guitar and always bragged to his friends about me. I don't know what, but something must have happened with their guitar player and Tony talked them into letting me play. I'm sure they were worried about whether or not I could do it. But I got up there and was able to handle it: it was all twelve-bar blues and standard blues-based covers like the Stones, which I had a feel for. I got free beers out of it, which is what made it truly professional.

There were a few guitar players in my circle of high school friends. I met a guy named Adam Greenberg who played drums and we found a guy named Ron Schneider who played bass and we became a trio dubbed Tidus Sloan. I still have no idea what that name means . . . I'm pretty sure that I got it off a guy named Phillip Davidson (who we'll get to in just a little bit). One night when Phillip was mumbling incoherently I remember being really curious about whatever it was that he was saying.

"Tidus ally sloan te go home," Phillip said. At least that's what I heard.

"*What?*" I asked him.

"Tid us all de sloans to ghos hum," he said. Or so I thought.

"Hey, Phillip, what are you trying to say?"

"I'm stelling you to tidus these sloans ta grow fome," he said. "Tidus sloans to go *home*."

"Okay, man," I said. "Cool."

I think he wanted me to tell all these girls in his house to go home, but I walked away from that situation thinking that Tidus Sloan, whatever the fuck that meant, was a pretty cool name for a band.

<hr/>

TIDUS SLOAN WAS A PURELY INSTRUMENTAL band because we never found a singer and I certainly wasn't going to sing myself. Basically, I don't have the personality to be a front man of any kind; it's enough of an effort for me to get out there and talk to people at all. All I really want to do is play guitar and be left alone. In any case, Tidus Sloan played early Black Sabbath, early Rush, early Zeppelin, and early Deep Purple without vocals—we were retro before there was a retro.

Slash and Ron Schneider, two-thirds of Tidus Sloan.

We rehearsed in Adam's garage, which drove his mom completely insane. She and the neighbors would complain constantly, which is understandable because we played much too loud for a residential neighborhood. His mom's name was Shirley and I drew a cartoon in her honor: it was a woman in the doorway of a room screaming, "It's too loud and I can't stand the noise!" at the top of her lungs. The floor of the room in the picture is littered with beer cans and on the bed is a kid with long hair playing guitar, totally oblivious.

My caricature of Shirley became the inspiration for my first tattoo, though the figure that I had inked on my arm looks nothing like her—my version has Nikki Sixx hair and huge tits, while the real Shirley favored curlers and was old and fat—though also with big tits. I got that tattoo when I was sixteen; it's on my right arm and it says Slash underneath it. Adam explained to me later that Shirley's frequent outbursts were entirely my fault: I had just acquired a Talkbox from Mark Mansfield's stepmom, which is a sound amplifier that allows a musician to modify the sound of whatever instrument is filtered through it by the movement of his mouth against a clear tube that's attached to it. Apparently the sounds that I made reminded Shirley of her late husband, who died of throat cancer just a couple years previously. He'd had to speak through an artificial voice box and the sounds I was making were too similar for her to bear. Needless to say I stopped using the Talkbox at her house.

There were a few other guitar players and bands around my high school, like Tracii Guns and his band Pyrhus. I had a moment of envy when I first started playing guitar, before I owned an electric; Tracii had a black Les Paul (a real one) and a Peavy amp, and I'll never forget how *together* I thought he was. We would check out each other's bands at parties and there was definitely a competitive vibe about the whole thing.

In high school I started hanging out with whatever musicians I could find. There were a few guys my age and a few older, left-over Deep Purple dudes, who were irretrievably brain-dead and well past their expiration date to still be hanging out with kids from high school. The best of them was the aforementioned Phillip Davidson: not only did he unintentionally name my first band, but he had a Stratocaster, which was a very big deal, and his parents never seemed to be home. He lived in this beat-up house in Hancock

Park that was overgrown with weeds and we'd just party over there all day and all night. We were teenagers throwing keg parties; no parents, just Phillip and his two stoner brothers.

I always wondered where his parents were; it was like the *Peanuts* cartoon, all kids, no authority figures. It was a mystery to me—I always thought that maybe his parents were coming home at any given moment, but they never did. I felt like the only one who was concerned; Phillip mentioned the existence of his parents, who owned the place, but they never seemed to materialize. There was nowhere they could be hiding either; this was a one-story house with three bedrooms. For all I knew, they could be buried in the backyard, and if they were no one would ever find them because the backyard was piled high with debris.

Phillip used to wander from room to room carrying his joint or cigarette or whatever combination of the two it was, while telling stories that were really *long* only because he talked really *slow*. He was a tall lanky guy with a true billy-goat goatee, long auburn hair, and freckles; and he was just *stoned* like *really* stoned. I mean, sometimes he would chuckle, but otherwise he was pretty expressionless. His eyes seemed perpetually closed—he was that kind of stoned.

Supposedly Phillip could play Hendrix and lots of stuff on that vintage Strat of his, but I never heard any of it. I never even heard him play anything at all. Whenever I was over there I only remember him putting Deep Purple records on the stereo. He was so burned out that it was just painful to hang out with this guy. I always see the best in people; it doesn't matter what their fucking malfunction is. But Phillip? I waited in vain for something brilliant to happen, just that small spark in him to ignite a flame that nobody else might see. I waited for two straight years of junior high and never saw it. Nope, nothing. But, he did have a Stratocaster.

I do not like to combine cocaine and guitar.

was pretty functional for a high school band. We played our school amphi-
theater and plenty of rowdy high school parties, including my own birth-
day. When I turned sixteen, Mark Mansfield threw a party for me at his
parents' house in the Hollywood Hills and my band was all set to play. For
my birthday, my girlfriend, Melissa, gave me a gram of coke and that night
I learned a valuable lesson: I do not like to combine cocaine and guitar. I
did a few lines just before we went on and I could hardly play a note; it was
really embarrassing. It's been the same the very few times since that I've
made that mistake: nothing sounded right, I could not find the groove,
and I really didn't want to be playing at all. It felt like I had never played
guitar before, or as awkward as the first time I tried to ski.

We did about three songs before I just quit. I learned early to save any
kind of extracurriculars for after the show. I can drink and play, but I know
my limit; and as for heroin, we'll get into that later because that's a whole
other can of worms. I did, however, learn enough to know to never carry
that kind of habit on the road.

The most extravagant Tidus Sloan gig was at a bat mitzvah deep in the
middle of nowhere. Adam, Ron, and I were getting high at the La Brea Tar
Pits one night and met some girl who offered us five hundred bucks to play
her sister's party. When she saw that we weren't that interested, she started
dropping the names of many famous people, her "family's friends," who
were going to be there, Mick Jagger included. We remained skeptical, but
over the course of the next few hours, she built this party up to be the big-
gest happening in L.A. So we packed our equipment and as many friends
as we could into our friend Matt's pickup truck and set off to play this gig.
The party was at the family's house, which was about two hours from
Hollywood—about an hour and forty-five minutes further than we expected;
it took so long that we didn't even know where we were by the time we got
there. The moment we turned into the driveway, I found it impossible to
believe that this house was about to host L.A.'s most star-studded party of
the year: it was a small, old-fashioned, grandparents' home. There were clear
vinyl slipcovers on the furniture, blue shag carpet in the living room, and
family portraits and china displayed on the wall. For the space available,
this place was *way* overfurnished.

We arrived the night before and slept in their guesthouse. It was a hospitable gesture but a horrible idea, and to tell you the truth, this very proper Jewish family looked truly shocked when we arrived. We set up our equipment that night on the veranda, where they'd set out the tables and chairs and a small stage, for the next day's performance. Then we proceeded to get completely annihilated on the load of booze we'd brought with us. We consumed it privately and did our best to contain ourselves to the guesthouse, but unfortunately, we exhausted our supply and were obliged to break into the family's house to acquire a few bottles of whatever was readily available. Those bottles happened to be the worst ones we could have gotten our hands on: mixing our vodka, and whiskey, with Manischewitz, and a bunch of liquors that were never meant to be downed straight from the bottle spelled the beginning of a very long weekend—for us, for our hosts, and for the many guests who showed up the following morning.

Over the course of the night, our band and our friends destroyed this family's guesthouse to a degree that surpasses nearly every similar episode that I can remember Guns ever getting into. There was puke all over the bathtub; I was sitting on the bathroom sink with this girl when it broke off the wall—water sprayed everywhere until we closed the valve. It looked as if we'd vandalized the place on purpose, but most of it was just a side effect. I am happy to say that I did not commit the worst offense of all: barfing in the stew. This dish, which was a traditional recipe served at every bar and bat mitzvah in the family, had been left to simmer overnight in the guesthouse so it would be ready to eat the next day. At some point in the evening, one of our friends lifted the lid, vomited into the pot, and replaced the lid without telling anybody—or turning off the heat. I can't tell you quite what it was like to wake up on the floor with a raging headache, broken glass stuck to my face, and the odor of warm vomit-infused stew clinging to the air.

Unfortunately the horror show continued for this poor family. We had drunk all of our booze and all of the booze we'd stolen from the main house the night before, so we started stealing booze from the outdoor bar first thing in the morning, as we began to rehearse. Later, when the relatives filed in for the afternoon's celebration, we were playing pretty loud and no one knew what to do or say, though a few suggestions were made.

A very peppy, very short old lady came up to offer her constructive criticism.

"Hey, you, young man, it's *too loud!*" she said, squinting up at us. "Do you think you could turn it down? Some of us are trying to have a conversation!"

Grandma was slick, she had Coke-bottle black-framed glasses and a designer suit and though she was short she had complete authority. She asked us if we knew any "familiar" songs and we did our best to accommodate her. We threw in all of the Deep Purple and Black Sabbath covers that we knew. They had a stage set up for us with chairs in front of it, but it was pretty clear that aside from a few six- and eight-year-olds, the entire party was plastered against the wall farthest from the stage. Actually, the guests were behaving as if it were raining outside, because when I looked up I realized that they'd packed themselves into the living room when there was no reason to flee the open air aside from the sounds of our set.

We'd completely freaked out the partygoers, so we tried to draw them in by slowing things down: we did a heavy-metal version of "Message in a Bottle." That didn't work, so we tried to play whatever other popular songs we knew; we played "Start Me Up," over and over, without a singer. It was no use; our half-hour instrumental verison of it didn't get anyone out on the floor. Out of desperation we played Morris Albert's "Feelings," as interpreted by Jimi Hendrix. That didn't do it either, so we made it our swan song and got the hell out of there.

<hr/>

IT MIGHT BE SURPRISING TO SOME, BUT even before I had a band, I started working regularly as early as possible to earn the money that I needed to pursue playing guitar. I'd had a paper route since ninth grade that was pretty extensive; I covered from Wilshire and La Brea down to Fairfax and Beverly. It was only Sundays; I'd have to be up at six a.m. unless I could convince my grandmother to drive me. I'd have two huge bags on either end of my handle bars, so leaning just a touch too much to either side spelled wipeout. I eventually upgraded my employment to a job at the Fairfax movie theater.

The amount of time I put into work and the amount of time I put into learning the guitar were simultaneous revelations to me: I finally knew why I was putting my nose to the grindstone. I guess it was the union of my parents' influence: my dad's creativity and my mom's instinct to succeed. I might choose the hardest way to get wherever I want to go but I'm always determined enough to get there. That inner drive has helped me survive those moments when everything was against me and I've found myself on my own with nothing else to see me through.

Work was something that I focused on and did well whether I liked my job or not, because I was willing to work my ass off all night and day for the cash to support my passion. I got a job at Business Card Clocks, a small mail-order clock factory. From September through December each year, I would assemble clocks for a bunch of companies' holiday gift baskets. I'd put an enlarged reproduction of their business card on a piece of masonite, insert a clock movement in the center, put a wooden frame around it, box it up, and that was that. I made thousands and thousands of these things. We were paid by the hour and I was the only person there who got crazy; I'd be there at six a.m., work all day, through the night, then I'd sleep there. I don't think it was legal, but I didn't care: I wanted to make as much money as I could during the season.

It was a great job that I kept for quite a few years, though it did eventually bite me in the ass: my boss, Larry, paid me by personal check, so I was never on the books at his company, and he never reported my salary to the IRS. Since I wasn't on the books, I saw no reason to pay taxes on my earnings. But the very moment that I made money with Guns a few years later, the IRS came calling, demanding all of those back taxes, plus interest. I still can't believe that of all the things I've done, the government nailed me for my job at a clock factory. I found out later how it went down: the IRS audited Larry and grilled him about a certain amount of money that couldn't be accounted for over the course of a few years so he was forced to confess that it had been paid out to his employee, me. The IRS tracked me down and put a lien on my earnings, accounts, and assets: any money that I deposited in a bank would immediately be seized to cover my tax debt. At that point, I had been broke for too long to give it all up once I'd finally gotten it: rather than pay it off with my share of Guns' first advance check, I had

my cut consolidated into traveler's checks, which I kept on me at all times. But we'll get to all that in just a little bit.

Another job was at the Hollywood Music Store, an instrument and sheet music shop on Fairfax and Melrose. As much as I was trying to earn my keep while pursuing what I really wanted to be doing, there were so many what-the-fuck moments. Here's one of them: there was a guy who used to come in and shred every day in the guitar section. He'd pick a "new" guitar off the wall, as if he'd never seen it before, and proceed to play it for hours. He'd tune it, shred on it, and just kind of hang out and play for what seemed like years. I'm sure there's one in every music store.

WHEN I STARTED JUNIOR HIGH, THERE. were so many great hard rock records for me to listen to and learn from: Cheap Trick, Van Halen, Ted Nugent, AC/DC, Aerosmith, and Queen were all in their prime. Unlike a lot of my guitar-playing peers I never strove to imitate Eddie Van Halen. He was the marquee lead player around, so everyone tried to play like he did, but nobody had his *feel*—and they didn't seem to realize that. His sound was so personal, I couldn't imagine coming close, or trying or even wanting to. I picked up a few of Eddie's blues licks from listening to him, licks that no one registers as his signature style because I don't think he's ever properly appreciated for his great sense of rhythm and melody. So while everyone else praticed their hammer-ons and listened to "Eruption," I just listened to Van Halen. I've always enjoyed individualistic guitar players, from Stevie Ray Vaughn to Jeff Beck to Johnny Winter to Albert King, and while I've learned from observing their technique, absorbing the *passion* of their playing has taught me so much more.

In any case, things had changed by the time I got to high school. By 1980, English punk had found its way to L.A. and had become something utterly ridiculous that had nothing to do with its roots. It was a swift, impossible-to-ignore fashion statement: suddenly every older kid I knew was wearing torn-up shirts, creepers, and wallet chains made of paper clips or safety pins. I never understood what the big deal was; it was just another superficial installment in the West Hollywood scene that revolved around the Rainbow, the Whisky, Club Lingere, and the Starwood.

Slash doing what he does best: playing constantly.

I never considered L.A. punk worth listening to, because I didn't consider it real. Around then the Germs were the big band, and they had many imitators, all of whom I thought couldn't play and totally sucked. The only bands that I thought were worth anything were X and Fear—and that was it. I respected the fact that the core of punk, from a musician's point of view, was about not being able to play very well, and not giving a shit about it. But I had a problem with the fact that everyone in the scene exploited that aesthetic for all the wrong reasons—there's a difference between bad playing and deliberately playing badly for a reason.

Coming out of London and New York, punk rock made an impression, and as much as it was misinterpreted in L.A., it did give birth to a bunch of great clubs, the Café de Grand being the best of them. That was the greatest venue at which to see true hardcore punk shows, but it wasn't the only one—the Palladium put on great hardcore shows, too. I saw the Ramones there, and I'll never forget it—it was as intense as surfing big waves. Other than a few exceptions, L.A. punk was as pathetic as the miles of poseurs lined up outside of the Starwood every weekend.

At that time, I had finally gotten to an age where I was the older kid. I had spent my life running around being the younger guy hanging with the older kids, getting into what they were into, always wanting to be a part of the cool stuff they were doing. Now I was that kid, and as far as I was concerned, the punk movement and this really horrible fashion thing that had followed it in the back door had ruined everything. I had just gotten old enough to appreciate and enjoy all the stuff that had gone on before that, and just as I had everything started to fucking suck.

From the time I was born up until 1980, everything was pretty stable. It was all sort of based on rock and roll, despite the pretty watered-down rock bands that came out: Foghat, Styx, Journey, REO Speedwagon, and many more. From '79 and '80 on, with the exception of Van Halen, everything went in a different direction, which instilled a whole different kind of rebellion, and what I was into more or less got phased out by trendiness.

I wanted to play guitar in a band that inspired that degree of devotion and excitement.

High for that social studies incident I found myself in high school limbo. Education has always been a priority for my mother; she let me live wherever I could, however I wanted, all summer long, as long as I agreed to move in with her, wherever she might be, come fall. She needed real assurance that I was going to school so nothing but my living under her roof would do. The summer after my expulsion, I enrolled for summer school at Hollywood High to try to earn the credits I needed to join Beverly Hills Unified High School with the rest of the class at the beginning of my sophomore year. But I also tried to get out of high school altogether by studying for and taking the proficiency exam. It didn't go so well: during the first half hour I took a smoke break and never went back.

During this period, my mom finally left her boyfriend, "Boyfriend" the photographer. Once Boyfriend began to freebase away, literally, everything in the house (he eventually ended up bankrupt), my mom and my brother packed up and moved out suddenly. I wasn't spending much time at home at the time, so I didn't witness it all go down firsthand. But when I heard, I was relieved.

My mom, brother, and grandmother moved into an apartment together on Wilshire and La Cienega and, per Mom's rules, I joined them there in the fall. Mom wanted me to graduate high school before I set out on whatever path I chose to follow, but I hadn't left her much to work with. My grades, attendance, and behavior record were less than stellar, so she did her best: she got me enrolled as a continuation student at Beverly Hills High.

Continuation is where they put kids with "adjustment" problems: learning disorders, behavior issues, and those who don't otherwise sync with the standard curriculum. Whereas at Fairfax I thought this was a situation to avoid, here it was perfect for me; I was allowed to work at my own pace, and I could set my hours to suit my new place in the workforce. I'd arrive at eight and leave at noon because I had two jobs at the time; aside from the Fairfax movie theater, the fall was high season at the clock factory.

My classmates in Continuation Education at Beverly Hills High were a real cast of characters. There were a couple of full-on Harley-Davidson

biker chicks, one that was a behemoth, whose heavy-set, fortysomething, Hell's Angels boyfriend picked her up every day. He'd arrive early and just sit there revving his engine; the other chick had her own Harley. There were also three Sunset Strip rocker chicks in class; their Aqua Net hair extended in every direction and their ripped-up T-shirts and spiked stiletto heels spoke for themselves. All three were attractive in their own way . . . they knew how to use lipstick and eye shadow, put it that way. I knew this other girl in class: her name was Desiree, the daughter of one of my dad's friends, Norman Seiff, a well-known rock photographer. We were playmates when we were little and we used to play naughty with each other back then. I had a crush on her all those years ago and I had so many more reasons to have a crush on her when I saw her again: she sat a row in front of me and wore nothing but loose sleeveless shirts and no bra. She had grown into a hot buxom punk rocker, who was still as cute to me as she had been when we were seven.

There was other riffraff in that class as well; we were a diverse and outlandish enough group that we could have been collectible figurines: there was the surfer-stoner Jeff Spicoli guy, the hot teenage mom-slut, the plump brooding Goth, the sad Indian kid who worked the night shift at his parents' 7-Eleven; all of us barely clinging to the fringe of high school society. Looking back, I'd like to know how every person in the classroom ended up there, at the otherwise ritzy Beverly Hills High, no less. We were sequestered together for the benefit of our "progressive" education in one classroom with one coed bathroom that doubled as our community smoking lounge. That is where I discovered why those three Sunset Strip rocker chicks looked like they did: they were the unofficial presidents of the Mötley Crüe fan club. They did free PR as well: they turned me on to Mötley during the first smoke break I shared with them.

I had known about Nikki Sixx, the bassist and creator of Mötley Crüe, since his first band, London, because Steven and I saw them play the Starwood one night when we managed to sneak in. London had true stage presence; combined with their low-budget pyrotechnics and Kiss-esque clothes, they were band enough to blow any teenage mind. I had no idea that Nikki had met Tommy and that they had found the other guys and

evolved into Mötley Crüe; neither did I know that they were spearheading a movement that would displace L.A. punk overnight. Mötley didn't look like Quiet Riot, Y&T, or any other Sunset Strip band of the day: they were as equally over the top but they weren't quite like anyone else. They were so into their own thing that there was no way that anyone, aside from me I suppose, could have mistaken these three girls for anything other than Mötley Crüe fans.

There are moments in life that only time can properly frame; at best you know the snapshot is special when you take it, but most of the time only distance and perspective prove you right. I had one of those moments just before I ditched education altogether: it was the day Nikki Sixx and Tommy Lee showed up outside of my school. Six years later I'd be doing lines with them off the flip-down meal trays on their private jet, but seeing them loitering outside Beverly Hills High is more memorable to me. They were wearing high-heeled boots, stretch pants, teased out hair, and makeup; they were smoking cigarettes; talking to girls in my high school parking lot. It was sort of surreal. I watched my newfound continuation friends, those three Mötley look-alike chicks, stare at the two of them with glazed doughnut eyes as Tommy and Nikki nonchalantly handed them posters to hang and flyers to hand out on the Strip announcing Mötley's next show. I was in awe: not only did these chicks find this band so exciting that they chose to dress like them, they were also willing to be their volunteer street team. Nikki had given them copies of their new EP, *Too Fast for Love*, and their job was to convert all their friends into Mötley Crüe fans. It was like seeing Dracula set his disciples loose on Beverly Hills to suck the blood of virgins.

I was impressed and objectively envious: I could never be in a band that looked or sounded like Mötley Crüe, but I wanted what they had. I wanted to play guitar in a band that inspired that degree of devotion and excitement. I went to see Mötley that weekend at the Whisky . . . musically, it was just okay, but as a concert it was *effective*. It was memorable because of the full-on production: Vince lit Nikki's thigh-high boots on fire and they set off a ton of mini flash pots. Tommy pounded away like he wanted to split his drum set in two, while Mick Mars shuffled around his side of the stage, hunched over like the walking dead. What affected me the most,

though, was the audience: they were so die-hard that they sang every song and rocked out as if the band were headlining the L.A. Forum. It was obvious to me at least, that soon, Mötley would be doing just that. And in my mind, that meant only one thing: If they can do it on their own terms, why the fuck can't I?

Slash shredding with Black Sheep in 1985.

Least Likely
to Succeed

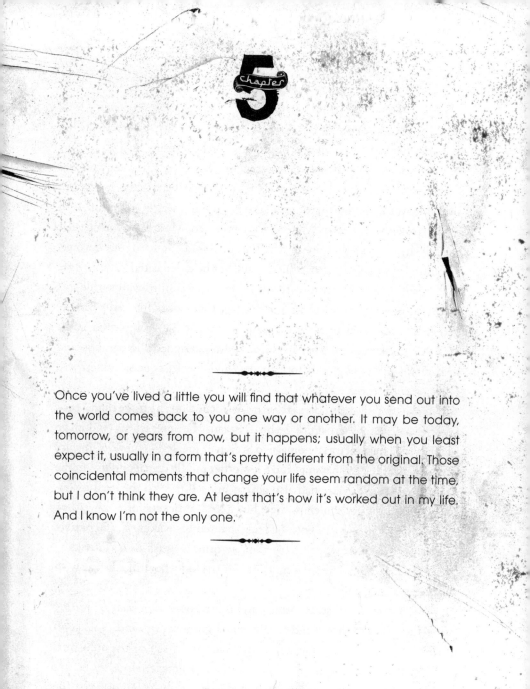

Chapter 5

Once you've lived a little you will find that whatever you send out into the world comes back to you one way or another. It may be today, tomorrow, or years from now, but it happens; usually when you least expect it, usually in a form that's pretty different from the original. Those coincidental moments that change your life seem random at the time, but I don't think they are. At least that's how it's worked out in my life. And I know I'm not the only one.

hadn't seen Marc Canter in about a year, for no other reason than that we'd each been busy doing other things. In the interim, he'd undergone a metamorphosis: when I'd seen him last, he was a music fan and was just beginning to take on a role in running the family business at Canter's Deli. He was by no means a total "rock guy"—that was more my angle, if broad strokes were drawn. When we reconnected, Marc was someone else entirely: he was a sterling specimen of the obsessed, die-hard rock devotee. I wouldn't have called it in a million years, but he'd dedicated his entire life to Aerosmith. He'd transformed his room into a wall-to-wall shrine: his Aerosmith posters were a continuous collage that looked like wallpaper, he had cataloged copies of every magazine that they'd ever appeared in, he maintained an orderly gallery, in plastic sleeves, of signed photographs, and he had amassed enough rare foreign vinyl and bootleg concert cassettes to open a record store.

Marc definitely didn't dress the part; he looked like no more than a rock fan with a taste for Aerosmith T-shirts, because he never let his fandom go so far as to inspire sartorial homage to Steven or Joe. It did, however, inspire stalking, stealing, trespassing, and a few other mildly illegal pursuits in the name of the cause. Marc had also gotten himself in with the local ticket-scalping community somehow: he'd buy a load of tickets for a show, then trade among the scalpers until he had bartered his way up to the perfect pair of floor seats. It was all a big game to him; he was like a kid trading baseball cards, but come showtime, he was the kid who walked away with the rarest cards up for grabs.

Once Marc had his seats sorted out, his little operation was just getting going. He'd sneak in a very nice, professional-grade camera and a collection of lenses by taking the whole apparatus apart and stashing the individual pieces in his pants, the arms of his jacket, and wherever else they fit. He never got caught; and he just caught amazing live shots of Aerosmith. The only problem was that he got into Aerosmith a little too late: when he started really digging them they broke up.

A cornerstone of Marc's collection of Aerosmith memorabilia was an empty bag of Doritos and a small Ziploc bag full of cigarette butts that he'd snatched from Joe Perry's hotel room at the Sunset Marquis. Apparently he'd staked the place out and managed to get in there after Joe checked out and before housekeeping showed up. Joe hadn't even played a show or anything the night before—at that point, he had quit the band actually. I thought it was a little weird, Aerosmith wasn't even *together*, but Marc was living for them 24/7. Marc has been one of my best friends in life since the day we met, so I had to support him by contributing to his collection: I did a freehand sketch of Aerosmith onstage for his birthday. I did it in pencil and then shadowed and highlighted it with colored pens and it came out pretty good.

That picture taught me a lesson that's been stated by the wise and otherwise throughout history: whatever you put out into the world comes back to you one way or another. In this instance, that picture came back to me literally and brought with it just what I'd been looking for.

The next time I saw the drawing I was at an impasse: I had been struggling unsuccessfully to get a band together amid a music scene that didn't speak to me at all. I wanted the spoils that I watched lesser players enjoy, but if that meant changing as much as I'd have to, I wasn't having that—I tried but I found that I was incapable of too much compromise. I won't lie now that retrospect is on my side and claim that deep down I knew it would all come together fine. It didn't look like it was going that way at all, but it didn't keep me from doing the only thing I could do: I did what felt right, and somehow, I got lucky. I found four other dysfunctional like-minded souls.

I was working in the Hollywood Music Store the day a slinky guy dressed like Johnny Thunders came up to me. He was wearing tight black jeans, creepers, dyed black hair, and pink socks. He had a copy of my Aerosmith drawing in his hand that a mutual friend had given him: apparently prints of it had been made and circulated. This guy had been inspired enough to seek me out, especially when he heard that I was a lead guitar player.

"Hey, man, are you the guy who drew this?" he asked a bit impatiently. "I dig it. It's fuckin' cool."

"Yeah, I did," I said. "Thanks."

"What's your name?"

"I'm Slash."

"Hey. I'm Izzy Stradlin."

We didn't talk for long; Izzy has always been the kind of guy with somewhere else that he needed to be. But we made a plan to hang out later on, and when he came by my house that night, he brought me a tape of his band. It couldn't have sounded worse: the tape was the cheapest type around, and their rehearsal had been recorded through the built-in mike in a boom box that had been placed on the floor. It sounded like they were playing deep inside a jet engine. But through the static din, way in the background, I heard something intriguing, that I believed to be their singer's voice. It was hard to make out and his squeal was so high-pitched that I thought it might be a technical flaw in the tape. It sounded like the squeak that a cassette makes just before the tape snaps—except it was in key.

AFTER MY INCOMPLETE STINT AT HIGH school, I lived with my mother and grandmother in a house on Melrose and La Cienega in a small basement room off the garage. It was perfect for me; if need be, I could slip out of the street-level window undetected at any time of day or night. I had my snakes and my cats down there; I could also play guitar whenever I liked without bothering anyone. As soon as I dropped out of school, I agreed to pay my mother rent.

As I mentioned, I held several day jobs while trying to put together or get into a band that I believed in amid the quagmire of the L.A. metal scene. Around this time, I worked for a while at Canter's Deli in a job that Marc basically invented for me. I worked alone upstairs in the banquet room, which wasn't suited for a banquet at all—it was more or less where they stored all kinds of shit that they didn't necessarily need. I didn't realize the humor in that back then.

My job involved comparing the waitstaff's checks with the corresponding cashier's receipts so that Marc could quickly and easily figure out who was stealing. It was so easy; a job that the biggest idiot could do. And it came with perks: I'd eat pastrami sandwiches and drink Cokes the whole

time, while putting those papers in two piles, basically. My job did have its place: through my sorting, Marc caught more than a few staffers who had probably been robbing his family for years.

After I left, Marc willed my job to Ron Schneider, my bass player in Tidus Sloan. Our band still played together sometimes, but we weren't taking things to the next level in any way—without a singer, we weren't going to ever gig on the Strip.

My job at the Hollywood Music Store was one of a few that I saw as stepping-stones to playing guitar professionally, full-time; I wasn't in it for the fame and girls, I wanted it for a much simpler reason: there wasn't anything else in the world that I enjoyed more. At the music store I was a salesclerk who sold—and played—every guitar on the floor, but that was by no means my only area of expertise. I also sold all kinds of shit that I knew absolutely nothing about. I could fake my way through explaining the ins and outs of bass amps, but when it came to drum sets, drumheads, drumsticks, and the wide array of percussion instruments I sold, I'm still impressed by my ability to put a shine on a pile of bullshit.

I liked my job in the music store, but it was a voyeuristic purgatory. I'd spend every idle moment staring through the front windows at Cherokee Studios across the street. Cherokee was a bit of a recording destination in the early eighties: not that I was a huge admirer, but every time I'd see the Doobie Brothers roll in there to cut a song, I can't say that I wasn't totally fucking envious. I was, however, totally fucking starstruck the day that I happened to gaze out the window to see Ric Ocasek walking down the street, heading to Cherokee.

Around this time Steven Adler returned from his exile in the Valley and we picked up precisely where we left off. Each of us had girls in our lives and the four of us became an inseparable unit. My girlfriend Yvonne was a senior in high school when we met; she was a disciplined student by day and a rock chick by night, and she managed those dual identities very well. Yvonne was an amazing girl: she was very smart, very sexy, very outspoken, and very ambitious—today she is a high-powered lawyer in L.A. After she graduated, she enrolled as a psychology major at UCLA, and since by that point I had begun to more or less live with her, on my days off she'd somehow talk me into accompanying her to school at something like

eight a.m. I'd spend the morning at the UCLA campus, sitting outside, smoking cigarettes, and watching the yuppies go by. Some days, whenever I found the course or professor interesting, I'd sit in on her larger lecture classes.

I don't even remember her name anymore, but Steven's girl at the time and Yvonne became fast friends because the four of us went out every single night. I didn't even want to most of the time, but there we were, out there hitting the Strip—and I didn't even like the music of the day at all, though I tried to be positive. The coup de grâce came when a very hyped, overrated "innovation" known as MTV first aired. I expected it to be like *Don Kirshner's Rock Concert,* the live, hour-long program that ran on Saturday nights from 1973 to 1981. That show spotlighted an artist a week and aired amazing performances by everyone from the Stones to the Eagles to the Sex Pistols to Sly and the Family Stone to comedians like Steve Martin.

MTV couldn't have been more of a polar opposite: they showed Thomas Dolby's "She Blinded Me with Science," the Police, and Pat Benatar over and over. I would literally wait for hours to see a good song; and usually it would be either Prince or Van Halen. I felt the same way when I explored Sunset at night: I saw a lot, I liked very little, and I was fucking bored the entire time.

Steven, on the other hand, was in his element. He was all about what was going down on the Strip, because it was his chance to realize his rockstar dreams. He'd never exhibited such ambition before: he did whatever it took to get into a club, to meet people, to make connections, and be in the mix to whatever degree possible. Steven posted up in the Rainbow parking lot every Friday and Saturday night, and he kept tabs on every band that ever played as often as he did everything but give his balls to get himself inside.

I rarely cared to go along, because I could never do what most often needed to be done: I was incapable of humiliating myself to go that extra mile. I don't know why but I had a problem hanging around parking lots and stage doors, looking for any way in that might present itself. As a result I was so infrequently present that Steven's never-ending morning-after tales of incredible bands and hot chicks eventually got to me. But I never saw

any of those mythical creatures when I decided to accompany him (against my better judgment). I witnessed nothing but a string of evenings that never achieved epic status.

I thought to myself just how hard it must be to be a girl.

One night that stands out started with Steven and me borrowing my mom's car (I was seventeen at the time, I believe) to go the Rainbow to mix it up.

We drove down to Hollywood and walked up to the club, and discovered that it was ladies' night.

"That's fuckin' awesome!" Steven shouted.

I had gotten into the Rainbow for years, thanks to my fake ID and Steady, the club's bouncer. He's still there, and he still recognizes me. For whatever reason, though, Steady wasn't having it on this particular night: he let Steven in and sent me packing.

"Naw, not you," he said. "Not tonight, go home."

"What?" I asked. I had no right to be indignant but I was anyway. "What do you mean? I'm here all the time, man."

"Yeah, I don't give a shit," he said. "Get out of here, you're not coming in tonight."

I was so fucking pissed off. I had nowhere else to go, so I followed Steady's orders and went home. I drowned my embarrassment in alcohol, and once I was good and drunk, I came up with the crazy idea to return to the Rainbow dressed as a girl. It made complete sense in that special way that drunken plans do: I'd show Steady—I'd get in the club for free thanks to ladies' night, and then I'd fuck with Steven. Adler hit on every girl in sight, so I was sure that he'd hit on me long before he realized who I was.

My mom thought my plan was hilarious: she outfitted me with a skirt and fishnets, piled my hair up under a black beret, and did my makeup. I couldn't wear her shoes, but the outfit worked—I looked like a chick . . . no—

I looked like a *Rainbow* chick. I drove back up to West Hollywood in my outfit; I parked a few blocks away on Doheny and walked to the club. I was both drunk and on a mission, so my inhibitions were nonexistent. I sauntered up to Steady and nearly laughed in his face when he waved me in with no pause for ID.

I was on top of the world; I had won—until I realized that Steven was nowhere to be found. It was like reaching the end of the roller coaster before the car had even gone over the first hill. The reality of the situation hit me square in the face: I was dressed as a girl, in the middle of the Rainbow. Once I saw the light, I did the only sensible thing—I left. On the long walk back to my mom's car, I thought that every shout was directed at me, I thought every laugh was at my expense; I thought to myself just how hard it must be to be a girl.

<center>◆━━◆×◆━━◆</center>

STEVEN'S GIRLFRIEND RAN INTO TOMMY Lee out on the town one night and Tommy invited her down to Cherokee Studios to hang out and watch Mötley record *Theatre of Pain*, the follow-up to their breakthrough album, *Shout at the Devil*. Steve's girl thought nothing of inviting Yvonne, Steven, and me; I guess she figured that Tommy's invitation included a "plus three." Steven and I should have known better. The four of us headed down there, all ready to hang out and watch the proceedings; when we arrived, we were informed, in no uncertain terms, that the girls could go inside—which they did—but Steven and I could not. It was suggested that we go home. We were fuming: we watched our girlfriends head into the studio, and spent the night in the two lounge chairs in the lobby trying to be cool while we discussed what they might be doing in there. It was not a good scene.

I'm not sure how, but somehow that experience didn't scar me enough to desert the notion of getting a job at Cherokee. I had been pestering the studio's day manager to hire me for an entire year. I'd stop by daily, like clockwork, during my lunch break at Hollywood Music across the street. I continued to do so, business as usual, but a few weeks later he finally gave in and offered me a job. In my mind, it was a milestone; I was now just one step away from becoming a professional musician. I was very wrong, but

my plan was that once I worked in a studio, I would make connections because I would meet musicians and producers every single day. In my mind, a studio was the place to meet other players who took it seriously and by working there at the very least I'd get free recording time once I got a band together. With that kind of bullshit in my head, I quit Hollywood Music feeling like I'd just won the lottery.

I was hired at Cherokee to be a gofer to the engineers, no more no less. I didn't care; I showed up to my first day, ready to run errands, take out the trash, whatever, whenever. Or so I thought: I visibly wilted when I discovered that my job for the week was to fetch whatever Mötley Crüe might need, day or night. Just over a week before, these same guys had refused to let me into the studio and might have had my girlfriend (I believed her when she said nothing happened, but still . . .), and now I would have to spend the next few weeks as their errand boy. Great . . .

The studio manager gave me one hundred bucks to fill Mötley's first order, which I was sure was just the first of many: a magnum of Jack Daniel's, a magnum of vodka, a few bags of chips, and a couple of cartons of cigarettes. I looked down at the money as I walked outside into the sunlight, debating the pros and cons of swallowing my pride. It was a really nice day. I stopped when I got to the liquor store to think about this for a minute.

I squinted up at the sky; I stared at the sidewalk, and then I started walking again—toward home. That was all she wrote for Cherokee and me: considering how many hours I've spent in professional recording facilities over the years since, it's almost ridiculous that I've never again set foot in Cherokee Studios. At this point I have no intention of doing so—I owe those guys a hundred bucks. The one day I did spend there taught me an invaluable lesson, however: I needed to pave my own way into the music business. It didn't matter that any idiot could fulfill the duties of fetching for Mötley Crüe, or anyone else for that matter—that job was something that I refused to do on principle. I'm glad that I did; it made it that much easier when Mötley hired us to open for them a few years later.

SO I'D DITCHED HOLLYWOOD MUSIC, thinking that my studio job would be the last day job I'd ever have before

I made it. Hardly. Things weren't looking too good for me at that point: I hadn't graduated high school, I wasn't going to college, and as far as I knew, I'd walked out on the only job that might have helped me on my way.

I was unemployed and undirected there for a while, which was a perfect moment for my mom to get me into school again—any school. God bless her perpetual commitment to getting me educated. This time she did the only thing that made sense—she knew that I loved music, so she enrolled me in some weird vocational music school.

I'm very disappointed in myself that I can't remember the name of this place, though I do remember how unfocused our teachers were. I'm now pretty sure that my mom found out about this place via a flyer at the Laundromat. In any case, I enrolled, I showed up, and within weeks my teachers had me out in the field laying cables and putting filters ("gels" they're called) over lights at various live venues. This place educated its students in the arts of sound and light engineering for live performance in a very hands-on fashion. There were about six of us in my class and almost immediately we were assisting techs on-site at venues like the Country Club, the FM Station, and various others in L.A. Actually it was a total sham: the school was clearly funded or run by the production company that put on these shows, so we, the students, were not only working for them for free, they had also taken our tuition money. Shady as it was, I did learn to run light and sound for live concerts. I enjoyed it, too, until the night I did the light show for a group of Duran Duran wannabes called Bang Bang. I realized two things as I watched their set: 1) it wasn't possible for a music performance to be more ridiculous, and 2) this sound-and-light gig was taking me nowhere fast.

———————◆·❈·◆———————

I WAS DESPERATE TO BE IN A BAND; SO I combed the ads in *The Recycler*—L.A.'s free musicians' paper—every week, looking for an invitation to something that appealed to me. For the most part it was futile: the ads were nothing but shredders seeking shredders. But one week, I saw an ad that intrigued me: it was a singer and guitarist looking for a fellow guitarist in the vein of Aerosmith and Hanoi Rocks. And more important, it expressly stated that "no beards or mustaches" need apply.

I called the number in the ad and made arrangements to meet them at this guesthouse that they were renting on some street up in Laurel Canyon. I showed up there with a girl that I was dating and recognized Izzy immediately from the day he came into the music store with my Aerosmith drawing. I then realized that the other guy must be that high-pitched singer I'd heard on the tape. I thought, *Cool, this might actually go somewhere.* Their little shack was more like a closet: there was room enough for a bed, with space to sit on the floor in front of it, and room enough for a TV—which was the only source of light in there.

I talked to Izzy for a while, but Axl never got off the phone, though he nodded his head in acknowledgment when I came into the room. At the time I thought it was rude, but now that I know him I understand that wasn't the case. When Axl gets into a conversation, there's no stopping him. In Guns, we used to call it a Twain Wreck: when Axl started telling a story, he was as long-winded as Mark Twain. That first meeting, though, was pretty uneventful: either they'd decided that they were no longer interested in a second guitar player or I just didn't look the part. Whatever the problem was, it went nowhere at all.

———◆—◗×◗—◆———

THE MINUTE STEVEN GOT BACK TO HOLLYWOOD, he proudly informed me that he'd learned to play drums at his mom's house out there in the Valley, which I am sure contributed to his being kicked out again. Steven was ready to start our band, even though at the time I was still halfheartedly playing with Tidus Sloan and answering the odd ad in the paper looking for a guitar player. I didn't take him seriously; to me Steve was my social director—and a bit of a nuisance: he started coming to Tidus Sloan rehearsals, and every chance he got, he insisted that he was a better drummer than Adam Greenberg. When I eventually found myself without a band, Steve had annoyed me so much that I wasn't even willing to watch him play, let alone play with him.

Steve's grandmother had given him her old blue Gremlin; a car that looks exactly like it sounds—stout and boxy. Apparently, every day, since he couldn't practice in his grandmother's house, he'd been loading his drum kit into this thing and driving out to the public park on Pico across the

street from Twentieth Century-Fox studios that includes a swimming pool and a golf course. I knew it well; I used to play soccer there when I was nine. As weird as it was, Steven would set up his drums next to a section of the walking path and just practice all afternoon and evening. I'm sure the seniors, joggers, ducks, and dog walkers were happy about it; a blond rock kid with teased-out hair playing a full-size double-bass-drum metal kit as hard as he can is bound to be a crowd pleaser in any setting.

I eventually agreed to check him out, though I continued to wonder what the hell I was thinking as I drove out to meet him. It was completely dark when I got there. I parked next to his car and wandered out to the jogging path and there he was, drumming away in the dark. He was back-lit by the distant floodlights, while the huge expanse of the park and the golf course loomed behind him. It was a very weird scene. I took that in for a while before I even paid attention to his playing. But once I did, I forgot about the backdrop. Sitting there in the dark, watching Steven play, I wasn't convinced of his abilities, but I was satisfied. Besides, I didn't have a better option open to me anyway.

STEVEN AND I WERE IN A SITUATION that was familiar and unwelcome—we were looking for a singer, and this time, a bass player as well. Steven was an asset in that regard, because he knew all the players: he was out so much that he had seen nearly every band there was to see in the L.A. rock scene at the time. Steven was also up on the gossip: once Mötley Crüe took off, Steve heard that Lizzy Grey, Nikki Sixx's cofounder in London, intended to put that band back together. That was huge—Steven and I had seen London when we were younger and they blew our minds. Izzy Stradlin was in that second version of London, but once he left, things fell apart a bit and there was a vacancy for a guitar player and a drummer. Steve and I auditioned for them at the space where the legendary funk band War used to rehearse and record on Sunset, down the street from Denny's. By this time that spot was nothing but a bombed-out hovel; today it's where Guitar Center Hollywood is, by the way.

So we rehearsed there with London for four days; we learned a ton of their songs, and even though it was a step up from nowhere, nothing ever came of it. If anything, the experience was interesting because I saw firsthand just how pompous those who believe themselves to be rock stars can be. The guys in London behaved like they were larger-than-life, as if Steven and me and everyone else in the world existed on the other side of an invisible fence. It took me back to my childhood and all of the rock stars that I'd met back then through my parents. Growing up around my mom and dad's clients and friends, I'd seen it all and had learned how to act and how not to act. I'd seen real rock stars throw temper tantrums and watched my mom deal with them. I'd learned through observation just how delicately to treat those personality types.

At the time I thought the guys in London were worldly and I was intimidated and impressed. Not so much now. I saw the guy who was singing for them at that time on the street in early 2007 while I was driving to the studio to record with Velvet Revolver. There he was, cruising down Sunset Boulevard wearing the same getup, still looking for a gig.

After that fruitless endeavor, Steven and I struck out on our own. We needed a bass player and a singer, but we figured we'd go about things logically and land ourselves a bassist first so that when we began auditioning singers, we'd actually have a whole band for them to sing over. We took out an ad in *The Recycler*; it was in the "Seeking" section, and it went something like this:

Bass player needed for band influenced by Aerosmith, Alice Cooper. Call Slash.

We got a few calls, but the only guy we wanted to meet was someone named Duff. He'd just moved out from Seattle and he sounded cool on the phone, so I told him to meet us at Canter's Deli at eight p.m. Steven and I got a corner booth right near the front; we had our girls with us—my girlfriend Yvonne had a big bottle of vodka in a brown paper bag in her purse. She was the one who introduced me to vodka, actually; before I met her, I drank nothing but whiskey.

No one remotely resembling a musician came into Canter's for a long while and the girls were definitely drunk when Duff did show up. I think

the four of us were debating what he might look like when this bone-skinny, six-foot-plus guy with short spiked blond hair rolled in wearing a Sid Vicious–style chain and padlock around his neck, combat boots, and a red-and-black leather trench coat in spite of the seventy-five-degree weather. No one had predicted that. I kicked Steven and hushed the girls.

"Check it out," I said. "This *has* to be him."

Duff had been in a series of punk-rock bands in Seattle: the seminal but mostly overlooked outfit the Fartz, for whom he'd played guitar, the legendary pre-grunge power quartet the Fastbacks (drums), and a few others. Just before moving down to L.A., he had taken up bass. Duff was as musically versatile as he was driven: he didn't leave Seattle because he wasn't creatively satisfied; he left Seattle because he knew that the scene (at that time, at least) was a losing proposition and he wanted to make it. He knew that Los Angeles was the West Coast music capital, so without a plan and with no friends waiting to take him in, he packed up his beat-up red Chevy Nova and drove down to L.A. to make a name for himself. I respected him immediately for his devotion: he and I shared a similar work ethic. It established a kinship between us right away that hasn't faltered at all over all of these years.

"So you're Slash," Duff said as he squeezed himself in beside me in our booth at Canter's. "You're not what I expected at all."

"Oh yeah?" I said. "Well, what were you expecting?"

"With a name like Slash, I thought you'd be much scarier, man," he said. Steven and the girls and all laughed. "I'm not even kidding, I expected you to be some kind of punk-rock psychopath with a name like that."

"Oh yeah?" I said smirking. We shared a laugh.

If that hadn't broken the ice, my girlfriend Yvonne made sure to smash it a few minutes later. We'd sort of settled into small talk: Duff was getting to know us and vice versa, when, apropos of nothing, Yvonne leaned across me and put her hand on Duff's shoulder.

"Can I ask you a personal question?" she said, louder than necessary.

"Yeah," he said. "Sure."

"Are you *gay*? I'm just curious."

For the first time in hours our table was silent. What can I say, I've always been attracted to outspoken women.

"No," Duff said. "I'm definitely not gay."

After that exchange faded the five of us went upstairs, piled into the bathroom, and broke out the vodka. And not long after that, we formed a band right then and there, and once again spent the next month or so looking for a singer. We auditioned Ron Reyes, better known as Chavo Pederast, when he was the front man for Black Flag for a few months back in 1979. There were a few other characters in there as well, but as usual, we couldn't find the right guy. All things considered, we wrote some really cool material: we came up with the main riff to the song that later became "Rocket Queen," and a few more great ideas.

Despite the creativity flowing between the three of us, I began to get really frustrated with Steven. He never kept up with the dedicated work ethic that Duff and I shared; though he maintained twice the social schedule. It was so aggravating to watch him expend his energy on partying when we had so much to do. At the time, it was obvious that should we find the right singer, we would really have a band that was worth something. The problem was, we didn't have a singer, but Steven was behaving as if we'd already been signed by a major label. In the end I was the one who broke up the band; I told Duff it just wasn't working and I broke off with Steven in every way for a while, too. Duff went on to greener pastures: coincidentally, when he'd moved to Los Angeles he got an apartment on Orange Avenue, directly across the street from Izzy. Soon enough, those two ran into each other on the street, and that was that; Duff became a player in the L.A. Guns/Hollywood Rose universe.

———— ◆◆◆◆ ————

THOSE WERE THE ONLY TWO BANDS COMING up behind Mötley Crüe that were worthy of note—L.A. Guns and Hollywood Rose, each of which were revolving-door outfits that shared a number of local players to an incestuous degree. L.A. Guns was founded by Tracii Guns, who had gone to Fairfax High with me—that band was nothing but a tighter, harder version of the sleazy blues shredding he played at keg parties back then.

Hollywood Rose was something else. I met up with Steven just after he'd seen them, and as he described their high-pitched singer, a guy who

could tear the roof off, I realized that for once, Steven wasn't exaggerating. I didn't put it together that I'd already heard this guy, probably because I'd heard him on what is most likely the shittiest, low-fi recording of a live band that had ever been made.

Steve and I went to see Hollywood Rose at Gazarri's and it was the first time that I beheld, hands down, the best singer in Hollywood at the time: W. Axl Rose. Much like the tape, the show was nothing more than an amateur garage band doing their best, but they had an amazing sense of reckless abandon and unbridled energy. At least two of them did: apart from Izzy and Axl, the band was pretty nondescript, but those two friends from Lafayette, Indiana, had an ominous presence about them. Izzy kept doing knee slides all over the stage and Axl screamed his fucking heart out—their performance was blistering. Axl's voice drew me in immediately; it was so versatile, and underneath his impossibly high-pitched shrieking, the bluesy natural rhythm he had was riveting.

As I said, Hollywood Rose (like L.A. Guns) was a revolving-door band whose players all knew one another and were always coming or going. Bass player Steve Darrow worked with Izzy delivering the L.A. Weekly during the afternoon, so they were tight, but Axl didn't seem to like guitar player Chris Weber for whatever reason. Axl apparently up and fired Chris without telling anyone else and somehow Steven heard that they were holding auditions for guitar players the next day.

It's all as vague and illogical to me now as it was then, but Steven convinced me to show up at their rehearsal space, which was a room in some hovel called Fortress on Selma and Highland. That place was the epitome of ratty Hollywood punk, because only punk rockers would have thought to trash it so extensively. Rock guys don't trash things until they've made it and are older; only punks do that out of the gate. I'm not sure what color it was originally, but the carpet at Fortress had turned a sick yellow brown, not only on the floor, but all the way up the walls and ceiling, where it had been installed to dampen the noise. Every corner was disgusting; the entire room was a lice-infested cube.

I started rehearsing with them and it was going fine—until Izzy took off during the second song. Now I know that bolting is Izzy's defense mechanism when he thinks things aren't quite right: he never makes a show

of it, he just slips out and won't look back. Apparently Izzy had no idea what I was doing there that day and understandably didn't like it that Axl had fired Chris Weber without consulting, or even informing, him.

Eventually, a while later after we'd become good friends, I asked Izzy about it. Izzy always maintained an aura of cool; he was never ruffled, he never let that guard down. But when I asked him about this, he leveled a deathly serious gaze at me, so I had no doubt that he was sincere.

"It's pretty fucking simple," he said. "I just don't like being *dictated to* under any circumstances."

In any case, he split. I'd been dragged into the middle of that situation, entirely clueless to it. After Izzy left, there was a short, awkward moment . . . and then we just started playing again.

I didn't even know that there was another concentric circle of tension around the move to bring me in: Tracii Guns had been vying for that gig. He'd been trying to recruit Axl and Izzy into a band for quite a while. I can't imagine that he was excited to hear that they'd chosen me over him. I had no idea about any of this, and even if I had I would have ignored all of it anyway. Finally, *finally*, I was in a band with a great singer—or a singer at all.

Slash in Hollywood Rose, bassist Steve Darrow is at left. Slash is playing the voice box.

Axl had been brainstorming on how to put together the right band, and he thought Izzy and I would make a great pairing, but since they'd never actually discussed it before he put it in motion, I was in but Izzy was gone. Hollywood Rose, as I knew it, was Axl, Steve Darrow, Steve Adler, and me. We booked gigs at Madame Wong's East and West and rehearsed in a studio called Shamrock on Santa Monica Boulevard between Western and Gower. That place was an incredible scene, where just about anything might happen; considering that it was located way past East Hollywood, anything really *could* happen without arousing the authorities. There were three studios in the complex and the owners threw insane parties every weekend, where it was always balls to the wall.

Axl and I became really good friends during this period because, for a while, he lived with my family and me. It wasn't because we were soul mates or anything: Axl never had a place of his own back then; he just crashed wherever he could. When he lived with us, he'd spend his days sleeping in my subterranean room surrounded by my snakes and my cats while I was at work. When I got home, I'd wake him up and we'd go to rehearsal.

All the same, I learned a lot about Axl during that time. We talked about music and the things we thought were great; we'd listen to a particular song and dissect it, and it was clear that we had a lot in common in terms of our musical taste. We had a mutual respect for all the bands that had influenced me.

Axl also had an interest in talking about life, both his own and in the greater sense. I didn't have a lot to say but I was always a good listener. So he told me about his family and the hard times he'd endured in Indiana; it was half a world away from anything I could comprehend. Axl impressed me then the way he always has: no matter what anyone might say about him, Axl Rose is brutally honest. His version of events might be singular, to say the least, but the truth is, he believes in what he says with more heart than anyone else I've ever met.

It shouldn't be shocking to hear that it wasn't always smooth sailing when Axl lived with my family. As I mentioned, my room was off the living room, down two flights of stairs, under the garage. For the most part, Axl kept to himself when I wasn't there, but one morning after I'd left for work, apparently he wandered up and crashed out on the couch in the

living room. In other households that might not have been that big of a deal, but in ours it was. My grandmother, Ola Sr., was our matriarch and that couch was the throne from which she watched her favorite TV shows every afternoon. When she arrived, right on time to enjoy her regularly scheduled programming, and found Axl there, sprawled out, Ola Sr. politely roused him. In her sweet, soft, old-lady voice she asked him to go back downstairs to my room, where he could sleep as long as he liked. For whatever reason, that didn't go over well: from what I understand, Axl told my grandmother to fuck off then stormed downstairs to my room—at least that's what my mom said.

My mom took me aside when I got home from work, and as easygoing as she is, she insisted that if Axl was going to live under her roof for even one more day, he needed to apologize to her mother and promise to never behave that way again. It was my duty to make it happen, which at the time I didn't think was that big of a deal.

My mom used to loan me her green Datsun 510, and as Axl and I drove to rehearsal that evening, I mentioned, in the least confrontational way, that he should probably apologize to Ola Sr. for telling her to fuck off. I hadn't known Axl long, but I already knew him well enough to understand that he was a sensitive, introspective person who endured serious mood swings, so I chose my words carefully and presented the issue in a very nonjudgmental, objective tone. Axl stared out the window as I spoke, then he started rocking back and forth in the passenger seat. We were driving on Santa Monica Boulevard, doing about forty miles an hour, when suddenly, he opened the car door and jumped out without a word. He stumbled, kind of hopped, and made it onto the sidewalk without falling. He steadied himself, then took off down a side street without looking back.

I was shocked; I did a U-turn and drove around in vain, looking for him for an hour. He didn't show up back at my house that night and he didn't come to rehearsal for four days. On the fifth day he appeared at the studio as if nothing had happened. He'd found somewhere else to crash and he never mentioned it again. It was pretty clear to me from that point forward that Axl had a few personality traits that set him very far apart from every other person I'd ever known.

THE LAST HOLLYWOOD ROSE GIG TOOK
place at the Troubadour and it ended eventfully. It was an "off" night all
around, basically a series of almost right moments. We went on late and
everything sounded terrible, the crowd was rowdy and disengaged, and no
matter how hard we tried, there was no turning the vibe around. Some
heckler in the front row antagonized Axl and soon he'd had enough; he
threw a glass at the guy or broke a bottle on his head—it doesn't matter
which, but it was a fitting expression of the pent-up frustration within the
band that night. As I watched the altercation with this guy build through-
out the set, it was such a big distraction during the show that I knew I was
going to quit as soon as the set was done. Axl going after him was like affir-
mation from the universe.

It's not like I hadn't seen it coming: I wasn't satisfied and the whole situ-
ation didn't seem very stable. We'd had only a handful of gigs in the few
months we'd been together and the lineup never felt quite right. By that
point, it didn't take much; and the bottle scene seemed uncalled for—it
distracted from the music to say the least. Here we were, a fledgling band
with enough internal issues trying to scratch out a name for ourselves, hav-
ing to contend with incidents like that. It meant something to Axl, of
course, but not everyone necessarily agreed with him. It was the way he felt
and, seriously, if it was called for, fine, but sometimes you gotta pick your
battles. Stopping the show to deal with this situation was a bit much. In
the spirit of rock and roll, I had an appreciation for the full-on fuck-you,
but as far as professionalism was concerned, it was an issue for me.

Axl is a dramatic kind of individual. Everything he says or does has a
meaning, a theatrical place in his mind, in a blown-out-of-proportion
kind of way. Little things become greatly exaggerated, so that interac-
tions with people can become magnified into major issues. The bottom
line is, he has his own way of looking at things. I am a pretty easygoing
guy, so I'm told, so when Axl would fly off the handle, I never followed
suit. I'd be like, "what?" and blow it off. There were such dramatic highs
and lows and extreme mood swings that being close to him always felt

like a roller-coaster ride. What I didn't know then was that this would be a recurring theme.

In any event, I told everyone in Hollywood Rose that I quit as soon as we got offstage. The band split up after that and Axl and I parted ways for a while. He went on to join Tracii Guns in L.A. Guns, which soon became the earliest incarnation of Guns N' Roses.

Slash on the circuit, 1985.

I went on to join a band called Black Sheep with Willie Bass, which was a rite of passage for a succession of talented musicians. Willie is a great front man; he's a really tall black guy who sings and plays bass and he had a penchant for landing the hottest shredder guitar players of the day, one after the other. He'd had Paul Gilbert, a virtuoso, Yngwie Malmsteen type; Mitch Perry, who had played with Michael Schenker; and for a time, me. Shredding was not my forte—I could play fast, but I valued classic rock-and-roll, Chuck Berry–style playing over heavy metal showboating. I took the gig anyway, because, after Hollywood Rose, I realized that getting out there and being noticed was essential: it was a way to meet other players and learn about other opportunities in a fashion that suited my personality more than networking on the Strip.

I took the gig and played to about eight hundred people out at the Country Club in the Valley, and it was a particularly good show, I must say. It was also the first time I'd ever played to so many. I enjoyed the exposure, though I remember thinking that I'd played terribly. I found out later that Axl was there, but I had no idea at the time because he didn't come up and say hello.

Black Sheep wasn't really doing much by this point; after that one gig, we didn't have any others booked; we'd just get together to rehearse now and again. My brief experience with them might not have been exactly what I wanted to do, but it did make me more public, so it seemed to me that if playing in a well-liked L.A. club band was winning me attention and putting my career on some kind of track, joining the biggest L.A. club band of the day might not be a bad idea at all.

Poison's guitar player, Matt Smith, called me when he decided that he was going to leave the band. His wife was pregnant and they had decided to move back to Pennsylvania to start their family. Matt and I had friends in common and he'd invited me to a few of Poison's parties. Matt was a good guy, he was down to earth—the least poisonous of the bunch. Matt knew that it wasn't my thing at all, but he said that it was a good gig that paid well and I already knew the band was definitely in demand. I was pretty against it, but Matt talked me into trying out.

Poison rehearsed in a big flat way down in Venice on Washington and La Brea or something like that, which was plastered with posters . . . of

themselves. I showed up to the audition wearing my typical uniform: jeans, T-shirt, and that day a pair of these really cool moccasins that I stole from the farmer's market—they weren't beaded, just really plain brown leather with short fringe around the ankle. I had learned four or five songs from a tape they'd given me and I just killed them when we ran through it all. They called me back for a second audition and I remember Bobby Dall, the bass player, looking me over as I played. The vibe was very different; there was a tangible attention to detail.

"So, like, what do you wear?" he asked me. "You don't wear those shoes on*stage*, do you?"

"I haven't given it much thought, to tell you the truth," I said. He looked concerned and confused.

I was one of three that they were deciding on, and I saw another guy at the callback that day. He had platinum-blond hair, a sparkly white leather jacket, and full makeup, complete with frosted pink lipstick. I got one look at him on the way out and knew that he'd get the gig. He did, of course—it was C.C. Deville. I had played the shit out of Poison's material, but that was the one and only way that I was a perfect fit for what they were all about.

nobody ever complained because they were shocked speechless.

IN 1984, AXL HELPED ME GET A JOB AT Tower Video and when he did it was bittersweet to see him again. When Hollywood Rose broke up, it wasn't exactly acrimonious but in the interim, another source of contention had come between us: Axl had hooked up with my then ex Yvonne.

I had met Yvonne through Marc Canter at a Ratt concert, where they were playing with Yngwie Malmsteen, at the Hollywood Palladium. She'd actually been Ratt front man Stephen Pearcy's girlfriend at one time. We went out to a late-night dinner afterward at this place the Beverly Hills Café that was one of Marc's favorite spots and that's where we got eyes for each other. We started dating after that. Yvonne was really cool—she was the person who turned me on to Hanoi Rocks and front man Mike Monroe, which was a band that I definitely appreciated. They were an influence on Guns N' Roses and are still an undervalued rock-and-roll institution as far as I'm concerned.

Anyway, Yvonne and I dated for a while, but during one of those spells where we took some time off from each other, Axl fucked her. I was not happy about that at all, but I can't say that I was surprised because it was obvious that he always had a thing for her. When she and I got back together, of course she had to tell me about it, under the guise of "being honest," when the real motivation was probably revenge for my dumping her.

I called Axl at his job at Tower Video to confront him. I was just *pissed*.

"You fucked Yvonne," I said. "What kind of cheap shot is that?"

I have to give Axl credit—he was honest and didn't try to weasel his way out of it. He told me that of course he did but that at the time I wasn't fucking her, so what did it matter? I didn't see it quite the same way, so things escalated from there until he invited me to try and kick his ass. I was going to go up there and duke it out but I let it go. Needless to say, it took some time to defuse the animosity. And one day, after hearing I was looking for a job, he told me about an opening at Tower as a peacemaking gesture. Axl always chose to patch things up with grand gestures.

Tower Video was located directly across the street from the Tower Records where I'd been busted shoplifting a few years earlier. Axl was living with one of the managers, and once I'd joined the ranks it didn't take me long to figure out that I was now one of a truly loony cast of colorful characters; I imagine that we were the most ludicrous and utterly negligent staff that any Tower location has ever employed. There were also

some great, senile alcoholics who worked at the Tower Classical next door.

Every night at about eight o'clock, after the general manager for records and video left for the night, those of us in video would stock up at the liquor store across the street, throw porno movies on the store's video system, and just drink. We'd put our friends' bands on the stereo and generally ignore every customer that wandered in.

It wasn't anything that the security cameras picked up because we didn't have vodka bottles next to the cash register, so it went on unnoticed for a long time—I imagine, though, that if those tapes were viewed, we'd come off as lazy and unhelpful. We'd mix our cocktails back in the office and walk around with them in plastic Solo cups; we'd be ringing up any purchases with one hand around a screwdriver. I'm sure the customers knew what we were up to the moment we breathed on them, but nobody ever complained because they were shocked speechless. All things considered, we were way too scary for most people; they just got out of there as quickly as they could.

Unfortunately, one of the tighter-assed managers caught on to us and when he did, Axl took the fall: he was fired for the antics that we were all guilty of. Even then, I knew why: Axl has the kind of presence and star power that threatens authority figures; they see someone like Axl as nothing but a "ringleader."

MY MEMORY IS HAZY ON THE VARIOUS events that led to the forming of Guns N' Roses, because, to be honest, for most of it I wasn't there. I'm not here to present the academic history of the band or set straight every misconception; I can only speak of my experience. In any case, sometime in early 1985, Axl and Tracii Guns started putting a band together; they brought in Ole Bench and Rob Gardner, who'd played bass and drums, respectively, in L.A. Guns. Not too long after that, Izzy joined their group and that is when Axl opted to change the name to Guns N' Roses for obvious reasons. Tracii had finally gotten his dream situation—as I said, he'd been after Axl and

Izzy to be in a band with him for a while. They did a few gigs, they wrote a few songs—in that order.

I was still working at Tower and had nothing else going on. I was envious, to say the least, when Izzy came in to give me a flyer for a Guns N' Roses show in Orange County. Somewhere along the line, Duff replaced Ole; they did a few more gigs and wrote a few more songs. I believe that during those Orange County shows Tracii and Axl had a major falling-out. Tracii quit pretty soon afterward and then one night Axl showed up at Tower to ask if I'd be interested in hooking up with Izzy to write some songs and give the gig a go. I stopped for a moment to think about what that meant.

Axl and Izzy were a unit, so any other players coming into their band had to work well with both of them, and Izzy had left Hollywood Rose too quickly to get to know me at all. I liked Izzy. He was, after all, the first guy I met and I enjoyed his style and admired his talent. In dealing directly with Izzy, I'd have something of a buffer with Axl. Axl and I got along in so many ways but we had innate personality differences. We were attracted to each other and worked together tremendously well yet we were a study in polar opposites. Izzy (and later Duff) would help. At the time, Izzy was enough to take the pressure off.

I showed up at Izzy's apartment a few days later and he was working on a song called "Don't Cry," which I immediately took to. I wrote some guitar parts for it and we fine-tuned it for the rest of the evening. It was a cool session; we both got a lot out of jamming with each other.

We found ourselves a rehearsal space in Silverlake: Duff, Izzy, Axl, Rob Gardner, and myself. Everyone knew one another, so we started throwing songs together that evening and it just gelled quickly; it was one of those magic moments that musicians speak of where every player naturally complements the other and a group becomes an organic collective. I had never felt it that intensely in my life. It was all about the kind of music I was into: ratty rock and roll like old Aerosmith, AC/DC, Humble Pie, and Alice Cooper. Everyone in the band wore their influences on their sleeves and there was not a bit of the typical L.A. vibe going on where the goal is to court a record deal. There was no

concern for the proper poses or goofy choruses that might spell pop-chart success; which ultimately guaranteed endless hot chicks. That type of calculated rebellion wasn't an option for us; we were too rabid a pack of musically like-minded gutter rats. We were passionate, with a common goal and a very distinct sense of integrity. That was the difference between us and them.

You Learn to Live Like an Animal

GUNS N' ROSES

Sat., Jan. 4th 11:00
Troubadour

"GET YOURSELF TOGETHER, DRINK TILL YOU DROP,
FORGET ABOUT TOMORROW AND HAVE ANOTHER SHOT!"

Happy New Year!

FROM THE BOYS WHO BROUGHT YOU THE MOST CHAOTIC SHOWS OF '85

SEND DONATIONS TO: GUNS N' ROSES
KEEP US OUT OF JAIL FUND
9000 SUNSET BLVD., SUITE 405
HOLLYWOOD, CA 90069

2.00 OFF
WITH FLYER

2.00 OFF
WITH FLYER

An early flyer Slash designed. The band always tried to come up with slogans.

We weren't exactly the type of people who took no for an answer. We were much more likely to give no for an answer. As individuals, each of us was street-smart, self-sufficient, and used to doing things his way only—death before compromise. When we became a unit that quality multiplied by five because we'd have one another's backs as fiercely as we'd stood up for ourselves. All three of the common definitions of the word *gang* definitely applied to us: 1) we were a group who associated closely for social reasons such as delinquent behavior; 2) we were a collection of people with compatible tastes and mutual interests who gathered to work together; and 3) we were a group of persons who associated for criminal or other antisocial purposes. We had a gang's sense of loyalty, too: we only trusted our oldest friends, and found everything we needed to get by in one another.

Our group willpower drove us to succeed on our own terms but never made the ride any easier. We were unlike the other bands of the day; we didn't take kindly to criticism from anyone—not our peers, not the charlatans that tried to sign us to unfair management contracts, not the A&R reps vying to hand us a deal. We did nothing to court acceptance and we shunned easy success. We waited for our popularity to speak for itself and for the industry to take notice. And when it did, we made them pay.

We rehearsed every day, working up songs that we knew and liked from one another's bands, like "Move to the City" and "Reckless Life," which were written by some version or another of Hollywood Rose. We had a piece of shit PA, so we composed most of the music without Axl actually singing with us. He'd sing under his breath and listen and provide feedback on what we were talking about in the arrangements.

After three nights we had a fully realized set that also included "Don't Cry" and "Shadow of Your Love," and so we unanimously decided that we were now fit for public consumption. We could have booked a gig locally, because, collectively, we all knew the right people, but no, we decided that after three rehearsals, we were ready for a *tour*. And not just a long weekend tour of clubs close to L.A.; we took Duff up on his offer to book us a jaunt that stretched from Sacramento all the way up to his hometown of Seattle. It was completely improbable but to us it seemed like the most sensible idea in the world.

We planned to pack the gear and leave in a few days, but our zeal scared the shit out of our drummer, Rob Gardner, so much that he more or less quit the band on the spot. It didn't surprise anyone because Rob could play well enough but he didn't fit in from the start; he wasn't of the same ilk, he wasn't one of *us*: he just wasn't the sell-your-soul-for-rock-and-roll type. It was a polite departure—we couldn't imagine anyone who had played those last three rehearsals not wanting to tour the coast as an unknown band with nothing but our gear and the clothes on our backs, but we accepted his decision. We would not be stopped, however, so I called the one drummer that I knew who would leave that night if we asked him to: Steven Adler.

We watched as Steven set up both of his silver-blue bass drums and loosened up with a few typical double-bass fills at rehearsal the next day. His aesthetic touchstones were off, but it wasn't an insurmountable problem. It was a situation rectified in a typically Guns fashion: when Steven ducked out to take a piss, Izzy and Duff hid one of his bass drums, a floor

tom, and some small rack toms. Steven returned, sat down, and started counting in the next song before he realized what was missing.

"Hey, where's my other bass drum?" he asked, looking around as if he'd dropped them on the way to the bathroom or something. "I came here with two . . . and my other drums?

"Don't worry about it, man. You don't need them, just count off the song," Izzy said.

Steven never got his extra bass drum back and it was the best thing that ever happened to him. Of the five of us, he was the most conventionally contemporary, which, all things considered, lent a key element to our sound—but we weren't going to let him hammer that point home all night long. We bullied him into being a straight-ahead, 4/4 rock-and-roll drummer, which complemented and easily locked in with Duff's bass style, while allowing Izzy and me the freedom to mesh blues-driven rock and roll with the neurotic edge of first-generation punk. Not to mention what Axl's lyrics and delivery brought to it. Axl had a unique voice; it was brilliant in range and tone, but even though it was often intense and in your face, it had an amazingly soulful, bluesy quality to it because he had a choir background from singing in church when he was in grade school.

By the end of his tryout, Steven was hired and the original Guns N' Roses lineup was locked and loaded. Duff had booked the tour; all that we needed was wheels. Anyone who knows a musician well, successful or otherwise, knows this: generally, they are adept at "borrowing" from their friends. It took one phone call and very minor convincing for us to enlist our friends Danny and Joe, whose car and loyalty we made use of very regularly. To sweeten the deal, we christened Danny our tour manager and Joe our roadie and the next morning drove Danny's weathered green tank of an Oldsmobile out to the Valley to pick up a U-Haul trailer that we filled with the amps, guitars, and drum kit.

Seven of us packed into this mid-seventies Olds and set out on what I don't think anyone but Duff realized was a trip of over a thousand miles. We were outside of Fresno, two hundred miles from L.A. and two hundred short of Sacramento, when the car broke down. Danny wasn't the type of guy to have splurged for AAA, so luckily we broke down within pushing distance of a gas station, where we discovered that it would take

four days to get the necessary parts to fix a beast that old. At that rate, we wouldn't make any of the shows.

Our enthusiasm was too great to allow for delays or thoughts of practicality, so we told Danny and Joe to stay with the car and gear until it was repaired and to meet us in Portland (about seven hundred fifty miles away), at one of the gigs on the route. From there, we decided we'd drive to Seattle together (about a hundred and seventy-five miles farther) to play the final show of our tour with our own gear. There was a brief moment when Danny and Joe campaigned for us to remain in Fresno together until the car was back on the road, but neither that nor the obvious option of turning back were ever considered seriously. We hadn't even considered how to get from one gig to the next, let alone that we might not find amps and drums ready to borrow when we got there. We really didn't give a shit about any of that; the five of us didn't hesitate—we hit the highway to start hitchhiking.

We gave Danny and Joe whatever money we could spare to pay for the car—probably about twenty bucks—and walked up the on-ramp to the highway, guitar cases in hand. A few hours without so much as one vehicle even slowing down to check us out didn't dent our confidence. We remained proactive, testing the efficiency of the various hitchhiking configurations available to us: five guys with no visible luggage; two guys hitching and three guys hidden in the bushes; one guy with a guitar case; just Axl and Izzy; just Izzy and me; just Axl and me; just Steven alone, waving and grinning; just Duff alone. Nothing seemed to work; the people of Fresno weren't having us in any way, shape, or form.

It took about six hours for our kind of misfit to come along; a trucker willing to take all of us on board, stuffed into the front seat and the small bench behind it in his cab. It was close quarters, made even closer by the guitar cases and the sheer intensity of this guy's speed habit. He shared his stash with us sparingly, which made his endless stories of life on the road more digestible: the five of us were all pretty cynical and sarcastic, so in the beginning we were thoroughly amused by this guy's insanity. As that night, the next day, and the day after that came screaming down the road at us through the windshield, there wasn't anyplace else I thought I'd rather be. When we'd pull over at rest stops so this guy could sleep for a while in the

back of his cab—which was a consistently inconsistent amount of time lasting anywhere from an hour to half a day—we'd crash on park benches, write songs as the sun came up, or just walk around kicking trash at squirrels.

After a couple of days of this, our chauffeur started to smell particularly pungent and his formerly affable, strung-out chatter seemed to turn darkly weird. We were soon collectively disenchanted. He informed us that he planned to take a detour to pick up more speed from "his old lady," who I guess drove out to meet him at regular spots on his route to keep him juiced up. It didn't look like the situation was bound to improve. The next time he pulled into a rest stop to take one of his endless naps, we were way too bored and broke to stick it out any longer. We decided to explore our options by hitting the blacktop to again look for a ride, figuring that if worse came to worst, the speed demon in the semi would find us and pick us up again whenever he woke up. He probably wouldn't even think we'd ditched him.

Our prospects weren't plentiful, because, among the five of us, not one of us bore an iota of mainstream appeal, from Duff's red-and-black leather trench coat to our black leather jackets, long hair, and a few days of road grime. I have no idea how long we waited, but eventually we hailed a ride from two chicks in a pickup truck with a shell. They drove us to the outskirts of Portland, and once we got within the city limits, all was well—Duff's friend Donner from Seattle had sent someone to get us who informed us that Danny and Joe had called ahead: apparently the car was too unreliable to make the trip so they had headed back to L.A. It's not like we cared; we were forging on, even though we'd missed every single gig along the way. It didn't matter to us so long as we had a shot at making our final show of the tour—it was scheduled to take place in Seattle, and what was meant to be our last gig became the first Guns N' Roses show that ever was.

Arriving in Seattle was especially victorious both because we'd actually made it (that last drive came off with no problems), and also because Donner's house was the closest thing I have ever seen to *Animal House*. The day we rolled in, they threw a barbecue in our honor that, as far as I could tell, never seemed to end—it was as raging when we dragged ourselves out of there as it had been when everyone first cheered the five strangers from L.A. who came through their door. There was an endless supply of pot, a ton of booze, and people sleeping, tripping, or fucking in

every corner. It was a fitting Guns N' Roses after-show party . . . that started before our first show.

We arrived at Donner's house a handful of hours before we were supposed to be onstage. We had nothing but our guitars, so we really needed to find ourselves equipment. As I said, before moving to L.A., Duff had played in legendary Seattle punk bands, so he could pull in some favors: he gave Lulu Gargiulo of the Fastbacks a call, and she came through for us by loaning us their drum kit and amps. She personally made the first Guns N' Roses show possible. And I'd like to thank her right now once again.

The club was called Gorilla Gardens, which was the epitome of a punk-rock shit hole: it was dank and dirty and smelled of stale beer. It was situated right on the water, on an industrial wharf that lent it a vaguely maritime feel, but not in a picturesque, wooden dock manner at all. That place was at the end of a concrete slab; it was the kind of setting where deals get made in East Coast gangster movies, and on top of all of that, it was cold and raining outside the night we played there.

We just got up and did our set and the crowd was neither hostile nor gracious. We probably played seven or eight songs—"Move to the City," "Reckless Life," "Heartbreak Hotel," "Shadow of Your Love," and "Anything Goes" among them—and it went by pretty quickly. That night we were a raw interpretation of what the band was; once the nervous energy subsided, at least for me, we'd reached the end of the set. That said, we had a very small number of train wrecks in the arrangements, and all in all the gig was pretty good . . . until we had to collect our money. Then it became as much of an uphill battle as the rest of our early career would be.

The club owner refused to pay us the $150 we were promised. We tackled this obstacle as we had the entire road trip—as a group. We broke down our gear, got it packed up outside of the club, and cornered this guy in his office. Duff talked to him while we crowded around, looking formidable and throwing in a couple threats for good measure. We blocked the door and held him hostage until he finally coughed up $100 of our cash. He had some sort of bullshit excuse about why he was shorting us $50 that was just fucking dumb. We didn't care to get to the bottom of it at all, so we took the $100 and split.

THERE IS ONE IMAGE THAT I HAVE OF our days in Seattle that sums it all up to me. It is of an upside down TV. I remember lying with my body half on the bed, my head hung over the end of the pull-out couch so far that the top of it was against the floor. There were equally rotted people that I didn't know lying on both sides of me and I was so stoned that I thought I'd found the best position in the world that a body might ever be in. The blood rushed to my brain as I dangled there watching *The Abominable Dr. Phibes*, starring Vincent Price, and there wasn't anything else I wanted to do.

After a couple of days of after-partying at Donner's house, we hopped back in the car with his friend, whom we'll call Jane. She was either crazy or just liked us enough to drive us all the way back to L.A.. I'm still not sure which. We drove through to Sacramento, which is about seven hundred fifty miles, before we made our first pit stop. By that point, we had to pause: Jane wasn't the type to have a car with functioning air-conditioning, and considering the summertime heat, it might have been lethal to keep going by that point.

We parked and spent the afternoon wandering around the state-capitol area begging for change to get something to eat. After a few hours, we took our earnings and hit the McDonald's and we barely had enough food to share among the six of us. Afterward, we lay down under the shade of a few oak trees in the park across from the capitol in search of some relief from the heat. It got so unbearable that we jumped the fence and took refuge in some convalescent home's pool. We didn't give a fuck that we were trespassing; actually, if we'd gotten arrested, it probably would have been an improvement—at least there would be food and better air-conditioning than Jane's car. Once the sun went down and it finally cooled off enough to get back in that thing, we got back on the road.

I didn't realize it until years later, but that trip cemented us as a band more than we knew; our commitments were tested on that journey. We'd partied, we'd played, we'd survived, we'd endured, and we racked up a lifetime's worth of stories in just two weeks. Or was it one week . . . I think it was one week . . . what do I know?

IT MAKES SENSE THAT GUNS' FIRST SHOW took place in Seattle because as much as L.A. was our address, we had as much in common with the average "L.A." band as Seattle's weather has with Southern California's. Our main influences were Aerosmith, especially for me, and then there was T. Rex, Hanoi Rocks, and the New York Dolls. I guess you could even say that Axl was a version of Michael Monroe.

So we were back in L.A. with our first-ever gig as a band behind us. We were all set to get back to rehearsing and keep the momentum focused. We got together out at this space in Silverlake and were all packed into Duff's little Toyota Celica driving home after rehearsal. As we pulled into an intersection to make a left turn, we were broadsided by some guy doing about sixty miles an hour. Steven broke his ankle because his legs were stretched out between the two front seats, and everyone got pretty banged up, myself least of all—I walked away unscathed. It was a pretty gnarly little accident; Duff's car was totaled and we could have been, too. That would have been a sick twist of fate: the band dying together after we'd just gotten together.

WE STARTED HANGING AROUND WITH A few of the seedier rock-and-roll people in the L.A. scene; they were part of an underbelly that the typical Sunset Strip rock fan didn't know about. One of the characters was Nicky Beat, who was the drummer for L.A. Guns for a minute, but mostly spent his time playing in lesser-known glam bands like the Joneses. Nicky wasn't necessarily seedy but he had a lot of seedy friends. He also had a rehearsal studio in his house in Silverlake where we'd go, set up our gear, and jam, and that is where the whole band really came together. Izzy had something called "Think About You" that we liked, and we revisited "Don't Cry," which was the first song I'd ever worked on with Izzy. Izzy had another riff for a song called "Out Ta Get Me" that clicked with me immediately when I first heard it—we had that one done in no time. Axl remembered a riff that I'd played him when he was living over at my mom's

house, which was ages ago at this point: it was the introduction and the main riff to "Welcome to the Jungle." That song, if anything, was the first real tune that the band wrote together. We were sitting around rehearsal looking to write something new when that riff came to Axl's mind.

"Hey, what about that riff you played me a while ago?" he asked.

"When you were staying with me?" I asked.

"Yeah. It was good. Let's hear it."

I started playing it and instantly Steve came up with a beat, Duff joined in with a bass line, and away we went. I kept throwing parts out to build on it: the chorus part, the solo, as Axl came up with the lyrics.

Duff was the glue on that song—he came up with the breakdown, that wild rumbling bass line, and Izzy provided the texture. In about three hours, the song was complete. The arrangement is virtually the same as it appears on the album.

We needed an intro and I came up with one that day using the digital delay on my cheap Boss guitar pedal board. I got my money's worth out of that thing, because as crappy as it was, that pedal provided the tense echo effect that set the mood for that song and eventually the kickoff for our debut album.

A lot of our earliest songs came to us almost too easy. "Out Ta Get Me" came to be in an afternoon, even faster than "Jungle." Izzy showed up with the riff and the basic idea for the song and the second he played it, the notes hit my ear and inspired me. That one happened so quickly, I think that even the most complicated section—the dual guitar parts—were written in under twenty minutes.

I had never been in a band where pieces of music that I found so inspiring came so fluidly. I can't speak for the other guys, but judging by the speed at which our collective creativity came together I assume they felt something similar. We seemed to share this common knowledge and a kind of secret language back then; it was as if we all already knew what the other guy was going to bring into rehearsal and had already written the perfect part to move the song along. When we were all on the same page, it really was that easy.

Slash, during Guns' short-lived glam phase.

WE BORROWED SHIT FROM CHICKS AND
initially we had that trashy glam look, though a lot more rough-edged.
Very quickly, though, we got too lazy to do the makeup and all that so our
glam phase was short-lived. Plus the clothes were a problem because we
were always changing girlfriends, and you never knew what the next "she"
was going to have. Besides, I don't think that look ever really suited
me—I didn't have the emaciated white-boy long-haired physique. Ditching

YOU LEARN TO LIVE LIKE AN ANIMAL

the whole idea worked to our advantage in the end: we were grittier, more traditional, and more genuine; more a product of Hollywood itself than the L.A. glam scene.

We were also the lunatic-fringe rock-and-roll band. We thrived on being out of place and took every gig we were offered. We practiced every day, and new songs came quickly; we'd test them in front of bawdy crowds at venues like Madame Wong's West, the Troubadour, and the Whisky. I looked at whatever we did each day as the next step along a path to where everything was possible. In my mind it was simple: if we focused on nothing but surmounting the nearest obstacle, we'd make our way from Point A to Point C in no time no matter how great the distance.

With every show that we played, we made more fans—and usually a few new enemies. It didn't matter; as we drew bigger crowds, it was easier to get gigs. Our fans, from the start, were always a mixed bag: we had punks, we had metalheads, we had stoners, we had psychos, the odd weirdo, and a few lost souls. They were never an easily identified or quantifiable commodity . . . in fact, after all of these years, I am still at a loss for a simple phrase that puts a bow on them—which is fine by me. Guns' die-hard fans were, I suppose, kindred spirits; misfits who'd made their outcast status their stance.

Once our profile started to grow on the local level, we hooked up with Vicky Hamilton, a manager who'd helped both Mötley Crüe and Poison in their early days. Vicky was a five-foot nine-inch overweight platinum blonde with a whiny voice who just believed in us and proved it by promoting us for free. I liked Vicky a lot—she was very sincere and meant well; she helped me get posters for our shows printed, took out ads in the *L.A. Weekly*, and dealt with the promoters at our gigs. I worked alongside her doing everything I could to further our cause; with her help, everything began to really take off.

We started playing at least once a week, and as our exposure increased, so did the need to get some new clothes—my three T-shirts, my loaner leather jacket, one pair of jeans, and one pair of leather pants weren't gonna cut it. I decided that I had to do something about it the afternoon before we played our first Saturday-night headlining slot at the Whisky.

I didn't have the financial means to make much happen, so I wandered the shops in Hollywood looking for odds and ends. I stole a concho belt

from a place called Leathers and Treasures that was black and silver, just like the one Jim Morrison always wore. I planned on wearing it with my jeans or my pair of leather pants (which I'd found in the Dumpster of my grandmother's old apartment complex) and continued browsing the various shops. I found something interesting in a place called Retail Slut. There was no way that I could afford it, and for the first time in my life, I wasn't sure how I could steal it—but I knew I had to have it.

A large black top hat doesn't easily fit under your shirt, though I've had so many stolen from me over the years that someone has worked out an effective technique that I don't know about. In any case, I'm still not sure if the staff noticed and, if they did, whether or not they cared as I blatantly snatched that top hat off the mannequin and casually walked out of the store and never looked back. I don't know what it was; the hat just spoke to me.

Once I got back to the apartment I was living in at the time, I realized my new "purchases" would best serve each other by becoming one: I cut the belt to fit the top hat and was happy with the way it looked. I was even happier to discover that with my new accessory pulled down as far as it could go, I could see everything but no one could really see me. Some might say that a guitarist hides behind his instrument anyway, but my hat added an impenetrable comfort. And while I never thought it was original, it was mine—a trademark that became an indelible part of my image.

WHEN GUNS FIRST GOT GOING, I WAS working at a newsstand on Fairfax and Melrose. I lived with my on-again, off-again girlfriend Yvonne full-time until she got sick of me, at which point we broke up once more, leaving me nowhere to live. My former manager at the newsstand, Alison, let me crash in her living room and pay her half of the rent. She was a very handsome reggae chick with an apartment on Fairfax and Olympic who was taking college classes at night. Alison was attractive, but I always thought that either she was a little old for me or that I was a little young for her; either way, we never had that kind of relationship. We got along very well, and when she left the newsstand for a better job, I was lucky enough to inherit her position.

YOU LEARN TO LIVE LIKE AN ANIMAL

Alison always treated me like the cute stray she'd taken in, and I did little to prove her wrong. As her tenant, I didn't take up much space. My worldly possessions were my guitar, a black trunk full of rock magazines, cassettes, an alarm clock, some pictures, and whatever clothes I owned or had been given by friends and girlfriends. And there was my snake, Clyde, in his cage.

Anyway, the newsstand job came to an abrupt end in the summer of '85 when a local rock station, KNEC, threw a party out in Griffith Park, complete with free charter buses that departed from the Hyatt on the Sunset Strip. I headed over there after work with two pints of Jack Daniel's in my jeans, not giving a shit that I was expected to open the newsstand up at five the next morning. It was a pretty debauched summer night as I recall; people passed bottles and joints as the bus made its way across town. There were plenty of local characters and musicians on board, and when we got there, music playing and a barbecue. The grass was full of people engaged in everything.

I got so fucked up that night that I brought a girl back to Alison's place and was fucking her on the living-room floor when Alison came home and caught us. She didn't need to say anything—her expression told me that she wasn't too pleased. I stayed up with this girl anyway until it was time for me to go to work. By the time I got her dressed and on her way, I was already late and my boss, Jake, had called. I was in the doghouse already because I used the phone at the newsstand to conduct band business so often that he'd started calling during my shifts to catch me in the act, which proved to be difficult. Those were the days before call waiting and I was on the phone constantly so it took Jake hours to get through just to yell at me. Needless to say he was pretty pissed off about opening up for me that day.

"Yeah, Jake, I'm sorry," I mumbled, still pretty drunk when he called for the second time. "I know I'm late, I got held up. But I'm on my way."

"Oh, you're on your *way?*" he asked.

"Yeah, Jake, I'll be there really soon."

"No you won't," he said. "Don't bother. Not *today*. Not *tomorrow*. Not *ever*."

I paused for a minute and let that sink in. "You know, Jake, that's probably a good idea."

lived across the street from each other on Orange Avenue. Duff had a working-class-musician mentality like mine—until the band really got going, he didn't feel right if he didn't have a job, even if his job was morally suspect. He did phone sales or phone theft, depending on your point of view: Duff worked as a telemarketer for one of those firms that promise people a prize of some kind if they agree to pay a small fee "in order to redeem it." I had a similar job before I got my job in the clock factory: I'd call people all day, promising them a Jacuzzi or a tropical vacation if they'd just "confirm" their credit-card number to cover their "eligibility fee." It was a nasty, cutthroat gig and I got out the day before it was raided by the police.

Axl and Steven would do anything not to work a regular job, so they got by on the street, or via their girlfriends' handouts. Though, as I recall, on occasion Axl and I took jobs together as extras on movie sets. We were in a few crowd shots at the L.A. Sports Arena for a Michael Keaton movie called *Touch and Go* where he played a hockey player. We didn't care as much for the camera time as we did getting fed and making money for doing nothing: we'd show up in the morning, get our meal ticket, then find somewhere to sleep behind the bleachers where we wouldn't be found. We'd wake up when they called for lunch to eat with the rest of the crowd, then sleep until it was time to clock out and collect our hundred-dollar check.

I liked being the industry's least industrious extra as often as possible: I found absolutely nothing wrong with free lunch and an afternoon of being paid to sleep. I looked forward to the same when I was scouted by a casting director for the film *Sid and Nancy*. Unbeknownst to any of us, the same casting director in various locales, scouted every single member of Guns N' Roses individually. All of us showed up to the first day of casting, like, "Hey . . . what are you doing here?"

It wasn't much fun; actually, it was like jury duty: there was a pen full of extras, but all five of us were chosen to be in the same concert scene, where "the Sex Pistols" are playing some small club. The shoot required showing up early in the morning, for three consecutive days, with the usual promise of a meal ticket and a hundred bucks each day. A three-day com-

mitment was too much for the other guys. In the end, I was the only one of us pathetic enough to show up for the duration.

Fuck them, I had a blast; for three days, they shot these "Sex Pistols" concert scenes at the Starwood, a club that I knew inside and out. I'd show up in the morning, clock in and get my meal ticket, then disappear into the bowels of the Starwood and get drunk on Jim Beam all by myself. While the other extras were doing their part playing audience members down on the floor in front of the stage, I watched the proceedings from a hidden corner of the mezzanine—and got paid the same wage.

<div align="center">—◆━×━◆—</div>

AS GUNS BECAME A CLUB BAND TO BE reckoned with, a few ridiculous L.A. managers started to circle us like sharks, claiming that they had what it took to make us stars. At this point we had amicably and temporarily parted ways with Vicky Hamilton, so we were open to offers, but most of those that we got were just retarded. One of the more convincing examples of how low those types will go and what would be in store for us should we make that mistake came courtesy of Kim Fowley, the infamous character who managed the Runaways the way Phil Spector managed the Ronettes; basically just a legalized form of indentured servitude. Kim gave us his best lines, but the moment he talked about taking a percentage of our publishing and making a long-term creative commitment to him, it was clear what he had in mind. His bullshit and demeanor spoke for themselves because Kim was too odd of a guy to fake it.

I liked him nonetheless and was happy to hang out and be entertained by him—as long as he didn't get too close. The rest of us were the same kind of animal: willing to take advantage of everything someone might have to offer without making any promises we'd have to keep. Axl would hang out as long as the conversation was worthwhile because Axl is a good talker. Steven was there if there were chicks involved. And I was willing to consume all of the free Denny's meals, cigarettes, drinks, and drugs in exchange for the conversation I had to put up with. Once the factors that had drawn us in were exhausted, one by one, we'd make our exit.

Kim introduced us to a guy named Dave Liebert, who was Alice Cooper's tour manager for a time and had worked with Parliament-

Funkadelic, only God knows when, and those two were intent on signing us as a team, and taking us for all we were worth. Kim took me over to Dave's house to meet him one night and I remember Dave showing us his gold records. His attitude was "Hey, kid, this could be you." I assume he intended to entice me further by inviting two girls over, who were young enough to be his daughters, that spent the night shooting speed in the bathroom. Dave dragged me in there at one point and it seemed like these chicks had no idea what they were doing. They were so inept that I wanted to grab the needle and inject them myself. Dave was into it and, in the unbearable fluorescent light of that bathroom, stripped down to his underwear and fooled around with these girls—who were nineteen at best—and invited me to join in. I remember thinking that of all the reasons why this scene was so very scummy, the lighting was worst of all. The thought of this guy managing our band and Kim Fowley with his collection of prehistoric gold records made it nearly impossible not to just laugh hysterically right in his face. It would have been professional suicide before we ever had something to lose. We'd never stand a chance if the management was as debaucherous as the band, anyway.

AS GUNS KEPT REHEARSING, WRITING, and gigging, working to define who we were, I started going out more. Suddenly there were actually bands I wanted to see because finally the scene was changing: there were bands like Red Kross who were a glam band, but were gritty, and at the other end of the spectrum, there were bands like Jane's Addiction who were great and that I related to but I wasn't on the same page with. We played shows with some of those more obscure, arty bands—I remember a gig at the Stardust Ballroom—but they never quite came off right. We weren't considered hip by the bands in that scene, because they thought of us as a glam outfit from the Troubadour side of town more than we ever really were. What those bands didn't know is that we were probably darker and more sinister than they were. Nor did they realize that we could not fucking stand our peers on the other side of town.

In fact, as our popularity grew, we began to wage war with the bands on "our" side of town. We never went out of our way to fuck with them, but

after a while everybody we played with was scared of us because Axl got a reputation for being volatile and flying off the handle at any given moment. I'd been out with him several nights where we got into these fucking major fights with total strangers for no real reason that I can recall. As far as Axl was concerned, there definitely was a good reason for it, but as far as I could tell, we were just fighting people in the street—literally in the street—because someone had looked at him the wrong way or said the wrong thing. Although I must admit . . . it was a hell of a lot of fun.

I'd say that my life lost all trace of a stable, "regular" existence once I was fired from my job at the newsstand. As I mentioned earlier, I'd been living with Alison, my former manager at that job, literally renting space on her living-room floor, but once I got fired, her charity and my regular paycheck dried up. With nowhere to live, I packed up my snake, my guitar, and my black trunk and moved into Guns' rehearsal space, where Axl and I soon became permanent residents. Izzy, Steven, and Duff had girlfriends that they crashed with—Izzy and Duff even had apartments of their own. Axl and I were the only two with nowhere else to go.

Our rehearsal "studio" was pretty raw; it was one of three storage units in a building off Sunset and Gardner that were meant to house boxes or cars, not people. The front door was a corrugated aluminum roll-up like the kind you find on a cheap garage, the floor was sealed concrete, and we were the only renters who chose to make our fifteen-by-twenty-foot space into a residence. The building came complete with a communal bathroom about fifty yards away, but most often, I preferred to piss in the bushes across the alley from our "foyer." We called the place the Sunset and Gardner Hotel and Villas.

Our rehearsal space had no business masquerading as a living space because it wasn't even meant to be a rehearsal space—it was barely even a decent storage space.

Eventually, Izzy decided that at the least, Axl and I should have a proper bed, so one day, he and Steven found some two-by-fours and built a makeshift queen-size loft over the drum kit. It was as welcome an innovation as the flush toilet had been in eighteenth-century England. We had one other implement that made our band "apartment" more of a home—a charcoal hibachi grill that one of us either stole or bought. I never used it, because

as much as I appreciate fine cuisine, I've never been bothered to try my hand at it, but somehow Steven and Izzy could turn out very decent meals on that thing.

We were industrious about writing songs and rehearsing every day in there, but since Axl and I lived there full-time, our practice space soon became an out-of-the-way, off-the-map late-night destination with no house rules. On a typical night, one of us would be getting laid in the loft or out in the open, another one of us might be passed out between an amp and the drum kit, and usually assorted friends were drinking and doing drugs in the alley until the sun came up. We wrote a lot of good songs in that garage, inspired by our surroundings. "Night Train," "My Michelle," and "Rocket Queen" among them.

"Night Train" was pieced together from a few different moments. I remember first working on the main riff of that song with Izzy, sitting there on the dank floor of that place, just before I moved out of Alison's. We didn't know where the song was going and we didn't have any kind of subject in mind, but the groove was so right and we locked in and felt it out. I remember feeling a bit off and the next day I came down with a bad case of strep throat. I was laid up sick on Alison's couch for two days but in the interim, Izzy played Duff what we'd done and Duff worked on it, filling out the groove and making our riffs into a proper instrumental.

None of us had any words in mind for this piece of music, but we were very inspired by it and it floated around in the band's consciousness until it found the appropriate vessel, which happened to be a celebration of our favorite drink, Night Train.

One night we were walking up Palm Avenue, which was an infamous street in our world because more than a few sleazy chicks lived there, a few junkie girls we knew lived there, and so did Lizzy Grey, the guitarist in London. We spent a lot of time on that block in those days, because we knew a few too many characters in that neighborhood, so every time we found ourselves walking over there we knew it was the start of something. That night we were sharing a bottle of Night Train, a "wine" that is about 18 percent strong and back then could be bought for less than two bucks a bottle. It is the cheapest low-rent wine that money could buy and we drank it like crazy whenever no one else was paying. It might not sound like much,

but it's definitely a trip; unless you've tried it, you probably won't understand why we found ourselves improvising lyrics in its honor as we wandered up Palm Ave.

I can't remember who started it, but someone burst out with the chorus: "I'm on the Night Train!" We all joined in and kept going as Axl improvised all of the lines in between: "Bottoms up!" "Fill my cup!" "Love that stuff!" and "I'm ready to crash and burn!"

It came to us in one of those amazing moments, just like "Paradise City." "Night Train" was an anthem that we came up with on the spot, not even knowing how much it really captured us as we were at that moment in time. In the same vein as "Paradise," there is an innocent quality to that song; it's a nursery rhyme almost, a cute melody sung by kids on a playground . . . sinister kids whose playground is a seedy back alley.

That song really got all of us fired up. I don't remember if we got to it later that night back at the rehearsal garage or the next morning, but within a day, we had it all worked out. Axl got the lyrics down, we smoothed out all of the parts and that was it. We tested it out at our next club date and it worked. It *really* worked. That song has a rhythm to it in the verses that from the start always made me go crazy. The first time we played it, even, I just started jumping up and down—I couldn't help it. When we had our huge stage much later on, I'd run the length of it, jump off the amplifiers, and lose it just about every single time we played it. I'm not sure why, but no other song we've ever played live made me move like that.

There was one more classic that we wrote back there in that garage: "My Michelle." The music originated there, I think over the course of a few afternoons. I believe Izzy and I came up with the basic structure, and then, as usual, Duff came through with exactly what the song needed to evolve. In any case, I didn't write the words, but I definitely know what they're about. The subject of the song is Michelle Young, who was friends with my first girlfriend, Melissa. I knew the both of them all through junior high, well before Guns was even an idea, let alone a reality.

The thing is, because of friends of mine like Mark Mansfield and Ron Schneider who were still close to me and part of the music scene to a degree, at the time, many of my old friends became involved in the Guns N' Roses universe once it got going. Because of our common friends, I reestablished

connections with people I hadn't seen since I'd left school, and many of them got sucked into our world—for better, and mostly for worse.

Michelle was one of them; even when we were kids she was always a nut case. When she started frequenting our circles, she ended up hooking up with Axl and they had a brief romantic interlude. He wrote those lyrics about her life, which tells the facts of her upbringing verbatim. Her dad was definitely involved in the porn business and her mom was a pill popper and drug addict who eventually committed suicide. But having my former school friend with whom I'd shared cigarettes in the bathroom back in junior high become the subject of one of our more intense songs was something else. I asked Axl about it one day, because I couldn't imagine the Michelle I knew being happy about having her story made public.

"Hey, Axl," I said to him at rehearsal after we'd run through the song, "don't you think Michelle is going to be offended?"

"Why would she?" he said. "It's all fucking true."

"Yeah it is, but I don't know if it's going to be cool if you say all those things. Can't you change it a bit?"

"No," he said. "It's the truth. Even if she doesn't like it, I'm going to do it anyway."

I expected the worst; even though we had nothing to sue for, I expected Michelle to come after us in some way. I at least expected her to hate the song and be mortified by having her business hung out there like that. I was very, very wrong: from the moment we played that song live through to when we recorded it for our album, Michelle loved the attention it brought her. Back then it was the best thing that ever happened to her. But like so many of our friends that were drawn into the dark circle of Guns N' Roses, she came in one way and went out another. Most of them ended up either going to jail or rehab or both (or worse), but I'm happy to say that she's among those who turned their lives around before it was too late. More than a few of our friends eventually moved to Minneapolis . . . maybe that had something to do with it.

"Rocket Queen" was inspired by a riff I came up with when I first met Duff. It was one of the more complicated arrangements on what became our album, mostly because we had to integrate the riff with Axl's more melodic chorus. The song is based on our mutual friend Barbie, who even

at eighteen had a notorious reputation. She was a drug addict and a queen of the underground scene back then. She'd eventually become a madam, but Axl was infatuated with her at the time. I hear she has managed to survive after all these years.

I was pulled under, I passed out cold, and fell off the chair and woke up sprawled across the floor hours later at daybreak.

IT WAS DURING THIS PERIOD OF WRITING and rehearsing at the Sunset and Gardner Hotel and Villas that I started to notice something different about Steven. He would show up to rehearsal a little too elastic; he seemed like he was drunk but he wasn't drinking anything. I couldn't quite figure it out because his playing was fine, so I was intrigued. Steven was dating a girl who lived with a roommate on Gardner just down the street from our rehearsal space. I started to go over there with him every night after we were done practicing and found it to be a pretty heavy scene: it was like time stopped when you walked through the door; everything moved very, very slowly.

I got to know Steve's girlfriend and her roommate, a girl so whacked out that it broke my heart. I have to admit, I also thought she was cute, so I started seeing her, and though I was aware that she was on something, I wasn't aware of what it was. I'd go over there with Steven after rehearsal and the four of us would listen to the Stones' *Goats Head Soup* all night

long while I watched them nodding off all over the place. It finally dawned on me that heroin might be the catalyst for everybody's subdued state. At first, none of them did it in front of me, so I figured it out later rather than sooner. But even if they had, I wouldn't have tried it because at that point heroin had no appeal to me. I didn't know much about it, and what I saw didn't make me want to try it at all. Why would it?

The roommate was one of those useless L.A. stories: she was eighteen or nineteen; a rich girl who had taken her family's money and done everything in her power to throw it in their face. In the process she'd fucked herself up pretty good, and she'd complain to no end about how her life was a shambles and how it was all her family's fault. Her solution was to piss and moan until she couldn't take it anymore, then get high and seek solace in nodding out, which, needless to say, got in the way of her limited, yet planned efforts to repair her situation. This movie came complete with the early-morning scene where her mother arrives unannounced to confront her and of course I made the mistake of getting in the middle of their horrible argument.

I didn't say much, but her mother was convinced that I was the cause of her daughter's condition. The truth is that I was the only one in her scene *not* on heroin. Her mother left that day hating me and leaving her daughter behind, but eventually she won out: that girl soon disappeared. After that, Steven's girlfriend moved out, too, and neither of us ever saw either of them again.

Up until I watched Steven and the girls do it and eventually did it myself, all that I knew of heroin were the antidrug movies I'd seen in school and the plot of *The French Connection*, which centered on Popeye Doyle's maniacal efforts to stop the import of a French cartel's huge shipment of it. At that point I had no idea that all of my heroes were on heroin. But I'd soon find out. It crept into my life like ivy up a wall.

Izzy and I were at Nicky Beat's rehearsal studio back in 1984, when I first chased the dragon with him, sucking up the smoke that rose from the foil through a straw as we heated it up. All it left me feeling was queasy and not very high at all. I didn't get the instant buzz, so I lost interest in it quick; feeling sick was not my idea of a good time. Izzy was cool; he could smoke it and get complete satisfaction that way.

A few months later I mainlined for the first time and that was all she wrote; after that, I'd never do it any other way than straight into my bloodstream. I was just like every other cheap-thrill user; I wanted it fast and I wanted it now. I've never been able to get high doing it any other way than with a needle. If I can't, I'd rather not bother; it's a waste of drugs, a waste of time, and a conscious decision to be inefficient. I had tried to do it the way it is supposed to be done; the ancient civilized method of chasing the dragon according to Chinese custom, but that didn't work for me. The Chinese were cool, collected, and composed about heroin, in the same way they were about opium. The intravenous method was developed much later, in the West, once people began using morphine recreationally. Needles were sought out for the instant gratification factor and that is what street people were after. In America, in the cowboy days of the Wild West, more women did it than men, all of them using needles, most of them hookers and barmaids.

One night really can change your life and this was the night that changed mine. I've thought about this a lot and I'm sure that it was probably because of all the Jim Beam I drank. We were in some chick's apartment I ended up at with Izzy. I was at her vanity table, in her bathroom; it was very dimly lit, very druggy. She tied me off, loaded it up, shot it . . . and a wave engulfed me from somewhere deep within my stomach. I got this huge rush and that was all that I remembered. I was pulled under, I passed out cold, and fell off the chair and woke up sprawled across the floor hours later at daybreak. It took me a second to figure out what had happened: there was a bottle of Jim Beam next to me that I'd been drinking and for a moment I forgot altogether that'd I'd done heroin.

I looked through the doorway and saw Izzy and the girl asleep in the bed and that was when I realized that I felt somehow . . . different. I wasn't sure what it was, aside from the fact that it wasn't familiar. It was all fine, though, because I was in the *best* mood. When Izzy and the girl woke up we hung out and I was just so content, so happy, and entirely at peace with everything. Izzy felt exactly the same way.

The girl's apartment we were in was off Wilshire near downtown L.A. and we left her that morning without a worry in the world. The future looked bright even though we didn't have any prospects at the time. As morning came over the city, we wandered all the way back up into Melrose in central

Hollywood and that's when I got the bright idea that we should go visit this girl I knew. She was a really attractive girl who went to Fairfax High who had a crush on me. Though I didn't know her all that well, I did know that her mom was at work every day, so we went over to her place and hung out and listened to the Beatles all afternoon. She had a big girlie bed with a fluffy comforter and the sunlight came into her room in a certain way; the whole space was very airy and white and pink and soft.

Izzy and I got there and fell out and listened to music. I was in love with the song "Dear Prudence." "Revolution" into "Dear Prudence" seemed to be everything that mattered in the world. "Norwegian Wood," that was good, too. We hung out there for the better part of the day, then left. On the way home, whenever we stopped walking, I would fall into that blissful nodding state that heroin brings. I realized that the buzz I'd gotten had lasted the whole day long.

This is the best thing I've ever done, I thought to myself. *Nothing was ever like this.*

I was nineteen years old.

OUR REHEARSAL SPACE/MY AND AXL'S apartment was where the band headed with our stragglers in tow at the end of the night. It was where we'd go after we'd played a show and whatever club it was had cleared us out. As our fan base grew, this ritual became an unwise proposition that wasn't going to end well but we engaged in it anyway. The Villas were deep enough into the cross section of Hollywood and downtown that no one but hookers and drug addicts were hanging around after dark— our neighbors were nine-to-five businesses on each side with the exception of the Gardner Elementary School right behind us, whose hours were more like eight to three. It was easy for fifty or more people to party all night, shooting smack, smoking pot, and breaking bottles against the wall without any trouble from the police. Soon that scene grew enough to fill our space, the alley, and the entire parking lot next to the building: people with liquor in brown paper bags could be found engaging in illegal and sordid activities, less than fifty yards off Sunset Boulevard at any hour of the night. We'd be up past dawn, but when the kids would start filing into the elementary school

in the morning, usually we started to wind things down. Luckily there was no interaction between our scene and theirs, although their playground did end at the back of our "studio" building.

Another band used the storage/rehearsal space next door to us and we could never remember their name . . . oh, wait, they were called the Wild. Dizzy Reed was in that band playing keyboards, and that is how he and Axl met and became friends. The Wild were a typical rock band of the day that I never went to see; I also never paid much attention to how they played. I did, however, party with them. Our entire rehearsal-space life was a scene defined by these two bands partying all night, every night in a dingy part of town.

The level of debauchery, for our part at least, got pretty outrageous. I remember being up in the bunk one night after a show with Izzy and some girl. We were taking turns having sex with her, but Izzy wasn't wearing protection, so when he pulled out, he fucking came on my leg, since I was right there on the other side of her. That definitely stopped me in my tracks. I sat up, looked over at him, and said, "Hey! Izzy . . . man. We've *got* to get a bigger place."

A scene that out of bounds wasn't going to last, and when it crashed it did so very dramatically. After one particular gig, as usual, our friends and whoever else was in the club came back to tear it up at our place well into the early morning. Now, most of the girls who chose to party in our alley-way until six or seven a.m. weren't the sharpest pencils in the box; but this particular night one of them lost it completely. My memory of the events is hazy, but from what I remember she had sex with Axl up in the loft. Toward the end of the night, maybe as the drugs and booze wore off, she lost her mind and freaked out intensely. Axl told her to leave and tried throwing her out. I attempted to help mediate the situation to get her out quietly, but that wasn't happening.

About a week later, Steven was there when the cops stormed in and turned the place upside down. They broke a few pieces of equipment searching for contraband and hassled anybody associated with us in any way; they threatened Steven with arrest if he didn't tell them where to find Axl and me because we were wanted for allegedly raping that girl. Steven got in touch with us and warned us, so we stayed away from home for the rest of

the day. I headed back there the next morning; it was raining and unseasonably cold, and I found Izzy when I got there, picking his way through the mess that the cops had left behind. I was completely puzzled because I hadn't done a thing that I could think of—I hardly spoke to the girl in question that night, nor had anybody else.

It was a bad situation, so I took my cue and split; I grabbed a few things and headed off to hide out with Steven at his new girlfriend Monica's apartment, which was within walking distance. Monica was a Swedish porn star who'd taken Steven in and I couldn't have asked for a better place to lay low because we used to have *awesome* threesomes. Monica was great, she was a really wonderful hostess that way, plus she had a phone, so I was able to receive constant updates on our legal situation. Generally, the news wasn't good: this was a real situation—Axl and I were charged with felony rape. The future looked grim and the band's progress halted immediately.

The girl's parents had contacts in the LAPD, and intended to press charges to the fullest. Axl took off to Orange County and hid out at some girl's place for a few weeks, while I stayed with Steven and Monica. For fear of arrest, we didn't book gigs and maintained a low profile. The truth was, Axl had definitely had sex with the girl, but it had been consensual and no one had raped her. For my part I hadn't even touched her! When we got our wits about us after a few weeks, we dealt with the situation through the proper channels.

Axl returned to L.A. and the two of us moved in with Vicky Hamilton and her roommate, Jennifer Perry, and Vicky hired a lawyer to handle our case. I'm sure Vicky regretted taking us in immediately: Axl and I took over the living room in her quaint one-bedroom apartment, and between the empty liquor bottles and the ceaseless parade of characters that seemed to trail along behind us wherever we went, overnight we converted it into a complete mess. Axl slept on the couch, I slept on the floor, and what was once a living room looked like a bomb had hit it. The kitchen was a fucking disaster; within a week there were dishes and trash piled a mile high. Luckily I'd convinced my ex-girlfriend Yvonne to watch my snake, Clyde, for a while. The case went to court, but somewhere along the line, the charges against me were dropped. Axl, however, did have to get himself a suit and

face the judge, but once the testimony was given, the charges were dropped and that was it.

———◆◆◆———

WE LOST WHAT SEEMED LIKE A YEAR OF our lives getting clear of that legal issue, because until then, every day had moved us forward with ferocious intensity. After that incident, we vacated our garage rehearsal space, and started playing out and working on new songs again. Our friends Danny and Joe were still in the picture; Danny's green Oldsmobile was still our band transportation. Danny was a great guy with a James Dean haircut and a very cool, confident vibe. He and I became drug buddies, too: once I got into heroin, we would drive that green beast all over L.A. looking for smack.

Joe was our roadie and my guitar tech back then, though he was pretty lousy: I remember headlining at the Roxy and one of Joe's duties was to bring me a slide during the solo section of "Rocket Queen," but by the time he actually got the slide on my finger the solo was over. I was so pissed off that I physically kicked him offstage. But all was forgiven later on, because Joe was a loyal, true-blue kind of guy that anyone would want to keep around. Joe was always the one to back any of us up when things got sticky and dedication like that can't be bought.

We weren't at all like the other bands playing clubs on the strip; we generally didn't care what they were doing. We did, however, as far as other bands went, have an unspoken disregard for Poison, because they were the biggest local band on the block and the epitome of everything that we hated about the L.A. music scene. We were scheduled to share a few bills with them at different points, early in our career, but each time something major went wrong. I believe once they didn't show up at all and we were forced to play two sets to cover for them, and I think another time the promoter pulled the gig at the last minute because of some shady move on their part.

One of our more memorable gigs from this era was an outdoor festival called the Street Scene that took place on six or seven stages in downtown Los Angeles that occupied a circuit of city blocks. It was our first time play-

ing it, and it was 1983, and we were scheduled to open for Fear, the only L.A. punk band that I really cared about. We drove down there in Danny's Oldsmobile and were unloading our gear in the designated band parking lot when we noticed a sea of people running our way. We continued to unload as people sprinted past us, literally as fast as they could—from what, we had no idea. It was as if Godzilla was coming or a guy had set off a shotgun behind them. We couldn't see what the problem was until we finally got close enough to the stage to realize there was no stage; Fear's fans had overzealously rioted and torn it down before the band even went on.

Our manager, Vicky, and I wandered around this huge mess in an attempt to find us a slot somewhere on the day-long bill. We pushed our way from stage to stage talking to the organizers, looking for an opening until we found one—playing after Social Distortion. It didn't sound like the best idea, following a loyally beloved local punk band, but it actually turned out to be one of the greatest gigs we ever did.

The audience was full on punk and still bloodthirsty after just having seen Social Distortion. We got up there and ripped into our set, and within the first thirty seconds, the show became a spitting contest between us and the first five rows: their fans fucking spit on us, so we just spit on them back. It was hilarious and memorably sickening: I remember going over to Izzy's side of the stage and standing there beside him spitting back and forth with these people because that's the kind of band we were. We were very tenacious, so no matter what any crowd ever did, we always turned it on them. By the end of our set, this disgusting war of the wills became fucking fun. We ended up with green phlegm all over us, and considering that it was warm out, not only was I shirtless, but the heat cooked the spit and made it start to smell pretty bad. It didn't matter, I was impenetrable: in the moment the energy of it all took over.

The next time we played the Street Scene was memorable, too, on a much different level. That go-round we were scheduled to open for Poison, who were headlining one of the bigger stages. It was going to be our biggest high-profile gig to date, and we were very ready to blow Poison off the stage. In the end we didn't even have to: we got up there and played, and everybody went nuts, climbing the scaffolding and pushing the stage to and fro in excitement. By the time we were done, the fire marshals decided to close

the place down. I remember seeing Poison roll up in all their glitter, ready to go on but unable to. I was quite pleased to see them all dressed up with no stage to play.

<center>⬥⟡⬥</center>

SO BACK TO HEROIN. IN THE WEEKS that followed that first time with Izzy when we'd spent the afternoon in that pink bedroom of that girl from Fairfax High, I developed a new interest. And I was dead-set to enjoy the honeymoon phase.

Yvonne was the only one who showed any real concern for my well-being at that point because she was from another world entirely. From her point of view it was easy to see that I was taking a casual stroll into the abyss. Our relationship had been on and off for a while, but she called me one day and asked me to meet her for lunch at Mel's on Sunset. I could tell that she was suspicious; as soon as we sat down, she started interrogating me in a subtle way, trying to figure out where I was at, what I was up to, who I was hanging with, what I was doing. The band was doing great, but in her mind we were still a little L.A. club thing—she didn't see what I saw at all. At the same time, Yvonne knew me very well, and she knew how ambitious I was, so I'm sure she had faith in what I had planned. What she couldn't put her finger on was why I wasn't my usual self—and that answer was obvious, but I wasn't going to tell her.

I remember her dropping me off on the corner of Clark and Sunset and going up to Vicky's apartment, where I was still crashing on the floor. I didn't turn around but I felt like she was looking at me; I felt like she knew something was up. A week or so later she called me over at Vicky's place, which was way out of line. She said it was important, she said that her grandfather had died and that she was so upset that she needed to see me. She asked me to come over that afternoon. Being the compassionate ex-boyfriend that I was, I didn't think twice—she picked me up and we went back to her house, all the while talking about the recently departed.

When we got there, it was probably about six p.m. and we went into her bedroom. I took my usual position at the corner of her bed, just watching TV and taking my cues from her. The doorbell rang suddenly.

"It's probably my mom," she said, and left the room.

Ten minutes went by, then the door opened again. When it did I saw two people I'd not seen in the same room in ten years: my parents. My attention was captured.

Yvonne came in and started feeding my mom and dad her interpretation of what was going on with me, which was very overdramatic; if anything, she sounded like the narrator in one of the antidrug films I'd seen in school, or at least the main character in an after-school special whose best friend is out of control. My parents were listening and studying me as well, just taking in the whole scene. I have two of the most liberal parents in the world, so once they didn't see anything wrong—I wasn't missing an eye or a limb and I seemed to be sitting up straight—they assumed that I was okay.

"So," my dad said, looking me in the eye, "is this true? Are you doing heroin, as Yvonne here has claimed?"

I didn't say no but I didn't quite say yes. I was loaded but hiding it as best I could, so there was no visible evidence of Yvonne's accusations—as far as I was concerned.

"It's really nice to see you guys in the same room," I said, grinning. "It's been a long time."

I went over and gave my mom a kiss, and that is when the entire mood shifted. Suddenly Yvonne's strategized intervention became a family reunion. I could feel her fuming as my parents and I spent the next half hour getting reacquainted. I kept up appearances while they were there, but the minute they left, I demanded that Yvonne take me home. Midway through the ride, I changed my mind; I asked her to drop me off at the Whisky. I didn't say a word to her the whole way over there. While I knew she meant well, we didn't speak to each other again for quite a while.

———◆◆◆———

THIS PERIOD WAS PRETTY INTENSE AS we made a name for ourselves, waded through the puddle of shady characters gathering at our ankles all while becoming the best band we could be. Eventually we found someone we could count on named Bridget, who was a lot like Vicky Hamilton but with slightly deeper pockets. Bridget wanted to sign us, but we never signed with anybody, so she was content just "working with us." Bridget was managing a band called Jetboy from San Francisco

that was pretty popular on the club circuit, so we rented a van and drove up there to open for them. We stayed at their house for a few days and got a glimpse of how a functional band, with a group apartment and a real roadie, actually lived. They were playing gigs all the time, and though we didn't dig the band very much, we respected their professionalism.

The coolest guy in the band by far was their bass player, Todd Crew, who became one of my best friends and a friend of the band for years—often to the chagrin of his bandmates. Todd had the best style: he was well over six feet tall, had this long straggly brown hair. He had a perpetual look of bemusement on his face, full-sleeve tattoos on both arms, and always wore some variation of a sleeveless leather vest, holey blue jeans tucked into his beat-up cowboy boots, and a cigarette between his lips at all times. Todd stood out from his band because he was classic rock and roll while the other Jetboys were typical glam poseurs. The singer did have a green Mohawk, though, which helped them seem a bit less transparent than Poison.

It was a great trip for us; our gig at this club called the Stone was great, and Todd's roommate was a reptile collector, so I was entirely occupied. I was really envious of his collection: he had snakes, a bunch of exotic monitor lizards, and a variety of crocodilians. On that trip we saw what was possible on a local level and realized that it was very much within our grasp.

The ride home was memorable, too. We were in our rental van, drinking and playing acoustic guitars, when I came up with the jangly intro to what became "Paradise City." Duff and Izzy picked it up and started playing it while I came up with the chord changes. I started humming a melody and played it over and over. Then Axl chimed in.

"Take me down to the Paradise City . . ."

I kept playing and tossed off some impromptu lyrics. "Where the grass is green and girls are pretty," I sang. I thought that sounded totally gay.

"Take me down to the Paradise City," Axl sang again.

"Where the girls are fat and they've got big titties!" I shouted.

"Take . . . me . . . home!" Axl sang.

It was decided that the "grass is green" line worked a bit better, and though I preferred my alternate take, I was overruled.

I expanded on the basic structure of the song as everyone improvised lyrics in rounds as if we were on a bus heading off to rock-and-roll summer

camp, which, as the L.A. skyline came into view, I suppose we were. After we got that whole chorus rolling, that's when I slammed into the big heavy riff that anchors the song. And that's the moment that "Paradise City" became my favorite Guns N' Roses song.

As atypically happy and gay as this all sounds for Guns N' Roses, it definitely went down that way; and it was sort of that kind of experience.

<center>❖</center>

OUR NEW MANAGER, BRIDGET, HELPED us succeed in taking our act to the next level, at least within the confines of the L.A. club circuit. The fact that we had played in San Francisco helped generate a bit of a buzz because the fact that we were able to play there meant that word of mouth was starting to spread; we had a fan base. Afterward we were able to book gigs with a more seasoned attitude, because those little things went a long way. We became one of the most-talked-about bands in L.A. at the time, which started to generate interest from the labels. The word was starting to get around, so much so that when Tom Zutaut of Geffen Records first saw us play at the Troubadour, he deliberately left after two songs, telling every A&R guy he saw on the way out that we sucked because he intended to sign us immediately.

Tom had become a legend after signing Mötley Crüe—he was the guy that every other rep in the industry watched because his instincts usually sifted the gold from the mud in the Sunset scene. The next time we played the Troubadour, Tom came backstage and introduced himself and I remember the whole band thinking that he was the only A&R rep that we'd met who deserved our respect, because his accomplishments spoke for themselves. His enthusiasm was also so real; he told us that we were the best band he'd seen since AC/DC and when he spoke about our music we could tell that he related to the songs more truthfully than anyone else had. We've been through years of ups and downs, but Tom still knows how to get my attention; when he really wants me to come out to check out a band he's thinking of signing, all he needs to say is: "I haven't seen a band rock this hard since I saw you guys that first time." There was something keenly sincere about Tom that night in the dressing room, and although we never told him so at the time, we had no intention of signing with anybody else.

Tom tried to fake out the competition, but it didn't work; word got around that he was interested in us and overnight every other label in town was trying to contact us. Bridget was still our kind-of manager, but since Vicky Hamilton was much better connected in L.A., all the A&R reps were calling her to get in touch with us. And that was enough to rekindle our relationship with Vicky.

It was a great time: we enjoyed as many free lunches, dinners, drinks, and whatever else came included from the major labels for as long as we could before signing. For the better part of the next two months, we were courted by Chrysalis, Elektra, Warner Bros., and a few others. We'd roll into these nice restaurants and order these extravagant liquid lunches, then sit there and just play the game. The only thing that we'd agree on was that we needed to meet again for lunch to discuss things further before we agreed on anything.

On and on it went until the day we decided to go down to meet David Geffen and Ed Rosenblatt and sign with Geffen Records. I sat there the entire time during our negotiations looking at David, whom I hadn't seen since I was about eight years old, thinking about all of the times I'd gone back and forth to his office with my dad when he was dropping off artwork, and wondering if David had any idea at all who I was. He didn't, of course, as my mom found out later. I made a point to visit the bathroom at Geffen, whose walls, as I remembered from my childhood, were a hippy collage, done very nicely in a very sixties style, of pictures from old rock magazines. I was happy to see that it was exactly the same.

The negotiations were quick: we demanded six figures, among other things, which was an unheard-of advance for a new, unknown artist in 1986. They accepted; Vicky Hamilton was our acting manager, so she hooked us up with Peter Paterno, who became the band's attorney. Peter wrote up our contracts and it was a done deal.

So Guns N' Roses was finally signed, but once we were, our new label didn't want us to play gigs anymore. They wanted us to lay low, build our mystique, and get our business in order: they insisted we find a *real* manager, and a producer, and focus on making a record. They wanted us to live off our advance and not be distracted by the routine of playing weekly while we took the necessary next steps. Little did they or any of us know that setting

L.A. ROCKS!

Vol. 1 Number 5 **Friday August 22 through Thursday September 4** **FREE**

JET BOY • JONESES
THELONIUS MONSTER
STAN RIDGEWAY
HANGMEN • BORN
LOSERS • **SHANGAI**
DAMN YANKEES
ALBERT COLLINS
RADWASTE
& THE SCREAM CLUB

interview with
GUNS & ROSES

interview with
LEGAL WEAPON

...AT PUPPETS
FIREHOSE
JAZZ BUTCHER
BUTTHOLE SURFERS
L.A. GUNS • LITTLE
KINGS • LORDS OF
THE NEW CHURCH
LAME FLAMES

SERVING L.A., ORANGE COUNTY, LONG BEACH, SANTA MONICA, PASADENA & THE VALLEY!

us loose with any kind of funds was a bad idea; they were sanctioning a degree of freedom that we had never known. Out of all of us, I was the most apprehensive about not playing any gigs. We were just going to sit idle with thousands of dollars to burn? That wasn't going to end well. The five of us had managed to make every day an epic on a budget that was determined by what we found in our pockets that morning; with our advance money in our hands and a record label behind us, much too much was possible.

As we all came to find out, back then and again and again, the worst thing that ever befell this band was having nothing to do and some money to spend.

While Guns played more clubs and our reputation spread, we got some early press in a local rock rag.

Appetite for
Dysfunction

Restlessness is a fickle catalyst; it can drive you to achieve or it can coax your demise, and sometimes the choice isn't yours. My restless nature is what earned me my nickname and it's kept me looking for the next thrill, the next gig, and the next mountain to climb for as long as I can remember. It's not the kind of thing that takes days off.

Before Guns got signed, I had no job and was living in a vomit-stained garage that was about as charming as a South American jail. All of my energy went into day-to-day survival and working to further the band, one show at a time. Once Guns was signed I didn't have to worry about money, food, or shelter. This minor sense of stability was unfamiliar to me; I had no concern for acquiring any of the trappings of normal life, so what seemed to be a blessing to me was almost a curse.

We were signed for something like $250,000, and our signing advance was around $37,000, of which my cut was about $7,500. I translated it into American Express traveler's checks that I kept in the right front pocket of my jeans, thanks to my trouble with the IRS. Saving my share wasn't an option, but I didn't celebrate by buying myself a new guitar or anything—I spent almost all of it on heroin. Each of us learned the same lesson in our own individual way before we got ourselves in line to do what we'd set out to do. It wouldn't be the last time that we'd need to rally against our instincts: whenever we earned ourselves some peace of mind, the same restlessness that fueled our success threatened to destroy it all.

It was obvious to everyone in our camp that Vicky Hamilton wasn't going to cut it as a manager once our operation increased in scale. It was also time to get a real crew: Joe wasn't a tech in any way, and Danny was a drug bud (whom I continued to hang out with in that capacity for years) but not any kind of road manager. We weren't entirely happy about making those changes, but it had to be done. It was the end of an era; we were no longer scrappy with nothing to lose: now we were scrappy with corporate backing.

Tom Zutaut arranged a few meetings with potential managers, the first of them being Cliff Bernstein and Peter Mensch of Q Prime, who managed Metallica, Def Leppard, and others, then as they do today. I went to Tom's office and they were late, so I passed out on Tom's couch waiting for them. For the record, I'm not sure if I was high or not. What I do remember is that the meeting didn't go well.

"Guns N' Roses just doesn't have a musical enough sound to be a band that we'd consider representing," one of them, I'm not sure which, said.

I sat there, pretty dumbfounded. *Huh?* I might have mumbled.

Basically, I took that insult lying down, because actually I was lying down, and that was the end of it. I didn't say anything, but my face must have registered a look of disdain or at least some skeptical confusion.

"You know those guitar solos you do?" the other one, I'm not sure which, said.

"Yeah," I mumbled.

"They just sound like noise to me, whereas if you listen to Metallica, their playing sounds really melodic."

"Okay, man," I said. *Whatever you say, Jack,* I thought to myself.

The whole time Tom did his best to mediate a potentially explosive situation by chiming in with comments meant to cheer things up and keep it positive.

"Well, the music really isn't well represented in the demo, guys," he'd say. "You really have to hear the songs properly produced."

Tom knew, as well as I did, that the music was *very* well represented in the demo—these guys, like so many others, just didn't get it. They passed,

of course, and they regretted it. Everyone Tom introduced us to in those days who passed on us regretted it—which in the end was a lot of people.

At the time Izzy was still living in his apartment and Duff was now living with this Hungarian girl, Katerina (whom he'd later marry), in an apartment on Hollywood Boulevard, coincidentally, next door to Sly Stone. I guess you could say that he and Duff had a tight neighborly relationship: Sly used to come by Duff's place unannounced to smoke PCP, crack, or a mix of the two, alone, in Duff's bathroom and then just leave. That blew our fucking minds. Apparently he did that all the time, but most of us didn't see it because we never really hung out at Duff's place—his girl wasn't the type to host a bunch of guys sitting around the living room. But I used to meet Duff over there before rehearsal, so I did witness it once.

There was a knock at the door, Duff opened it up, and there was Sly.

"Hey, man," he muttered because he never remembered Duff's name. "Is it cool if I use your bathroom?"

"Oh yeah, sure," Duff said.

And that was it. Duff said that Sly might be in there anywhere from a few minutes to a few hours.

Duff also made the acquaintance of West Arkeen while he lived in that building. The only place I knew West to live on a regular basis back then was in his beat-up El Camino. I think at that point he was parking it outside of Duff's building, so he was a tenant by extension. I was introduced to him through Duff and he became friends with the band; much more so with Axl than with me or the rest of us at first. At that point especially I was wary of meeting new people because all manner of riffraff had started to hang around us, so I was standoffish to newcomers. It takes a lot for me to trust someone, though after a while, West and I became friends.

West was a guitar player from San Diego and a consummate party guy who became more of a fixture than the average friend of the band: he even cowrote some of our songs like "It's So Easy" and "Yesterdays" with Duff and "Bad Obsession" and "The Garden" with Axl. Duff and West would hang out and write songs and I would join them sometimes, but West and Axl got really tight. In addition to writing with Guns, he cowrote songs for Duff's and Izzy's solo projects and all of us contributed to his project, the Outpatience, in the late nineties, just before he died of an overdose.

West was a hard-drinking, hard-living good-times guy, so he fit in with us just fine. He was the kind of character who was so secure in his own skin and content with his own existence that if you weren't nice to him, he'd still be amiable to you; that's probably why he won me over in the end. For better or for worse, West was the guy who introduced the rest of us to what was then called speed and what is now called crystal meth. Speed was his thing; he always had a lot of it, he had major connections to it down in San Diego, and everyone in his orbit was always on it.

Eventually West somehow got the money together to rent a nice house in the Hollywood Hills; it was three stories, right on a cliff, tucked away in the trees. He lived there with "Laurie" and "Patricia," these two speed-demon chicks that might have been attractive if they weren't so strung out. Laurie somehow held down a job in the film industry and drove a nice Suzuki jeep, while Patricia never seemed to work, but she always seemed to have money. I could never get my head around how they maintained some appearance of a normal life, with a house, money in the bank, and all that—all while doing speed with the utmost abandon. But then again, I didn't know much about speed then.

I used to crash there whenever I had nowhere to crash, and as West became closer to all of us, there was one thing I could never figure out: how he, too, always had money. Especially as things got crazier for us, West became the only thing like a friend that our band had in the world. He was the only one that always came through when any of us needed anything; for a long time he literally was the only one we could trust.

<hr />

AS SOON AS WE GOT OUR ADVANCE money, we collectively managed to do one practical thing, which was to rent an apartment. We got turned down by almost every management office we approached because it's not like we had good credit—or credit at all. But finally we found a place on the southeast corner of La Cienega and Fountain; a two-bedroom, two-bathroom, ground-floor apartment. We actually got a bit domestic for a moment and went out and rented some furniture—two beds and a kitchen dinette set. We rounded out the decor with a couch we found in the alley behind the building and a TV that Steven's mom donated to our

cause. When we first moved in, Steve's mom also kicked us off with some groceries. It was the only time that we ever had them—for maybe a week, if you opened our fridge it actually looked like somebody lived there.

Steve and Izzy shared a room, and Axl and I shared a room, and that apartment is still there; I drive by it all the time—it's the space with the big bay window on the first floor overlooking the intersection. When we first rented it, Izzy was still living with his girlfriend Dezi on Orange Avenue and Duff and Katerina were on Hollywood Boulevard, but mutual interests dictated that Izzy spend much of his time over at our place. Following some sort of domestic dispute, he became a full-time resident for a while.

To me, our place was deluxe; I even relocated my anaconda, Clyde, from Yvonne's to join me there. Unfortunately, moving out of our garage into an ostensibly nicer apartment didn't curtail our debauched delinquency; we ended up getting evicted after the three months we'd paid for—and never got our security deposit back. It didn't work out as efficiently as planned, but being in the same place was more or less a step toward organized productivity as a band.

Everything was great until we got evicted, as far as I was concerned. We'd just gotten some money and I tried to be as frugal as I could in the smack-buying department, just making it stretch as far as it could go. In spite of my efforts, our place became a real shooting gallery: we'd cop down in East L.A. and it seemed like there was an endless supply in the street. Mark Mansfield came by one night, and unbeknownst to each other, we'd both become junkies, so it was *great* to see him. He was working with a Texas band called Tex and the Horseheads, who were also all strung out, so all of us hung out over at our place. Before this, I did dope when I could get it here and there, but I could never afford to get it consistently. At this point, though, I could finance a daily habit, and I was enamored enough of drugs that I didn't know or care what I was getting myself into.

The label had rented us a rehearsal space at a place called Dean Chamberlain's over in Hollywood, where Jane's Addiction rehearsed as well. We'd roll in there every day at about two or three in the afternoon and play for about four hours. This little box was about eight feet by twenty feet, just very narrow and long, and was lit up by unpleasantly bright, hospital-strength fluorescent lights. Basically it was like rehearsing in a 7-Eleven.

Ironically, one of the first songs we worked up there was "Mr. Brownstone," a track that was conceived under much dimmer circumstances. Izzy, his girlfriend Dezi, and I were up at their apartment one night when we came up with it. They had a little dinette set that we'd sit around cooking up our shit and then we'd just jam. We were sitting there complaining, as junkies do, about our dealers, as well as just complaining about being junkies, and that's where that song came from. It basically described a day in the life for us at the time. Izzy had a cool idea, he came up with the riff, and we started improvising the lyrics. Dezi considers herself a cowriter on that track and for the record she did come up with maybe a noun here, perhaps a conjunction there. When we had it all together, we wrote the words down on a grocery bag. We brought it down to the Fountain apartment and played it for Axl and he reworked the lyrics a bit before the band worked on it at our next rehearsal. Axl could always take a simple Izzy melody and turn it into something fantastic, and that is just one of a few examples.

Tom Zutaut was eager to find us a producer and to get us on the road to recording—little did he know how long that road would be. The first candidate he sent our way was Tom Werman, who was a big fucking deal. Werman had recently produced Mötley Crüe's *Shout at the Devil*, which sold a few million in 1985, and before that had made a name for himself producing Cheap Trick, Ted Nugent, and Molly Hatchet. Werman went on to work with Poison, Twisted Sister, L.A. Guns, Stryper, Krokus, and Dokken—basically he became the sound of eighties metal.

But he couldn't handle us. We never even got to properly meet him. He came to our rehearsal space and we were playing "Mr. Brownstone," at jet-engine decibel levels. Izzy and I had just gotten brand-new Mesa Boogie stacks and I was playing a new guitar: it was a Les Paul that had belonged to seventies blues guitarist Steve Hunter. I'd traded my BC Rich for it at Albert and Howie Huberman's place, Guitars R Us. That store was an institution for every L.A. musician who couldn't afford Guitar Center, it was *the* musician's pawnshop. It was where I got rid of all of my shit and got new stuff. Or, when the money dried up, it was where I sold my equipment for cash to score more smack.

In any case, we were playing "Mr. Brownstone" so brutally loud that Werman walked out immediately. He came in with his assistant, paused in the

doorway, then turned around and disappeared. We finished the song and I went to the door to see if they were outside and found an empty street.

"I guess it must have been a little too loud," I said to the other guys.

We shrugged it off, but I was bummed because I thought we sounded great. Then again I was used to people not getting it.

Guns was the type of snarling beast that thrived in pits like that.

The most well-known figure that considered working with us was Paul Stanley of Kiss, who was looking for the right band to launch a side gig behind the mixing board. Izzy, Duff, and I couldn't have cared less; we told Zutaut that we had no idea what Paul Stanley could bring to the equation. Steven, of course, was beside himself—Kiss were his heroes, so we figured we'd let Steven have his jollies and agreed to the meeting. The process began with Paul coming down to our apartment to "discuss music." By this time heroin had become a daily thing, so when Paul arrived, Izzy and I were doing all that we could to keep from nodding out; just barely keeping it together enough so that it wasn't obvious . . . or so we thought. Izzy and I parked ourselves on the couch, and since we didn't have a chair in the living room, Paul sat on the floor next to Steven and Axl.

"First things first," he said. "I wanna rewrite 'Welcome to the Jungle.'" According to Paul, the song had real potential, but it lacked an impactful structure. What it needed was a chorus that was more memorable, more singsong, more anthemic—in a word, more like a Kiss song.

"*Ugh*," I grunted under my breath. As far as I was concerned, that was the end of our relationship. He was the epitome of the guy with the nice clothes, the trophy wife, and the nice car "stooping" to our level to tell us what to do. I didn't take kindly to that.

Paul was persistent, though. We saw him again not long afterward when we played a showcase that Geffen had set up. Basically, Tom arranged it because we needed to play a gig, so it was this industry-only, invite-only

"concert." It took place at Gazzari's (today it's the Key Club), which was a venue that we'd never, ever played on the circuit because it was totally against everything we stood for. It was so glam and gay that there were radio ads for it where the owner, Bill Gazzari, proclaimed in his thick East Coast accent, "All my bands got foxy guys in 'em! If they don't got foxy guys, they don't play on my stage." Gazzari's was where the *really* plastic glam metal could be found. And we definitely weren't trying to be foxy. The only time I'd ever even been in there aside from this gig was to see Hollywood Rose back in the day.

Anyway, Paul Stanley attended that show, and he actually bullied the sound engineer into allowing him to man the soundboard and control the mix. We didn't find out until later, but when we did, I cringed at the thought: Paul Stanley had mixed Guns N' Roses—at Gazzari's. Really, how much more cliché could it get? I do remember that we got paid, because I remember counting and dividing our money and saying to Izzy, "I gotta go cop!" That was all that I cared about at the time—and that's what I did; I took off out of there to meet up with my dealer friend.

Paul still wanted to win us over, so he insisted on coming to our next gig, which we knew once and for all would show him who we really were and what our producer needed to capture. It was a week later, at Raji's, which was a total dive, probably a twenty-by-twenty-foot room that reeked of beer and piss with a PA that sounded like an outdated console permanently in the red. The stage was a foot high, packed against the farthest wall from the door; the bathrooms were more disgusting than CBGB's. In other words, it was Guns N' Roses' natural habitat. I think in Paul's mind, he was coming down to prove to us once and for all that he understood where we were coming from. He was going to "hang out" on our "turf," because, after all, he and Kiss had played dives back in the day. His intentions were good, but I can't help but think that pretty quickly he realized that where we were coming from was somewhere he hadn't seen in a long, long time. Guns was the type of snarling beast that thrived in pits like that.

That show was fucking amazing: it was as dirty, muddy, shoddy, and teetering on chaos as Guns ever was in my mind. It was as honest and true as Guns N' Roses ever got, because I did a big hit of smack before we went on, which, mixed with the liquor I had already been drinking, made my

stomach so rotten that I'd turn around and blow chunks over the back of my amps every five minutes. I had a new guitar tech, Jason, who had to keep jumping out of the way to avoid getting coated. The overwhelming heat in there didn't help the situation much. The show was so rambunctious, the audience so full of unruly diehards, that Axl ended up getting into a fight with some guy in the front row—he might have smashed him in the head with the base of his mike stand. The whole show was a fucking riot; there was so much energy packed into that tiny little overheated box of a room. It was *fucking awesome.* There's a picture of that gig on the inside sleeve of *Appetite for Destruction.*

I can't imagine where he stood during the show, but Paul Stanley materialized after the set with his blond-bombshell girlfriend/wife, each of them in outfits that probably cost more than the market value of the entire building. There wasn't a dressing room at Raji's; there was a hallway between the side of the stage and the back door with a small set of stairs, where our entire band sat down after we were through playing. Paul and his girlfriend/wife were so out of place but they tried to sit there with us anyway. We were sweaty and gnarly, and after puking about eight times onstage, I was doing my best not to lose it all over him as he said to me, with his Ivana Trump lady on his arm, "Hmm, well, that was *interesting.*"

The next day we made it official: I told Tom to let Paul know that we were going to continue our quest for a producer, thank you very much. I'm sorry to say that not long afterward, I retold this story to the *L.A. Weekly* with an excessive degree of attitude directed at Paul. I meant no harm; I was so enthusiastic about what we were doing that to me everyone who didn't get it was just *wrong.* I didn't even remember insulting Paul publicly and therefore had no qualms about calling him a month or two later to ask for a favor. We'd begun recording, at that point, but I'd pawned my best guitars for dope and I hoped that he would be able to hook me up with some studio-worthy gear via his sponsorship deal with BC Rich.

"Hey, Paul, it's Slash," I said. "It's been a while. How are you, man?"

"I'm good," he said.

"Hey, listen, I know you've got that deal with BC Rich. Do you think you can get me some guitars?"

"Yeah, I could, it wouldn't be a problem," he said, followed by . . . silence. "But I *won't*. Here's a piece of advice: you should be careful about airing your dirty laundry in public. Good luck to you."

Click.

Dial tone.

It took a while, but in 2006, I got the chance to apologize to Paul at Vh1's *Rock Honors* show, where I was part of a tribute to Kiss along with Tommy Lee, Ace Frehley, and others. It was all okay; it was water under the bridge. Looking back on it, I see exactly why I behaved that way: I was arrogant back then, and when you're arrogant, regardless of who you are as a person, the fact that you're not a fan of someone's band is a legitimate enough reason to be a prick.

There was no way in hell that I was going to county with fingernail polish on.

WE WOULD PRACTICE EVERY DAY; WE wrote new songs, and we partied every night. As I mentioned before, smack was easy to find so I wasn't keeping track of how often I did it. In my mind, it was strictly recreational—it wasn't supposed to be the center of the universe.

The first time I realized that I had a problem was the first time that there wasn't any around. I didn't think too much of it—ignorance is bliss. On that particular day when it all caught up to me for the first time, Izzy and I decided to go to Tijuana with Robert John, the photographer and good friend who's shot us since day one and became our official photographer on the road all the way through 1993.

Anyway, it was a great day trip: we drank a few bottles of tequila, we wandered the streets; we watched drunk Americans be ripped off by whores

in every dive bar and brothel shack on the strip. As the day wore on, I just thought I was tired and drunk and catching a cold; I had no idea of what was really going on in my body. When we got back to L.A., I remember, I passed out immediately. I woke up later that night still feeling sick, so I figured that a few whiskeys at Barney's Beanery would cure me. I headed down there around ten p.m., and after my first couple of drinks, I didn't feel any better; actually I felt worse. I went back to the apartment and assumed the air-raid position: I got on my knees with my head between them and my hands on my head, simply because there was no other position that felt comfortable to me. I remember that night vividly because Marc Canter popped by unexpectedly late that evening. He was as far removed from the junk scene as you can imagine. He eyeballed me curiously.

"You really don't look good," he said. "Are you all right?"

"Yeah, yeah, I'm fine," I said. " I have the flu."

The reality was that I was dope sick after just one day without heroin. It was hard for me to admit that to myself. As I lay sweating alone in my bed that night, I was still unwilling to regard it as anything else but the worst flu I'd ever had.

I cut down I guess, but I continued on more or less the same path until the next time I was forced to face the fact that I had a habit—thanks to the long arm of the law. I was cruising around with Danny one night looking for dope and we managed to cop some shit, but it was very little; it was just a taste. We took it over to my friend Ron Schneider's place (my bass player in Tidus Sloan) and we did it, hung out, and listened to Iron Maiden with Ron for a while and then left to head home at about four a.m. We were coming up La Cienega when the blue and red lights went on behind us. When we slowed down and pulled over, we were, literally, right in front of our apartment, spitting distance from our door.

These two cops were clearly out to fulfill their nightly or monthly quota, because we weren't speeding or doing anything suspicious at all. We had nothing on us, but Danny had forgotten the needle he had in the breast pocket of his shirt, which gave the cops carte blanche to do whatever they wanted. They started by shining their flashlights in our eyes.

"Have you taken any drugs tonight, sir?" one of them asked me.

"No," I said, squinting at him through my hair.

"Are you sure about that? It looks to me like you have; your pupils are pinned."

"Yeah, that's because you're shining a flashlight in my eyes," I said.

They weren't having any of it: they impounded Danny's car and arrested him for possession of paraphernalia. They cuffed me, too, but wouldn't tell me on what charges. And it all came down within ten feet of my front door.

They stuffed Danny and me in the back of the patrol car and continued on with their unstated mission to bust every long-haired "vagrant" in sight on their way back to the station. Less than a mile down the street, they picked up Mike Levine, the bass player from Triumph, who was exiting a 7-Eleven and heading to his car with some beer under his arm, on the premise that he *intended* to drink and drive. They put him in the back with us, and continued on. A bit farther down, on Santa Monica Boulevard, they busted a girl for "public drunkenness," literally three blocks from the sheriff's office. The girl wasn't visibly drunk at all— she was just walking down the street. Since there wasn't any more room in the car, one of the cops opted to walk her across the street to the station.

They put all of us males in the same holding tank and we sat around the jail cell for a few hours. Mike Levine got bailed out, and after Danny had sat around long enough, they let him go, too. He was booked for having the needle and was given a court date, and all of that. I was the only one left, and since I thought that I hadn't done anything, I figured that I'd get out any minute now. It was Saturday by then, about eight a.m., and as the hours stretched on, I tried, unsuccessfully, to get the guards' attention to ask why I was still being held.

The only answer I got was being shuffled from the small cell of the night before to a larger cell with high ceilings, a rubber mat on the floor, one common toilet in the corner, a lot of inmates, and the rank smell of piss. I had no idea of what was coming next. My high had started to wear off; I was a few hours away from complete withdrawal. After a while we were loaded onto one of those horrible black-and-white transformed school buses with gates on the windows. I was shackled at the ankles and wrists and chained to the guy in front of me. I still had no idea why I was there, but I realized that I was going to the county jail, so I immediately started chewing off my black nail polish. There was no way in hell that I was going to county with fingernail polish on.

It took hours to get there because the bus made stops at several jails along the way to pick up more people; all while I got sicker and sicker. At each jail we were loaded off into another group holding cell to wait while the new additions were processed. The county jail itself was about twenty miles away, but getting there, with all of those stops and red tape, took all day. We hit about six jails and finally got to county in the late afternoon. The process was no less endless when we finally arrived: they logged in my belongings and put me in a series of holding rooms with the other new inmates until my paperwork was complete.

It was the most tedious bureaucracy I've ever seen in my life, and it didn't help that I was genuinely dope sick during it all. Up until then, I knew about being dope sick in the abstract sense; I had heard stories, but even after I'd experienced a bit of it after that day in Tijuana, I regarded it with the same carefree bravado that had gotten me hooked in the first place. Faced with the reality of being dope sick, I figured that the best way to avoid it was to always know where to get more junk. It hadn't been a problem in Hollywood. But being locked up in the county jail for a few days with no access to heroin was something else entirely: it was a forced detox in the worst possible setting.

I was housed in one of those big old-fashioned rooms with a few rows of cots, where I sweated it out, nauseous, sick, and exhausted. I'm not sure exactly how long I was there altogether; I suppose close to three days; then all of a sudden they let me out, again with no explanation, and I had to go through the whole fucking entrance process in reverse. Axl had put up the bail, and had Danny pick me up, but I didn't know that as I made my way through the exit procedure in my little jumpsuit, waiting in long lines, sitting in a series of rooms, sweating and coughing and sniveling and fidgeting, smelling really bad and looking and feeling fucking miserable. When they handed me my clothes and belongings, I was finally informed why I was there: I'd been hauled in for a six-year-old jaywalking ticket. There had been a warrant out for me after I'd not shown up in court or paid the fine. Of all the things I've done, I got busted for jaywalking. Well, at least I did my time and paid my debt to society.

I walked around outside of county, bumming cigarettes for about an hour wondering who had bailed me out, until Danny suddenly showed up;

we then drove straight down to Melrose and Western to cop. When I got back to the apartment, Axl was sleeping, so were Steven and Izzy, and Duff wasn't around. I got high, took a shower, and when those guys woke up, I realized that they hadn't even noticed that I'd been gone for a while. I wasn't expecting much, but it would have been nice to get some degree of fanfare. When I found out later that Axl was the one who scraped together the bail money; I was touched. That was pretty cool of him.

<center>◆━◆×◆━◆</center>

DESPITE OUR LIFESTYLE AND ITS unconventional set of priorities, we did get a lot of things done in that apartment. We wrote an acoustic version of "You're Crazy" that ended up as an electric version on *Appetite* and in its original form on *Lies*. We worked that one up at Dean Chamberlain's, giving it that edge by speeding it up about twenty beats per minute from its original state. Axl, Izzy, and I had some really great creative times in that apartment. But regardless, our advance, both collectively and individually, had dwindled, so our quest for a manager was suddenly important: we had lost our lease and two of us had more or less devolved into everyday junkies that needed somewhere to live.

Tom Zutaut introduced us to Arnold Stiefel, a manager whose biggest clients at the time were Rod Stewart (whom I believe he still handles), and the actor Matthew Broderick, who was about to become a huge star off the back of *Ferris Bueller's Day Off*. That didn't impress us any. But after a few great meetings with Arnold and his partners, somehow we walked away with the most ideal situation imaginable: they hadn't signed us outright, but they agreed to put us up in a house until we found a producer and made an album, at which point they'd decide if they wanted to sign on as our managers. I have no idea what kind of deal Tom made with them to make that happen, but this was the perfect short-term fix: they were willing to let us "evolve" on their tab.

I felt sorry for Tom by then. We were this self-destructive mutation of a band that he'd had the utmost confidence in and we were paying him back by showing no promise of ever getting it together. To us it seemed funny that none of the producers or managers seemed fit to do the job, but Tom was very aware that we were slowly but surely narrowing the "interest" gap

between everyone in the industry and no one at all—I'm sure he was panicked: after two years he might lose his job if he didn't make it work.

The only good thing that Tom, as an A&R man, got out of this was that when he picked us up and signed us, we had a couple of really good songs, but this period of time allowed us to write a bunch more *really* good songs. Maybe in the back of his mind, there was a method to Tom's madness, maybe he knew that we needed this time and did everything he could to make it happen, because in the end he got the good stuff out of us. It was never stated as his intent, but I'm sure he looked at the bright side that way. This band took up so much of his time from the moment we were signed to the time we got our record done and got out on the road that it must have driven him insane. There was nothing that he could do to mold us or move the process along at all, because anything he tried failed. The band's overall attitude and extracurricular activities opposed the right direction at every turn.

Out of desperation, Tom did manage to get us into the studio with Manny Charlton, the guitarist for Nazareth, at Sound City Studios on Whitsett and Moorpark out in the Valley. We worked on demos of "November Rain," which was about eighteen minutes long in its original version, so needless to say we really needed to sit down and focus on arranging it. We also worked on "Don't Cry," and almost every other song that made it onto *Appetite*, except "Sweet Child o' Mine," because we hadn't written that one yet. It was a great day in any case, hanging out in the studio recording everything live in this great big room. Unfortunately, Manny didn't feel right. The demos sounded great, but they were just that: a bunch of great demo tapes. We knew enough about ourselves to know it wasn't okay.

<hr>

SHORTLY AFTERWARD WE MOVED INTO the Stiefel house, as we came to call it, a brand-new home in a gated community called Laughlin Park located way out in Griffith Park near the Observatory, the Greek Theater, and the L.A. Zoo. It was way out in East Hollywood, about a twenty-minute drive from where we used to live. That doesn't seem like much, but since none of us had cars, this became the most unsocial period we ever knew.

We were stuck out there in a new house, in a new complex, in the woods. There were two bedrooms upstairs—one was Axl's and one was Steven's and Izzy and I shared a bedroom downstairs . . . due to our "shared interests." We lived there for four or five months but had little furniture to speak of; we had beds, one table, and a couple of chairs in the entire house. Axl somehow managed to conjure up a proper bed, a lamp, and a dresser from somewhere: his room was a well-equipped oasis guarded by a padlock, but the rest of the place was basically empty. The lighting situation was equally meager: there was one lamp in Izzy's and my room, an overhead light in the dining room, and no lights in the living room or above the stairs or in any of the hallways. The entire time we lived there, it looked as if someone was about to move in.

We did have a fireplace, and since we never bothered to buy lamps, once the sun went down, we lit fires and generally restricted ourselves to the living room or the kitchen, which also had an overhead light. We were so out of our element: for once we were living in a neighborhood where household items weren't available for free on the street, in other people's trash. The upside was that we were in such a far-off residential area that when we didn't feel like playing acoustics, we could jam all night on our electric guitars. And if we'd owned practice amps we probably would have.

The drug lifestyle was a dominant reality in our lives, and it played a major role in everything we did at that point. Once it showed signs of wear, there was definitely light at the end of the tunnel . . . whether we liked it or not. It was obvious to us all that the free and easy overindulgent smack days we'd enjoyed in West Hollywood were done: we'd run out of money, most of the shit on the street had gone dry, and because of our new address, we were at the mercy of the only drug dealer willing to travel. It was not good at all: what had been very fun a short time ago was now a major pain in the ass. Unfortunately, we were in no shape to just up and quit and forget about it. We were forced to be conscientious and frugal as we strove to scale ourselves back.

When we did score, Izzy and I wrote a lot because back then heroin was a great catalyst for us. I thought it was the coolest of all the drugs because it made me feel really at ease with everything; it melted away my inhibitions and insecurities. On smack, I was cool and confident so collaborating was

easy. As soon as we'd get high, Izzy and I would start jamming and working out ideas, just trading riffs and chords back and forth. Something always seemed to come out of it naturally, it seemed so inspired.

I HAVE A WAY OF SITTING DOWN WITH the guitar and coming up with these hard-to-play riffs; they're unorthodox fingerings of simple melodies. It's my way of getting into playing or finding something interesting to do as opposed to just practicing scales. To this day, I still do it; rather than doing obvious "exercises," I invent runs of my own design that both loosen up my fingers and keep my ears engaged, because if practicing doesn't sound good, why bother with it at all.

That is what I was doing one night as Izzy sat down on the floor to join me.

"Hey, what is that?" he asked.

"I don't know," I said. "Just fucking around."

"Keep doing it."

He came up with some chords and since Duff was there, he came up with a bass line, as Steven planned out his drum beat. Within an hour my little guitar exercise had become something else.

Axl didn't leave his room that night, but he was just as much a part of the creative process as the rest of us: he sat up there and listened to everything we were doing and was inspired to write lyrics that were complete by the next afternoon. They became an ode to his girlfriend and future first wife, Erin Everly, daughter of Don Everly of the Everly Brothers.

We'd found a rehearsal studio in Burbank called Burbank Studios, which was nothing more than a big warehouse owned by this old Asian couple, which is where we really started to work on the preproduction for *Appetite*, perfecting the songs we'd already demoed. At our next session, we worked our new song into a complete movement: we wrote a bridge, added a guitar solo, and so it became "Sweet Child o' Mine."

That was all fine and well, but we still didn't have a producer. Tom came up with the idea to try out Spencer Proffer, who'd worked with Tina Turner, Quiet Riot, and W.A.S.P., who Axl liked a lot back in the day, so we went for it. We took our gear down to Pasha Studios, which was where Spencer

operated out of at the time and we agreed to work on "Sweet Child" together as a test. Spencer was a great guy; he was actually the one who suggested that the song needed a dramatic breakdown before its ultimate finale. He was right . . . but we had no idea what we wanted to do there. All of us sat around the control room, listening to it over and over, devoid of a clue.

"Where do we go?" Axl said, more to himself than the rest of us. "Where do we go now? . . . Where do we go?"

"Hey," Spencer said, turning the music down. "Why don't you just try singing that?"

And so became that dramatic breakdown.

We worked up a solid demo of "Sweet Child," and worked with Spencer on demos for about half the tunes on *Appetite*, but by the end of the process we just didn't feel confident that he was the producer for us, so our quest continued.

<div align="center">———◆◆◆◆◆———</div>

IT WASN'T LOOKING GOOD—I'M SURE Tom was at his wit's end, but right at the breaking point, we found a manager. Technically, we were supposed to be managed by Stiefel and company, whose house we were living in, but since neither Tom nor we had any interaction with them, we continued to take meetings with potential managers. The one that stuck to the wall so to speak was Alan Niven, a guy who knew right away what he was walking into by working with us.

Izzy and I met Alan at a bar and I could barely keep my eyes open sitting there on my stool, but that didn't seem to bother Alan at all. From the start he thrived on the reckless energy of our band and was excited to get us over the initial hump that had stalled us on our way to recording and touring and becoming a professional entity. I was very jaded and, as I mentioned, I was very paranoid about anyone who aimed to get inside our circle. But I respected Alan before I even met him: he was the architect behind the Sex Pistols' signing with EMI so I knew that he had skills. He was a charming, raffish New Zealander who took to Izzy right off the bat and knew that we were worth the effort. Alan didn't try to exert his will in the creative arena—he left that to us—he just did what he did best: marketing and management; that was his forte.

Alan met everyone while we were still working with Spencer down at Pasha and listened to all of the demos we'd done and decided that we should take those takes, add a live audience track, and release it all as a live EP. He thought it was essential for us to get some product out while we still had a strong buzz in the industry; it would keep the excitement alive while we recorded our full-length album.

We came up with the idea of releasing the EP on our own label, which we insisted was financed by Geffen. It would appear to be a "live" EP on an "indie" label but in truth it wouldn't be either. We called the label Uzi Suicide and the EP *Live Like a Suicide*. It was untouched demos of four songs we'd been playing since our first rehearsal: Aerosmith's "Mama Kin," Rose Tattoo's "Nice Boys," and two of our own, "Move to the City" and "Reckless Life." They're raw I guess, but if you ask me they still sound pretty fucking good.

Playing the Troubadour circa 1986.

So now we had a manager and now we had half an album of "live" tracks and Zutaut was happy. He believed the EP would attract eligible producers. It definitely got us noticed: I remember leaving Alan's house in Redondo Beach with Duff and hearing "Move to the City" played on KNEC, this great heavy metal station out of Long Beach. The EP was a clear indication of our aesthetic, not to mention our lifestyle, and as it had always been, there weren't too many easy-to-find like-minded souls. To say the least, it took a few dry runs to find the right guy.

IT WAS AGREED THAT PLAYING A FEW gigs would keep us visible and keep us from losing momentum. I, for one, knew that if there wasn't any concrete work commitment on the horizon, it was likely that I'd treat every day like a vacation. We went back up to San Francisco to open for Jetboy at the Stone, followed by a gig two nights later opening for Ted Nugent at the Santa Monica Civic Center.

At the time we were still living at the Stiefel house officially, though once we chose Alan as our manager, we began to vacate in anticipation of letting Stiefel know the bad news. Axl moved back to Erin's, I don't know where Steven was staying, and Duff was where he'd always been, so Izzy and I became the only full-time residents, living in comfortable squalor in the downstairs back bedroom. It was a gypsylike scene; our friend Danny crashed there much of the time, too, amid the sparsely appointed rooms.

Finding dope in L.A. had become difficult suddenly, so Danny and I scoured the streets regularly looking to score. One of those nights we got lucky and managed to pick up a sizable amount. We were elated; we drove back to the house and stashed it all in a gun-shaped lighter of mine. We hid it in my drawer because the next morning we were off to San Francisco. I saw no reason to bring any along, because in San Francisco, I'd never had a problem scoring top-grade China White.

We packed all the gear in the van we'd rented; Danny and Izzy and I drove up in Danny's car, and when we got there, Izzy and I went straight to someone's apartment, where we planned to score our shit. The dealer didn't get there before the show, so we went and did the gig, which was a

blur because all that I could think about was getting my smack afterward. The rest of the band packed up, Danny included, and headed back to L.A., while Izzy and I offered to drive Danny's car back ourselves because we wanted to score. We went back to the apartment and waited around for the shit to show up. We waited . . . we waited . . . we waited . . . *nothing.* At that point, we were getting jumpy, and when the dealer finally showed up it was crap—just useless. We looked at each other, both realizing that we were a fuck of a long way from home, and we didn't have much time before we turned into pumpkins.

It was well into the next morning when we hit the road, but we knew that, at the very least, I had a bunch of shit stashed back at the house. All was well, we were making good time . . . until we ran out of gas. We lost a good hour there what with hitching to the gas station and back. Once we got on our way again, speeding to make up for lost time, as the itchiness stalked us, we got a flat tire. Changing a tire is never fun, but when your internal clock is counting down the seconds to your demise, it's something else altogether.

We finally got home that night, thinking that we were cool and all was well. There's a dope camaraderie that kicks in between junkies who are about to get high together, and as Izzy and I headed into the house, we were the greatest friends, just as tight as can be; all arm in arm and laughing about everything we'd just been through getting there. We went into my room, I opened up my stash drawer . . . and discovered that all my shit was gone.

Then I called Danny.

"Hey," I said. "Didn't I stash my shit in my lighter?"

"Yeah," he said innocently.

"It's gone."

"No way."

"I can't find it."

"That really sucks."

"Get over here and help me!"

Izzy and Danny and I proceeded to tear the bedroom apart, then the rest of the house. I knew that I had put it there and I knew that Danny was the only one there with me when I did, but I was willing to give him the benefit of the doubt.

"Man, you know what?" Danny said after we'd exhausted every possible stash spot. He shook his head. "I hid it. I hid it when I was high. I'm going to try to remember where . . . let me think."

After Danny thought about it long and hard, he came up with a few corners we hadn't checked; a few wild goose chases. Then he went home again, leaving Izzy and me with the impossible task of trying to hook up with Sammy, our Persian dealer—our only dealer at the time. It was not looking good: we beeped Sammy every ten minutes and he never called back.

The next morning, Izzy's girlfriend Dezi came over and she could tell that the situation was dire: we'd been up all night, we'd driven from San Francisco, we'd been paging dealers unsuccessfully all day, and we had to open for Ted Nugent in a few hours. Izzy and I were tripping out, nothing was happening, we had no one else to call, and we were wrecked. We were starting to jones pretty hard; we were like vampires out of *Blackula*, just rolling around on the ground and going to the bathroom to puke every five minutes.

Our show with Ted Nugent was all the way down in Santa Monica, at seven-thirty p.m. Sammy was not calling us back, so we had to figure out how we were going to get something in our system—anything at all—to make us human enough to make the show. We were in no condition to perform, let alone even drive ourselves to the gig. In desperation, Dezi called her friend Melissa, who lived up in Hollywood, in Izzy's old apartment. She had heard from Sammy and was going to meet him shortly.

That was enough to motivate us: we drove over there somehow and hung out waiting for Melissa to return with our drugs. It looked like we might have taken care of one problem, but at the same time, it was around five p.m. and we were about an hour from the gig. Finally she returned, Izzy and I got our shit, we did all that, and *what a relief that was.* Fuck! We were once again functional. We had barely enough time to join our band, who were waiting for us so that we could play our first arena, to a sold-out crowd of three thousand.

We hightailed it over there. We had no artists or parking lot passes on us, and after the night we'd had, we looked like scabs off the street. We left Dezi to park the car and climbed the fence at the back of the arena for lack of a better plan. In the process I got caught on the chain links and the but-

ton of my jeans popped off, so I spent the rest of the night making sure my zipper didn't go all the way down leaving me hanging out there, because I've never been the type to wear underwear.

Izzy and I somehow snuck into the loading area and made it up to the backstage area, and as we started down the hallway toward the stage I saw Gene Simmons. He was standing at the other end giving us a foreboding stare, which is something he is very good at doing. I had no idea why he was there, but it added to the surreal quality of the last twenty-four hours. Izzy and I got to the dressing room with less than ten minutes to spare. The guys may have been annoyed at first, but they were soon relieved. Disaster averted . . . we took one look in the mirror and headed to the stage.

And that was the first time we ever played "Sweet Child o' Mine" live. I hadn't at all mastered the signature riff to the degree that I could execute it on a whim, but I pulled it off anyway and the band as a whole played it *really* well. The whole set was good, and we had a collection of friends there: Yvonne, Marc Canter, and a few more of my "normal" friends. Even better, right after we got offstage, Izzy got beeped back from Sammy, who was going to meet us at the Stiefel house. Yvonne and her friends were there backstage, and at the time she and I were together again and the whole intervention incident was bygones. She didn't know exactly where I was in terms of drugs—and I didn't feel the need to tell her.

She was just there being a very supportive girlfriend, cheering her boyfriend on at his first big gig at a live arena. All things considered, she was letting me do my thing. Of course she wanted to celebrate afterward, which was a problem. I couldn't wait to get out of there and get home to do drugs, but I didn't want her to know so I tried to tell her that I'd call her and we'd meet up after we dropped off our guitars, but she wasn't having it—she and her friends were going to meet us up at the house.

Izzy and Danny and I couldn't think of a better way to celebrate our show than with some smack, so we flew back toward Griffith Park to score. It was so early that it wasn't even dark out yet, so as we cruised up Fairfax and stopped for a red light at Fountain, it was easy to see our dealer Sammy's car in the lane beside us. It added to the elated, epic mood of the day—and cut Sammy's commute in half. At this point, I felt like I stood a chance of getting high at the house before Yvonne arrived.

We scored from Sammy, sped up to the house, and ran inside like lu-
natics: Izzy ducked into our room and slammed the door and I locked
myself in Steven's bathroom, which was lit by a red bulb he'd installed. I
was in there trying to navigate my fix, all while shaking and huffing and
puffing from nerves in this unnatural red light, when suddenly there's a
knock at the door.

"Hey, babe," Yvonne said. "Are you in there?"

"Oh, yeah, I am!" I said. . . . "Yes I am. But I'm taking a shower. I'm all
sweaty from the show." Then I turned on the water.

"Let me in, babe," she said.

"I'm in the shower," I said. "I'll be right out."

I finished what I needed to do, I threw some water on myself, and I went
outside. I'm pretty sure she knew about it. Yvonne didn't want to stay over
at our house—I can't imagine why—so I agreed to go back to her place with
her. And that was the night that I decided fuck it, I'll just kick. I'd fixed in
the early evening, so it wore off at about one a.m. and for the next few days
I did a cold turkey there in Yvonne's bed. It wasn't the last time I'd do so
before we all got it together to record *Appetite*, but each time I did, I never
told her what was really going on. I acted like I had the flu and played down
how terrible I felt. Yvonne was busy; she was in school, so most of those days
I was on my own in bed, in hell. The truth was, she was happy enough that
when she left I was there and when she came back I was there, even if I was
just a shadow of myself on my back, in her bed.

I kicked at Yvonne's that time for a whole week, and despite the poten-
tial fiasco surrounding the gig, no one knew about it for better or for worse.
Everyone in the band was on such a high after that show; I only regret that
I didn't meet Ted Nugent that night, because he'd been such a huge influ-
ence on me when I was young.

Danny eventually admitted to Izzy and me that he'd done all of that
dope I'd stashed, and I've never forgiven him for it. It was a cold-blooded
thing to do that nearly ruined Izzy and me in the eyes of our bandmates.
If it had all gone wrong, it would have caused our band untold professional
embarrassment at a very crucial point for us. But that's the thing about
smack—it's the devil. It is so alluring and seductive that it turns you into a
dishonest, backstabbing demon. Being a junkie is akin to what we imagine

vampires are: it has an enticing aura at first but it becomes a hunger that must be fed at all costs. It completely takes over, and it reels you in. It starts with a taste here and a taste there and then you're doing it all the time. You think it's your choice, but it's not that way—soon you *need* to do it all the time. Then you're hooked into a really vicious cycle before you're even aware that you've become just another statistic.

IN TRUE GUN'S FASHION, I DON'T THINK we ever formally informed Stiefel and company that we weren't going to sign with them—we just deserted the house, leaving a sea of trash and property damage in our wake that Tom Zutaut had to deal with. Alan was our manager and that was that.

Releasing the *Live Like a Suicide* EP afforded a small advance, so Izzy and Steven rented a small apartment just south of Sunset right near the Rock 'n' Roll Ralph's—the supermarket in West Hollywood where every local musician buys beer and whatever else they subsist on. Duff was where he always was, living with Katerina, and Axl lived with Erin. I was the only blatantly vagrant member of the band, shacking up with Yvonne or other girls or crashing on whichever floor I found at the end of the night.

At this point in time, there were many strippers in our midst. All I can say is God bless them all. Many a band before and after us have had this connection. Strippers who hang together are virtually like a band themselves, and we related to one another. They were generous and thought we were cute or dark, mysterious musicians, or just lost puppies that they had to tend to and found attractive. And maybe they felt protected around us, too. The fact that they usually had this uninhibited sexual energy didn't hurt. All in all, they were entirely appropriate for guys like myself.

There was one named Christina who had a roommate, and I'd shack with either one of them on any given night. I lived there for a while and would sleep in one or the other's room, or with them both, depending on how things went. Those girls lived down the street from Izzy and Steven in an apartment building full of strippers on La Cienega. I was hooked up over there, you could say, and called that place home as the band proceeded through another waiting period, which, as usual, spelled nothing but trouble.

Steven, Izzy, and I had a lot of fun over at Christina's: dope was more readily available now that we were all back in Hollywood, though still nowhere near as plentiful as it had been when we'd lived there last. After I got clean, though, I did my best to stay off it. I remember one night I was hanging out with Axl and Izzy over at the stripper house and trying my best to abstain. I didn't have any money on me that night: dope was scarce enough that it could be found but not easily enough that people were willing to share for free. I thought I could just hang out and not do it, but I couldn't—I had to get out of there. Not long after that, I was back on it—it was no use.

I crashed wherever I could, and did whatever came to mind, and there was a point in there when I hooked up with Dave Mustaine of Megadeth. We became friends; he was strung out on smack and crack and he lived in the same neighborhood, so we hung out and wrote songs. He was a true, complete fucking maniac and a genius riff writer. We'd hang out, smoke crack, and come up with *major* heavy metal riffs, just fucking dark and heavy as hell. Sometimes Dave Ellefson would join us; we got along great, we wrote some great shit. It got to the point, in our drug-fueled creative zone, that we started seriously entertaining the idea of my joining Megadeth. Guns was in a holding pattern, after all, and I was high enough to consider all kinds of bad decisions. Dave Mustaine is still one of the most genius musicians I have ever jammed with, but still, in my heart of hearts, I knew I couldn't leave Guns.

Another place I frequented, as did many of us, was Hell House, a pit that embodied our collective mind at the time. It was a very obvious Rorschach test for anyone who might consider working with us or knowing us at all. Hell House was a West Arkeen production; it was a place—in theory, a "home"—that he'd rented with a few of his Harley-Davidson biker friends who had relocated from the East Coast.

The house was a ranch with three bedrooms along one end from front to back. The rear bedroom was occupied by Red Ed and his girlfriend/wife. Their room was off-limits to all because Ed was the biggest biker in residence and his girl was an even more formidable threat—you knew on sight not to fuck with her—but they were both sweet as could be. No one ever disturbed their room; in fact I don't think anyone had ever even been in it. The middle bedroom was where these other bikers, Paul and Del James, lived.

Their place was set up to be a small home recording studio, and West had the bedroom in the front, which was such a pigsty that no one wanted to go in there. All you could do was lie down on the bed; it was such a mess you couldn't stand in there and you couldn't sit down.

I hear that there was a backyard at Hell House . . . I'd love to know what it looked like. During all of the time that I spent there, including my time as a resident, I never made it past the kitchen. That was one of the areas, along with the living room, where transient members like me gathered and left the formidable bikers and their girlfriends well enough alone in their rooms. Visitors were allowed in the living room, the kitchen, and that other room . . . I guess it was the "den." There was also the pantry, where West often chose to pass out. As chaotic as it was, some kind of unspoken law applied where no one disturbed the legal residents, while every common area was a free-for-all war zone where everything in sight could be broken or lit on fire no problem.

I can't imagine who decided to rent those fuckups their property because they turned it into a communal crash pad more gruesome than anything else I've ever seen in a first-world country. It was the second-to-last struc-ture on the block; it was surrounded by apartment buildings, and the front lawn sloped up so that it looked like it was on a hill. It was just south of Sunset on Poinsettia, and as you came down the block, it stuck out like the house in *Psycho*. There were a few things that only spending a night there could teach you, the most important being that if you lay down anywhere there was a two-to-one chance that you'd leave with crabs. I'm still not sure why the lot of us weren't just hauled in by the cops every single night. There were always cars and bikes on the lawn and trash all over the place; there were always people coming and going and loud music at all hours of the night. Hell House was so raucous that from a distance it appeared to be vibrating.

One of the regulars to be found at Hell House was Del James, a true oxymoron: he was a biker guy with tattoos and the whole thing, but he was a writer. Del was tight with all of us at one point but he became tighter with Axl as time went on. Axl really took to him, responding to his intellect and how Del patiently listened to Axl express himself deeply. They did a lot of writing together and I think they still do. Del ended up writing treatments

for some of our videos, as well as having written the short story that inspired Axl to write "November Rain."

During this bit of band downtime as we searched for a producer, we frequented Hell House a bit too much, but I was the only one vagrant enough to live there on and off as well. I even did a few early interviews there. When I read them I couldn't believe how shocked the journalists were by the surroundings. To me there was nothing crazy about it at all.

she gave each and every one of us crabs.

MY OTHER MAIN SOCIAL SCENE, ASIDE from Hell House and the stripper complex across the street from Izzy and Steve, revolved around the ladies of the Seventh Veil, which is a strip club on Sunset that is still alive and kicking. I liked to shack up with a few of the girls who worked there who shared an apartment off Hollywood Boulevard where we'd usually drink ourselves senseless all night long. One of the girls in that scene was named Cameron. Every single one of us fucked her at one point or another, and Steven ended up dating her for a while, and across the board she gave each and every one of us crabs. It was ridiculous; we started to call her Craberon—to her face. I gave her the benefit of the doubt; I thought that maybe I'd picked up crabs over at Hell House or any of the other questionable places I chose to sleep at the time, but that wasn't the case. Craberon had a nice little apartment of her own in West Hollywood and the one time I slept with her over there I got crabs there, too.

Another stripper worth mentioning is Adrianna Smith, the girl that both Axl and Steven dated and that Axl forever immortalized on our debut record . . . but we'll get to all of that in just a little bit. My little universe over at the Seventh Veil was great: I'd show up around eleven p.m., gather some tip money from the girls, head down to the liquor store, stock up on Jim Beam (the poor man's Jack Daniel's), and have a party started for them

back at their place when they got off work. As someone with no place of his own, it was the best setup I could imagine: a cool, reckless spot full of girls where I could get away with drinking or doing whatever else I wanted to do without anyone giving me a hard time.

In the back of my mind, I was aware that we were no closer to choosing a producer and that the inertia was destroying us. I was strung out, drinking, doing drugs when I could, with very little money—and the rest of us weren't much better. I was back to relying on friends and living on couches and living the street life once again—but this was worse than the old days. Back then it was fun because the band and I were working toward something. Now it felt like we were too disorganized and fucked up to be anything other than vagrants and we'd "made it." I knew deep inside that I needed to get my shit together, that I couldn't last in the abyss much longer.

Around this time, our dealer Sammy got busted, and that was a real turning point. I was at Izzy and Steven's that day and Izzy's girlfriend Dezi had gone out to meet Sammy for us at one of his regularly scheduled spots where all of his clients came out of the woodwork to score. The cops had planned a sting, and when Dezi left and never came back we got worried. Much later on we got her phone call from jail. They'd taken in all of Sammy's clients, and were going to spring her, but Sammy was not coming back for a long, long time. That was a big reality check for us; I remember Izzy and I desperately scouring the streets looking for some smack. It was a mess. I ended up going back to Yvonne's and kicking there for the third time. I just stayed up for days and didn't feel well, claiming I'd caught the flu again.

Meanwhile, Tom Zutaut was at his wit's end. He called us into Geffen one day, we thought to discuss another handful of producers that he wanted us to meet. Once he got us in his office, he just stared at us for a while. I was nodding out, still a mess from drying out at Yvonne's, and the rest of the guys looked rough as well.

"What the *hell* can I do for you?" he said. "Take a *look* at yourselves. Do you even think you're *capable* of making a record?! You guys have to get it together! Get focused! Time is running out!"

His comments hung in the air, but they made an impression because slowly but surely, without making a big deal about it or even acknowledging it, we got ourselves together.

ALAN NIVEN AND TOM ZUTAUT HAD SENT every producer in town to meet us, and just when it seemed hopeless one finally stuck—Mike Clink. We did one session with him and recorded "Shadow of Your Love," which was the best song in the set the first time I saw Hollywood Rose. Our version of it didn't make the album, but it was eventually released on a Japanese EP.

In any case, when we listened back, it was all there: finally we heard ourselves on tape exactly the way we wanted to. It was just us, but refined; Clink had captured the essence of Guns N' Roses. Finally all systems were go. We'd spent seven months in limbo, barely playing and intermittently recording with producers that weren't right. It felt like an eternity; because the way we lived, a few months would have decimated a lesser band.

Mike Clink had what it took; he knew how to direct our energy into something productive. He knew how to capture our sound without losing its edge and he had the right kind of personality to get along with everyone. Clink's secret was simple: he didn't fuck with our sound—he worked hard to capture it perfectly, just as it was. It's amazing that no one had thought of that. Clink had worked with Heart and Jefferson Starship, but what sold us was that he'd worked on UFO's *Lights Out*. That record was a standout to all of us, because Michael Schenker's guitar playing on it was both outstanding and sounded amazing.

I've always found that producers are the type of people who have all the answers to other people's problems but never to their own. They're the first to tell other people what to do, how to play, how to sound—all of it. They often don't have their own identity, which makes them hard to respect. Mike was different, he was amiable, he was never intrusive, he was easygoing, quiet, and observant. And he knew who he was. Rather than make suggestions as if he knew better, he chose to take it all in. From the start we completely respected him.

We booked ourselves time at S.I.R. studios and with Mike at the board, the band felt free to be ourselves; at our very first preproduction session, we started writing what would later become "You Could Be Mine." At another session, we started to work up "Perfect Crime," which was something

that Izzy brought in. We weren't in there to write new material, but we were so comfortable that it just came to us.

We started to demo all of the songs that we were considering for *Appetite*, and went through them with Mike pretty much as we'd done them before with very few changes. The only creative shift that occurred was one of Alan's suggestions actually. In "Welcome to the Jungle," originally we repeated the section where Axl sings "When you're high, you never want to come down." Alan suggested taking one of them out. He was right. It made the song tighter. But aside from that, all of those songs were captured as they were in one or two takes. It's a testament to how well things were going in the studio and how great a mood we were in. We *never* listened to suggestions—from anyone. But we were willing to give it a shot, and we found out that it worked. Alan was already managing Great White at the time; he also produced them and served as a cowriter. It's a very good thing that none of us were aware of that at the time, because that session might not have gone so well and "Welcome to the Jungle" might have been a very different song. It never bothered me once we found out about Alan's connection to Great White, but it had quite a negative, snowball effect among some of the other members of our band.

I can only imagine how ecstatic Tom was that Guns N' Roses now had a real manager and a producer that we wanted to work with. It took a couple of years, but it finally looked like this group of lunatics that he'd convinced the label to believe in was actually going to turn out the way he'd promised we would.

Alan set us up in Rumbo Studio in Canoga Park, where Clink liked to work, to do our basic live tracks. Canoga Park was close to where Steven grew up in the Valley, which was a foreign country as far as I was concerned. I think that might have been the point—they thought keeping us out of Hollywood would force us to focus on recording. Alan rented us an apartment at the Oakwoods, which are these generic fully furnished complexes all over the world. He also rented us a van for transportation. For some reason, I can't imagine why, I became the designated driver.

Mike hired some real professionals to help out his street rats: Porky, a famous guitar tech, and Jame-O, the drum tech. They'd done hundreds of records, total pros who were also fun-loving partiers. They were invaluable to us.

Recording a real album in a proper studio was new to us: we'd done

demos in various locations around L.A. Some of them were epic: we did the earliest versions of "Don't Cry" and "Welcome to the Jungle" at Hollywood Sound, in the same studio where Led Zeppelin recorded their second album. Some of our sessions were epic in a different way, such as the time we got into an altercation over payment with the owner of some shitty studio in Hollywood. He was so coked out that he pulled a gun on us.

"You're gonna fucking pay me," he said, his eyes opened far too wide. "Right now!"

"Oh, you're right," we said. "Yes, we're wrong . . . you're right; we're just going to go."

Someone grabbed our tapes on the way out and thankfully no one got shot.

The first day of recording, we commenced with "Out Ta Get Me," doing the same thing we'd always done, but in an entirely new setting: we set up in a big live room and just jammed. When I heard the playback, I realized that I had a huge issue on my hands: my guitar sounded like shit coming through a real studio's soundboard.

During my period of recklessness, I'd managed to hock nearly all of my equipment, including Steve Hunter's Les Paul. I'd convinced Marshall to send me some amps when we had our rehearsal space out in Burbank but I'd never paid for them, so they took them back. Basically I had nothing: at the time I had three guitars. Two were Jacksons, one of which had been made especially for me: it was a black Firebird with my Shirley tattoo on the body (it sounded like shit). The other was a Strat-like prototype with an arch top that they had loaned to me, and I never gave back. It was one of only two that were ever made. My third was a red BC Rich Warlock. And none of them sounded good through the studio monitors.

I was so frustrated and nervous. We'd come this far, and I was determined to have my guitar sound perfect on the record. But I didn't know how I was going to make that happen, because I was more or less bankrupt. I tried to downplay how I felt during those basic tracking sessions by drinking a lot and jumping around while I played with the band, knowing that somehow I had to figure this out and rerecord all of my parts. The other guys weren't going to need to do that—Izzy, Duff, and Steve were so tight right off the bat that those tracks needed no improvement at all.

Recording was going great, but life in the Valley was not. After we wrapped each night, Tom Zutaut, Axl, Duff, and Mike would go home. Theoretically, Izzy, Steve, and I were supposed to go to the Oakwoods and do the same. Usually we were much too excited, so we'd try to go out and we quickly became problematic residents of Canoga Park. We figured that there must be nightlife somewhere, so we sought out anything at all that appeared to be a rock club, a pub, or a bar. We'd roll into what always turned out to be a very conservative neighborhood disco, if that even makes sense, or some bar ruled by a suburban country-music situation. A scraggly mini-gang of long-haired guys in either of those scenarios was an instant clash.

At the time Alan had hired a guy named Lewis, who was posing as our security guard, to look after us. Lewis weighed somewhere between three hundred and four hundred pounds and drove a late-seventies sedan with the driver's seat pushed completely into the backseat just to accommodate his girth. He was a really sweet guy from Houston and I loved him, but when he was supposed to be on security detail, he was usually eating. Lewis had this way, and I don't know how he did it, of going around to the back door of any place we might go to and procuring a huge carton of food from the kitchen. They would literally give him a cardboard box full to the top of take-out containers with everything on the menu in there. This wasn't a burrito or a taco kind of handout—Lewis had entire entrées, like four of each of them. It was something the likes of which I've never seen. He'd take this haul out to our car and just *eat*.

Meanwhile, inside, usually the three of us got into or just barely avoided full-on bar fights. We were psycho enough to scare people off most of the time, but sometimes it got ugly. Luckily, we weren't ever hauled out to the parking lot by a mob of redneck shitkickers—if we had, we might have interrupted Lewis's meal.

Valley nightlife got so tedious that one night when we came home after a great day in the studio and a few hours of heavy drinking, we did the only thing that made sense: we destroyed our Oakwoods apartment Keith Moon style. We tore down everything that wasn't nailed to the wall, and smashed everything else beyond recognition. We turned the beds over, we smashed the nightstands, and we pulled the kitchen counter out of the wall. We smashed the huge sliding-glass doors, we broke the windows and every

mirror, glass, and plate in the place; we destroyed the TV, and the armoire the TV was in. There were splinters and glass everywhere. I woke up on the couch, which was broken, too, with an insane hangover and surveyed the room through squinted eyes.

"Uh-oh," I mumbled . . . to myself.

Once my accomplices and I were awake enough, we agreed to lie: we decided that someone had broken in when we weren't there. We came back late that night and passed out, opting to deal with it in the morning. We told Alan that exact story that day at the studio, because by then he'd become the band's mother figure, a lot like Malcolm McLaren was for the Sex Pistols.

We had every intention of sticking to our bullshit version of events, but as Alan began to ask questions, our story got more and more confused and transparent. Before he called us out, we admitted everything. The funny thing is, after considering his options, Alan decided to go back to the Oakwoods and feed them the same story we'd invented. They didn't buy it either—I can't imagine why—so it went on our tab. For a while there we were banned from all Oakwoods properties worldwide. Apparently the ban was lifted somewhere along the line, because I lived in another of their locations briefly five years later. I managed to be a problem once more, this time by mistake: my snake—I can't remember which one I had with me—got adventurous and crawled down the toilet. It resurfaced in a neighboring room and scared the shit out of someone. Sorry about that . . .

WE WRAPPED UP THE BASIC LIVE recording in just a few weeks and everything sounded great—except my guitar. Alan had booked me time at a studio called Take 1 to rerecord my parts, but I still hadn't found a proper guitar. I didn't know what I was going to do; I tried to play it cool and not show signs of stress, but as our time drew to a close, there was no solution in sight. On our very last day at Rumbo, Alan came into the control room and laid a guitar case on the small couch behind the soundboard. The little cubby where the couch fit was lit by one overhead light, which perfectly spotlighted the guitar as Alan opened the case.

"I picked this up from a local guy in Redondo Beach," he said. "He makes them by hand. Try it out."

It looked good: it was an amazing flame-top 1959 Les Paul replica with no pick guard, and two Seymour Duncan pickups. I felt it out and I liked it, but I didn't get to plug it in until I arrived for my first session at Take 1.

I have romantic memories of those days at Take 1: from the first to the last moment, the entire process was magic to me. It was a small place with no frills—basically just a glorified home studio, but it was my first time recording guitar parts, and what we accomplished there can never be duplicated.

The moment I plugged in my new guitar I thought it sounded pretty good; I was ready to find the right amp. We started going through different Marshall heads—many of them actually, and it was an arduous process. I remember taking every rental amp, putting it in the studio room, miking it, and plugging in. I'd play a few chords, then my tech, Mike Clink, and I would tweak the head, then I'd play a few more. Mike might make some adjustments in the control room or come out and move the positions of the microphones, then I'd play a few more chords and we'd do it all again. It was all entirely worth it. Mike Clink is such a genteel and laid-back guy that he just let me do what I needed to do even if it wasn't necessary: I kept renting and returning amps; we went through about eight before I found the one that sounded exactly how I wanted it to. It was like an act of God because this amp wasn't stock—it was a Marshall that had been customized by someone.

I used it on the entire record and I intended to make it mine when the sessions were done; I told the rental company that it had been stolen from the studio. Unfortunately, my own guitar tech returned it without telling me. Once S.I.R. received an amp that I'd reported stolen, they weren't exactly ready to send it back out to me: when I called they told me that it had already been rented out to someone else.

Anyway, when I heard my guitar through that amp, I knew that it was right immediately; it was a truly magic moment. I plugged into it, as I had all of the others, and casually hit a few chords—and that was it. It was that perfect Les Paul/Marshall combination where the depth of the guitar's tone and the crunch of the amp come together perfectly. It just sounded *amazing*.

"Hold on," Mike said. "Don't move. Don't do *anything*."

He made a few minor tweaks to the head and it sounded even better. And that was that—no adjustments were made to my guitar setup for the

entire session—no mikes were moved, no knobs turned, nothing. We'd found the sound I'd been looking for and we weren't going to lose it.

That guitar has been with me ever since. It was made by the late Jim Foot, who owned Music Works in Redondo Beach. He made about fifty of those Les Paul replicas entirely by hand with no detail overlooked. It became my only guitar for a while, and has become my mainstay in the studio ever since. It has sounded different on every record I've done, but it is the same exact guitar. It just goes to show how volatile recording is: the size and shape of a room, the soundboard used in recording, as well as the molecular quality of the air all play a part—humidity and temperature affect a recording tremendously. Where the guitar and amp is placed, how it is miked; all of these things can drastically influence the result.

I didn't know any of that at the time, but I am glad that we didn't move the amp or guitar one inch for the *Appetite* sessions—it was just fine where it was. But now I understand why I have never been able to re-create my exact sound on that record ever since. It is more than just setting up the same equipment in the same booth, because believe me many have tried. There has been a lot of interest in the equipment and the exact technical specs of the amp that I used for *Appetite* but it can never be replicated. I've actually played a modified Marshall amp that is supposedly identical, but even with that original guitar, it didn't sound the same. It couldn't—because I wasn't in the same studio under the same conditions. Those sessions were one of a kind.

❖❖❖

I DID ABOUT A SONG A DAY. I'D SHOW up, make myself a coffee and Jack Daniel's—or was it a Jack Daniel's and coffee?—and get to work. Izzy's stuff was one take—there was no way he was going to come down and rerecord it, and he didn't have to: his playing is so here and there, just the essence of great rhythm guitar, that spending too much time on it, or recording it on top of the live track, is just silly. Basically, what Izzy played was the simple heart of the songs, no matter who wrote them; if everything else was taken off one of our songs, you'd hear the grace of Izzy's simple scratch rhythms.

As a unit, the entire band had a simple but effective way of playing together. Steven would watch my left foot to determine the tempo, and he'd look to Duff

to cue every drum and bass fill. Those two had a really cohesive relationship—they would communicate the changes and subtleties of every single song through eye contact. Meanwhile, Izzy played all around the riffs that I'd be playing beside Duff: he and I would do Led Zeppelin–style single-note riffs while Izzy brought simple chord patterns that fell around the beat instead of on it. For every downbeat, Izzy had an upbeat. It made for a pretty complex-sounding rock-and-roll band, but at its core it was very simply executed.

The first song I worked on in the studio with my new rig was "Think About You" and the very last was "Paradise City." Duff came down there and hung out every day, because now that I wasn't doing dope, I'd switched to booze again with heartfelt abandon, so he and I were drinking buddies. I would pick Duff up at the apartment that he shared with Katerina on Crescent Heights and he and I would show up at the studio around noon. He'd hang out, listening in until I wrapped it up sometime in the evening, then we'd go out looking for trouble in Hollywood every single night. At the time, trouble was most easily found at the Cathouse.

The Cathouse inhabited the building that used to be Osco's, the ridiculous disco that was featured in the movie *Thank God It's Friday*. I remember Osco's being the spot for all of those "crazy" people when I was a kid, but I never went in there. It was enough for me to see it from across the street: all of their matching slacks and coats, silk shirts and thin belts, shiny shoes and flashy girls in red, blue, or yellow silky dresses, bouncing all around. By then the space looked different, and now it was ours; it more or less became our club, though we didn't realize it at first. It was as if we already had a table there in the VIP, but nobody had told us so.

We were sort of shy and meek when we first started hanging out there until we realized how much the owner, Riki Rachtman, *really* wanted us there. Once we discovered that we could get away with anything at that place, we exchanged shy and meek for crazy and out of control; it was as if we'd been given psycho carte blanche. I was known to break a beer bottle over my head for no reason when the mood caught me and I thoroughly enjoyed stair-diving headfirst down the long flight of stairs leading up into the Cathouse, so long as it was packed with people filing in. Whenever I watch *Jackass* it makes me nervous. I never put a fishhook through my cheek but I definitely had that mentality back then.

I remember one night Mike Clink politely asking if he could come down and hang out with us, and he showed up on a first date with the girl that he eventually married. I did my best to behave and make conversation, but as I walked away from them, in a very Sid Vicious type of move, I stumbled into a huge plate-glass window, which shattered all over me.

Guns rocks the Cathouse.

The Cathouse became our haven during the final stages of making the record. I got to know Nikki Sixx really well at the Cathouse, because he was there a lot. I ran into Yvonne on occasion over there, too. It was such a spot for us that Axl even went, which always brought us added attention—even *we'd* get excited because he didn't often hang out with us at the clubs and bars. Duff, Izzy, and I were gutter rats, but Axl was more sophisticated,

and always brought a different edge to the proceedings. At the very least, he usually wasn't passing out like we were.

Almost every night after leaving the Cathouse, I ended up at someone's house—usually someone I didn't know. Most often, they were girls, and if I was fortunate, they'd let me shower there in the morning before I headed out in the rental van to pick up Duff on my way to the studio to work on the next song. That's the way it went—I had no money at the time but I got by. I got lunch on the studio budget—it was always Taco Bell. Duff and I were so broke that before we headed to the Cathouse to scam free drinks all night, we'd head to McDonald's for dinner, where we'd use these game coupons to cobble together a meal. If you bought anything you'd get one of these scratch-off tickets and receive free fries or a free Coke or a hamburger. There was some kind of McRib promotion called Mac the Knife, so I developed a taste for those. We'd pool our resources into a meal, then whip back over the hill into Hollywood.

Another pastime of mine was taking my frustrations out on the rental vans that Alan provided for us. There was no rhyme or reason, I'd just kick the windows out, break the mirrors—anything glass was in danger. I drove one of them through an industrial-strength fence and destroyed both the fence and the van's front end. I treated those things as if they were battering rams. I would walk up to a brand-new one and smash the headlights out before I even got behind the wheel. One night I drove this girl home, all the way up to Edinburgh and Santa Monica, thinking I was getting some for sure. The next thing I knew it was eight a.m. and I was double-parked, slumped over the wheel, with the lights on and the passenger door wide open. Apparently she'd left me there passed out at the wheel. It was hilarious—only because I didn't get caught. I remember waking up, taking stock of the situation, and hightailing it out of there. I can't imagine how the fuck I got away with that.

One of those vans is immortalized in a great picture that Robert John took of me. It features the one other guitar that I used on *Appetite*—a 1960-something Gibson SG that I managed to borrow from Howie at Guitars R Us, that sounded great once I got it in the studio. It was really heavy-sounding, so I used it on "My Michelle." Anyway, that afternoon I decided to stick it through the hole I'd kicked in the windshield (from the inside) of the van I was driving at the time strictly for Robert's entertainment.

My van abuse demanded that we became familiar with a few different rental companies and a few different locations; Hertz, Budget, Avis, we knew every franchise within a five-mile radius. What I would do is pick up the van, destroy it over the course of two or more days, then return it in the middle of the night—I'd just leave it in the parking lot with the keys in the ignition. Then I'd go to a different location and pick up a new one. Eventually Alan had to take me aside.

"I got a call from Budget," he said. He was pissed off. "The manager of the location insisted that I come down there. I kept asking why and he said that I needed to see the damage that had been done to the van to understand the scope of the problem. And I have to say that he was right."

"Oh yeah?" I said, almost proud. "Was it really bad?"

"It was but that wasn't all," he said. "The manager chewed me out for an hour as he showed me every inch of damage that had been done to the van. Then he asked me if I had any idea what kind of psychopathic horrible people I was involved with. After seeing that, I'm not sure that I do."

What can I say? Those vans were mobile hotel rooms—they got a lot of wear and tear. At the time I didn't even have a hotel room: all of my belongings were in an empty storage room at Take 1. Every day when I'd return from whatever I'd gotten into in Hollywood the night before, I'd head in there to change my clothes; I'd be happier if I'd managed to get a shower wherever I'd crashed. That place was the biggest closet I've ever had—it is actually where we took the photo on the back cover of *Appetite*. I loved it in there; it was all nice and quiet and the only sanctuary I had then. The studio wouldn't let me sleep there, unfortunately. They said that it was an insurance issue, but you know what? I never believed them.

There were only two things that I found difficult while recording my overdubs for *Appetite*. The first was the solo at the end of "Paradise City," which was always easy live but wasn't in the studio. In concert, it could last anywhere from one to two minutes, but on the album version of the song, it was designed to be exactly thirty seconds. So it wasn't easy for me to focus the same narrative and emotion into thirty seconds, and when the red light came on, it threw me for a loop—I actually got gun-shy. I remember going at it a few times and getting so frustrated that I just left the studio completely disappointed; the next day, though, I came in fresh and nailed it.

My other issue was recording "Sweet Child o' Mine." Steven watched my foot to keep time; and for that song I'd count him in because my riff kicked off the proceedings. There was no high hat through the beginning and we hadn't recorded a click track for it, so when I went in to do the overdubs it was a guessing game: I'd be sitting there anticipating the start of the song, hoping that in my mind I'd timed it right so that when I started playing, my timing was right. This was years before digital recording, so there was no signifier to guide me in any way. It took a while, it took many takes, but we got it in the end. Other than that, the album came together so quickly and naturally that it felt like it was meant to be. Obviously it was.

Once I was done at Take 1, I had to find somewhere else to stash my shit, and theoretically myself, so I shacked up with my friend Todd Crew of Jetboy, who had moved down to L.A. from San Francisco. He was living with his girlfriend, Girl—that was her name—and their roommate Samantha, who had the biggest set of tits that I've ever seen on a petite girl like herself; that was enough to inspire me to be a one-girl guy for a minute. The four of us had a blast and were a complete and utter spectacle: we went to the Cathouse every single night, just carousing and making a general nuisance of ourselves during the few weeks that Axl took to finish up his vocals.

<div align="center">◆◆◆◆◆◆◆</div>

ONCE THE RECORDING WAS DONE IT was time to get it mixed. Tom Zutaut took me to New York—it was my first time there—to introduce me to a few candidates as well as some East Coast industry folk. Tom loved to show off: he liked showing his talent the luxury of business class, and showing his talent how important he was in the industry—that was the motivation behind this trip as much as finding us a mixing team. I met Rick Rubin, who was just hitting it big with Run-DMC and Def Jam and his new signing, the Beastie Boys. Rick took us out to his favorite spot to eat, White Castle in Queens. Rick was great; we talked about all kinds of records that we liked, and just shot the shit, because he'd already passed on mixing us. A lot of people passed on mixing us, and once again—all of them regretted it later.

The pair that took us on in the end was Steve Thompson and Michael Barbiero, whom I met on that trip. We had Thompson and Barbiero mix

"Mr. Brownstone" while we were there and we sent it back to the rest of the band. At the same time Alan Niven did a mix because he wanted a shot at doing the album. Alan's version wasn't bad—I remember that Izzy liked it a lot, but the other guys' take was much more in-your-face. They had a tight midrange to their sound that fit our band perfectly. Theirs was ballsier and meaner; there was good interaction between the guitars, while Alan's was more linear, two-dimensional, and hollow.

We set two weeks aside to mix the record and then Axl, Izzy, and I, along with Alan Niven and Tom Zutaut, returned to New York and stayed at the Parker Meridien in midtown while it got done. Tom had his own room, Izzy stayed with Alan, and Axl and I shared the other room. At the time I had a broken wrist and a cast on my arm; an injury I'd sustained during a recent trip to Seattle with Duff. We were partying at his friend Donner's place, which was as rowdy as ever, and somewhere along the line, I met some girl, and while she was on top riding me, the record player started skipping. It was ruining the moment, so I punched the floor, a bit too hard, obviously, to get it to stop.

In any case, my cast didn't stop me from trying to wrestle Alan to the ground and destroying our entire hotel room during one of our first evenings in New York. I don't even remember how it started—I'm sure it was nothing more than my being fearless, and drunk, and Alan being a big bear of a guy that I wanted to tackle. I woke up with rug burns all over my face and chest—apparently I lost the match.

Our stripper friend Adriana Smith made an appearance on that trip as well; she was on the East Coast visiting friends who lived in Alphabet City. It was good to have her there, because Adriana was a fun-loving, high-spirited individual, but once Axl coaxed her into his bed, I had to put up with listening to them fuck all night in the room we were sharing. Adriana is a very vocal individual so I opted to spend most of my nights out, usually as late as possible.

I spent one of them with Steve Thompson, who took me to the China Club, which was the epitome of eighties New York nightlife—lots of coke, little substance, and much too expensive all around. I was in there in my top hat, leather jacket, and leather pants tucked into my cowboy boots amid a room full of the type of New Yorkers who say "Yo, how you doin'?" all the

time and try to impress one another with their expensive Italian blazers and the sack of blow they've got in their pocket. Steve, of course, was pretty dialed into that scene—he was in the music business after all.

Once I decided that I'd had it with that place, I slipped out without telling anyone as I'm sometimes known to do. It has gotten me into trouble before—for example, when I opted to wander off in rural Canada—because usually I just get lost. Such was the case that night: the club was in midtown, less than ten blocks from the hotel, but at around four a.m. I set out the wrong way on an all-night journey in an unfamiliar city. It was very surreal: I wandered down Broadway all the way to Houston Street, over to Avenue C, and by nine a.m. somehow found my way back uptown to the hotel. New York isn't really the city that never sleeps: I managed to find pitch-black stretches of street with no one else around aside from the occasional bum. As it did get quieter and quieter I began to feel more and more alone. A montage of New York City movies came to mind as I looked at blocks that were both familiar and totally strange to me. Once I finally admitted to myself that I had no idea where I was going, it came together and I started to recognize a few landmarks. Before I knew it, I found the hotel. As usual, there was hardly a welcoming party. I wandered in and found Axl and Adrianna asleep.

Mixing the record was an incredible experience. It was the first time that I learned the process of sound manipulation, and looking back at it now that digital technology has changed the recording industry forever, I feel privileged to have made and mixed that record in the days before things changed. There was no automated interface back then: Thompson and Barbiero manually worked the faders, making minor adjustments to each channel, as per our request, each time we listened back to each track. Those two guys were amazing; they had a system, pretty much an unspoken language between them. Steve was the energetic, in your face guy and Michael was the reserved, analytical, calculated guy. And they got on each other's nerves constantly, which somehow fueled their creativity.

The way they'd work was that Barbiero would set up the basic mix—the drums, the bass, and all of the EQs. Then Steve would come in and they'd start taking passes, with Steve doing all of the frenetic tweaks to the guitars and the vocal jumps throughout the mix—he did all of the dynamic rocking parts, while Barbiero laid the sonic foundation. Since mixing was entirely manual, done

while the song was playing, it was a one-take affair. When they took a pass, the song would start, they'd have all four hands on the board and they'd immediately start jumping around each other, adjusting knobs and faders in real time as the music played. If they got just one thing wrong, they'd start over. And on top of that, they had all of us in the room backseat-driving.

One of the funnier episodes was the day that Izzy got up bright and early to head down there and oversee the mixing of "Sweet Child o' Mine." He totally rode their asses. Usually they'd have a mix up by noon and would have it done by four. That day Izzy called us around one and told us all to come down immediately because it was finished and it sounded great. When I walked in, the first thing I saw was the traumatized look on Mike Barbiero's face—the guy looked like a prisoner after a long night of interrogation. He played us the mix, which was ridiculous; it was nothing but Izzy's guitar and Axl's vocals with everything else faded into insignificance. I could hardly hear the drums, the bass was nonexistent, and my guitar was audible only in the intro and the solo. Let's just say that Izzy has a sparse way of looking at things and that was very indicative of his point of view. Obviously we redid it.

As we mixed down the song "Rocket Queen," Axl felt that the bridge needed something; some other element to elevate the drama. He suggested that Adrianna Smith, who was with us in the studio that day, fuck him in the live room so that we could record her vocals and layer them over the breakdown. We'd been drinking Jack pretty heavily all day, so it seemed like the most natural thing in the world. I was all for it; I knew too well what she was capable of vocally—she had kept me up for the past three nights. So we lit up some candles for atmosphere, then she and Axl went out into the live room, got down on the floor by the drum riser, and we recorded Smith's performance in all of its honest moaning and groaning. Enjoy it—it's right there in the final mix. That breakdown said it all; I couldn't think of a better song to close the album and I couldn't think of a more telling slice of our lives at the time to hand to our fans.

it encourages you
to drink responsibly
and behave politely.

of how to best exploit every situation to our advantage; he was excellent at spreading the word and generating excitement. While the album was mastered and prepared for release, he kept us rehearsing and booked us a three-gig run in London at the Marquee, and arranged for some interviews over there. He did everything he could to introduce us to England ahead of time, which was a smart move on his part. Before we could go, however, I had to get myself a new green card, because I'd recently lost it when I left the black day planner in which I keep all of my important papers on top of the van as I pulled out of rehearsal with Duff one night. It ended up all over Santa Monica Boulevard, and even though I was able to find most of it on the street, the one thing I never found was my green card—it's possible that there is an illegal immigrant walking around L.A. with the name Saul Hudson. If so, I hope my name has served him well.

I made the mistake of bringing Todd Crew and West Arkeen with me to wait in line down at the immigration office when I went to replace it: it's always a first-come, first-served basis, so after the third day of unsuccessfully getting in, I needed company. We showed up at four a.m. to ensure that I'd make the cut and we were so drunk that we were stumbling around the place like the Keystone Kops. We'd brought some booze for the road, of course, so once the office opened we were a total mess. Todd almost got arrested because he started playing with some rubber plant in the hallway while holding my place in line, which made the other people there very uncomfortable.

We got over to England and stayed in two apartments, Axl and Izzy and Alan in one and Duff and Steven and I in the other. We had a tour manager named Colin and we got there a week before our shows to rehearse and do some press. We were staying in Kensington High Street, which was too far from the twenty-four-hour culture of Soho. It was not at all a rock-and-roll neighborhood; it was very proper with nothing to do but drink in the pub on the corner, which of course we did. It reminded me of the time we spent in Canoga Park: we explored everything and found nothing that was quite our scene. Except in London no one paid attention to us.

Todd Crew and Del James met us out there, which elevated the tempo considerably. Todd had tickets to Paris that his parents had given him for his college graduation. Looks can be deceiving: to the naked eye he was a

burnout, but Todd was a college grad and was very well schooled. He'd never taken that trip, so he and Del used those tickets, just two long-haired American rock-and-roll guys totally lost in France living their version of *European Vacation*. After a couple of days they took the ferry over and then the train and crashed out at our place. They were unruly Americans trying to navigate Paris to London via ferries, cabs, and rail. Del used to call people like me and him "lugheads." I can't even imagine how those two lugheads ever made it.

Our average day in London consisted of rehearsal, after which we might go to one of the clothing shops in the area because that was all that there was to do. One time my guitar tech Johnny took me to a really nice guitar store. He made a big deal out of me: I was Slash, the guitar player for Guns N' Roses, the next great American rock band from Los Angeles. While he was schmoozing the owner I lay down on the floor to get comfortable, and passed out cold. They had to carry me out. Apparently that incident made a big impression on the English press and kick-started a handful of nicknames—"Slash Crash" and "Slashed" (as in pissed or drunk) were a couple. It established my "legendary" reputation there. I can't imagine why.

Once our friends from home arrived, we did carouse more intensely. We'd drink in every pub we saw, rehearse for a few hours, then drink in every other pub we saw until the pubs closed. We weren't nearly as rambunctious or destructive as we were in say, the Valley, because there wasn't much that we could have possibly done to bring life into Kensington High Street. Just walking down the street, looking at the manicured parks and gardens, was quite sobering at any time of day. Our rehearsal space had the same cold London environment. In a clinical room or neighborhood like that, you don't feel right busting things up: it encourages you to drink responsibly and behave politely.

Once we ventured to Soho and beyond, however, we found our peers. One night Duff and I were motivated to see a band (I can't remember at all who) at Town and Country, which was a converted coach house way out in East London. We were smashed when we got there and we were more smashed when we left, and we had never stopped to consider that we'd be more or less stranded after the show. The trains had stopped running and I'm sure there was a bus, but we

knew nothing about that. We started walking, just trying to make sense of which way was up, looking in vain for a cab. And of course it started to rain.

I was not happy about our situation at all, and apparently I became such a belligerent ass that right then, on some street miles from where we had to go, Duff found it necessary to straighten me out. We didn't get in a fistfight exactly but there were definitely words exchanged. I don't know how we got home, I don't remember passing out; after our "altercation" I remember nothing. We did get back to the apartment somehow where Del lay in wait. Del was fond of taking pictures whenever one of our friends ended up in a compromised position, so I've learned through visual evidence that I slept through most of the next morning on my hands and knees with my boots on and my head buried in the corner of the couch. My top hat had been reduced to a complete puddle by the rain, but I'd held on to it—it was sitting there in a heap beside me. I wasn't happy about that at all—for the rest of the trip. I was like a beaten puppy: "What? No top hat?"

One of our weirder excursions in the week leading up to our gigs took place on a Sunday, which no one bothered to tell us was off license, meaning no liquor stores, pubs, or grocers were allowed to sell booze. Of course you can always find the odd lawbreaker, but that day we had our work cut out for us, because no one was feeling kind to our cause in the proper lanes of Kensington High Street. As we wandered around looking for an open pub, we amassed a few odd stragglers. One of them was a weird young girl who was a rock fan, and was really shy but was somehow . . . off. She latched on to us and began to follow us wherever we went. No one was really talking or interacting with her much—she just hung around. We weren't sure if she was a runaway, a groupie, homeless, or emotionally disturbed, but by the end of the night it was clear that she intended to stay wherever we were staying, because it didn't seem like she had anywhere else to go. She was harmless enough, so we let it happen. Between Del and Todd and the rest of us, our flat was full of people sleeping on the floor, crashed out wherever. I was passed out on the floor myself and I remember that this girl was across the room before I lost consciousness. But sometime during the night, I woke to find that she had unzipped my pants and was sucking my dick. I acted like I was still asleep but I must admit that I didn't stop her because it was pretty good. In the morning she was gone and we never saw her again.

WE REHEARSED AT JOHN HENRY'S, A famous studio where everybody who is anybody has done the same. It's the eqivalent of S.I.R. in L.A., but with an English sensibility—it's just a bit more "proper." It was very cool, because lining the hallways were road cases that said MOTÖRHEAD, IRON MAIDEN, and THIN LIZZY. The place had an amazing vibe. We chose to spend our per diems, which were a few pounds a piece, at the pub, so we'd raid the little café at the studio for as many coffees, Danish, and sandwiches as we could stand. We'd get bags of crisps at the corner shops for a few pence and fill up on those before drinking the rest of our money at the pub around the corner.

Our three shows were at the Marquee Club, the famous little sweatbox where everyone from The Who to David Bowie to the Sex Pistols had played. On show days we sound-checked there, then Duff and I spent the evening drinking outside on the street with the curious locals who had come to see us. After a week in Kensington High Street, we were starved for any taste of the rock-and-roll culture that we were used to. I'm not sure if it was that afternoon or after that first show, but hanging out like that I managed to land myself a girlfriend named Sally, who was a hot "Page Three" girl at the time. "Page Three" is a fixture of the English newspaper *The Sun* that features aspiring swimsuit and lingerie models each day, because, they are, after all, newsworthy. I was infatuated with Sally immediately. She made the rest of the English trip much more fun because she also knew where to go. We hung out at a couple of stable Soho rock-and-roll spots. One of them was the Intrepid Fox, where I nailed Phill Magg, the front man of UFO, with a shot glass. I don't remember why.

I also hung out with my hero, Lemmy Kilmister. The entire band met Mötorhead that trip and that made our journey perfect.

Those Marquee shows were loud and hell-bent; what I remember, I remember fondly. We did AC/DC's "Whole Lotta Rosie" and Aerosmith's "Mama Kin," and all of our original stuff. One of those nights was also the first time that we ever played "Knockin' on Heaven's Door," which we put together at sound check on a whim. I'd always loved that song and loved that live version—it was much more raw than what ended up on *Use Your*

Illusion. Those shows went over well enough that, from the start, we were never even considered part of the same league of L.A. hair metal bands who had come through England. We were seen as something else, which was what we'd been saying all along. Finally, it felt like we'd been justified.

<hr />

AFTER THAT TRIP, WE RETURNED TO L.A.
to put the finishing touches on the album. Axl had brought us a print of a Robert Williams painting that we all agreed should be the cover—it's a manic scene of a robot about to avenge a girl who has just been raped by eating her attacker. We thought it was perfect; we even adopted the title of the painting as the title of the album: *Appetite for Destruction.*

Everything was great, the album went out as planned with the Williams print on the cover, and no one had a problem with it. That was until Tipper Gore and her lobbying group the PMRC got ahold of it. They were very effective at censoring music at the time, but we didn't care—we welcomed as much controversy as Tipper could dish out.

Our wish was granted: Geffen got so many complaints that our album was banned before it was ever even properly stocked at the national chains. We were told that most retail stores wouldn't carry it and most others required that we wrap the album in a brown paper bag unless the cover was changed. Faced with selling nothing now that we finally had something to sell, in a rare moment of common sense, we decided to compromise and agreed to redesign the cover: the Williams print was put on the sleeve inside. A guy we knew at Hell House did a painting of the five of us, as skulls, on a cross, which was *incredible* so we used it for the cover, and Axl had it tattooed on his arm as well. It was a cool enough design that as much as we were unhappy about eating crow, we ended up with something new that we loved. A first edition of that original cover is a collector's item by the way.

Since I have some illustration skills, I had always been very involved in the design of the band's art and posters. I remember the day when I took out a bunch of *Guns & Ammo*–type magazines back when I had my newsstand job and flipped through them until I found the perfect gun to copy for our logo. I took the picture home with me; at first I wasn't sure how to tie it all together. I was living over at Yvonne's and one night, after she and

her mom had gone to sleep, I was sitting up at their kitchen table and it came to me. I took out that picture of the gun and drew it freehand, then I drew another one of them crossed with roses underneath. That simple design stuck; it became the logo for the band.

Anyway, once we agreed on the new cover design, I wanted to go to New York to oversee the new album art layout as well as to meet with our merchandiser about our T-shirts and our new booking agent, Bill Elson at ICM. It was going to be a very busy trip.

At the time I was "dating" a porn actress, Lois Ayres, whose work I appreciated, and while the shocking nature of her performance might have deterred other suitors, I was intrigued by it. We got together somehow or another in L.A. and I had been crashing at her place for a while. When I was scheduled to go to New York, it just so happened that she was scheduled to go as well because she had a few feature performances to do at a couple of strip clubs in Times Square. She had a room booked for her at the Milford Plaza on Eighth Avenue and Forty-fifth Street so I crashed with her when I arrived.

My second morning there, I was awoken at seven a.m.

Ring! Ring!

Ring! Ring!

I picked up the phone and hung it up.

Ring! Ring!

Ring! Ring!

Obviously it wasn't going away.

"Yeah? What?" I shouted.

"Hello, sir, there is a Todd Crew here to see you," the voice said. "Is it okay to send him up?"

"Uh . . . yeah . . . sure," I said hesitantly. I had no idea what Todd could possibly want at seven a.m., in New York, no less.

Apparently he'd come out on a last-minute invitation from an actor friend because he'd needed to get out of L.A. fast, for his own good: he and Girl had split up, which was a *major* deal—those two had been together for years and were more or less one person. He'd also been fired by his band, who hated the fact that he hung out with us so much. He was soon replaced by Hanoi Rocks' Sam Yaffa with little to no discussion. At that

point they'd not only kicked him out, but they'd kept all of his gear and were refusing to give it back. So Todd was not in a good way to say the least. He arrived at my door already fucking drunk, with a full liter of what we liked to call Toad Venom in one hand: vodka and orange juice disguised in a 7UP bottle. I had an entire day of meetings all across town, beginning at ten a.m., but I could see that Todd needed tending to. Girl wasn't taking his calls, he didn't have a band, and there was no way that I was leaving him alone.

I had no choice; I took him to all of my meetings, which was quite the endeavor. They were all within a few long midtown blocks of one another, which was fine with me; I'd planned to go to each of them on foot—it was a long way to go, but I was actually looking forward to it. It was one of those oppressively hot New York July days and Todd insisted that I first take him to a Western Union about ten blocks out of my way to pick up some money. He was so distraught that I agreed, and to this day I wish I hadn't: if I had refused to go to Western Union with him, it might have ended differently because he wouldn't have had any money on him.

We proceed to the street to get on our way and, as I said, Todd was already fucking wasted: he'd start to fall over every time we stopped at a traffic light. I was holding him but he was half a foot taller than me and just big all around. I'd try to lead him down the street and he'd collapse in the middle of the intersection while a crowd of people darting to work at eight a.m. forked around him where he fell. We got to the Western Union one step at a time like that, then we got his money, and got up to my first meeting at Geffen about ten minutes late.

I left Todd in the lobby and I'm sure whoever the secretary was that day still remembers him. He passed out cold on the couch the minute he hit the air-conditioning, so I left him there, this big, snoring long-haired tattooed guy, who scared everyone unlucky enough to be waiting in the lobby that day. When it was time for me to go, it took two assistants to get Todd into the elevator. Sleep had helped him a little, but not much. Still, somehow, I maneuvered him through the streets and got to the rest of my appointments on time: one was at Brokum to discuss the T-shirts and the other was at ICM. All the while I dragged a drunk bass player along with me, treating it like he was the invisible elephant in the room no one talked about.

He was like the cop in *Up in Smoke*, trying to give directions on the highway with the hot dog stuffed in his face.

By the early afternoon my business was done. Todd was a little bit more coherent, but definitely in need of a nap, so I thought taking him to Central Park would do the trick—at the very least he could sleep it off on the grass in the sun. I managed to steer us up there, and just as we were heading into the park we ran into three musicians from a local L.A. band that we both knew. I don't remember why they were in town, but they wanted us to head down to Alphabet City with them to cop some heroin. Todd was all for it, but I wouldn't let him; I had just done my time in that pit of hell and the thought didn't interest me at all. On top of that, I had a record on the way and the risk of arrest or worse wasn't worth it.

I kept the party hounds at bay by suggesting that we buy a bottle of Jim Beam and take a carriage ride around Central Park, which we did. That was quite a scene: me, Todd, and these Goth-looking dudes with some tattoos and piercings taking in the summer sights. We chased it with some pizza and a round of drinks at this little dive bar afterward. And once we were on to the second round, smack came up again. I did everything I could to put the brakes on it, but I was overruled. My personal concerns at that point mattered less to me than Todd's well-being: I didn't like what I saw and I did everything I could to keep him from going darker. Todd had done heroin, but he wasn't all that experienced; even if he had been, he was in no state to be messing with drugs. As I said, I was unanimously outvoted: Todd got them to agree to go get the dope for us so I wouldn't be at risk of getting busted. To say the least, he *really* wanted some. We headed downtown and waited for them in a bar on St. Mark's Place in the East Village while they scored the dope.

We ended up at their friend Chosei Funahara's place; he was the bass player for the Plasmatics. I shook his hand but I never really got a chance to talk to him because Todd was so desperate to get high that we went directly into the bathroom within the first two minutes of being in his apartment. I was wary about this stuff, because you never know what you're getting when you buy shit off the street—you always have to be careful. I didn't really want to do it, but I sampled a little bit and since I could tell that it wasn't strong at all, I cooked up a little shot for me and Todd.

We hung out there for a while and we made plans for our friends to meet us later at my hotel room, before Todd and I made our exit. The sun was starting to set by the time we got to Times Square, and as we walked along the rows of movie theaters, I decided, as I stared at the marquee, that I really wanted to see *Jaws 3-D*. Todd agreed; all he really wanted to do was drink anyway. We bought a case of beer and snuck it into the theater, which might sound odd by today's standards, but in 1987, New York's Times Square was still gritty enough that the odd movie house that wasn't showing porn 24/7 wasn't going to eject two guys who'd brought their own beer.

Jaws 3-D wasn't that great; and neither was that shot of heroin. I noticed, halfway through the film, that I wasn't high and that I'd drunk about two or three of those beers, while Todd had downed the rest, one after the other, just pounding them. Then he suddenly left the theater to call Girl. He was gone for a really long time, and I hoped that was a good sign—maybe they were patching things up. Unfortunately, that wasn't the case: when the show was over I found Todd slumped on the floor by the pay phone completely beside himself because Girl had rejected him, apparently in an extremely harsh manner.

I steered Todd back to my hotel doing what I could to sort him out, hoping to get him settled down. He was completely distraught, but after a while, I managed to get him relaxed, lying down in bed, slowly edging toward sleep. And that was precisely when our "friends" from earlier in the day knocked on the door. They were all set to shoot dope and hang out and Todd suddenly perked up and was eager to join in. It was another losing battle, so I got on board, I shot almost all of my dope because this stuff still had yet to kick in. At the same time I was monitoring Todd to be sure that he didn't have too much, because he had been drinking heavily for about eighteen hours. I can't say what happened for sure, but I'm almost positive that he got a shot from someone else who was there that night when I wasn't looking. What I gave him wasn't strong enough to cause what happened.

Maybe an hour after everyone showed up, Todd stood up in the middle of the room, kind of leaning to one side, then suddenly collapsed. His breathing was slow, he wasn't responding, so I got him into the bathtub and doused him with freezing-cold water. I shook him, I slapped him, I did everything I could to wake him up. All while our "friends" gathered themselves and fucking split without so much as a word.

There I was with my best friend, Todd, in my arms in the bathtub. I was freaking out; I'd OD'd before but I'd never dealt with anyone else OD'ing on me. I did everything I could to keep him conscious. I was confused because I did, as far as I knew, twice the amount that Todd had done and I wasn't even high. I started to wonder what else he had in his system that I didn't know about. I didn't know what the fuck to do. Suddenly Todd came around: he was semiconscious, he was breathing, and for a few fleeting moments his eyes seemed to focus on me and the room around him. His breathing became regular and finally I felt comfortable. I dried him off and got him into bed.

I sat there next to him, watching his breathing, and called our mutual friends to tell them what was going on in an effort to calm myself down a bit. I also called the only person that I knew in New York well enough to confide in—a girl named Shelley who worked at ICM, with Bill Elson. I was speaking with Shelley, watching Todd carefully, when all of a sudden, his breathing stopped. I dropped the phone and shook him, and slapped him, while holding him up. I beat on his chest in desperation but he wouldn't come around. I called 911, then threw water on him, but nothing worked. I couldn't save him—Todd, all of twenty-one years old, died in my arms. I was flooded with every emotion, fear, panic, anxiety . . . and where the *fuck* were the paramedics?

When they finally arrived, they were complete assholes. It had taken them nearly forty minutes. They came in the room and stared at Todd as if he were a bag of garbage.

"Oh shit," one of them said, a bit too loud for my taste. "What is this, now?"

"I know," the other one said. "This is stupid, he's long gone."

"I don't know why we even bothered. . . . Glad we didn't rush!"

They took the body away and left me there in the room with Todd's wallet, cowboy boots, and his other belongings. I had barely begun to grasp what had happened when the police arrived. They gave me the whole good cop/bad cop interrogation, asking if I knew where he got the dope, asking me where the syringe was. They set themselves up in two separate rooms in the hotel and they sent me from one to the other for about three hours. Once they were done and satisfied, they split and told me that I'd need to be at the station at eight a.m. the next day to sign papers confirming "receipt of the body."

That statement alone was way too much for me; once they left I went down

to the street, sat on the sidewalk with my back against the wall of the hotel, and tried to figure out what had happened. I saw the sun come up and before I had any kind of answer, it was time to scrape myself off the pavement and get down to the precinct. I've never been so disoriented in my entire life.

That place was as ramshackle as *Barney Miller* and I signed whatever it was that I needed to sign—which was as impersonal as filling out a form for lost luggage. I returned to the hotel in a daze. Lois had yet to return from the night before. I was lying in the bed when I heard an inhospitable knock on the door. It wasn't housekeeping—it was serious. The manager and a security guard stood there, telling me that Lois had not only not come home but she'd bailed on her bill, and the hotel had no intention of granting me a late check-out.

I returned to my perch on the sidewalk, and after a while, not knowing who else to call, I called Alan. He arranged for me to go to Shelley's place and get some rest. Once I did I just passed out from the exhaustion. The next thing I knew Alan was there; he'd flown in to make sure I got back to L.A. in one piece. I'm glad he did, because I was numb and paralyzed.

That was the worst thing that had happened to me up until then—or since. Todd was my best friend and he was gone. It didn't end there. When we went up to San Francisco for the funeral, I had to deal with finger-pointing from Todd's obviously distraught family and the guys in his band—everyone thought that his death was my fault. Todd's stepbrother was friends with Del James—he knew me and even he thought I was to blame. It got very ugly. Todd's family even hired a private investigator to check me out for a while; so on top of the mourning, an unjust black cloud of accusation followed me around, while I'd been the one in the end who had done everything possible to keep Todd alive.

It was a hell of a wake-up call: not only had I come face-to-face with the realities of the voracious lifestyle I lived, but I also learned that by living so overtly I would always be an easy target—even to those I trusted—those who knew me the best of all.

Off to the Races

I can say one thing about the "musical highlights" of 1987, it's that they were more stereotypically eighties to me than the entire decade put together. In 1987, Bon Jovi's "Livin' on a Prayer" spent February 14 through March 7 at number one—more weeks than any other single that year. In 1987, Whitney Houston became the first female solo artist to have an album debut at number one. Robert Palmer took home the Grammy for Best Rock Vocal Performance for "Addicted to Love" and the Eurythmics took home the Grammy for Best Rock Performance by a Group for "Missionary Man."

Dirty Dancing and *Three Men and a Baby* were the big movies of that year and every song that came on the radio was saccharine and overproduced: Madonna's "Who's That Girl?," Peter Gabriel's "Big Time," Steve Winwood's "Back in the High Life Again." The music industry was full of other bad ideas in 1987: compact discs were already out, but the powers that be decided that "cassette singles" were the future—and launched that format with a Bryan Adams track called "Heat of the Night" that withstood the test of time just about as well as cassette singles did.

As for straight-ahead hard rock in 1987, Aerosmith made their comeback with *Permanent Vacation,* but other than "Rag Doll" and "Dude (Looks Like a Lady)," the songs most played on the airwaves were nothing but the weak and weaker. There was Whitesnake's "Here I Go Again," Heart's "Alone," Great White's "Once Bitten," and Billy Idol's cover of "Mony Mony." And somewhere between the two there we were: neither Guns N' Roses nor *Appetite for Destruction* fit into any preexisting niche in the musical landscape of 1987. As much as we'd "made it," it was the same as it ever was: we had to build a space of our own.

Appetite for Destruction was released on July 21, 1987, to little or no fanfare at all. To be kind, I'll say that it was a hit on the underground circuit; it had a small cult following, transmitted by word of mouth, like Metallica's *Kill 'em All*. We found early fans in The Cult after their lead singer, Ian Astbury, saw us play at the Marquee in London; later on he told me that he knew immediately that we'd be huge. He got us signed up as the opening band on a two-month leg of their North American tour in support of *Electric*.

That album was produced by Rick Rubin and was a major departure from The Cult's Goth-influenced roots. It made sense that they'd want a hard-rock band like ours supporting them because *Electric* sounded like it was recorded in 1973. The Cult had a huge worldwide audience by then, and though *Electric* would be the album to do it for them, they hadn't quite hit it big in America. I was exposed to that record through the girl I was sleeping with at the time. Chicks were good for finding out what was cool at the moment—they always seemed to be up on the records of the day.

Before we took off on The Cult tour, we shot the "Welcome to the Jungle" video, which was our first. It was a two-day shoot. The first day we shot all of those little vignettes that define each of us as individual characters in the video: Axl gets off a bus, Izzy and Duff are seen out the street, etc. If you blink, you miss my appearance: I'm the drunk sitting in a doorway with the brown-bagged bottle of Jack. We shot those scenes on La Brea, outside of some little storefront that our director, Nigel Dick, had found. I was not unfamiliar with the long and arduous process of making videos: I was an extra in a Michael Schenker video for a song off his *Assault Attack* album in 1982.

Over the course of the evening as I waited for my call time for "Jungle," I got plastered drunk. I found the constant cycle of "hurry up and wait" that is standard on any kind of film or video shoot so boring that by the time they were ready for my scene, it was more of a candid portrait. That video captured where I was at in that moment: a minute after the director called "Cut," I got into a fight with our manager, Alan Niven, over what I

have no idea—and neither did he. I told him off and then I wandered into the night and hitchhiked to who knows when.

The next night we shot at the Park Plaza Hotel, which was the location of Dale Gloria's Scream Club. Dale is a local nightlife celebrity in Los Angeles who has owned and run a variety of clubs—Scream was the most legendary. That second day, yet again, was another long shoot on location, but at least we shot the band performing the song live. We made it an event: we did the song on a closed set, then we opened it up and filled the club with an audience and played it three times in a row. That was cool. And that was a wrap on our first video.

A day or two, maybe a week, later, we set off on tour with The Cult to support them during a two-month, August-and-September swing through Canada, the West Coast, and the South. That tour was great; none of the usual bullshit happened where the headliner predictably sabotages the opening band by turning down their sound so that they make that much more of an impact when they take the stage. I think The Cult had circumvented that issue by choosing us; a band from L.A. that no one had heard of. Whatever it was, there was great camaraderie among our bands. Ian and Axl got along very well and Duff and I hung out a lot with bassist Stephen "Hagus" Harris. Still, I'm not quite sure that they knew what they were getting when they hired us. One thing was for sure: this outing confirmed my passion for touring. These were meager beginnings, but they launched my enduring love affair with the road—I remain an irretrievable road dog as of this writing.

Another pattern that has endured in my life established itself again at this time: I had ditched heroin as a daily habit and made the smooth transition into booze. We were working now, so I'd predictably replaced one addiction with another, exchanging smack for full-tilt drinking. I was naive to think that I was so tough that I'd gotten myself all clean and had no problems with addiction whatsoever—the truth was I hadn't changed anything. I'd only substituted the substance. I transitioned my addiction from illegal to legal; because alcohol was acceptable to everyone. It was an expected facet of everyday life in rock and roll, so if I was drinking heavily but not shooting up, those in my circle were fine with that. What did they know?

From that point on, aside from a few isolated incidents, it was a few years

before I had serious heroin issues again. The interesting thing is that in the interim, my entire point of view on heroin changed: soon it was as if I'd never tried it at all. Somehow I totally forgot about it, and lost all interest in it, even when people around me did it in my presence. I still don't get it. I did take my drinking to an all-time high as a replacement, though I tried really hard to be mindful of never exceeding my limitations before a gig.

A long time ago someone had taught me that the best cure for a hangover was another drink—the hair of the dog that bit you. That became my philosophy, because it worked; the only problem was that during this period, the parties never seemed to stop, and so began a cycle. I woke up with a hangover every day, so I started every day with a fresh drink, and then drank through to the next party that night. In no time, the parties blurred: I was drinking all night into the next day and into the next night into the night after that. There really wasn't a day when I took time off from drinking because there was generally a party to get to every day; it was all part of my daily routine.

We were a gang of heathens who thought we knew everything but in reality we knew nothing.

ON THE CULT TOUR, WE STAYED IN cheaper hotels than they did, but that didn't stop us from wreaking havoc at theirs. Often, the night ended with Duff and me being kicked out either by

the hotel staff or the band themselves, and being faced with the challenge of finding our way back to wherever the fuck our hotel was. One night I was so drunk that I passed out on a couch in the lobby of The Cult's hotel and Duff left me there. I woke up at around five a.m. after just having wet myself in my sleep. To make matters worse, I didn't have my hotel-room key and had no idea where we were staying. The staff at the hotel would not help me at all, probably because I was soaked in pee and smelled like a bar. I headed out into the Canadian cold; it was freezing, and I wandered around, just hoping I'd find my way. The only hotel that I could see once I got outside was a long walk away, but lucky for me it turned out to be ours. I was even luckier to be wearing my leather pants, because I wasn't as frozen as I might have been. That's a wonderful side effect of leather pants: when you pee yourself in them, they're more forgiving than jeans.

I was just so excited to be on tour *anywhere* with an *actual tour bus*, no matter how shitty or unreliable it was. As a band, we were like the scrappy underdog team in a sports movie; we had inferior gear, and nothing but the clothes on our backs, but we had enough heart to win the championship—we were a rock-and-roll version of *Slap Shot*. We were even playing in hockey rinks in Canada: the tour started out in the eastern provinces and continued on to the West Coast, down into the American Pacific Northwest, south through California, then across Arizona and Texas into Louisiana and the Mississippi Delta region. It was a trek.

In Canada, nothing shocked us but we shocked everyone. Too often I felt like we were the Blues Brothers in that scene when they show up to play the redneck bar and they're pummeled with beer bottles. We had the attitude to back it up whenever we found ourselves unexpectedly in a hostile environment, which was good . . . because a few times we did.

Even when we didn't, all across Canada, we got weird looks wherever we showed up. We thought we were normal, but I could see pretty clearly that the way we carried ourselves was not normal to these people at all—or other people for that matter. We were a gang of heathens who thought we knew everything but in reality we knew nothing. I imagine that The Cult looked at us like a volatile piece of equipment: we were interesting to some of them because we had a unique timbre; but we were a machine that might crap out at any moment.

Cult singer Ian Astbury was really entertained by how explosive we were: he enjoyed it; in his mind, we were ferocious and really hungry and all of the qualities that seasoned rock people envy. He was right: we were all that and more—we were like an M80 in a Coke can. Cult guitarist Billy Duffy, on the other hand, just seemed like, "Yeah, whatever." He either wasn't interested or wasn't buying it. In any case, more often than not, they'd stop by to take a look at our antics.

<hr>

WE GOT UP THERE AND DID OUR GIGS every night on that tour, but the truth is that I never felt satisfied doing those shows. We had yet to become a solid touring entity; we weren't seasoned pros just yet and that ate at me. It probably made us entertaining because we were so loose around the edges: we showed up with no experience; just the clothes on our backs, the gear on the stage, and a handful of songs to play for people who had never heard of us. I think we were the only ones who knew we had a record out.

We played hockey rinks, theaters, and a few small festival dates with a handful of bands on the bill. And as much as I was happy to be out there touring, which I thought was the greatest thing ever, I couldn't get over the fact that it wasn't quite as good as it should be. We never got there in my mind because our presence on a large stage just wasn't up to par. But that's just me being overly critical, which is definitely a part of my character. I was unable to write those gigs off like I imagine the Sex Pistols would have.

That said, it felt like a homecoming when The Cult tour arrived at the Long Beach Arena. I remember rolling in there late the night before and staring at the building, completely starstruck. I'd seen Ozzy, AC/DC, Black Sabbath, Judas Priest, Billy Idol, and countless others there and for so long, I'd thought playing there meant you'd *arrived*.

I'd even seen Ratt there against my will: as I mentioned, Yvonne had dated their singer, Stephen Pearcy, back when they were still called Mickey Ratt. When she and I were together, the group headlined there and she was still so proud of him that we had to go, even though he was a complete moron. She was thrilled that Ratt had made it from living together in one cheap apartment to headlining the Long Beach Arena. And now I had and I can't lie; when we

got that gig, I had a tremendous feeling of accomplishment. To a big touring band, in the grand scheme of things, playing to five thousand or so at the Long Beach Arena didn't mean shit—but to us at the time, it was *everything*.

It was an appropriate homecoming, too. We pulled into the arena and parked the bus on the street outside of the hotel. Somehow we managed to pick up two girls who were right there on the sidewalk, and a couple of the guys took them into the back of the bus. Then we checked in to the hotel and I remember sipping my drink while looking out across the parking lot at the arena, where that building loomed on the horizon, larger than life. The next day our friends from L.A. came out, and when we went on, they gave us more attention than all of the Canadian crowds combined had done. It was great, we were *home*.

These were the type of any-band-anytime equal-opportunity groupies that were down to fuck everyone all the time.

WE TOOK TO THE TOURING ROUTINE PRETTY naturally; we were off to the races, right away. We were built for it; we went through the paces without trying too hard. When we got to Arizona, I believe it was, we experienced groupies for the first time; not the kind that wanted to fuck us because they were fans of ours—we'd already had our share of those back home. These were the type of any-band-anytime equal-opportunity groupies that were down to fuck everyone all the time.

Overall, groupies were usually between seventeen and twenty-two; if they were in their mid-twenties, they'd most likely been around the block a few times—maybe too many—and there were those older than that, which often involved some bizarre mother-daughter combos. But in a way, the groupies in the sticks were more understandable than the groupies in L.A.: culture was at a minimum where these girls lived, and they had devoted themselves to getting as big a piece of it as they could when it passed through town. It was almost respectable.

Whenever we weren't performing, Axl holed up in the back lounge, resting his voice and sleeping. Sometimes when we'd have a day off, he'd sleep back there instead of checking in to the hotel. Still, he'd come out every so often to hang out with the rest of us and that was always cool. Everything was really good at this point—put it this way, we got on stage on time. The camaraderie was high; we were the perfect bunch of guys for touring together . . . not that I had anything else to compare it to. But we were all quite content.

Until the compressor on our shitty bus broke down, taking the air-conditioning with it, somewhere in the middle of Texas. As we sat there suddenly sweating bullets in the heat, it occurred to us that there had to be a class above touring on the level we were at.

West Arkeen came out to Texas for a few days, which took the party up a few notches in spite of the Sahara-like conditions on the bus: West left us four or five days later looking like a shadow of his former self. I estimate that he lost about eight pounds in sweat. We had three days off in Texas after that, in this resort hotel in the middle of nowhere, and during those three days we fired our bus driver and a tour manager we'll call "Cooper."

Cooper was a character; he wore a newsboy cap all the time and drove a yellow Lotus. He was this skinny, wiry English guy with a very jumpy demeanor—I guess that was due to all of the coke he did. The problem with Cooper was that he had turned into a self-centered rock star and forgot that he was a tour manager. We'd gotten sick of Cooper luring the chicks we'd picked up to his room with the promise of coke, and keeping them there in the hopes of getting laid. He'd even lie to us when we'd call his room, asking where the girls were. He'd say they'd split and we believed him until the one time we stormed down there and caught him red-handed.

He also had a bad habit of promising Izzy and me a gram of coke if we got up in the morning to do interviews. He'd give us the smallest taste, but once when we were done at the radio station or on the phone or whatever, and demanded the rest, he usually tried to back out of his promise. That was just stupid—if you promised us drugs and didn't deliver, we were the kind of people who'd kick your ass.

The last straw was a situation where Alan had entrusted Cooper to take care of the band and he just lost it and got us to a gig very late. It was a big-time fuckup and that was it for him; Alan sacked him and the bus driver at once. They were just gone. The next we heard was that Cooper was selling phone books door-to-door.

I was impressed when Alan booted Cooper without so much as an explanation—that's when I knew that he was serious. It was an example of the overly protective, paternal, and possessive stance he took toward us. It was comforting because we were such hell-raisers that someone needed to give a shit.

It was great that Alan trimmed the fat; but the reality was that after those days off, we needed to get to the next gig in Houston and we had no tour manager and no bus driver. We had to seek out other transportation on the spot. I don't remember what the other guys did, but Duff and I drove in this Trans Am with this girl I'd picked up. All was fine until we got caught in a torrential rainstorm because her car had no windshield wipers. The rain was coming down so hard that I had to lean out of the passenger-side window and use my upper body as a shield to keep the rain off one half of the window while I wiped the other half with my arm so that she could see well enough to drive.

Our Houston gig was killer, and after that we saw more of the South. Louisiana was right up my alley, especially New Orleans, with all of the voodoo and the presence of African religion and black magic. We went to a really authentic bayou restaurant in the swamplands where I ate rattlesnake and blackened alligator. It was such a great time for me; I came to realize that there was no other place that I'd rather be than on the road and that I'd hit it right in terms of a career.

WE LOCKED OURSELVES INTO A SET
road crew for this tour as well, a cast of characters that became our team for years. We'd rehearsed before the tour with Mike "McBob" Mayhew as the rhythm-guitar-and-bass tech; and "McBob" used his keen sense of humor to remind us of just how low we were on the food chain by constantly pointing out the pedestrian nature of our traveling accomodations. He had years of experience on the road, and his little comments here and there were all the reminders we needed that the Shangri-la of our tour bus was a mirage.

McBob has been with Duff and me to this day—he is part of the Velvet Revolver crew—and after all this time one of the more entertaining aspects of having him around is his still endless supply of road stories. Many of them end with Mike landing himself in the hospital due to all sorts of ailments and injuries that are typically self-inflicted or an unforeseen effect of partying. One of the most memorable stories in his arsenal is about the time he got so drunk that he fell out of a car, skidded on his head down the pavement, and woke up in the hospital with a metal plate in his skull. Sometimes it sets off the metal detectors in airports. McBob was like Robert Shaw—Captain Quint—in *Jaws*, sitting there on the bow of *The Orca* dropping these heavy war stories on us like a one-man atom bomb.

Our crew was rounded out by Bill Smith, my guitar tech, whom I soon realized was in it solely for the beer. He was a sweet guy, he loved to party, and he sat there on the side of the stage, watching the show more than helping run it behind the scenes. I'd say he probably changed five guitar strings the entire tour; he was able to swap them out okay, it was just that he didn't get it done on any consistent or logical timetable. Thanks to Bill, I learned to play more carefully—I tried to never break a string because if I did, I never knew when I would get that guitar back. I only had two guitars on the road, so I'm not sure what was taking so much time. Needless to say, I had to replace Bill. All things considered, between our crew and our inexperience with touring on a professional level, our operation came off like the Bad News Bears.

———◆◆◆———

THERE IS AN ESSENTIAL MOTIVE FOR
touring that never dawned on us back then: we were completely ignorant that

touring was intended to promote our record. We thought of it as all for the sake of playing. It was, to me, work for the sake of work, because without a tour, I'd have nowhere else to be. We were too into the experience to think of promoting our "product" day to day as we walked onstage, but Alan was trying to figure out how to market this thing, probably so he'd have something else to boast about as much as just making it succeed.

Alan wasn't doing a good job, and neither was Geffen, because the one thing I was painfully aware of when we played every night was that nobody was aware of our record whatsoever. We felt as unheard of as any other band you've never heard of. So we kept it moving, we kept touring regardless of how we were received, and Alan and Tom Zutaut kept pumping *Appetite*. The only other option would have been to go home, and we had no intention of going home ever again if we could help it.

For an entire year, from August 1987 to sometime late in 1988, we didn't see L.A. for more than a few days; we just bounced from tour to tour. Alan Niven booked us a tour across Europe opening for Aerosmith, with Faster Pussycat on the bill, that was to kick off a few days after The Cult tour ended. Aerosmith had just returned to rock and roll, and we couldn't think of anyone we'd rather support. But it wasn't meant to be this time—at the last minute Aerosmith canceled, so instead of going home, Alan sent us out there with Faster Pussycat and a great Japanese band called EZO to fulfill our obligations.

It was our first headlining tour; it began in Germany, at the Markthalle in Hamburg on September 29, 1987. It was great to headline, but we had a few issues. Faster Pussycat was one of those bands we hated from L.A.; they were exactly the kind of people we tried to avoid. The tour was also a bit of a culture shock: Hamburg still felt like it was a post–World War II casualty—the place had a pretty narrow viewpoint. It was a dark, industrial, sort of sour city that seemed, as a whole, as if they'd rather not have us there if they could help it. That kind of environment always inspired us to show our true colors more than usual, which didn't go over well. Every time we'd walk into a restaurant, every head cranked around and the room got quiet. And when it did, we were all the more determined to order a bunch of drinks and smoke and carry on more than we ever would have done in the first place.

That tour was our first experience with Doug Goldstein, too, the new tour manager that Alan appointed to look after us. I remember we got in late at night—a full day after Faster Pussycat—and the next morning I got up and went to Doug's room to collect our per diems before we set out sightseeing. All across Germany, and especially in Hamburg, there are outrageously graphic porno shops, usually in a very-easy-to-find, central location, and that is where we went. I was excited to no end—I'd never seen anything so obscene in my life. I was like a kid in a candy store, pulling these insane graphic magazines off the shelf—bestiality, pregnant women, just the most depraved things imaginable—holding them up for the other guys like, "Have you fucking *seen* this?"

We were staying in the same hotel as Faster Pussycat and we ran into them in the lobby and said hello before we took off that day. We were civil, I'll say that, but not what I'd call friendly. Regardless, once we let them know that we were going to head out to see the city, Mark Michals, Pussycat's drummer, insisted on coming along with us.

His band looked a little bit nervous. "No, no, stay here with us," one of them said.

"No, that's cool, I'm going to go," Mark said.

"Really, you should really stay, we're going to go out later," another one said.

"Yeah, it's cool, I'm going with these guys," he said.

We did nothing to encourage him, let alone invite him. I even remember one of us blurting out, "No, stay with them," but there he was tagging along with Izzy, Steve, Duff, and me for the day. Our first stop was lunch at Euro McDonald's. I had become a huge McRib fan during the recording of *Appetite*, so that was the height of cuisine to me. I was happy to see the McRib on the menu in Hamburg, and to the naked eye, it looked like the real deal, but it wasn't: instead of barbecue, it had some kind of anonymous brown sauce on it. There went my one meal for the day. The reason why we were so emaciated back then was that we never really ate anything.

In any case, we wandered around all afternoon, and when it got to be evening, we headed to the Reeperbahn, which is a street that is five straight blocks of brothels where no women are allowed—just like Amsterdam's red-light district, every type of girl you can imagine is available. We were

in heaven: we'd never seen anything like it and at the time we didn't have friends in bands who had been around more than we had, so no crew of seasoned guys had told us anything about this place. I was tripping out. I think in the first fifteen minutes Steven blew his entire per diem on hookers. We were walking along when he suddenly disappeared into this subterranean garage, where there were all manner of prostitutes just hung out against columns under colored industrial-strength fluorescent lights.

It was getting later and this guy Mark was still trailing us. We left the Reeperbahn and went to some bar that was one of the places the Beatles played when they were starting out. Once again, we walked in there and we were the scourge of the earth, but we didn't care; we drank Jack with one cube of ice per drink (because that's all that they would put in the glass) until they closed. We walked back to the hotel and this guy was *still* with us—at that point we'd stopped talking to him altogether. It had been a long day, so I went to pass out in my bed while Mark did the same in the other bed—which was Duff's. Now Izzy was always the Great Instigator: he could stir things up without getting involved, so he didn't let this opportunity slide.

"Hey, Duff," he said. "That guy is sleeping in *your* bed."

"Yeah, he is, isn't he," Duff said.

"You gonna let him do that to you, man?" Izzy said. "Fuck that! He can't do that to you."

"No way! Fuck no, man!" Duff said.

"Who the fuck *is* that guy anyway, man?" Izzy said.

"Yeah, who the fuck does he think he is?" Duff said, now getting pretty heated. "Fuck that guy!"

They tried to wake him up pretty roughly, but Mark was out cold.

"I know what we should do, man," Izzy said. "Let's tape him up and put him down the elevator shaft."

"*Fuck* yeah!" Duff said.

"We'll put him down the elevator shaft. He can sleep on top of the elevator."

They taped this guy up pretty good: his arms, his hands, his ankles, and his mouth were all totally bound. He was a medium-size guy, about 140 pounds, so they carried him off and got him to the elevator, and that's when

he woke up and started squealing like a stuck pig. They quickly abandoned the original plan and just threw him in the elevator and sent it down to the lobby. The hotel staff dealt with him from there. They got the tape off, and once he told them who he was, they went through the chain of command until they got in touch with his band, who had to come retrieve him because he had no room key, no ID, no money, no nothing. That was the last night I spoke to him; I just nodded at him for the rest of the tour. Come to think of it, that was the last we heard from any of them.

The next night we did the gig, the first one of our headlining tour, and it's good that it didn't set a precedent. The venue was on the water; it was this really industrial, dark room with benches and long tables on the sides. Everything in there was painted black—it was the blackest club I've ever seen and it just reeked of stale beer. On the walls were signatures and graffiti from every single heavy metal and thrash band who had been through there, which appeared to be many.

The audience was without a doubt the most lackluster crowd we had ever played to in our lives: as I recall, they were as cold and miserable as the weather. I remember that before we went on and the second we got off, the club played nothing but Metallica, nonstop. It was obvious that any American band, or any band at all, that didn't sound like Metallica wasn't going to go over. And I was right. We got through the show and the only thought going around in my mind when we finished was *I would fucking hate to have to do this again tomorrow.*

I was extremely apprehensive about how the rest of the tour was going to go—particularly since we had more than a few dates to do in Germany. We had a few days to go before the next gig, during which time my worry escalated. But once we got to Düsseldorf, an airier city with more trees and fewer bomb shelters, it was such a drastically different scene that I realized just how big and how diverse a country Germany is: the individual vibe of each city is unique.

--------◆◆◆◆◆--------

AS WE MADE OUR WAY ACROSS EUROPE, the band started to get really tight; our spontaneous interaction was becoming really pro and playing was getting fun. We did most of the driving on

our European tour in a sightseeing bus that we'd converted into a communal crash pad by removing most of the seats and filling the floor with cushions. Izzy had picked up a German girlfriend along the way and she brought a friend along that I started hooking up with. I always liked to find a girlfriend in each territory that we'd travel through; and since I already had my English girl, Sally, waiting for me, I had to end my German romance abruptly once the tour crossed the Channel. I told my German girl, literally the moment before I entered the room where Sally was waiting for me, that she had to go home immediately.

When I think of Europe, aside from the gigs, I remember spending most of my days off in and out of a variety of VD clinics. Back in L.A., I was dating a porno chick as well as this sweet little junkie jailbait girlfriend I had. Right after we'd shot the video for "Welcome to the Jungle," I remember waking up and discovering these three weird little red marks on the left side of my stomach. At the time, AIDS had really kicked in and become a national health issue. It started a strange hysteria among rock musicians; everyone was alarmed but most of us still felt immune to the whole thing. We figured that no one needed to worry about it until David Lee Roth got it.

All the same, I had just read *Time* magazine's cover story on AIDS and the pictures of HIV-related lesions looked exactly like the marks on my stomach to me. It was probably just psoriasis or an irritation, but I was convinced that between my porno chick and my junkie girlfriend that I'd caught it, because I hadn't used protection with either of them. I remember walking up Melrose near San Vincente after leaving the junkie girlfriend's place to go to a clinic for an AIDS test. I thought I was a goner; I was convinced that this European tour would be the only international tour I'd ever do before I died. Luckily, the test was negative.

It didn't help that on top of that, I'd picked up venereal warts, probably from the porno chick—which intensified my AIDS terror. I'd been pretty promiscuous up to that point and never used protection, but I never thought anything more serious than crabs could happen to me. When these things showed up . . . I thought, What the fuck is *this?* I went to a clinic before we left and they tried to get rid of them a few times, but nothing worked; they kept coming back. When we started on the tour, they had gotten so painful that I couldn't sleep on my stomach. I spent all of my time in and out of

clinics in every country we went to, keeping these things at bay. I wanted to get rid of them permanently before I met up with Sally. Eventually I got them off properly so they didn't return just before we got to the U.K.; Sally never knew a thing.

If I had to choose my favorite show of the tour, it was the Paradiso in Amsterdam. The venue is amazing; it is a dark, foreboding building that used to be a church. Inside the main hall are high ceilings, arches, and great acoustics. So many legends had played there, from the Sex Pistols to the Stones, so I was excited to do it. I remember Axl going off on old rock stars that night during the set: I don't recall his exact words but the gist of it was that any older-generation rock star who felt that we were ripping them off was right—we were, but we were doing it better. I think he capped that speech off by telling Paul Stanley to suck his dick.

That show was so great that Izzy and I decided to celebrate by scoring some dope. We were in Amsterdam after all, where soft drugs are basically legal and hard drugs aren't hard to find—at least that's what we thought. We spent half the night looking for dealers, and eventually copped some smack that was so stepped on and weak that it wasn't even worth the effort. Obviously we were pegged as tourists.

We took a ferry from Holland to England, and for the crew guys who had tour experience it was no big deal, but for us it was huge. You could smoke as much pot as you wanted until you got there. It was wild, all of the crew guys and the band smoking themselves to death, trying to consume the rest of whatever they'd bought in Amsterdam. There was a main bar area, and Axl got so high that he went to sleep on one of the couches there. We were the only ones in there when he did, but soon the place filled up, and all of the other passengers sat around him and kind of leaned on him. I remember opening the doors to the various cabins, where one or another of our crew, like Bill, my guitar tech, would be smoking every single last crumb of their weed so they wouldn't have to throw it over the side before we got to England.

We ended the tour on October 8, 1987, in London and it was amazing. The band was really coming into its own; we'd had enough road time by then to know what we were doing. We had become comfortable as players: we knew one another well enough that we didn't have to think much about

what we were doing the moment we went on. Once you have that familiarity, you can improvise and build from there and make every show unique. The Hammersmith Odeon show was explosive; die-hard fans that I run into to this day tell me that it was the best show of ours they've ever seen. When a show really clicked, as we did that night, we would have a great interaction going between me and Izzy because we had that indescribable guitar relationship; or I could be in sync with the rhythm section, Duff and Steven; or there was the great interaction between Axl's energy and my emotional interplay with him. It was just great energy as a whole—we'd throw it out at the crowd and they'd throw it right back at us. It couldn't have happened in a better venue: the Hammersmith Odeon is the famous room where everyone from Motörhead to The Who to Black Sabbath to the Beatles to Johnny Cash has played; and it's where Bowie did his final gig as Ziggy Stardust in 1973.

<hr />

WE RETURNED TO THE STATES AND landed in New York City and went directly to do MTV's *Headbangers Ball*. Immediately afterward we'd have to get on the tour bus to do an overnight drive and meet up with Mötley Crüe to begin our stint opening for them. We'd flown all night, hadn't showered, and were in no mood for the MTV experience. From the moment we entered the building at ten a.m., it was a huge clash between hungover, sweaty, unclean touring-in-the-same-clothes-for-weeks rock musicans and the corporate world of MTV. We got to reception and there was a Geffen representative waiting to meet us who was all smiles and bullshit gracious posturing. We got our little name tags, we filed through the turnstile into the elevator and into a room to wait; some green room with nothing in it but two couches and a table. There was no rider, no amenities, nothing in there at all. I had my bottle of Jack with me, of course, so I was fine.

It was obvious that we weren't happy, so someone up there sent VJ Downtown Julie Brown in to say hello and keep us occupied for a minute. I got the feeling that it wasn't her idea; she didn't want to be in that room at all. She went through the paces but wasn't anything close to her trademark bubbly self; she looked nervous and apprehensive. Clearly she had the worst precon-

ceptions of our band; for someone who lived in New York and was supposedly "downtown," she turned my stomach. If I'd been further through my bottle of Jack, I probably would have shouted what I was thinking: *Shut the fuck up already, we don't want to be here either, but we all have to get through this day.*

When we got on set, we met JJ Jackson, the host, and he was really cool. They had this big set, and somewhere along the line, we joked that we should destroy it on camera. That idea stuck, and among ourselves we decided that we were going to do just that. So we got into the interview, and Axl talked, answering all of JJ's questions. I sat there quietly; the other guys were quiet, too. We waited until the show was just about over and then in ten seconds flat we totaled the set. I didn't think about it at the time or again until a couple of weeks later when I saw the episode. We looked like savage zombies straight out of *28 Days Later*. That was our first real exposure, our first step up from just having a video on MTV; that was us, inching our way into mainstream consciousness.

We left MTV, got on our bus, and the next day set off with Mötley. It was surreal to follow up a week spent in a converted sightseeing bus headlining in Europe with a Midwestern tour of America supporting Mötley Crüe: they were touring *Girls, Girls, Girls*, were enjoying the apex of their popularity, and were a band who spared no expense. I had always liked Tommy from the moment I met him—he's probably the most genuine, true-blue, heart-of-gold person to emerge from that scene. I always liked Nikki because he was the brains, the marketing, and ideas guy behind that band. I'd always respected his dedication and his passion to his vision and how he'd made it a reality. Mötley was the only band from L.A. that came out of the glam metal scene that was 100 percent genuine. They might not have been the most original—after all, Nikki shamelessly lifted entire parts from other bands. But whether it was Kiss or any of their other influences, Mötley wore those influences on their sleeves and were so sincere and devoted that you could not fault them for it—and Nikki embodied all of that in my mind. On that tour Duff and I could usually be found in close proximity to Nikki because we knew that he was always holding a huge bag of blow.

Those guys were very generous with us; they took us in like proud parents, and like proud parents, they showed off the house that their hard work had built. This was their third big headlining world tour, so they had their entire

stage show going: a full arsenal of pyrotechnics, a huge crew, months of sold-out arenas to play—the full rock-and-roll dream. They had developed this convenient system of communication involving walkie-talkies and numeric codes: everyone in the band's production had a walkie-talkie with a key taped to the back of it explaining what the various numbers represented. There were codes strictly for the crew relating to gear, lighting equipment, load-in, etc. Then there were the band's walkie-talkie codes, which covered their day-to-day needs. For example, "1" stood for blow, which was listed under a nickname; "2" was a code word for chicks; "3" stood for booze, and so on. It was great, at any given time, as the situation required, they'd just get on the line and say, "Hey, it's Tommy, I need a number one, a number three, and if you see a few good number twos along the way, bring all of that to my dressing room. And, uh, please hurry. Thank you very much!"

We hung out with those guys a lot during the tour, but Nikki was always very aware of how much he was showing off their success and making the band's status known to us. He and Tommy were the only ones inviting us over to enjoy their spoils: we never saw Vince and for that whole tour I never met Mick Mars. To this *day* I've never met him, actually. As much as it felt like Nikki was sharing with us, it was clear to me that he was doing it to boast a little; especially because we only saw him and enjoyed their privileges when Nikki felt like hanging out. There was always an agenda with him: in the touring situation he was never out of control—whenever he did lose control he was always in a situation where he'd be taken care of. I respected that: Nikki didn't like to make himself vulnerable. And hanging out with the likes of us was not at all conducive to retaining control.

Mötley were traveling by private plane as often as possible at that point, and for one of the longer travel legs between gigs, Nikki invited us to join them on the plane. It was more than most headliners would have done and flying Mötley Air was enjoyable; the trip came complete with drinks, lines, and aisle surfing during takeoff and landing—a sport that involves standing sideways in the aisle and riding the plane's momentum. If you get the chance, do it; I highly recommend it.

At the time, there wasn't a more debauched double bill than Guns and Mötley; and as much as we lived up to it, that reality quickly became business as usual. That gig was my first exposure to first-class professional

touring, which, unlike Steven, had never been something I coveted, although it's become a regular part of my life. To me, those moments onstage, playing guitar before a crowd, is what it's all about. That is what has always mattered to me; that is what makes all of the boredom and drama that comes with being in a touring rock band worth it.

So I did everything possible to put distance between yesterday and the present.

Although I'd been around show business all of my life, on the Mötley tour I finally realized, firsthand, that entertainment was equal parts tedium for each moment of magic—it demanded commitment. Even in the best of situations, life on the road is monotonous: you get up at whatever time; you pass the time until the gig; you do the gig; and you party, usually while traveling to the next one, where you do it all again. Touring, to this day, every day I do it, is still a new experience.

That said, it has never become cliché to me; I've always known where I am. Touring, to this day, is still not a cliché to me; every room is not the same. Back then as now, I've always made a point to do a sound check to get the vibe of the venue. I wasn't always able to do so when we were an opening band, but what I could do was learn a bit about the city we were in. I never cared about what was going on in any given city culturally, but I did care to learn what I could about our audience and what they were like.

Unfortunately whatever conclusions I'd drawn about the people who'd come to see us wherever we were would most often be left in the urinal of whatever bar I went to after the gig. In my mind I'd have these moments of enlightenment that would be forgotten entirely en route to the next city only to be relearned on the next tour. I had a finite amount of memory, and

since I eagerly awaited the next moment, the past faded fast. If anything touring to me is like the Stephen King story "The Langoliers," where the past is eagerly munching away at your heels as you desperately try to stay one step ahead.

When you are that gung ho to get where you're going, there is never enough time in a day. I don't remember sleeping or resting at all during this period; there was a fever pitch to everything and I didn't want to miss a thing. It felt like if I slowed down, time would catch up and then all of it would stop.

So I did everything possible to put distance between yesterday and the present. I've always been that way and I still am. It is why I don't have any memorabilia to speak of: I don't have gold and platinum records, only the guitars that mean something to me. My wife, Perla, was so shocked by that fact that she recently had the record company remake me platinum copies of all of my records. She hung them on the wall leading up the stairs in our house. I think they lasted a week; they drove me so nuts I took them down one night and put them in storage. I don't need accolades on the wall to remind me who I am.

MY ONLY TANGIBLE CONNECTIONS TO the past outside of my memories are the meticulous day planners I've maintained for most of my life—until I gave up on them after having too many stolen or lost. But I have saved all of those that survived and a few have come in pretty handy when ugly legal situations or something like this book have popped up and I've needed to recall specifics. It was how I kept track of my life and I did note every significant event. That said, unfortunately, this tour with Mötley is a black hole because, for the first time in my life, someone stole that day planner, along with all of the very few clothes I had with me on tour. It wasn't hard for them to do—all of it was stuffed into the pillowcase that doubled as my luggage. Our security guard Ron Stalnaker would always handle our bags—he was one of those kind of guys who against all rhyme or reason had this need to carry things and exert himself. His mind-set was robotic, "I must pick up and carry . . ." It was fine with us because we never used bellboys or porters anyway because back then we couldn't afford the tips.

So Ronnie had set our bags up against the side of the bus and gone back into the hotel wherever we were to get more bags from the lobby. Some kid had been waiting there and grabbed the first two bags set down—which were Duff's and my pillowcases. We hardly did laundry; we didn't have anyone to take care of our shit. On occasion—and I mean on occasion—we'd go to a coin-op laundry and clean our clothes. We wore what we had and just kept getting new T-shirts whenever possible. Basically, once my jeans were worn out, I wore my leather pants for the rest of the tour. Duff, Izzy, and I definitely lived by the seat of our pants (pun intended) clotheswise; we'd throw our shit in one laundry bag or pillowcase, both the clean and dirty all together. That bag that was stolen contained everything I needed that day: socks, a new T-shirt, my day planner, plus everything else that I had to wear. We meant enough at that point for someone to want to steal my "luggage," as if it were a prize. I guess that's cool. At the time it was a drag because I had no other clothes and I was late for a radio interview. I had to do it in person, live on the air, in a towel, since I'd told Ronnie that it was okay to take my "luggage" to the bus while I took a shower—I'd planned to get dressed en route. At least I got a T-shirt from the radio station.

MÖTLEY WAS THE ONLY BAND FROM THE L.A. scene that we came upon that we ever worked with on a national, professional level. It made sense; they were the only band we respected, the only one with whom we could share a camaraderie. I was still convinced that no one knew who we were, but apparently they did because it was quite the ticket and the shows were amazing. It was the ultimate "bad boy" bill and we behaved accordingly.

There was the night that Nikki Sixx and I got into a drinking contest. Depending on whom you ask, either I started it, claiming that I could drink both Tommy and Nikki under the table, or Nikki dared me to outdrink him. In any case, he and I ended up sitting at the hotel bar wherever we were and getting into a shot contest. Nikki had a system. He would order four shots and I'd down my two right away, while he'd down one of his and leave his second lingering, which I'd end up downing because it was just sitting there as kind of a community thing. I was aware of what he was do-

ing, but I was still slamming quickly, and whether it was the conversation or whatever, I started to lose track. Soon enough, the more shots that were there, the more I'd drink. In the heat of the moment I'd do mine, while he'd be nursing his, and there was that extra one so down it went. I'd never drink like that alone and I wasn't fooled; I was totally aware of what he was doing . . . to a point.

In theory, we were going shot for shot, but since I was drinking half of Nikki's rounds, I'd say that by the end of it I downed twenty shots of Jack Daniel's to his ten. I got so drunk that I've been told that I barfed right there at the bar, between my legs, onto the floor, and tried to hide it. I don't remember that at all, but I do remember doing what I always liked to do when I was drunk—wrestle some guy who was much bigger than me. In this case it was Nikki, whom I tackled, bar stool and all, out of nowhere. Nikki is pretty tall, and at that time he was pretty heavy, too, so he ended up turning it around: he slammed me on my back and sat on me. Once I was sedated, they took me upstairs and put me to bed in Tommy's drum tech Spidy's bed. I woke up there the next morning completely unable to turn my head; I was in the worst pain I'd ever felt in my entire life. I managed to limp to my room and called Doug, our road manager, to tell him that I needed a doctor right away. Apparently I'd dislocated four vertebrae in my neck.

I could barely play because supporting the weight of my guitar across my shoulder was excruciating. I spent the next few weeks just standing in one place onstage with my top hat pulled down as far as it would go. The vertebrae that were injured were too far up and too close to the base of my skull to have a chiropractor put them back in line. So I had my first experience with acupuncture and that proved to be very helpful; I got it before every single show and a few times a week for a few months afterward. Until the swelling subsided, I walked around like a rusted Tin Man.

That wasn't the only painful experience to come out of that night. Apparently, after I passed out, Tommy and Nikki made me the subject of a photo shoot: they took a picture of my face, with Tommy's balls dangling above it, and the next morning made copies of it, had them laminated, and passed them out to everyone on the tour. I think the photo even became the official image for their All Access passes. I'd been tea-bagged for all the world to see.

Never before or since did Guns have that kind of a relationship with a band we toured with. And never was there the same level of debauchery going on. Mötley was the only group around with a like-minded self-destructive mentality, combined with a raging sense of competition and one-upsmanship. That entire tour we tried to outdo each other on every level and it made the shows that much better. The only thing I've experienced that came close was when Skid Row opened for Guns N' Roses years later, and as much as I hate to admit it, I think with Sebastian Bach on board, we took it all a little bit further.

Mötley did have a great finale in store for us: they honored the age-old tradition of punking the opening band's set the last night of the tour. Their crew kept it secret, and we really had no idea what was coming. As we launched into our last song, twenty pounds of flour fell from the rafters, and as cool as we might have thought we were, in an instant we looked ridiculous. It took me weeks to get that shit out of the crannies of my guitar.

All of it was definitely a learning experience. Mötley were at the top of their game and were a well-oiled machine, but I'll never forget the look of terror in their manager Doc McGee's eyes whenever I ran into him. He was dealing with a band on the edge: on that tour, at the end of every single night, Tommy was usually so fucked up that he looked like he was on the brink of dying. My last memory of that whole experience was watching Doug wheel Tommy through the airport in a baggage cart to catch their flight. Tommy was completely passed out at the time; he was a heap of lanky limbs that hung over the side with his head leaning all the way forward, his chin bobbing against his chest.

<hr />

AFTER WE WRAPPED THE MÖTLEY TOUR, it was slim pickings—there weren't too many appropriate outlets for an act like ours. But there was one perfect fit—Alice Cooper. It seemed like a marriage made in heaven. We'd done a show with Alice back in 1986 in Santa Barbara that, if it were another artist of his stature, would have disqualified us immediately. When we did that show, we were supposed to do the hour-long ride out there together, but Axl insisted on driving

with his girlfriend Erin at the very last minute. We were all against it, as was Alan, but Axl convinced him that there was nothing to worry about. We got to the gig; Axl was nowhere to be found, but was apparently on his way. It came time to take the stage—no Axl—so Izzy and Duff and Steve and I got out there and started playing without him. Izzy and Duff sang "Whole Lot of Rosie" by AC/DC and a few other covers. We were opening for Alice Cooper but basically that set was a drunken jam fit for a bar—except we were in an arena. It got so bad that at one point we asked the audience to sing lead and then asked if there was a lead singer in the house. We were friends with the crowd for a minute, but that quickly changed; we ended up insulting them and throwing things at them. It was ridiculous.

We stayed up there for the allotted amount of time and then retreated from a totally embarrassing disaster. We got out of there immediately and drove back to Hollywood, so pissed that we talked about kicking Axl out of the band that night and looking for a new singer. Izzy and I went right to West's house and I was upset enough to use smack again; as we got high in the bathroom, Izzy and I talked about the fucked-up show and what we were going to do about it. It wasn't the first time we'd had these talks; I'd say that the subject of firing Axl came up six times, very seriously, in the life cycle of the band. Izzy and I were in the middle of really strategizing how to do it when Axl showed up. He came into the bathroom and sat down on the bathtub and he started talking.

The amazing thing about Axl is that he didn't understand, in situations like this one, that he had done anything wrong; it wasn't within his frame of reference. He walked into that bathroom believing he had no reason to apologize as far as I could tell. All the same, he spoke at length and as much as the conversation left the subject of his absence at the gig, he did make a type of very vague apology. And when he did, he also explained, with much more passion than he lent to the apology, why he'd done what he did. His reasoning for his actions was so involved that all that I came away with was the impression that he was totally unaware of the implications of his no-show and what had transpired in his absence that he literally didn't get it at all. There are certain protocols that Axl just didn't heed; since he's not

in the same mind space as other people, the accepted norms just don't occur to him.

Explaining those norms might or might not make a difference; you'd never know. Axl is superintelligent, yet at the same time he lives in a place where the logic that governs other people does not apply. He doesn't ever realize what an inconvenience his choices might be for others. He means no harm; it's just the way he is. It's very hard to try to even explain it. He is as sincere as someone can possibly be, but it comes down to the fact that Axl, regardless of the world around him, insists on existing according to rules that hold true only in the universe that he has created around himself. That Alice Cooper show was a clear example: I remember being really angry and Izzy felt the same way that night. But as pissed off as we were, sitting there in that bathroom, discussing how we were determined to find a new singer, when he showed up, Axl still won us over. Slowly but surely, we found it in our hearts to just let it go. Of course it didn't hurt that we'd been doing smack . . . we were so loaded that after a while none of the drama seemed to matter anyhow.

In any case, that was then and this certainly was now. Apparently, Alice had gotten a kick out of that performance of ours; I think he'd seen a bit of his younger self in us. Alice was supporting *Raise Your Fist and Yell*, and hadn't had the best year: he'd almost been killed onstage when his famous guillotine stage prop malfunctioned and nearly decapitated him. Alice had cleaned up his act at the time, too, so aside from a few rowdy members of his band, we were the only obviously bad apples to be found on that outing. We set off on a leg of his U.S. tour with yet another entry-level, burned-out, unforgettable bus driver. This guy was a long-haired musician who liked to talk about the music he was always writing, and as much as he was "fun" to hang out with, he consistently did stuff that made life harder than it had to be for us. The biggest problem was that he always wanted to go out with us, so instead of parking the bus in one place and letting us find our way to wherever we wanted to go, he'd offer to take us there on the bus and inevitably got us lost on side streets. Needless to say, he didn't last long.

When we first came on the tour Alice was superkind and supportive. He welcomed us on board with no agenda; there was no hierarchy and no bullshit. He genuinely liked our band and what we were about—and we

completely looked up to him. We took lots of pictures with him, put it that way. It was an interesting transition: being around Mötley, we'd seen a large-scale production going on and a predictable performance every night. With Alice, it was the same at a whole new level. As much as we'd been fans for years, based on his records and lyrics and persona, it was something else to tour with him. He had a keyboard player, a weight-lifting behemoth of a guitar player, as well as Kip Winger on bass, another guitar player, and a drummer. He was backed up by a bunch of hired session guys and had all kinds of props, and it was interesting to watch how Alice interacted with all of it. He had an eight-piece band, backup singers, actors, costume changes, . . . it certainly was a show.

Slash has had the thrill of sharing the stage many times with Alice Cooper over the years.

He also had a snake, which I was excited to see. But Alice wasn't a snake collector; he didn't have one at home, it was more of a prop as well. He did have a guy there to take care of it, a guy that wasn't very knowledgeable about how to care for this poor boa constrictor as we traveled across the frozen Midwest, so I gave him some tips. Regardless, we kicked ass on that tour.

Because of the production, we were right up against the front of the stage, right up against the audience, and that was a catalyst. Those shows were dynamic, with minimal lighting and venues smaller than those on the Mötley tour; all in all, it was a huge and swift departure from where we'd just been. That was the one theme that characterized this time for us: we changed gears constantly. Drastic as they were, those changes forced us to learn a lot in a short amount of time. If we didn't adapt we would fail; it was that simple. For a band stuck in its ways, it was good for us to be forced into all of these different situations with no warning.

———————◆·▸◁◀———————

WE WERE IN CENTRAL MICHIGAN IN some nowhere town; I was having a drink at the hotel bar when our tour manager told me that the gig was canceled because something had happened with Alice. A few hours later we learned that his father had died; and for the next few days we waited in the hotel bar wondering if the tour would go on. The second night of that vigil, Steven Adler completely lost it. Steven could get very emotional at the drop of a hat, and his way of showing it was complete and utter defiance. In this little town, there was a sports bar, a restaurant or two, the hotel, and no other distraction for miles. Duff was with him that night; they had gone out drinking and for some reason Steven got so worked up that he punched a street lamp. He broke his hand entirely and was sidelined for something like six weeks.

Alan had booked us four headlining dates back in L.A. that were to follow the Alice tour weeks and we realized that Steven wasn't going to be out of his cast in time, so we put out the word that we needed a drum-

mer to sit in for a few shows. Within a day, we hooked up with Fred
Curry, the drummer for Cinderella, and he was great in a pinch. Fred
learned all of the songs right away, and we rehearsed with him in the
lobby of the hotel in Michigan; Izzy and Duff and I on our guitars while
Fred played along on drum pads.

After a few days, we heard that Alice had canceled the tour, so we flew
back to L.A. and prepared for the Perkins Palace shows. We were all re-
senting Steve at the time; we had no sympathy for the fact that he'd woken
up the morning after the street-lamp incident with a cast on his arm,
knowing he'd gotten too drunk and done something stupid. He'd fucked
up—he had to deal with the consequences.

When we got back to L.A., Steven and I moved into the Franklin
Apartments, furnished short-term units on Hollywood and Franklin, for
the few nights before we did the four Perkins Palace shows in Pasadena
and for a while after that. When I checked in, I had Sally in tow. She'd
shown up at the Drury Hotel in Missouri—which we called the Dreary
Hotel in Misery—with a green card and was all set to stay with me for a
while. She is from Sheffield and is a real English girl, so she was out of her
element immediately, touring with us, but she survived. She and I moved
into a place right next door to Steven.

We had a few weeks before those four Perkins Palace shows went
down in Pasadena, and as usual, given a few days freedom in L.A., I
dove headlong into lunar activities. One of those nights Lars Ulrich and
James Hetfield from Metallica came over and we did some outrageous
partying. Sally was there and I remember that there was a girl that
James wanted to fuck and I let him take her into my bedroom. They
were in there for a while and I had to get in there to get something, so I
crept in quietly and saw James head-fucking her. He was standing on
the bed, ramming her head against the wall, moaning in that thunder-
ous voice of his, just slamming away, and bellowing, "That'll be fine!
That'll be fine! Yes! That'll be fine!"

Steven, Sally, and I caroused extensively every single night. One time
we went to the Cathouse, which had relocated to Highland and Melrose,
and that night we ran into the infamous Mark Mansfield as well as Nikki

Sixx. Our little group all got together: I was on an antiheroin kick for the moment, so I wasn't interested, but Mark had some junk, and he, Steve, and Nikki wanted to get high. I wasn't even privy—they left to head back to Steve's place to go do it.

Later on Sally and I went home; we had a few more drinks in our room and I passed out. Sally stayed up; I think she was aware of the scene going on Steve's unit. I don't know the series of events because I wasn't there, but those guys had done their shit and at some point Nikki wandered into my place. Apparently, he had done one too many shots because he OD'd in my apartment.

Sally tried to wake me up when she found Nikki in a heap in a corner. I was so drunk and tired that she had to pull me into the shower to bring me around. That hardly worked: I got belligerent and thrashed about and broke the glass shower door. Meanwhile, the paramedics were hoisting Nikki out of the bedroom. Steven was there, too, all high, of course. Thank God for Sally; she was the one who called 911. Nikki might not be here otherwise.

A few hours later, Christine, Doc McGee's assistant, came by to pick up Nikki's stuff. We found out that he'd gone to Cedars-Sinai, been revived, and then he'd checked himself out a few hours later. I'm not sure what he did after that but legend has it that he did more smack and immortalized the evening in the song "Kickstart My Heart." In any case, if looks could kill, Christine would have done me in. She treated me as if Nikki's overdose was my fault; as if it had been my junk, my idea, as if I'd forced it on him. Christine was someone who was usually nice to me, but she was now sending me full-on daggers. I've never spoken to her again.

In spite of all of that, the Perkins Palace shows were some of the best shows we'd ever done . . . and Fred Curry was playing. It was awful for Steve: he was standing there in his Clint Eastwood shawl, with one of those batter's helmet hats with the two straws leading into cans of beer and his arm in a cast. I sort of felt sorry for him. He played tambourine; he was so pissed off. He was nice to Fred, but barely. I could understand that: he had to sit there and watch us play that well—without him—to a homecoming, friendly crowd the likes of which we'd never seen.

OFF TO THE RACES

overdose, but the fact that it happened in my apartment was reason enough for the powers that be to punish me by exiling me, Sally, and Steven from Hollywood to a Holiday Inn down in Hermosa Beach. It was the first of a few times that management devised ways to get me out of town to locations with less activity in an effort to keep me in check. Their intentions were good but their execution never was. Hermosa Beach was certainly eons away from Los Angeles, and one thing was for sure—I was stuck there in that little one-bedroom with its little TV and two chairs because I didn't have a car. There wasn't a proper kitchen, there wasn't a proper anything, and it was too far from a town that could fulfill those needs. There wasn't even room service.

Steven was next door to Sally and me; and I have to say, this was the beginning of Steven's downward spiral. The few times I saw him he had all kinds of shit going on in his room; he was doing tons of blow and always had one girl or another keeping him company. I can only say this in retrospect, because at the time, he seemed happy. I was there drinking bottle after bottle of Jack, as my relationship, such as it was, with Sally came to a dramatic head. We fought nonstop once we relocated to Hermosa Beach. She became progressively more belligerent, and once I finally lost my patience, I shipped her off to L.A. For the next few years, I'd run into her, and one time, she even materialized at the foot of my bed . . . but we'll get to all of that in just a little bit.

We did *Lies* during this period; we got the acoustic stuff all down and I did my guitar over dubs. That kept me occupied for a fucking second, which was great, because every day that I spent in Hermosa Beach I was one day closer to exploding. The guitar parts on *Lies* took me exactly two days; if anything, I was so excited to be back in L.A. that I ripped through them too quickly—I wish it had all taken longer.

It seemed like my exile lasted an eternity; it was the kind of reality where twenty-four hours took years. I wasn't real popular down there either: I'd go down to the local watering holes and there was nothing fun to do, and the locals' vibe wasn't all that welcoming. That place was a beach-and-surf scene, and when a town adopts that as its cultural identity there's nothing interesting about it at all—at least to my gutter rat sensibilities at the time.

WE HUNG AROUND FOR A WHILE THEN we headed out to New York City to play a few headlining dates. We had Zodiac Mindwarp opening up for a few, as well as EZO. These gigs were staggered, but I remember playing the Limelight. We didn't take it all that seriously: our plan was to just fly in and use some other band's equipment. I took sleeping pills before the flight in L.A., and when we missed our flight because Axl was running late, I somehow managed to stay awake.

We always traveled together on the road, and while we waited for Axl and the next flight I kept drinking Jack. By the time we got to New York City, it was time to go right to the show; and the combination of booze and pills had really kicked in. I'd slept maybe an hour on the plane, so basically I was the walking dead. We go up there unannounced, and all things considered, it was a pretty good night. The only problem was the dreaded moment when we had to play "Sweet Child o' Mine." It took me ten minutes to get those first eight notes together. I'd start and stop and start and stop until finally I figured it out. It was embarrassing but funny at the same time. I think that was the same night that I stage-dove and the crowd parted like the Red Sea and let me hit the floor. I lay there for a moment taking stock of whether I'd broken any bones or not. Then I got back on stage and tried to maintain some semblance of cool.

The Ritz show in New York we played that trip was hugely popular on MTV. It wasn't one of our greatest shows by any means: Axl was having vocal problems, and though we didn't play badly, we'd played so much better in the recent past. In any case, it was loose and out of tune and punk rock, and for those reasons alone, it is something to be recognized. That footage is important because it is the essence of the band. The crowd was great, and like so many memorable moments, it was over and done before I even knew it.

We did a slew of gigs on the East Coast afterward, and that was Guns in our prime. I remember one particular night at L'Amour in Brooklyn, which was one of the most classic metal/hard-rock venues that anyone could ever play in New York City. Izzy got totally drunk downing beers

backstage while we were waiting around to go on. But he remained cool in his own way—Izzy was always funny like that. That night he let on like nothing was wrong, spending the entire show sitting on the tiny ledge between the top and bottom cabinet of his rig. It was hilarious to watch.

Those were great gigs—all of the fans that were there know it as much as I do. During that period, when we headlined, we had a certain majestic presence. Something happened in those months when we made the move from opening band to headliner; by then we knew how to make our forty-five minutes a no-holds-barred experience. We were a great opening band, and when we were billed to play more, we were even more bang for the buck. Headlining had a personal vibe to the set; those nights when we had free rein of the room, we were everybody's band.

<center>◆ ⊰※⊱ ◆</center>

WE LANDED BACK IN L.A. AND WE SHOT the "Sweet Child o' Mine" video, which kept us busy until Alan could get us back on the road. That video was fine; it was just another long two-day sit-around shoot. As long as there was a live-performance element to it, I was okay with the whole thing. That particular video featured every band girlfriend of the moment, which, looking back on it now, is amusing.

At the time, Alan had assigned Ronnie, the security guy, to look after me. He was fiercely loyal and committed and I turned that aspect of his personality into great fun. Alan had the best intentions in mind, but I got into more trouble once Ronnie was around than I otherwise would have because I began to focus on fucking with him as my new pastime. He'd have to lock me into my room and hide in the hallway in case I tried to escape—because I would. Ronnie was great; he played along, he never really lost his temper even in those moments when I devoted all of my energy to sneaking past him. All things considered, he was a great asset until it all went south. We'll get to all of that in just a little bit.

<center>◆ ⊰※⊱ ◆</center>

OUR NEXT JOB MADE EVERYONE APPREHENSIVE before we even said yes: it was opening for Iron Maiden, starting out in

Canada in May 1988, on their tour in support of the album *Seventh Son of a Seventh Son*. We weren't overly excited about it, as we didn't feel like we were the perfect match. I had nothing against them, I had gotten into them via Ron Schneider from Tidus Sloan, who loved Maiden, Rush, Armageddon, and Sabbath—so I was very familiar with Iron Maiden's entire catalog. I'd spent many an afternoon when we'd ditched junior high watching Ron play his Rickenbacker bass along to the Maiden records. I liked *The Killers* record most of all. After that one, I lost touch.

Iron Maiden's theme on that tour and on that concept album was some kind of polar holocaust: the set looked like a huge glacier from which their mascot, Eddie, emerged, unfrozen from his ice tomb or whatever. Apparently the album was a big hit for them in the U.K. and is considered one of their best. To us, the whole thing was ridiculous; we hated their stage show on sight and had a hard time playing with that ice-scene backdrop behind us every night. We showed up for the first gig and couldn't do a sound check because their crew hadn't gotten the whole glacier together yet. Not to mention the Yeti.

Back then, we didn't have day rooms paid for in the hotels, so we either hung out at the gig or on the bus until showtime. Those were interesting shows; we were so out of place that it was a challenge. We did our best to play well and we were well received for the most part; we weren't hated and we weren't loved—for every show where we really connected, there were plenty where we didn't.

Duff and I, for our part, tried to connect with the Maiden guys. That band is a British institution, and we realized that; they've been around forever, they have their crew, and what they do is what they've done for years. We were an American upstart band, all frayed at the edges, fucking with their very established system. Duff and I respected that and we hung out one night with them, and played darts and forged a momentary kinship and that was great. It wasn't hard: they were amazing at darts and we weren't, and we were totally cool with losing to them.

For a short moment there, it seemed like we had found common ground between Maiden and us. But that didn't last. A few dates later, Axl walked into the commissary, which was loaded with crew guys from both camps, and made a statement. The commissary is a kind of sacred

place to bands on tour: it's a neutral zone, it's a shared area; if anything, it's like the chow line in prison or the army. It is the one place on tour where everyone puts up with everyone. So we were halfway through this tour, and Axl walked up in there and fucking *lost* it: he flipped a table over and stormed out. He seemed so frustrated and at the end of his rope about the tour.

There was already an uneasy tension between Maiden and Guns. This obviously sent the tension level to Yellow—Red being nuclear. The buzz went around the crew network, and from that point on, there was no socializing at all between the two bands. It was awkward but we were determined to hang in there and see it through.

The Maiden tour wound its way through Canada and headed south into Seattle and Northern California. I'm not sure, but I think that it was a Bay Area date when Axl refused to leave the hotel to do the gig. If I remember correctly, he was still in his room when the rest of us left for the venue, and Alan was with him. Not long after, we got the call that Axl wasn't feeling well and couldn't perform. The crowd awaiting Maiden was pretty large, so Alan insisted that Duff and I go out there and let them know that Axl was sick. When we first walked on stage, there was a ripple of excitement and cheering, until they heard what we had to say. It was a huge deal—it sucked; I wish that it didn't have to happen. For better or for worse, when Duff and I delivered the news, it wasn't well received—and that was the first time that we'd ever gotten such a reaction in our career. The crowd was upset to the point that it was obvious that they really did care—and we weren't even the headliner. We hadn't expected much from Maiden's fans. We had no idea that we'd crossed over the way that we had. It was a nice surprise.

There were just a few Maiden dates for us to do in California to end the tour, and as much as none of us wanted to do them, we were all committed. There were two shows at Irvine Meadows, but Axl's throat was such that he just couldn't do those last two shows—there was just no way. I'm not sure how that went over, but it was registered early enough that Alan had time to scramble to fulfill the contract. In the end, L.A. Guns were hired to play the opening slot so long as enough of us showed up to jam with

them. Duff, Izzy, Steven, and I showed up reluctantly—at best—to play at least a few songs. We got up there and our crew told me after that L.A. Guns had tried to sabotage our gear; they'd turned down all the amps to make us sound bad. I guess Tracii was worried that I was going to outplay him. Whatever it was, they tried to nip it in the bud, but our people caught it and fixed it. In any case, that show ended any sort of "civil" relationship between Tracii Guns and me.

———◆·✕·◆———

THOSE SHOWS WERE THE LAST DATES ON our schedule. When we got back to L.A. I started hanging around with West Arkeen and there was a rumor and general worry in the band's circle that I was back on smack. The truth is, I got high once and that was it. But their intentions were good: they were worried that I might do myself in if we had nothing to do. And they weren't exactly wrong. I had a penchant for being unruly and they could never nail me down. With that in mind, Alan decided that Doug should take me to Hawaii to chill out for a bit.

Doug and I went to Maui and he's a total golf head, so he was completely absorbed because we stayed at a premier resort that he picked for that very reason. I was supposed to soak up the sun and "relax" . . . it was a nightmare. The place was entirely bungalows; we had a rental car for the week and stocked our little huts with groceries. It was as expensive as a hotel but wasn't like a hotel at all. We were scheduled for a two-week stay, but after five days I was ready to leave. I started calling Doug demanding plane tickets to somewhere more interesting. "I can fly anywhere, man!" I shouted. "Fuck this place, why am I here?"

"Slash, relax, it's cool," he said. "Okay, where do you want to go?"

"Anyplace! *Fuck.* I'm going to fucking New York City!"

In the end, instead of flying me out, he agreed to fly in this hot stripper I'd met in Toronto. Doug arranged it all and then I was happy. I was supposed to be chilling out, but I still got really drunk on that trip. One night in particular I tied one on with her and for some stupid reason I found it necessary to smash all of the glass louvers in the front door of our bungalow. I didn't think about

it at all; it seemed perfectly natural at the time. Suddenly there was a knock at the door that night as we sat on the couch and this enormous Samoan guy who was a guard at the resort was out there and he was not happy at all.

"Did you break all of this glass?" he asked.

"Yeah," I said. "So what?"

"You've got to clean it up," he said ominously. "You're going to clean up this mess." He was right; morally, yes, I should have cleaned up the glass I'd broken. But I was paying nearly a grand a night just to be there, and at those rates, I wasn't about to clean up anything.

"Why don't *you* fucking clean it up, man?" I told him.

The guy stared me down for a second, then he grabbed me by the neck and slammed me up against the wall. I didn't know what he had planned; all I knew is that I could hardly breathe and that my naked back was seriously feeling the stucco wall.

My girl went crazy and jumped on the guy's back, totally raising Cain. It didn't matter much; he was locked onto my neck like a pit bull: he swung at her with one arm, but the other one never loosened its grip on my throat. This whole scene was pretty loud; after a few minutes we attracted a crowd. This couple from next door came over, and when the Samoan guy saw them, it was like kryptonite: all of a sudden he straightened up and just ran away. The next day I tried to find him, but it was no use: he disappeared and never came back; he left his job and all of it behind, apparently.

<center>◆━◆━➤◆◆━◆</center>

WE DID A MINI-TOUR SHORTLY AFTER that: it was something that Alan booked to keep up our momentum. We played a theater in Phoenix with TSOL, and I remember that when I arrived there, everyone in our camp was happy and relieved to see me. I was suntanned, and Doug was very proud; according to him, he'd taken me down to Hawaii and straightened me out. I found that pretty funny.

We did the first gig and it was fine, but the second night Axl didn't show up: he refused to leave his room. I don't know how intensely Doug

and Alan tried to get him out of there, and I still don't understand why he wouldn't come out, but it was a serious blow to morale in my mind. We in the band were beside ourselves; we were headlining and we couldn't just forgive this. There aren't too many reasons to miss going onstage—if there's a death in the family, or you're dead yourself, or sick or at best deathly ill, it's excusable. Aside from that you crawl onstage if you have to. It set off a chain reaction—the floodgates of dysfunction were open from that point.

Steven found someone who was holding in Phoenix and I got loaded, he got loaded; I'm not sure what Izzy and Duff were doing, but Steve and I were three sheets to the wind. All that I remember of that night was that our hotel seemed cavernous; the distance from my room to Steven's seemed like six miles. That hotel was dark and moody: there were a significant number of people who had gotten rooms there strictly to party after going to the show and they were in full swing, so there was a sinister, druggy vibe hanging about the place.

As the sun came up, Doug and Alan called a band meeting over breakfast. Duff, Izzy, Steven, and I filed into whatever restaurant and sat down with Alan and he delivered us the business. He told us that we were on the verge of ruining everything we'd worked so hard to achieve. It took all of my strength just to keep my head up for two seconds while Alan went on about how we couldn't go on like this. We made a point of expressing our disappointment with Axl's disregard and the fact that he didn't even show up for the meeting. But we also knew that we couldn't go out and just get a new singer. It seemed like Alan was with us and was going to talk to him. It didn't make a difference, of course.

We returned to L.A. and canceled the rest of our tour. Next up: opening for Aerosmith. The controlled environment of being an opening band seemed like it would be good for us at the time. Their manager, Tim Collins, had spearheaded their sobriety and the band had spent millions getting themselves cleaned up and into a sober universe. And they'd hired an opening band that was falling apart at the seams. I can only imagine the lies that Alan came up with about how great we were doing to close that deal.

Steven Tyler, Slash, and Joe Perry.

Tom Zutaut, Alan Niven, and Doug Goldstein were read the riot act about endangering Aerosmith's sobriety by Tim Collins and we then met with him as well. We showed up to his hotel room in L.A., where we ordered about $1,000 worth of booze from room service when he went to the bathroom. As they wheeled in this huge cart of drinks and food, Tim didn't say anything, he just smirked.

"Sorry, man," I said. "We were hungry . . . and thirsty."

It was our way of showing him that we weren't willing to relinquish our lifestyle, but we were open to following a few essential guidelines. All alcoholic drinks would be consumed in unmarked cups and all bottles of booze would be kept out of sight, and of course no mention would be made of heroin or cocaine. That wasn't a problem: it was never hard to lie when we were holding drugs because none of us were ever the sharing kind.

The tour started in July and lasted for two months, and I couldn't have been happier about supporting one of the bands that meant so much to me. Aerosmith's new album, *Permanent Vacation*, was the first that was written by outside songwriters and contained the first hits that the band

had enjoyed in years, but as much as I didn't think that the use of song-writers was particularly cool, I was happy to see them resurrected from the dead.

The first night of the Aerosmith tour was tumultuous: it started in Illinois, and while the rest of us showed up early enough to watch them sound-check, Axl was missing in action until half an hour before show-time. I remember Steven Tyler coming up to me and saying, "Hey . . . so where's your singer?" It's become a recurring punch line; it's his standard greeting whenever he sees me. Axl showed up at the very last minute, which obviously caused tension to be high all around, but we played well enough to make up for it.

We played Giants Stadium on that tour, with Deep Purple on the bill. That stadium is so huge and we had so much room on that stage that we could really run around; we were always good at that. We did a forty-five-minute set and we played "Paradise City" twice because we were shooting it for a video. The crowd just freaked. That stadium can hold eighty thousand, and even though it wasn't completely full, we'd never played to a crowd that large. The energy was incredible. It was one of those moments when I truly realized how popular we were becoming in the "real" world. It was a moment of clarity.

I remember sound-checking that day; I walked out into the middle of the arena, this huge expanse, and played my guitar, just for a while, to take it all in. We'd walked into so many situations since that first gig in Seattle, and that same chemistry and energy was still there. If anything, we were stadium-worthy from the start; we had an irrefutable way of doing things that needed very little adjusment once we made the leap to a grand scale.

We came offstage and I was on cloud nine, so I went onto our bus and celebrated with about five lines of coke and a few deep tumblers of Jack Daniel's. Literally the minute after I'd finished my last line, Gene Kirkland, a photographer I knew, burst in and said that he was there to shoot Joe Perry for the cover of *Rip Magazine* and Joe had requested that I be a part of it. The coke was really hitting me and the Jack wasn't helping much; I felt like Frosty the Snowman.

Slash pretends he didn't just do three grams of blow. Joe Perry knows Slash just did three grams of blow. Note Slash's clenched jaw and stiff arms.

I told Gene that I'd be there in a few and pounded as much Jack as I could stomach, then I tore the bus apart searching in vain for my sunglasses. I checked myself in the mirror, took a few deep breaths, and headed outside as nonchalantly as possible. I strolled over to Joe trying not to twitch, hoping that my smile looked more relaxed than it felt. Coke makes you paranoid and this particular batch was some speedy New Jersey, stepped-on Sopranos coke so it was hard to hide the effects. I'd met Joe before but I did not want to be around him all coked up. Every time I see the resulting picture of us, I have to laugh, because anyone who knows me at all knows that I never smile like that or ever hold myself quite so stiffly. Somehow I managed to keep my jaw in line but it wanted to swing like a barn door in the wind.

We did a pretty good job of behaving ourselves that tour, but Steven Tyler was convinced that we were high out of our minds all of the time. He was so inquisitive about what we were up to and what we'd done the night before. He'd come over to us every afternoon and say, in that rhythmic, rapid-fire delivery of his, "What'd you do last night? You get high? You fuck some girls?" It got hard to live up to his expectations.

The only near disaster that we had with Aerosmith was at a venue somewhere in the Midwest. There was a long drive from the hotel to the venue, Axl was running late, and the first car was full, so I decided to wait for him. The other guys got there fine, but we got totally stuck in a line of cars heading into the venue on a two-lane highway. We were fucked, just crawling along, and the clock was ticking. Axl was cool but I was completely anxious. We somehow managed to get a police escort and make it with five minutes to spare. I remember walking into the dressing room, throwing on a new shirt, and running up to the stage. I passed Joe Perry in the hallway and he was standing there with one leg out the way he does, just watching me, with this slight grin as if to say, "Ha-ha. *This* time you made it."

In hindsight, it was clear that despite Aerosmith's radio hits, we were soon the main attraction. It happened very fast for us, thanks to MTV's chronic rotation of "Sweet Child o' Mine": within a few weeks of the single's release in early June, it hit number one and we became the most popular band in the nation. We heard things from management, but it didn't sink in with me until *Rolling Stone* showed up on tour: they'd sent a writer out to do a cover story on Aerosmith, but after a few days of

watching the crowds' reaction and seeing us play live, the magazine opted to put us on the cover instead. By the end of the tour, we were absolutely fucking huge, generating the kind of excitement that pretty much baffled me night after night.

That said, we were still a scrappy group of gypsies without a clue, so Aerosmith's manager, Tim Collins, sent us off with a parting gift that we desperately needed: luggage. They gave each of us an aluminum Halliburton suitcase that I still have today. Tim realized that we were each the type who might stay on the road for ten more years without a proper suitcase—and he wasn't wrong. I remember how grateful and excited I was to have it; I ran over to Joe and Steven's dressing room and thanked them from the bottom of my heart. They looked at me like I was crazy; now I realize that they probably had no idea that management had sent us a gift at all.

WE SHOT HALF OF OUR THIRD VIDEO during our tour with Aerosmith. The live footage seen in "Paradise City" was captured in two locations; the first was Giants Stadium in New Jersey and the second was at the Monsters of Rock Festival at Castle Donington in the English Midlands a month later on August 20, 1988. By the time we got to Donington, "Sweet Child" and "Welcome to the Jungle" had charted around the world and our album had broken the Top Ten. At that show we experienced a frenzied reaction like nothing we'd seen before. The festival broke attendance records that year, surpassing the hundred-thousand mark. There couldn't have been a better place for us to record live footage . . . except for the fact that two people were trampled to death at the front of the stage during our set.

The audience was crazy, just this sea of surging people. Axl stopped the set a number of times in an effort to control the crowd, but there was no calming them down. We had no idea that anyone was actually hurt let alone killed; after we'd done the gig and were celebrating in a nearby pub, Alan came in completely distraught and gave us the news. It was horrible; none of us knew what to do: something that had been a cause for celebration a moment before had become a tragedy. It was the first of many strange, surreal, and contradictory times.

LESS THAN A MONTH LATER, GUNS PERFORMED "Welcome to the Jungle" at the MTV Video Music Awards and took home the Best New Artist Award. I'd like to know where that trophy is today; I think I left it in a cab, which, now that I think about it, is as much as it deserved. Then on September 24, 1988—nearly a year and two months, to the day, after its release—*Appetite for Destruction* began a three-week sit-in at the very top of *Billboard*'s album chart. And so began our reign of terror. The truth is, all we ever cared to do was top the bullshit hair metal bands that enjoyed undue success for their subpar existence. We—well, I at least—never wanted to be Madonna; that kind of pop-star reality had nothing to do with what our band was about, according to me. But before I knew it, that's where we landed almost overnight.

After nurturing us through making the record, then waiting a year for it to take off, Tom Zutaut wasn't going to let this upswing lose momentum: he convinced us to package the acoustic recordings we'd just done with the *Live! Like a Suicide* album and release it immediately. We called it G N' R *Lies* and it was released on November 29, 1988. The album hit the top five a week after it was released, and suddenly this band that Geffen had nearly dropped was breaking records: we were the only act to have two albums in the top five at the same time during the entire 1980s.

We had broken in America and the U.K. already, so Alan booked us on a tour of Japan, Australia, and New Zealand, where the record was just starting to take off. Japan was such a culture shock; the first morning that I woke up there and looked out of my window, and all of the Japanese toys and every *Godzilla* movie that I'd been a fan of suddenly took on a whole new meaning. Izzy had it worse than I did: he'd gotten really strung out the week before we left, so to get through the ten-hour flight without a hitch, he took a bunch of time-release Valium the moment we got on the plane. He slept all the way there and was so out of it that we had to carry him through immigration. We did our best to hold him up the whole way through the process, but it didn't seem like he was going to make it.

When he woke up in his hotel room, he had no idea at all where he was,

so he called the front desk, unsure if any of us were even in the same hotel. They transferred him to Steven's room.

"Hey man, it's Izzy," he said. "Uh . . . where am I?"

"Hey man!" Steven said. "You're in Japan!"

"No."

"Yeah, man! We're in Japan!"

"Get the fuck out of here," Izzy said. "No way."

"Yeah, man, look out your fuckin' window!

Like every other hard-rock or heavy metal band that plays Japan, we hung out in Roppongi—we stayed at the Roppongi Prince Hotel, actually. Between the watered-down drinks and the bad blow, I burned out on it immediately because I had no idea where else to go. I stayed locked in my room for most of that tour, a room that I should mention was about ten feet by ten feet, but just *so* incredibly *efficient*. There was the language barrier, of course, but above and beyond that, I couldn't deal with the Beatlemania element of Japanese music fans. They met us at the airport, they followed us to our hotel, and they pretty much waited in the lobby or hotel hallway in case any of us thought about leaving. I was flattered, but I thought it was pretty strange. The few times I cared to go out, I was escorted to the Hard Rock and a few other clubs, and found no reason to make that effort again: the pseudo–dance club/rock scene full of exported American models did nothing for me at all. Luckily, I did run into a girl that I knew from L.A., and that made things more bearable. Otherwise, my memories of that tour come down to three things: sticky rice, sake, and Jack Daniel's.

We did five dates total and took the bullet train to the shows outside Tokyo. Our promoter throughout Japan was Mr. Udo, who was famous for handling all of the big hard-rock acts in those days; he saw the rowdiest of bands from Van Halen to Mötley safely through his country without a casualty. As is customary, Mr. Udo hosted a dinner for us, which included executives from our Japanese record label and important promoters—who, we were told, were members of the Yakuza, the Japanese Mafia. We were instructed not to show our tattoos that night because our Yakuza hosts would be offended: in Japan, tattoos carry much more weight than they do elsewhere, and tattooing is elemental to Yakuza culture. Of course we didn't listen: Axl wore short sleeves and I took off my jacket and rolled up

the sleeves of my T-shirt without thinking about it. The dinner ended up being very pleasant, and Mr. Udo gave each of us cameras as a parting gift at the end of the meal. Those cameras were a kind gesture that turned out to be a problem in the end: none of us were savvy enough to declare them as gifts when we passed through customs, so the Japanese authorities detained us when they found them. Some of us, at least: I'd lost mine by the time we got to the airport, and I think Steven had as well. Duff somehow got through, but the other guys got held up. After an hour of questioning, Izzy made the camera a moot issue by smashing it in front of the guards. Axl, however, did not, and he was searched to the maximum degree; I believe he was strip searched—everything. In any case, we missed our flight waiting for him.

Our next stop was Australia; we did a short tour that hit Sydney and Melbourne, and since our record was just barely cracking their consciousness, we resuscitated a few covers, like "Marseilles" by the Angels and "Nice Boys Don't Play Rock 'n' Roll," which is by one of Australia's greatest rock bands, Rose Tattoo. We made a point of getting in touch with them and arranging to meet, and I must say that the leader of their band, Angry Anderson, was everything I thought he'd be. Angry had more tattoos than anyone I'd ever seen, and he was every bit as real and honest as I'd hoped for.

By this time, we were showing signs of wear and tear from the physical demands of excessive touring. It was taking its toll. We'd also been spoiled by the sheer enthusiasm of the crowds in America, so Australia was a little bit of a letdown when we needed a lift. The chicks were standoffish and independent. They weren't clambering all over themselves to meet us the way they did everywhere else. At this point, heroin started to rear its ugly head again: Izzy and I ran into someone who had some and we copped a little. We soon discovered that there is a long-standing heroin culture in Australia. We kept it together, though, just a taste here and there, so it didn't evolve into another full-time habit.

We did manage to get the most out of it and did some good writing while we were there. "Civil War" was an instrumental that I had written just before we took off for Japan. Axl started writing lyrics to it and we worked it up into a proper song at sound check in Melbourne, first the beginning part then the heavy section. That song came together very quickly.

After our five dates in Australia, we popped over to New Zealand, and at that point I realized that I was completely burned out. It had been two long years on the road. At the same time I didn't want to go back home because I had nowhere to go.

When we got back to L.A., I treated myself to a rare indulgence: a guitar. Somehow this collector got in touch with our management because he wanted to sell me Joe Perry's 1959 Les Paul—the tobacco-colored sunburst he'd been photographed with countless times. Joe's ex-wife had sold it back when he was still on drugs and they had come upon tough times. And this was it—the guy had pictures of it and all the documentation. I knew that guitar well—Joe was holding it in the Aerosmith poster I had on my wall growing up. It had a distinctive nick in it; this was the real deal.

The guy wanted eight grand for it, and though I had never spent eight grand on anything before in my entire life, I had to have it. It was a pretty amazing moment when I finally held that guitar in my hands; the same instrument that played an essential role in the path I'd chosen in life was now in my possession (and I would use it on the "November Rain" video). I truly felt like I'd arrived.

If memory serves, it was around this time that I finally retired to storage the guitar that I'd used on *Appetite*, my Les Paul replica (and the backup for it that I'd bought). I abuse my guitars when I play live, and by this point it was severely banged up after all of that touring. It did make a cameo in the "Sweet Child O' Mine" video, however, as it did in the "Paradise City" video. Actually, I used it in most of our videos, with a few exceptions, one of them being "November Rain" where I used Joe Perry's 1959 orange Les Paul.

In any case, I was in need of new touring guitars, so I asked Gibson for two Les Paul Standards. They appreciated my dedication, but since I wasn't very high-profile at that point, they wouldn't give them to me for free; they'd only sell them to me wholesale. That was fine: I got two red-and-orange Sunbursts and I immediately got them refinished so that they'd look less brand-new and brightly colored. I wanted them to be a bit duller and weathered. I used the main one through the rest of our *Appetite* touring, through the entire *Use Your Illusion* tour, and on both Snakepit tours. The other one remained a backup.

They saw some living to say the least. When Velvet Revolver started, those guitars were so banged up that I decided not to retire them but to use them minimally on stage—I call upon them whenever we play "Fall to Pieces." To fill that void, I asked Gibson for a couple more and this time apparently I was a bit more high-profile so they gave them to me, no questions asked. They actually took it even further: they made me a Slash model Les Paul that is an exact replica of those 1988 Standards that I'd bought from them way back when. I now use those onstage and they are such exact replicas that the first time I opened the case to look at the prototype, number 001, I thought that I was looking at my original guitar that they were returning to me. The replica has every single nick, scratch, and cigarette burn that my guitar has. It even has a crack in the neck from that time when it exploded in my face and was rebuilt—we'll get to that story in just a little bit. In any case, it's called the Slash Signature model and it's every inch exactly like mine. I'm honored that they did that for me, especially considering they did the same for Jimmy Page: they replicated the guitar he used for *The Song Remains the Same* and all of the greatest Led Zeppelin albums.

At the bike track in Rescda, practicing. The blond kid is Chris, Jeff Griffin's younger brother. He thinks he's beating Slash, but Slash has the inside lane.

1971, age six.

Slash's elementary-school photos.

Slash was roughhousing that day; he was being difficult for some reason.

Slash and his mom, Ola.

Slash and Axl onstage, July 1988.

Guns, circa 1987 (top) and 1992 (bottom).

Gilby Clarke, Duff, and Slash on the Use Your Illusions tour.

Duff, Izzy, Matt, and Slash at Mates rehearsal studio, jamming pre–Velvet Revolver. They may or may not have been working on a song called "Snafu."

Duff and Slash.

Slash playing with Lenny Kravitz; note Lenny's dreds at left.

Slash on the set of the video shoot for "Estranged."

Slash during his forced exile in Hawaii. He was sent there by management for two weeks to stay out of trouble.

Slash fatigued at the end of a long set during the final notes of "Paradise City."

Opening for Aerosmith at Giants Stadium, New Jersey.

Slash and Ronnie Wood.

Slash and Steven Adler.

Izzy and Slash.

Iggy Pop and Slash after an Iggy gig either before or after Slash recorded with Iggy on his Brick by Brick album, 1990.

Good buddies Tommy Lee and Slash backstage at some awards show, probably KROQ.

A grumpy morning on the bus.

Perla gives Slash a special kiss in the lobby of the Hard Rock Hotel in Vegas. He's standing in front of the Guns N' Roses display in the lobby.

Charlie Sheen and Slash in a private jet, most likely headed to Vegas. Slash used to keep that necklace he's wearing loaded with coke.

Ron Jeremy and Slash judge some kind of Miss Nude pornography-related beauty contest in Indiana. Note the intense concentration.

Slash and Perla and Johnnie Walker.

Self-explanatory Slash.

Slash and good friend Robert Evans, legendary film producer.

Once the final leg of the *Appetite* tour was over, I was back in L.A., pretty shiftless and uncomfortable; for the first time in two years I had no predetermined place to be, no job to do when I woke up. I had been away so long that nothing was satisfying and the everyday business of life seemed alien to me. I wasn't sure how I was supposed to go to the store for groceries after I'd played arenas in Japan the week before. I'd been on tour long enough to forget that I once bought my own liquor and cigarettes, and what I really couldn't shake was the thrill of playing every night. I expected each day to hit that same dizzy climax. I had to fill the void. With the band on break, I embarked on a solo tour that never left L.A. I was more decadent than I had ever been; because when things stop, when things slow down, and when I don't know what to do with myself, I'm the most self-destructive person I know.

I don't see it as some kind of fault. I see it as a natural side effect. After two years of touring, it will take anyone at all a long time to wind down. I had been living at breakneck speed wherever I lived; I had no idea of what was going on with me. I'd done nothing at all to slow or calm down, so I sure as hell wasn't prepared to stay in one place. Our career had meant working constantly just to make it take off. And then it kept on. It was five years, it was eight years . . . I was eighteen, I was twenty-three. I'd done it; we'd done it. And now I was home; I smacked up against the wall.

At one point in my life I was so obsessed with heroin and opium and anything derived from poppies that I went to the library to study the culture and the science of them every day. I read what I found; from the textbooks that explained the chemical makeup of the drugs to the history books that chronicled the evolution of the Triads and the other Chinese gangs who ruled the trafficking and smuggling of it. I also read about all of my rock-star heroes . . . all junkies. All things considered, I did manage to come into that part of the drug culture without an image in mind that I was trying to portray or mimic. It was a simple contradiction that made complete sense to me: everyone in town was doing heroin, and because of that I wasn't interested in it at all. But once I actually did it, I was *very* into it . . . I just felt no need to advertise my interest.

The first and last rock-and-roll books that I ever read were loaded with heroin and drug use, and were much too sensational. I read *Hammer of the Gods* and *No One Here Gets Out Alive*, histories of Led Zeppelin and The Doors, respectively. They mention the drugs throughout, and I was so obsessed at the time that I read them for the drugs only; I wasn't interested in whatever else they had to say. To me, those books were basically written for the authors' own entertainment; they seemed inaccurate and full of shit. And after that I never read another rock-and-roll biography again.

In that way I never did my "homework"; I never studied the lives of other junkies in rock and roll. But at the same time I didn't have to: I got hip to Keith Richards and Eric Clapton and Ray Charles later on in life. I think that anyone who is a true junkie has an innate kinship with other junkies. Somehow I knew that we shared mutual interests; that addiction speaks to you. Without knowing it, you're attracted to them.

Heroin was novel to me then, it was an adventure, it was a private hideaway in my own body and mind. After I'd been through withdrawal and gotten clean more than once, the inescapable discomfort never discouraged me. I may have realized how crippling addiction was whenever I got clean, but after I was clean awhile, I'd reminisce about how much I loved to get high.

to discover it all again. It was 1989: We'd toured most of America, Canada, Europe, Japan, and Australia. We'd watched our album sit around and do nothing for a year before breaking the Top Ten and having a number one single; we'd shot three videos that became mainstays on MTV, a channel that helped us out, but that we didn't care for. We performed at the American Music Awards, playing "Patience" with Don Henley on drums. We'd toured with our friends and heroes. Finally and suddenly we were the band that we'd always known we were . . . just better.

When we landed in L.A. at the end of the *Appetite* tour, each of us, one by one, set off to rediscover whatever we'd left behind: Duff went home to his girl Mandy (whom he married in 1988), Steven headed to his chick's place (whoever she was at that point), Doug took off to San Diego, Alan returned to Redondo Beach, Axl went to Erin's, and soon enough Izzy and I were sitting there alone at LAX, with our brand-new Halliburton luggage and no particular place to go. Each of us became a boy in a bubble at that point. We had taken home enough money from touring and now money was starting to roll in off the sales of *Appetite*, so that the need to survive was no longer a motivation. Everyone was, I suppose, stopping to smell the roses; I'm just not sure that any of us knew how.

Izzy made a call and we went over to a friend of Seymour Cassel's who we'll call "Bill." We'd gotten a taste of smack again in Australia, so the craving was there by the time we got home. Besides, after two years of touring, subconsciously, we both felt that we deserved it. Anyway, Bill had a taste for drugs and always had plenty of every variety; he was also very generous.

When you start to get famous at all, a few typical things start happening: in Hollywood, if you're out at a bar, everyone wants to buy you a drink, you can get into any club; whether you like it or not, you are suddenly a figure on the nightlife circuit. When that started happening to us, there was nothing less interesting that I could have imagined doing with my time. That Hollywood scene was the same old shit, and the more recognizable I was, the less I liked it. The amount of "dudes" who wanted to "party with me" had quadrupled, so I became entirely insular. Even on the rare occasion when I wanted to go out, I

found that the Hollywood scene we'd known was dead: the Cathouse was closed down and there was nothing else in L.A. that I found interesting at all.

Everyone in the band needed time to decompress; looking back, it makes complete sense to me that I allowed myself to slip into that seductive heroin comfort zone. It was the one aspect of success and fame that wasn't vapid to me; there was really nothing else. I didn't want to go to strip clubs or look for hot chicks or otherwise exercise my newly found status. All I wanted to do was hang out at Bill's and do drugs.

The only stability that I'd enjoyed in my life up until then was the constant traveling, which was a contradiction not lost on me. I was twenty-three and I hadn't had a stable life or home since I was thirteen; home for me was living with girlfriends or being on a bus with the band. I lived for playing my guitar and being on the road, plain and simple.

Like I said, Bill wasn't a real dealer, he just liked to get high casually. He always smoked heroin and he had lots of self-control about everything he did. Meanwhile I was the opposite: I had a fiendish, obsessive/compulsive attitude toward heroin and was always eager to get around it and get more of it. That first night over at Bill's I didn't have any gear to shoot it with, so we all smoked it. But I couldn't wait to grab a bit and leave the next day in search of a rig. It turned out to be the start of a long and nightmarish obsession with heroin that lasted from 1989 through 1991.

BILL'S PLACE WAS ON FRANKLIN AND Western in East Hollywood way off the beaten track; he and his wife and their friends were really cool. Izzy and I hung around there on a daily basis and fit in just fine. Bill never allowed shooting up at this place, so I would smoke a little there, pocket some for later, and shoot it up at my leisure when I cut out to do my errands or go to appointments.

One of them was a photo shoot with Izzy for *Guitar World* with Glen La Ferman. We were both so high; we'd spent at least a week over at Bill's. I remember that we showed up with our guitars, and that we passed out on the floor . . . not much else. It wasn't on purpose; I'm not sure that we were even aware that we'd done it. I just remember that afterward we went back to Bill's.

For the record, that shoot contained the famous picture of me that is in the Rainbow, where I'm laid out with my hat on the ground and a bottle of Stoli, my guitar, and the rest of it at my side. If you have decent vision and you take a look at Izzy and me in those frames, you will easily see how out there I was. I was high off the entire success of touring and we were both in search of the kind of excitement you will never find walking around Hollywood playing rock star. I was in search of someplace dark.

Eventually Bill got arrested and was sentenced to thirty years to life for being caught three times with illegal drugs in large enough quantities that they qualified for "intent to sell." In the end Bill served eleven years and got out. But at one point before his arrest, he was under surveillance from his phones to his home; every move was monitored. Two of the people who made regular appearances, of course, were Izzy and me, and Bill told me later that the cops were particularly curious about us. Supposedly they were willing to bargain with Bill if he dropped a dime on us because by then we were famous, to a degree. But Bill wouldn't do that. God bless him.

<hr />

EVENTUALLY I DECIDED THAT, IN LIGHT of the band's success, I should rent a place of my own. My apartment on Larrabee was the first that I'd ever had to myself, under my own name, and I was proud of that. It was just one room, a fully furnished, perfect studio, laid out exactly like a hotel room—and that's exactly what I liked about it. Unfortunately, like every other apartment I'd lived in before then, I was pretty quickly evicted.

I kept it up for a while; well, Ronnie Stalnaker did, actually—one of his jobs was to keep drugs and trouble away from me and me from them. He'd regularly come through and clean the place up, probably as a way to see if I was behaving. I never did; it was much too fun of a challenge to figure out how to sneak my druggie friends into the apartment without Ronnie finding out. It was always a feat because Ronnie lived right next door.

It wasn't going to end well with Ronnie—he got a bit obsessive about his job and went a bit Single White Stalker—but at this point he'd done nothing but prove himself to be a very loyal bodyguard, despite all of my efforts to fuck with him. For example, one night, while we were on tour somewhere, I decided

to end the evening by throwing my bottle of Jack into the TV set in my hotel room before I passed out. It exploded, of course, and Ronnie came in. We were a number of stories up, but Ronnie decided that we weren't going to pay for that TV. He climbed out of my window, across the ledge of the building, and into an adjoining room, where he stole that TV and replaced it with the one I had broken. *That* is dedication.

Another time when we were in Dallas, Duff and I had adjoining rooms connected by a door and we invited over too many friends with piles of coke. Our party lasted all that night and well into the next afternoon. Things got out of hand, of course, and a big glass coffee table got smashed, and I walked all over it barefoot and bled everywhere. At some point someone kicked the dividing door off the hinges and tipped the beds over and smashed all of the lamps. There were too many of us behaving badly for Ronnie to deal with, so he came up with a plan to get us out of the hotel without the management noticing. He somehow herded us into a service elevator and snuck us out of a loading dock and onto the bus. The hotel had heard all of the noise and was very aware of the party going on, but Ronnie had kept security out of there somehow for an hour or so. We thought we'd gotten away, until the cops pulled us over a few miles down the road at a convenience store where, if memory serves, I'd actually just stolen a bunch of candy.

We were lined up against the side of the bus and taken in for trashing the hotel rooms. It was *expensive* and I can say in all honesty that it was the last time I've ever *really* destroyed a hotel room. Sure, I've been through a couple of TV sets and done a few other stupid things since, but that was the last time I engaged in total annihilation because *I* got the bill for that one.

Ronnie was clearly dedicated but regardless, it wasn't easy keeping my first apartment in shape. The first blow came when my younger brother, Albion, or "Ash," stayed there while I was away on tour. Ash is a great graffiti artist, and when I returned, I found that he'd covered every wall with an amazing mural that I had no interest in having in my home. I was so pissed off but I only told him that what he'd done was "inconsiderate." He was only sixteen after all. Since then Ash has gone on to form Conart, one of the most cutting-edge T-shirt companies around; the designs are based on his art.

Ronnie painted over the mural, he cleaned up, he did everything else to keep us in there as tenants. That place was pretty simple: I had a microwave,

I had a refrigerator full of the usual bachelor-pad supplies and condiments. There wasn't much, but even so it all got beaten up pretty fast. After all, West Arkeen came by all of the time and the two of us got to smoking a lot of crack together. We'd hit the pipe and listen to music and slowly climb the walls. In those tweaked-out days I spent with West, I fully realized what a great guy and an awesome fucking mess he was. To complement his influence, I had another musician friend, Jay, whose place I went to a lot to get high on smack. All things considered, slowly, despite my financial resources, but surely my living conditions became as gritty as they'd been when I was living in a storage unit.

<hr/>

I WENT THROUGH AN INTERESTING succession of girlfriends at this time; just a handful that I'd see over at my place, each on different nights. At some point during these months my manager had the brilliant idea of having me present some award to someone or other at the MTV Video Music Awards. I can't even remember who we gave it to, but my copresenter was Traci Lords, the porn star, and Alan thought that it would be funny for me to be up there with her. Obviously he saw the advantage of the sensational aspect, which was not a bad idea at all.

So Traci and I met backstage and we started talking and then we started dating immediately. She was really good-looking and a bit of a dichotomy— as I soon found out.

I was in a strange place; I was mildly famous, I was infamous, but I was still stuck in a raggedy, heathen mentality in terms of my quality of life. At that time, I could have had $15 million in the bank, but I wouldn't have changed my lifestyle at all; I didn't have a car, I was happy to have my one-room apartment that looked like a generic hotel room, and needed nothing more—that was where my head was at. At the same time, I knew how to be a gentleman, which is entirely what Traci Lords expected on a date. So somehow we hit it off.

But Traci didn't want any part of being seen in public with me; if we ever went anywhere where anyone might be paying attention, she'd put me through this stupid ordeal where I'd have to come in after her and meet her inside, as if by accident. Obviously I was recognizable, so she always insisted

that we scoot in some back alley entrance. Personally, I don't think anyone who ever saw us gave a shit; it just made going out in public with her a huge pain in the ass. Call me naive but I didn't get it; I had no idea who she was hiding from. From what I understood she wanted to keep a low profile because she didn't want to be exposed as a groupie slut or one of the porno chicks that guys like me dated. I was never one of those guys who was judgmental about that stuff and never understood those who were; in fact, the only reason I knew her was that I'd seen her in this movie where she was bent over holding her ankles and she looked *amazing*. I truly appreciated that, so I figured everyone else appreciated that, too. I didn't get her whole charade at all.

At that point, Traci was done with porn and was working on her singing career as well as trying to cross over into regular movies. That was why she didn't want to be seen as a porno actress fucking a rock star—she wanted to change all that. She had talked me into playing on one of her songs and coming to the studio somewhere in Vancouver where she was recording her album. All I can say is that she was hooked up with the least talented, shadiest "music producers" I've ever seen and I told her so. Nonetheless, I helped her out on a few tracks, but nothing was going to keep that whole album from being a joke.

Everything we ever did together was very overly formal and very proper; it always seemed to me that she was living up to some idea of herself that wasn't anywhere close to who she really was. Honestly, all that I wanted to do was get into her pants.

Of course, once I started dating her, West brought over a copy of *New Wave Hookers* so we could check it out. It was very entertaining but somewhat of a tease because after a month of dating we still hadn't slept together. Our "relationship" was starting to become more of a bother than it was worth.

Traci had called me early one week to make plans and that same day West came by with a huge pile of crack. We stayed up for the next two days, and by the time Traci showed up to go out with me, West and I were crawling around on the carpet looking for rocks. I knew she was coming but I couldn't help it: we were a mess, the only person that would have been okay with it would have been a crack whore. My place was a fucking pigsty on every level and it didn't help that West was there like some resident pygmy:

he was only about five four and had stringy blond hair that was really greasy after two days of smoking crack. West always had this permanent grin on his face that became more and more disturbing the more wasted he was. This particular afternoon he was so wasted that he openly leered at Traci. He was so high, that he thought nothing of going over to my bookshelves, retrieving *New Wave Hookers*, pointing to the cover, saying "That's *you*, isn't it! You're Traci Lords!" He kept grinning at her.

Now Traci was the kind of girl who was after a man who was going to provide her with the things she wanted in life: nice clothes, nice cars, a nice life. And while I could have done that, I was nowhere near mature enough to realize that that is what most girls are after—especially girls like her. I didn't see it that way at all back then, because the way I'd been living, I had barely paid attention to the finer things. But there she was in the middle of the afternoon, in a completely dark apartment that smelled like burning tires after our forty-eight-hour crack party. And there was West, short, shiny, and drooling. And there I was, too.

Traci took a long slow look around. "I'll be right back," she said in her pouty little voice. "I forgot something in my car."

"Yeah, cool," I said. "Then we'll take off." I was high, and not particularly aware of time passing, but I soon realized that she'd been gone far too long to ever be coming back.

I was this lone guitar player with a snake, just doing my thing, shooting my scene.

251

I rented up in the Hollywood Hills, and that lasted for about a month. It was partially furnished with all the basics that one might need—beds, a microwave, all of it. We had fun while we were there and I also managed to write a lot; I wrote "Coma," and the two of us wrote "Locomotive" in that house; there was some creativity going on.

Adam Day shacked up with us as well. He is the guitar tech that has been with me for nineteen years. Adam moved in and, as much as our professional relationship has thrived since, that was the last time he ever tried to live in close proximity to me.

Around then we shot the videos for the *Lies* album, which was topping the charts, along with *Appetite*. We shot the "Patience" video in two places; one was the Record Plant, where we had actually recorded the songs; that is where we shot the footage of us playing live. The rest of it—the various band member scenes—were done at the Ambassador Hotel, where Bobby Kennedy was shot. At the time it was closed to the public but open for movie and video shoots.

I had two snakes that had been given to me when I had my apartment on Larrabee: one was a six-foot red-tailed boa constrictor named Pandora that was a gift from Lisa Flynt, Larry's daughter. The other was a nine-foot female Burmese python named Adrianna. Both of them lived in my bedroom closet and both were in the video. I had just moved them to the new house and I remember that the day of the video I sent Adam to get them and he came back completely freaked out—and without the snakes.

"Um, yeah, well, I tried to get them," he said nervously. "But they are out of the cage, loose, and on your bed." So I had to go back to the house to fetch them—no one else would.

I remember that day pretty well; I was just starting to become one of those junkie musicians that assumes that what they're doing is so commonplace and accepted that they almost do it out in the open. I showed up at that shoot, breezed by all of the lighting and camera guys who'd been huddled around all day preparing for this scene, and locked myself in the bathroom. I was now that guitar player whose reputation preceded him and I lived up to it: I stayed in there for eight minutes, then came out loaded and lay in bed with my boa around me. I didn't do much as they shot what they needed. I don't

think I said a word to anyone. It must have been surreal; it wasn't the sixties anymore; it was actually the end of the eighties. In the sixties musicians traveled with their entourage and did shit like that. I was this lone guitar player with a snake, just doing my thing, shooting my scene.

<hr />

AFTER RENTING FOR A WHILE, I DID what anyone with new money should do: I bought a house like my business manager told me to do. I still had no clue as to my future or how to handle finances; I had no material aspirations at all. I didn't spend much on anything at that point; money was still an abstract concept to me. Possessions had never mattered to me, though suddenly everyone around me began to be very concerned with them.

I found a house off Laurel Canyon, which was the area of L.A. that set my mind at ease: it reminded me of the best memories I have of my youth. I bought my first house on Walnut Drive, just off Kirkwood, which is just off Laurel Canyon, and it was forever known as the Walnut House. Incidentally, Walnut Drive was just off the street where Steven fucked the thirty-year-old at Alexis's party so many years before.

The Walnut House was a two-bedroom, funky little tucked-away pad in need of interior design, so it seemed natural to me to hire the team that had styled the "Patience" video to transform my new house into a similarly gypsylike environment. They found all of the furniture at thrift stores and antique furniture shops, and while they got it all together, I moved in with our international publicist, Arlette. She had been hired on back when we played those first three English dates at the Marquee. She'd taken a maternal shine to me, probably because I was such a stray puppy at the time. She let me bring my snake Clyde over, who'd been living with Del James for a while, as well as Pandora and Adrianna. Actually I moved a bunch of other snakes in there, too, into the living room of her two-bedroom apartment off Cynthia and San Vincente in West Hollywood, where Arlette still lives. She was incredibly generous to let me bring all of my pets there; unfortunately, she also had to deal with my rampant heroin habit: every single night one shady character or another came around back and knocked on my window . . . her window, technically. I knew she wasn't a huge fan of

my reptiles, but she was less a fan of me staying up all night, shooting dope, and having undesireables stop by in the wee hours of the morning.

A funny thing happened with the snakes, though. Arlette was scared of them at first but she became, with no encouragement from me, a true snake freak. I eventually gave her a baby Burmese python that grew to fifteen feet long. They became great friends: she took him swimming with her, she'd take baths with him, and she talked to him like he was a dog. She was convinced that the snake was human and understood everything she said, and I must say that he acted like it.

Arlette was very concerned for my welfare when I lived with her and she pointed out the obvious: I had transformed myself from a happy-go-lucky alcoholic into a fiendish monster junkie who bore no resemblance to the guy she'd known all those years. I knew she was right; I knew I didn't look all that healthy and I didn't feel all that healthy. I stayed with her for three or four months but I did little to change.

Instead, I occupied myself with the redesign of my house. It was turned into the gypsy opium den I wanted: they refinished all of the molding and wood, and painted every room in dark colors. The kitchen was a deep forest green; my favorite drug bathroom was entirely black. Another room was painted midnight blue and the living room was deep purple. There was a sepia tone to another room, as if it were out of an old Western movie. I also bought myself my first car to go with my first house: it was a Honda CRX, and like every car I've ever had, it was black inside and out.

I was pretty out of control at the time. I remember showing up to meet the contractor to talk about redoing my bathroom and thinking that breaking out a few lines would be a good way to break the ice.

He and I stood in the bathroom as he walked me through the work that needed to be done.

"Yeah, yeah, cool, man," I said. I slapped down the toilet-seat cover and cut out four thick lines of coke. "You want one?"

He looked pretty uneasy. "No, no thanks. I'm on the job," he said.

"Okay, right, that's cool," I said. "I'll do yours, then."

"It's not just that, it's also eight o'clock in the morning," he said smiling apologetically.

At that moment I was every single nightmare cliché of what that guy had ever heard about rock stars, rolled into one: even more so because he had been hired to turn my extra bathroom and its huge corner Jacuzzi into a massive snake terrarium that took up a quarter of the room. He was going to build glass walls from the floor to the skylight to enclose the tub, which was elevated, plus add a set of Plexiglas stairs so that you could see my pets wherever they might be. I couldn't wait to fill it with trees and all the other shit that snakes like. In the Walnut House I kept about ninety snakes and reptiles: I had lizards, caimans, all kinds of animals.

When the work was done and I finally moved into the Walnut House, I commemorated it by getting really high. I had this great round Oriental wooden table with intricate carvings and a glass top in the den. It was to be the centerpiece for all kinds of cutting over the years, but that first night, Izzy and I sat there with one lightbulb on, on this dark red velvet couch. Needless to say, I didn't clean up right away.

Not long after I moved in there, I saw my ex-girlfriend Sally again. My bed in that house was a loft, on the second floor, in a room that was pretty pitch-black aside from the light cast by a lamp next to the pillow. I had these boxes around the end of the bed that were full of magazines and had remote controls mounted on the inside of them for the TV that rose from a cabinet at the foot of the bed. That bedside lamp was an antique with a salmon-colored glass lampshade that threw off the softest light; I loved it. Anyway, I remember that night very well. I'd gone to sleep earlier than usual and suddenly woke up with a strange premonition. I turned on the lamp to get my bearings and there she was. Sally was towering over the end of the bed; just this silhouette on the ceiling and wall—at first I didn't know who it was. It was pretty scary. At that point in my life I had guns, but I didn't have them with me and I'm glad; if I did, it's possible that I could have shot her, she'd scared me so.

Getting inside wasn't easy; she'd had to jump a fence, walk down a steep set of stairs, and she'd been lucky enough to find my extra key under the doormat—which, of course, was forever removed from there afterward. She was not in a good way, so I let her sleep over that night, and in the morning I drove her down Laurel Canyon and dropped her at the corner of Sunset. It wasn't the last time I saw her, but it was the last time she ever

got inside my house like that. From what I heard, she hung around L.A., and got into trouble. The very last time I saw her was in New York, where she was hanging around with Michael Alig and the notorious Limelight crowd; after that I heard she went back to England. And is much happier now.

It's tough to be the kind of person who hangs around the edgier fringes of society if you're not a musician or someone who has a purpose being there. Everyone else is a disposable player out there in the void on the scene. Most of the girls who dated us back then were these innocent chicks whose lives were changed forever after one of us came into it for however long it lasted. We were like a vacuum back then that sucked people up and spit them out; a ton of people around us fell by the wayside that way. Some people died, not because of anything we did to them, but as a side effect of being too close to the flame. People would get attracted to our fucked-up weird life and just get it wrong and drown in our riptide.

<hr />

STEVEN AND DUFF PURCHASED HOMES close to my new place, just over Mulholland Drive, on the Valley side of Laurel Canyon. They were on opposite ends of the same street. As I mentioned, Steven was building his version of domesticity with some chick, and Duff and his future wife, Mandy, were settling into their home life together. Duff was always very good at maintaining a household; he never fell into the transient kind of lifestyle that I did. I might have lived less than two miles from those guys, but I didn't see them too often; if they'd been drug dealers, I'm sure that I would have.

All things considered, I realized that I had to clean up a bit before we'd be able to get rehearsing again. Duff didn't want to write with me when I was high and I couldn't blame him for that. When there was a bit of a drug drought in L.A., and it became a huge pain in the ass, my subconscious trigger of needing to play superseded my drug craving. I just locked myself up in my house and with the help of Dr. Stoli and his assistants I got through my withdrawal.

Once I got off the smack, Duff and I got reacquainted and we scheduled rehearsals. At that point we did so without any confirmation from Axl. The

only messages I got from him came officially through management via Doug Goldstein, who spoke with Axl on a regular basis.

It didn't matter that we weren't all there; Steven and Duff and I started jamming at Mates, our go-to spot. Izzy wasn't quite up to joining us: he'd spent a bit too much time around Bill's house and was on a path as dark as mine. He came to rehearsal every so often, but we never waited for him. At least we were trying to be productive; I have no idea what Axl was up to at the time because we didn't speak, probably because a few of us were chemically out of control.

Drinking excessively became the thing again for me. I would drive home from rehearsal totally plastered, passing people on the wrong side while going up Laurel Canyon. I'd be doing ninety miles an hour in my little Honda CRX; I would have died easily if I'd hit anything. I'm thankful that I didn't hurt anybody, get arrested, or die—someone is watching out for me, given how often I've come close to death and made it back alive.

One particularly outstanding night I turned off Laurel Canyon onto Kirkwood, the street that led to my street, Walnut Drive. There was a guy stopped at the corner of Walnut who was preparing to make a left onto Kirkwood. He was way too far over, in my lane; and in my mind he was in my *way*. Rather than stop or slow down, I just plowed into his car—on purpose.

I tried to back up and take off, but our cars were stuck together; I'd smashed him on the driver's side by the rear wheel and my car's front end was attached to his car. At that point it dawned on me that I probably shouldn't have done that.

I sat there trying to back up and split; I pulled my bumper to pieces because it was severely mashed into this guy's car. As I was doing so, he got out and walked up to my window.

"So?" I asked, and stared at him for a minute, squinting.

The guy reeked of booze; he was completely wasted and now totally confused by me.

"You're fucking *drunk*," he said, his speech a little slurry.

"No, I'm not," I said. "*You're* fucking drunk."

I lit up a cigarette as he and I slowly came to the realization that both of us were pretty fucked up to the degree that police involvement was a bad idea.

"Do you have insurance?" the guy asked. "I don't."

"Listen . . . I can't afford to get in trouble with the law," I said.

"Let's pretend this didn't happen," he said.

"Fine by me."

We managed to pry our cars apart; that guy bolted and I drove up my little hill as fast as I could. I put the car in the garage and sat there for a moment. My heart pounded as the reality of what could have happened sunk in. I had a much-needed moment of clarity: the repercussions of that misadventure would have halted everything for me.

It didn't take a clairvoyant to see that if we would ever be a band again, Izzy and Duff, Steven and I, would need to write some music and get Axl interested and back in the mix. We had a few songs going but we had to keep up the pace and stay focused. We were already almost there: it was becoming exciting again; the original hunger was returning and the fire was alive. We wanted to make Guns music our top priority.

We kept rehearsing, and once we'd gotten a few songs all together, we went over to Izzy's place on Valley Vista and Sepulveda in the Valley to do some writing and see where his head was. It didn't take me long to figure it out: I was in the bathroom over there taking a leak when I noticed the two-inch-thick layer of dust in his shower and bathtub. That thing hadn't been used for weeks—Izzy was that far gone. Even Axl showed up that day, and regardless we started working on a song that became "Pretty Tied Up." I remember that Izzy had taken a cymbal and a broomstick and some strings and had made a sitar out of it. Needless to say . . . Izzy was pretty fucking high.

We didn't have to confront him at all; he had a serious scare one night that set him straight. Whatever it was, Izzy got too shook up to even talk about it. He just called his dad, who came out from Indiana, and took him back home, and that's how and where Izzy got clean. He's been clean ever since.

The rest of us continued to work, and once we had some material and were communicating with Axl again, he let us know that he and Izzy wanted to write the next album in Indiana. I couldn't imagine why; both of them had left Indiana as soon as they could to come to L.A. and they never seemed too fond of the idea of going back. In any case, our situation was so unpredictable that I wasn't going to move to a wheat field with no guarantee that

we'd even get anything done. Their whole intention was to get away from the distractions of L.A. and I respected that; Axl wanted us to go somewhere where we could have our privacy to focus on writing. I wanted to do the same, but at least be in a major metropolitan area, so in the end we agreed on Chicago. It was close enough to Indiana that Izzy could join us when he felt ready, or go back there easily if he felt like his sobriety was threatened.

Doug Goldstein and I went to Chicago to scope out where we would live and rehearse. We chose the Cabaret Metro, the famous rock club on the north side of the city: it's a concert space that houses a separate club called the Smart Bar in the basement, and also has a theater upstairs. It was perfect; we took over the theater and when we were done for the day, the coolest bar in the city was waiting for us downstairs. We rented out a two-unit, brown brick apartment building a few miles down the road on Clark Street, right by the elevated train, to live in.

We all moved out there, with our techs, Adam Day and Tom Mayhew; our production manager; and our new security guard, Earl. Duff, Steven, and the crew guys moved in downstairs, and Axl, Izzy, Earl, and I lived upstairs. That was fine by me because I had the place to myself for the most part—it took Axl more than a month to join us, and Izzy was there for less than an hour. It takes Axl an indeterminate amount of time to decide what he is going to do from the inception of an idea to the point of carrying it out, which always keeps things interesting. All in all what we were doing wasn't business as usual for us, but it was a start.

For a while, it didn't matter to me that we'd just relocated the entire band in order to satisfy the only two guys who weren't there because by then Duff and I were such enthusiastically social boozers that the miles of bars along North Clark Street were a new playground for us—all within walking distance. My personal consumption at that point was a half-gallon bottle of Stoli per day, plus whatever I consumed when I was out at night. I'd wake up in the morning and fill a Solo cup 85 percent full with vodka, ice, and a bit of cranberry juice. I called it breakfast of champions. Duff was in the same league, though I believe that he made a fresh drink, packed with ice, before he went to bed and left it next to his pillow; that way the ice would keep it cold enough while he slept that it would still be nice and fresh first thing in the morning.

I'd sit on the floor sipping my breakfast and watching TV each day until the rest of the guys were ready to go rehearse. We'd jam at the Metro for most of the afternoon, sometime into the evening, and then spend the rest of the night in and out of bars. We were more or less hanging out and writing riffs here and bits of songs there. When we were working we were focused, but we could never complete any of our ideas without all of the players in attendance.

I've learned that it is essential for everybody to be present at all times— our producer Brendan O'Brien insisted on it during the writing of Velvet Revolver's last album, *Libertad*. Everyone in Guns was focused at this point—even Axl—but we didn't have very good group skills and had no idea at all how to govern our work situation. The desire was there, but we needed *regulation*. If one of us didn't show up, we'd work anyway, which was one of many things that held us back from getting it together properly. For one thing, Duff and I were intent on drinking all the time and considered that normal because it never interfered with work, but we were so ferocious about it outside of rehearsal that it was off-putting to Izzy. He couldn't be around that kind of behavior then and he's like that to this day. We weren't aware of it at the time, and even if we were, we might not have cared—all we knew was that he wasn't showing up to work and we couldn't accept that. I'm sure Axl had his reason for doing things his way, too. But we didn't have a good line of communication among us about any of these issues, so the end result was serious misunderstanding. Since these points of interest were simply never discussed, since there was never a conversation about how to adjust our game plan to take everyone's needs into account, we kept doing things the way we had in the past, which considering that we'd all changed caused us serious internal tension.

Instead of coming up with a new method to account for our issues, all of the problems just snowballed. This was when a good manager might have turned the situation around, but we didn't have one. Throughout this process, Doug and our management were useless; they didn't seem to want to take the time to deal. Alan was still in charge, and Doug was our day-to-day man, and he wasn't doing anything but enabling us. Their attitude was that we were supposed to know how to do this shit ourselves. And we did; we accomplished creatively left to our own devices . . . but only when

we were living together as one, living five similar lives. Now that we'd become a band who had to set up shop, and we were coming from different perspectives, that dynamic was gone. There is no one to blame; we did the best we could.

We'd had to get going without Axl there, and we found his absence disrespectful, and that disrespect built up into such great animosity that when he did finally show up, the rest of us were pretty resentful. We were an out-of-control band with some some semblance of integrity who had lost their ability to properly channel it all: for the life of us, we just could not get on the same page. We also made no effort to pursue the adult way of handling things. I wouldn't call it innocence or naïveté looking back, but we all played a hand in mixing the pot. None of us stood back and took a moment to ask one another or ourselves, "How do we do this? How can we get everyone together and working and satisfied?" We needed to be clear-headed about it; if one thing didn't work, we'd need to keep trying. But we didn't do that. Outside of the fact that our management didn't care to take the lead, the biggest catalyst to the demise of the band was the lack of communication among the members.

Admittedly, I was pigheaded; I didn't want to always feel like I was bending over backward. I thought of us as equals, and I was making a conscientious effort to get things going, but I didn't have the wherewithal to understand what Axl was expecting, or the patience to sit down and talk it out with him. As with any relationship, when someone lands on your bad side, it gets hard to be empathetic. My guard by then was *way* up. With all of that going on, it was much easier to just enjoy the summertime in Chicago because the bars were mighty inviting.

In our plentiful free time, Duff and I also did our personal best to stay in shape. I had one of my BMX bikes out there and I used to ride it between the apartment and the rehearsal space, bunny-hopping over everything in sight, riding on the sidewalk. It was a good workout. Some days Duff and I even went to the gym, usually just after our morning vodkas. We'd go down to one of those big public YMCAs with our security guard, Earl, to pump iron. We'd be down there in our jeans, doing sets between cigarette breaks—it was invigorating. We'd usually cool down afterward with cocktails at a sports bar. It didn't matter how big we were back home or how

many records we'd sold or the shows we'd played; in Chicago, we were nobodys. We were just a couple of regular Joes to our fellow bar patrons; and there is not a bigger haven for regular Joes in America than the sports bars of North Clark Street.

Every night we hung out at Smart Bar, which was very cool, but a much different rock scene than L.A. It was 1990, and that place was all about techno and industrial music like Ministry and Nine Inch Nails. We didn't really gel with people there, because we were clearly of a different variety, but we made a circle of friends anyway. We had dozens of chicks; it was a like a shooting gallery in that place, but eventually I settled on one. Her name was Megan; she was nineteen. Megan lived with her mom and younger brother in a nearby suburb and she was really exotic-looking, a heavy-chested, bubbly, sweet girl.

I began to settle into a cozy little relationship with her, and was getting used to the routine of jamming however long by day and hanging out with her all night. And that is when Axl showed up, which changed the dynamic immediately. Despite the resentment, we were so glad to see him that no one wanted to aggravate the situation by confronting him about his lateness. We started to work with him on the days that he actually came to rehearsal, but we were never quite sure which days those would be. If we'd decide that we'd all start jamming at four p.m. or six p.m., he might show up at eight or nine, or not at all. When he did come down, Axl generally tinkered around on the piano or sat and listened to some of the ideas we'd worked out. All things considered, we managed to produce a few good tunes: "Estranged," "Bad Apples," and "Garden of Eden."

Over all, I found our time in Chicago to be a huge waste, which will always be a point of contention between Axl and I. He seemed to think that we were really getting somewhere and that I was the one who ruined it all. I might have felt differently if he'd been there the whole time, but after almost eight weeks—six of them without him—I felt we didn't have enough material to show for it, and I was frustrated and unwilling to wait around to see if we'd get it going consistently. The vibe among us was just too dark and not conducive to real creativity. We were also being so frivolous with our money that I couldn't ignore it: we had moved our entire operation to the Midwest

and come up with nothing but a few complete songs and a handful of rudimentary ideas, many of which we'd brought out there with us.

I did try to stay the course once Axl got to town, but two incidents put an end to my time in the Windy City. The first was the night we came home after drinking to find a feast of Italian food on the sidewalk in front of our apartment. I got a bird's-eye view of the mess because, as I recall, I had insisted on spending the entire night lying on the roof of the car whenever we drove from bar to bar. Our favorite Italian place was right on the corner and apparently Axl had unloaded the band's entire dinner on a few people who had found out that we were living there and were heckling him from the street. (By the way, this was not the inspiration for the title of *The Spaghetti Incident*; that came from one of the complaints against the rest of us that Steven listed in his lawsuit—which we'll get to—after he was fired. I'm not even sure what he claimed . . . something having to do with Axl throwing spaghetti at him, I believe. I guess that was a theme in those years.)

Anyway, after Axl chucked our dinner at the hecklers, he proceeded to trash the entire kitchen and break every glass item in the apartment. And, as we'd find out a few days later, sometime during his tantrum, Izzy arrived, having driven in from Indiana. He took one look at what was going on from down on the street and turned his car around and left immediately without even entering the building.

I suppose that the rest of us should have noticed that Axl was unhappy and acting out after that first incident, but by then we'd gotten to the point where we just let him do his thing and tuned it out. Who knows, maybe if we listened to what he wanted to do and just complied a bit more he wouldn't have freaked out so hard. Still, who could fathom what he was unhappy about? He showed up with this very sort-of-bitter attitude that seemed to be coming from a very depressing place. But, to be honest, I was more worried about Steven than Axl by then: he was a huge problem; he was doing tons of blow and his performance had become irregular. I didn't catch on at first; he kept his coke hidden in the refrigerator in the downstairs apartment where he lived.

We would be hanging out and sharing a bit of blow, but I couldn't figure

out how Steve was always that much more wasted. He'd just get this twinkle in his eye and say, "Hey man . . . butter tray," and point at the fridge.

"Yeah, okay, Steve. Sure," I'd say. I'd go to the refrigerator, fix myself a drink, and come back with nothing remarkable to report. I didn't think he actually wanted me to look in the butter tray. He was that fucked up that I didn't take it seriously.

"Did you see?" he'd ask, grinning wildly. He'd just keep pointing at the refrigerator and saying, "*Butter tray.*"

"Yeah, man, I saw it," I'd say. "That's a great refrigerator you've got there. Really nice butter tray, man."

"Butter tray."

"So, Steven . . . what are you trying to say?"

Tom Mayhew discovered it eventually: Steven had a steep supply of coke piled up in that butter tray of his.

At this point, I really had no choice but to see that we were all unraveling. No matter how in control I felt I was or thought everyone else was, I realized that Steven was growing irretrievable. As soon as the band ended its stay in Chicago, Steven and I had less and less interaction; he was completely isolated once we got back to L.A. We were tight as a band gangwise, but during our two years on tour, Steve and I developed a distance between us as individuals that grew nothing but worse.

One of the few things we had in common as a band at the time, in Chicago though, was a shared interest in Faith No More's album *The Real Thing*. It was the background music for that entire trip. It would be playing all the time on the different stereos in our apartments.

There is the background; in the end this is why I left. The last straw involved some girls that were brought back to our place one night. My girlfriend Megan had gone out and I was at home in bed. Late at night, I heard some commotion; the sound of a few people filing in and heading past my bedroom down to Axl's room. Until then, Axl had spent most of his time in there alone, constantly on the phone. This night was clearly an occasion.

My room was at the front of the apartment, separated from Axl's by our living room and a long railroad-style hallway. So I went down there to see what was going on; I found our security guard Earl, Tom Mayhew, Steve,

and Axl hanging out with two happy-go-lucky Midwestern girls that they'd brought back.

We all hung out, and as it got later, it was suggested that the girls have sex with all of us. They were willing to blow everyone in the room, which seemed reasonable to me, but they didn't want to fuck us. For whatever reason, that really pissed Axl off. The girls had a very intelligent rationale for their point of view, but Axl begged to differ. This debate continued for a moment, and it was pretty relaxed, but suddenly Axl exploded. He threw them out with such rage it was shocking. The way it went down was completely unnecessary. The coup de grâce was that one of the girls' dads was a prominent officer with the Chicago police, or so I was told. Later that morning I packed up my stuff and flew back to L.A. A few days later, I had Megan move out and join me.

———◆◆◆◆———

GUNS WAS A BAND THAT MIGHT BREAK apart at any second; that was half of the excitement. When we had a common goal, that was less likely to happen. The more time we spent apart, as our communal, creative vibe became more a memory than a reality, our lack of communication and the disadvantage of not knowing what was truly going on with one another disabled any ability we might have had to deal with change.

At the creative level, things between us had changed drastically. Until *Use Your Illusions I* and *II* Guns wrote songs one way: start with an idea that anyone would come up with and then we'd collaborate. Axl is so prolific lyricwise and has such a heartfelt sense of melody that combined with Izzy's songwriting skill and Duff and myself, creating great guitar parts was easy, and so we'd have amazing songs in no time. Izzy and Axl had such great chemistry because Axl knew how to transform one of Izzy's simple structures into a perfect, well-rounded, melodically and lyrically rich song. A great example is "Patience": Axl really elevated that song of Izzy's into something else entirely. I have such a powerful sense of melody and riffs that I'd tie it all together. A lot of the time I would start the core writing of a song with a guitar hook that Duff would expand upon with a great bass line, or I'd come

up with a bridge and chorus section that would inspire Axl to write incredible lyrical hooks.

When Izzy and I brought a song to the band, usually some or all of the words were there, but when Axl sang them his way ... it would *really* come together. Back then it was easy; but by 1990 we'd lost that communal inspiration to produce. The desire to get together and write songs is one thing: that's like a day job. It's quite another to be *inspired* by a mutual collaboration. That was the harshest reality for us to come to terms with. For the first time we had to work at it; all the same when

Slash kicking back on a balcony with some toad venom.

we finally got down to it, it was great and it came quickly, but everything along the way was a complete fucking *chore*.

I WAS PRETTY DISILLUSIONED ABOUT the band when I got back to L.A. from Chicago. I moved back into the Walnut House, with Megan. I'm not quite sure what I was thinking because I hadn't known her long, but there she was. Everyone else in the band, aside from Izzy, was still in Chicago, and after a day or so, they realized that I was gone. They started to trickle back, but in the end Axl stayed behind for about two weeks after I left. Considering that he was furious with me for ending our "creative reprieve" there, he didn't spend that time writing down in our prepaid rehearsal space. From what I understand, he spent the time sleeping and threw a few more apartment-wrecking tantrums, as well as sending me berating messages, via management, usually Doug on a semiregular basis. Doug would call me as if he was Axl's boy, and I can't say I automatically trusted whatever he had to say, but I'd respond as honestly as possible and hoped he'd convey the truth about why I'd left to Axl. Regardless, Axl just stayed out there and sent messages to all of us for a while, I guess.

Guns was a band that might break apart at any second; that was half of the excitement.

Axl and I had a very interesting sort of love/hate relationship, and always did. Most of the time Axl and I were like fishing buddies who don't have much to talk about unless they're fishing. Then there were times

when he and I had a great rapport, when he'd come to me to talk when he had a lot on his mind. For all of those periods, there were stretches when we were so obviously on opposite sides of some invisible fence that we didn't communicate at all. During the months before we got to writing again, Axl and Erin were having very serious problems in their relationship and he and I had many deep talks about it. What they were going through was very serious: in fact, one time after Chicago I had to go over to Erin's house to help defuse an argument they were having. Every couple has their inner workings, and if there is one thing I would never try to claim is that I understood the inner workings of theirs. Still, I was friends with both of them so I could help mediate. Despite all the shit going on with Guns, we were still bandmates and friends. If Axl ever needed me for something, I'd always be there.

<hr />

MY RETALIATION WHEN I GET FRUSTRATED creatively is to be self-destructive with drugs. It's my excuse to go down that path. It's a common phenomenon for junkies. So shortly after I got back to L.A., considering the state of affairs with the band, when the opportunity presented itself, I was too eager to take advantage.

Megan and I had settled in; we were happy in our new home. She turned out to be quite the homemaker, and took to keeping the place up, cooking, and being domestic very naturally. She would go to bed early and get up and go to the gym and then clean up and make dinner. After a few weeks her friend Karen came out from Chicago and they spent a week shopping. That was the first day that I had to myself and I ran into a friend that I hadn't seen in years: a chick from back in the El Compadre days. It's this amazing Mexican restaurant on Sunset and Gardner, and when Guns was still coming up, Duff and I would hang out there constantly, holding court as if we owned the place: we'd bring chicks in there and they'd suck us off or fuck us under the table and just do all this crazy shit.

This old friend that I ran into used to cut hair—mine included—and mentioned that she still did so, but she also sold dope here and there—it was all the encouragement I needed. She came over later with a bag of clean rigs, and before I knew it, before Axl even got home, and before Megan and

Karen returned from their tour of Melrose and Beverly Hills, I was back on smack with a vengeance again.

Megan was one of those chicks who dated the wrong guy and got dragged through the mill with me. She was pretty innocent; she might have thought she'd fallen in love, but I don't think she had any idea of what she'd gotten into or what was going on with me once we returned to L.A. She'd met me when I was a complete drunk; and, as I've mentioned, to the naked eye, a clever heroin addict doesn't act that much different, unless you count their drinks. Megan was so innocent that she didn't pick up on the fact that I'd suddenly stopped consuming a half gallon of vodka per day, though, if anything, I was acting just as drunk—if not more so.

We continued a very sweet, very twisted, almost 1950s kind of relationship. She would tend to the house, then head to bed at ten or eleven p.m. and I'd stay up all night, downstairs in the living room, shooting up every few hours in the black bathroom. Some nights I'd write songs on the couch, some nights I'd just stare at the snakes. Before I noticed, it would be morning and Megan was up and we'd hang out and have a great time until I got tired. She never asked questions and we got along that way for a while, very happily. We had pet names for everything. Everything to her was either "cute" or "sweet," and I was usually "sweetie." Looking back on it, Megan sounded a lot like Jennifer Tilly.

Megan was also, as I mentioned, really domestic. She fixed the place up, especially the kitchen, and made it all entirely livable. She liked to have people over for dinner, if the occasion presented itself. I remember that I had Mark Mansfield come by once, more to get high and catch up than have any kind of meal, but Megan made us a feast: she served us some variety of chicken with several side dishes, garlic bread, and a nice salad, all served on place mats—the whole thing. She was really pleased, and didn't seem to notice at all how dark a state both Mark and I were in. We were so stoned that we just kind of played with the food. It didn't matter; at the end of the night, Megan told me that she thought Mark was *charming*. Megan was interesting in other ways: more often than not, rather than screw, she liked to just jerk me off and watch it . . . I guess we did have a pretty strange relationship.

the act of shooting up always turned me on.

through management continued when he got back from Chicago through to my last days in the band. But the start of it maybe woke Alan and Doug up a bit, because suddenly they seemed desperate to get us in the same room regularly again. The success of *G N' R Lies* had created a huge demand and we hadn't released anything since. We could have sold out a worldwide tour on the basis of a debut record that was three years old, plus an EP with just four new songs. I suppose most other bands don't enjoy that kind of demand, but we weren't going to rush the next record, probably because we couldn't settle down to write any of it.

For my part, I got darker than ever; I started speedballing heavily and really enjoyed the unique brand of hallucinatory paranoia that comes with it. No one had taught me to speedball; I just thought it would be like a narcotic Reese's Peanut Butter Cup. Coke and heroin were two great tastes that I knew would go great together.

It took me some time to figure out how much of each resulted in the effect I desired at the time, and it was endless fun experimenting. I had a few different techniques, but usually I'd shoot my coke first and then follow it up with a shot of heroin. Mixing the two was also a good time, but I often did them separately because I loved the ritual of the needle; the act of shooting up always turned me on.

Speedballing was the greatest roller coaster I've ever ridden: the rush of the coke would send me up and then the dope would kick in and the trip would take a wonderful turn; and the two would weave in and out of each other from there on out. I'd always end up shooting all of the heroin before I'd mowed through the coke, so usually I'd get wired to the point of an impending heart attack. At the end of those nights, I was also often left

with the distinct feeling that I was being watched, so I started to think that walking around my house armed to the teeth was a good idea.

I bought a bunch of guns: a shotgun, a .38 Special, a .44 Magnum, and a few revolvers. I used to keep my .38 in the back of my pants, and after Megan went to sleep, and after I'd shot up enough coke and heroin, I'd walk around the house thinking about things while watching the little hallucinatory figures that started to pop up in the corners of my vision. I'd see them dive and roll off the top of the curtain rods or run along the baseboards in my peripheral vision, but every time I tried to look at them head-on, they'd disappear. Around then I stopped talking to everyone I knew and started doing a great deal of drawing. Throughout my life, my drawings have always reflected what I was into at the time. During this period, I drew nothing but dinosaurs and assorted graphic designs and logos.

I should have been drawing the little demon men that I could never quite see or seem to capture on film—believe me, I tried. As soon as I started to speedball regularly, those little guys were everywhere. They were small, wiry, translucent characters that I saw from afar until eventually they'd crawl up my jacket whenever I got high. I wanted to get to know them in a way; as I lay on the floor, waiting for my heart rate to relax, I'd watch the little Cirque du Soleil show that those guys would put on all over the room. I often thought about waking Megan up so that she could check it out. I even took pictures of them in the mirror when I found them perched on my shoulder and in my hair. I started to talk about them and see them so clearly that I even freaked out my drug dealer. On the rare occasion when I'd leave the house to score my drugs, I'd usually shoot up right away at his place and then start seeing those little guys crawling up my arm.

"Hey, do you *see* that?" I'd ask, extending my arm. "You *see* that little guy, right? He's right *there*."

My dealer would just stare at me expressionless. This guy was a drug dealer who was pretty used to strange junkie behavior. "You'd better go, man," he'd say. "You're *way* too out there. You should go home." Apparently I was bad for business.

One night I was patrolling the house with my shotgun and came down

the bedroom stairs into the living room. Then I went up the stairs to the bedroom landing and up to the loft, where Megan was asleep. As I got up there, the gun went off and blasted through the ceiling opposite the loft. Megan didn't even wake up, which is amazing.

I was still awake when the fire trucks came. I was lying there pretty rattled as I heard the sirens. I just lay still and thought, "Oh, boy."

My house was cut into a steep hill, so the small, square, second-floor bedroom window was actually just above street level. I heard the commotion and figured someone was coming for me, so I tucked my .45 in the back of my pants and ran upstairs to the window, pulled the shade aside, and stared at the firemen preparing to break down my door. I asked them what the problem was and they told me that my fire alarm had been ringing for thirty minutes.

I averted that situation; I assured them that there was no fire, and Megan was none the wiser. Another time that she might have caught on to my nocturnal activities but didn't was the morning that she woke me up on the couch in the living room. Apparently I'd nodded out with the needle right there next to me.

"Sweetie," she said. "I think the cat is playing with something."

I looked down to see one of my cats smacking my needle around like it was a mouse.

Not too long after that, Duff started stopping by because he was worried about me. I'm not sure why; all of the conversations we'd had while I leaned out of my bedroom window and he stood in the cul-de-sac were pleasant enough. I always had a gun in my belt and never invited him in, of course, but it was cool because he never seemed to want to come in either.

"Hey man, how you doing?" I'd ask.

"Fine," he'd say. "Hey, what's up?"

"Not much."

"Okay, then," Duff would say, kind of sizing me up. "See you later."

"Hey, you want to come in?"

"No."

"Okay, that's cool. See you later."

heart trouble my whole life up until she died. When she passed, I was utterly distraught. I never thought that she would die so young; she was only in her late sixties. I saw her in her final moments at the hospital; it was the only time I can really remember breaking down.

The night after I saw her dead in her hospital bed, I went to the Rainbow Bar and Grill and I borrowed a couple hundred dollars from Mario, who owns the establishment. Even though I had money, I never had any cash on me; my business manager was reluctant to give me any for obvious reasons. Mario had no idea what the money was for and it was the first time I'd ever asked for any. I went down to East L.A. to cop some dope, then came back to Hollywood and fixed in the front seat of my car on a side street. For some reason I called Izzy; he had recently rented an apartment in Santa Monica, and I asked if I could crash at his place. He said it was cool so I drove my little Honda CRX down the Pacific Coast Highway high out of my mind. Before I went to Izzy's, I spent a few hours speeding around some Santa Monica side streets like a maniac. I remember actually jumping my car off dirt mounds on a construction site. How the car survived, I don't know. I was literally out of my mind. . . . I don't know how I didn't get busted either. When I finally got to Izzy's, he set me up on the couch for the remainder of the night. I remember that while he slept I watched the movie *Performance*, which he had rented. . . . Then I passed out.

Now, at this point in 1990, Izzy was on probation for having an altercation with a stewardess on a commercial flight, which is a federal offense, so he was keeping his nose very clean, so to speak. He had an appointment with his probation officer early the next morning, and left me at the apartment. I got off the couch with the apartment to myself, and proceeded to the bathroom to take a shower because my grandmother's wake was later that morning.

After my shower I tried to do my fix, still high from the night before but believing it was entirely necessary. I couldn't find a vein; I got blood all over the bathroom, the towels, the walls, the sink—you name it. I kept at it until I hit an artery. Then I hid my works in Izzy's living-room closet and headed out to my grandmother's wake, leaving Izzy's apartment in blood-stained shambles.

When I arrived at the wake I was a junkie mess. I greeted my mom and brother, but for some reason I was not prepared to see the rest of my family on my mom's side and made it known. I paid my respects to my grandmother and then went into the bathroom to fix again—it was all too much. That's what kind of fiend I was. When I emerged, my mother realized that I was unfit to be out in public, so she suggested I go home. I went home with my old girlfriend Yvonne, who was at the wake. I hung out at Yvonne's for the better part of the afternoon, but I was too out of my head for her to put up with. I took a cab home only to be greeted by a message on my answering machine from an extremely pissed off Izzy Stradlin. Izzy had found all the syringes and the spoon I had hid in his closet, and was none too happy about it. Seeing that he was on probation and could be searched by his probation officer at any time without warning, he had every reason to be angry.

Looking back on these events, I realize how insane and self-destructive I was, but I didn't know it then. Now it seems shocking, but back then it was no big deal—to me at least.

My grandmother was the most unselfish, giving person I've ever known. She'd give you her last nickel no matter how strongly you'd protest. She was also very supportive of me in all that I did, but especially with music. She had had classical piano training when she was young and she was musically inclined. I got the feeling that she was relieved when I picked up the guitar; she financed my first pieces of gear. She probably figured that music was safer and more sophisticated than terrorizing innocent people on a BMX bike. Little did she know how wrong she was. Her son, my uncle Jaques, lived with her and was about twelve years older than I. He had Down's syndrome. He was big into music as well, and his taste was pretty eclectic because he was a pretty childlike, animated individual. He listened to the Village People, ABBA, the Partridge Family, but he turned me on to James Brown and The Runaways—go figure.

My grandmother passed away of heart complications in 1990 and left my mother to take care of Jaques, but before she left us, she was very proud that I had made a career out of playing music. My uncle Jaques passed in 2004.

have killed Guns off before we even got going if it weren't for the Rolling Stones. At the height of this period, when I was speedballing like Belushi, we needed a reason to rally more than we did when we had nothing but determination and nowhere to go. I remember the day I got the call.

"Hey Slasher, we got a call from the Stones, they want you to open for them." It was Alan. "It would consist of four shows at the L.A. Coliseum."

"Really?" I said. "That sounds like a good idea."

"They're starting their tour soon and they're doing production rehearsals in Pittsburgh."

"Well, let's go out there," I said.

They booked our flights and Alan, Doug, and I headed out there to see the Stones rehearse. I packed up a few syringes, enough dope to get me through a few days, and I was ready. I hadn't counted on one problem, which had been a problem for our band from the start: on the way to Pittsburgh, Alan had booked a stopover in Ohio to check in on Great White. Great White . . . there really wasn't a band other than Poison that stood for everything we hated more than Great White, and our manager, Alan Niven, managed them. This enraged Axl on a daily basis, particularly after Alan forced Guns to fill in for them at the Ritz in New York at an MTV concert in 1988; an appearance they couldn't make for some reason. Once we took off and Alan started piggybacking off our popularity to further *their* career, it became a huge issue with us, so stopping off to see a Great White show on the way to the Stones was a stupid move on Alan's part.

I had no interest in seeing them play, so I stayed behind in my room to shoot drugs until our flight in the morning. I was pretty good at hiding syringes and dope by then; the lining of my jacket was always good, and the inside of a pen was an easy cover for a dope balloon. There were various other techniques, too, but those must remain secret. On this trip I was sloppy, though, and I'd somehow broken my syringe.

It wasn't a problem; I called down to the front desk.

"Um, hi, is this the front desk?"

"Yes, sir, it is, how can we help you?"

"I have a bit of an emergency situation going on here. I am the guitarist for Great White and I am a diabetic and my insulin syringes were in a bag of mine that was stolen. I need to be onstage in an hour and I need to take my medication beforehand. Is there a pharmacy close by that you could send someone to for me?"

"Yes, sir, I'm sorry to hear that. I can most certainly manage that."

"Thank you very much. I really appreciate it."

When the syringes appeared at my door, I was blown away. A junkie can be very persuasive and manipulative when it comes to dope and getting it done. In any case, I was back in business in no time, having a blast in my hotel room all by myself. Over the course of that night I'm not sure if I actually lost one of my heroin balloons, but I took that hotel room apart as if I had. I turned everything over, I looked under every surface; basically it looked like some kid had built a very ambitious fort with all of the available furniture.

I had such a party that night and made such a mess that we didn't get to Pittsburgh on time. I'd shot most of my stuff the night before, but I needed a fix so bad once we got there that I told Alan to let me have a nap before the show. I fixed and passed out and slept through the entire Stones gig. Alan and Doug called me numerous times but I never heard the phone. The two of them saw the show and the next morning told me how great it was.

Alan looked me square in the eye. "Slasher, I'm going to turn this down," he said. "There is no way you can open for these guys. You are in no shape at all to do this."

"We can do this, I promise you," I said. "Just book the gig."

Despite his reservations, he did.

I was a fiend, though other people seemed more concerned about it than I was. Most of my dealers had started avoiding me. The few that would sell to me were cool, but they never wanted me around them; they'd only drop shit off at the back door of the Walnut House and never come inside.

Around this time, I saw my mom and even she was worried. She suggested that I get on the phone with David Bowie, because Mom thought that his advice would help more than forcing me into rehab.

David was engaging, and wise in the ways of chemical abuse. He asked me about what I was doing drugwise and what I was going through emotionally, psychically, and with the band. I rambled on for a while, but once I

started talking about my little translucent friends, David interrupted me. The conversation as a whole was way too involved to have with someone that he hadn't seen since they were eight years old, but he'd heard enough.

"Listen to me," he said. "You are not in a good way. If you are seeing things every day, what you are doing to yourself is not good at all. You are at a very spiritual low point when that begins to happen." He paused for a moment. "You are exposing yourself to the darker realms of your subconscious being. You are making yourself vulnerable to all kinds of negative energy."

I was so far gone that I didn't agree: I thought of my hallucinations as my good-time entertainment.

"Okay, that's cool." I said. "Yeah, I suppose that's bad . . . Duly noted."

ONCE THE STONES GIGS WERE BOOKED, everybody became duly responsible about getting to rehearsal on time and it seemed like we had our incentive once again. At this time Duff was our most responsible member: he'd pick Steven up every day, after waiting for him to do however many lines he needed to do to get straight; then he'd pick me up. I made them both wait outside while I did my prerehearsal shot.

The day before the Stones gigs we did a warm-up show at the Cathouse and it was killer. It was the first time we'd played in a while, and we had so much energy to get out; we sounded amazing and it was a classic Guns show. It wasn't without its unpleasantness, though, because Axl insulted David Bowie so much from the stage that Bowie left in the middle of the set.

David was there with my mom, sitting at a table near the front, and apparently Axl was convinced that backstage before the gig, David had been hitting on Erin Everly. It was such a ridiculous notion that afterward my mom asked me what the fuck was wrong with Axl. It was an uncomfortable situation, but I just blew it off and tried to focus on the positive. That evening was captured for posterity in the video for "It's So Easy," which was never accepted by MTV or aired in the States because we refused to edit out the profanity in the song.

We were booked into the Hotel Bonaventure for the four nights of the Stones shows and that's where I was the morning before the first one when

I got the call that Axl wasn't going to do the gigs. His reasoning was that Steven and I were on smack. We were . . . but that was beside the point; we were opening for *The Stones*. Somehow we coerced him into doing the first show, and it was a disaster.

"Enjoy the show," Axl said when we took the stage, "because it's going to be our last one. There are too many of us dancing with Mr. Brownstone."

I was so pissed off about that and he was so pissed at me for being a junkie that I spent the better half of the show facing my amps. Nothing was together that night, the band sounded horrible. In my state of mind I walked offstage, got right into my limo, and went to get high in my room.

The next day, Doug told me that Axl would play the remaining shows as long as I apologized, onstage, to the audience, for being a junkie. That was a pretty hard pill to swallow. In retrospect, I understand why Axl singled me out rather than Steven. I am the stronger of the two of us and Axl relied on me more. My presence was important to him; he felt that I was a link in the band that couldn't afford to be out of control. Still, I didn't think a public gesture was necessary. When you're high, you're arrogant and there was no way I was going to take the blame in that way. I didn't think that smack was causing the problems in the band and even if it was, now was not the time to make an issue of it.

But I had to do something. So when the time came, I walked out there, and rather than apologize, I went into some banter about heroin and what it can do to you and how we'd been around the block a few times, how I'd done my time with the seductive beast. It was more amusing than anything else, because I didn't want to bring the audience down at all. I have a way of mumbling when I talk anyway, so I think the mention of "the reality of drugs" and whatever else I said came off as an apology enough. We did a long intro to "Mr. Brownstone" as I spoke, so from an audience perspective, it seemed like an impromptu introduction to the song.

Whatever it was and wasn't, once Doug told Axl that I did it (because he refused to leave the dressing room until I did), Axl was pleased and the vibe of the whole band turned around as he walked out onstage and we launched into "Mr. Brownstone." Suddenly our camaraderie returned; once those personal issues were handled, we were able to focus on the playing.

That second show was fine, and the third was even better—we really got it all down by then. The fourth show was fucking *amazing*—we were at our best. Those dates were an experience, to say the least. They are renowned on the bootleg circuit and anyone that was there remembers them very well: even on the nights that we were off, they were nonetheless entertaining.

The Stones watched us for all four nights I've been told, because we reminded them of themselves back in the day. Not that I spent any time hanging with them. I was too strung out. Despite whatever I'd said onstage, all I cared about was getting my fix as soon as possible once the last chord was played. I did it in the parking lot usually; I couldn't wait to get to the hotel. As much as I was inspired by those shows, I started to look at the band and writing our album as something I'd get to "once I got clean." It's a famous junkie mantra.

To get the drugs I needed during those four nights, I once had to leave the hotel to drive into Hollywood and wait for my smack, then go back downtown for the gig. You can be on such a level—playing the Coliseum—but if you're a junkie you also exist in this scrungy reality of copping your shit in the street, grassroots style. You do it and then go back to your other reality.

I didn't want that to happen again, so for the third gig, I gave this dealer we'll call "Bobby" backstage passes so that he could come down and bring me my shit . . . and see the show. I was backstage waiting for him to show up, and as it got close to showtime I started to feel ill. The clock was ticking and I was at the point where I was unable to play; I was full of anxiety because if he didn't get there in time then I wouldn't be able to go onstage. I was waiting, I was beeping him, and I was trying to keep up appearances. I was beeping him. He was not answering. Literally ten minutes before we went on, Bobby showed up. I locked myself in the bathroom in the trailer we called a dressing room and I got high and breathed a sigh of relief. It was not good. Axl had every reason to make the point he did—that kind of existence just couldn't work at the level we were at. When you're that caught up in heroin it's not about the music anymore. I had forgotten that. Steven was in an equally bad place, but until I got clean again, I didn't have any idea of what was going on with him at all.

been and where we had to go; and since the Stones shows had established a functional creative rapport within the band again, we set about tackling the issue as best we could. Doug thought that he could pull off a soft intervention with Steven by taking him on vacation to an exclusive golf resort in Arizona. Steven was excited by what the band had just done, so, at least in theory, he wanted to get his act together. He agreed that a week away from L.A. chilling by the pool, in the desert, was all that he needed.

I was a more complicated animal: suggesting rehab wasn't going to go over well, and neither was being looked after. Actually, no one could tell me shit at the time; they had to trust that I was going to get it together on my own. And I fully intended to; I thought about how to go about it over the course of many nights spent high up in the Walnut House. I had a doctor prescribe me Buprinex, which is an opiate blocker. He'd get me bottles of that and syringes. It was a very expensive treatment, but this guy was kind of a Dr. Feelgood; not the type of guy who had a real legitimate practice to speak of.

I brought all of that with me the night that I spontaneously decided to join Doug and Steven in Arizona. It made complete sense at the time: the Arizona sun was a *great* place to begin scaling back my habit. I told Megan that I had some band shit to do and that I'd be back in four days. I booked my flight, I called a limo, and I called a drug dealer that I knew who was located on the way to the airport. I had it all figured out: I copped enough coke and heroin, and packed all the Buprinex to get me through a nice mellow long weekend at a golf resort.

I hadn't called Doug or Steven to let them know I was coming, so when I landed there that night, I was on my own. There wasn't much going on around town, but I didn't care.

"Hey, how far is this place?" I asked the limo driver.

"About forty-five minutes, sir," he said.

"Okay. Listen, can you stop off somewhere to get me some silverware?" I asked. "I've got some food back here that I really want to eat."

The driver drove for about twenty minutes and stopped at a Denny's. He came out and handed me a knife and a fork, wrapped in a napkin. *Great,* I thought.

"Hey," I said. "Listen, is there anywhere else we can stop? I need a *full set* of silverware."

After another fifteen minutes we stopped again and this time I got the spoon. I promptly put up the divider between the driver and me, got my drugs out, and cooked up my meal.

I did my fix and relaxed while we drove to the hotel. The scrappy underbrush of the Arizona landscape suddenly looked much more inviting and the tinted glass made it look even more lush.

When we got to the resort, the Venetian, I took my one-man party into my room. It wasn't the kind of place that I was used to, because it didn't look like a hotel: it was a collection of bungalows along a beautifully manicured golf course . . . a lot like that place Doug took me to in Hawaii, come to think of it. My room was great: there were these sheer white curtains around the bed, a small adobe-style fireplace, and a bathroom with a glass-enclosed shower—it was like a well-appointed spa. It was so relaxing that I could think of no better therapy than shooting coke and smack all night to soothe my soul.

I soon forgot that the shit I brought was meant to last me four days—I was acting as if I had something to celebrate. Within hours I was out of heroin. It's a common problem for junkies: when you're high, you're in a nice contented state, everything is good and mellow, and that's when you make your plans; that's when you figure out how much dope you need. Then you start doing your dope and everything changes. You reposition everything as you're going; you find reasons why you can and *should* do a hit right now. And once you've done that, you find a reason why you should just finish what you have because, hey, you won't need it later.

You do all of this crazy, psycho shit, because when it comes right down to it, the day you first did heroin, the time you did it and loved it, when your system was pure and unadulterated, that was the best time you will *ever* have doing it. You spend the rest of your using career chasing that high that you'll never find again, so you convince yourself that you will get back there if you just keep at it. You try all different methods of getting there, but you're chasing a ghost. You end up needing to get high just to feel well: you want just enough to not feel bad, just enough to get you to feel fine. But when you have a nice amount of it, you still try to find your original high—and before you

know it, in one night, you've gone through what you planned to ration your-self over four days. Your careful planning is fucked.

That was no reason to stop the party, as far as I was concerned, since there was plenty of coke left to shoot. No matter how meticulous you are with the smack, it will always be done well before the coke. And when you start really shooting coke, the hallucinations you get are so real that you can no longer tell yourself that you're just high and that it's your mind play-ing tricks on you. It's like being on acid, but with a whole different attitude. It's scary and realistic, and not at all psychedelic. In my case, it got violent and terrifying. I had enjoyed that element of the drug in the past, but this time I went over the edge.

I kept shooting coke that night just to keep shooting; I've mentioned how I liked sticking the needle through my skin, into the vein, and feeling the drugs enter my body and take over. I also loved the ritual; the cooking, the straining, and the tying off almost as much as the high. I was pretty content with myself just going through those motions for a few hours.

And then things got weird. I started shadowboxing monsters that I saw on the other side of the sheer curtains that framed the large king-size bed. I was bobbing and weaving, as if I were working out at a gym. This shadow-boxing continued all night long until the sun came up, drowning every shadow in the room and ending my activity. Once I snapped out of that trance, I figured that I should probably head out in search of Steven and Doug.

First, I decided to shower, to straighten up a bit. But before that, I opted for one last shot of coke. I felt great when I got under the big rain-style, luxury showerhead. And as I was there under the nice warm water, the coke hallucinations hit me harder than they had that night or ever before: full daylight was coming in through the skylight, but I watched as long shadows emerged from the corners. They crept up the floor toward me, up the glass of the shower, and took the shape of the shadow monsters I'd boxed earlier. They were right in front of me, filling the glass door, and I wasn't going to let them get me, so I punched them as hard as I could, sending the entire pane of glass into pieces all over the floor. I stood there with a cut hand, under the water, paralyzed, paranoid, scanning the bathroom for other assailants. And that's when my little buddies showed up.

They always looked like the creature in *Predator* to me, but a fraction

the size and translucent blue-gray; they were wiry and muscular with the same pointed heads and rubbery-looking dreadlocks. They'd always been a welcome, carefree distraction, but this hallucination was sinister. I could see them gathering in the doorway, there was an army of them, holding tiny machine guns and weapons that looked like harpoons.

I was terrified; I ran across the glass on the floor and slammed the sliding-glass door to the bathroom shut. Blood began to form in a pool under me, issuing out from my feet, but I didn't feel a thing; I watched in horror as the Predators squeezed their limbs between the door and door frame and began to slide it open. I put all my weight against it in an effort to hold it shut, but it was no use; they were winning and I was losing my balance on all of the broken glass.

I decided to flee: I broke through the sliding-glass door, cutting myself further and spraying debris all over the room. When I ran out of the bungalow, the bright sunlight, the shocking green of the grass, and the colors of the sky were overwhelming; everything was jarring and vivid to me. Everything in my room had been so real that I was not prepared, in my condition, to be so suddenly transported from the drawn curtains into the shimmering daylight.

I just ran . . . fully naked and bleeding, down the fairway, away from the army of Predators I saw over my shoulder every time I turned to look. I needed a reprieve from the harsh daylight, so I ducked through the open door of another bungalow. I hid behind the door, then behind a chair, as the Predators began to fill up the room. There was a maid in there, making the bed, and she started to scream when she saw me. She screamed louder when I tried to use her as a human shield to protect myself from the small hunters on my trail.

I fled again, running at top speed through the resort with a translucent army at my heels; the colors and scenery only added to my dementia. I made it to the back of the main clubhouse and went through the back door and into the kitchen; all of the cooks and activity were dizzying, so I ran out of there, right into the lobby. There were guests and staff everywhere and I remember grabbing a well-dressed businessman standing there with his luggage, once again using him as a human shield. He seemed so together that I believed he could hold the Predators at bay, but I was wrong. They

actually got to me at that point and started climbing up my legs, loading their little guns. The businessman didn't want anything to do with me; he shook free so I backed into a utility closet somewhere near the kitchen. As a crowd gathered, I ran out of there again, back outside, eventually finding darkness and shelter in a shed on the fairway, where I hid behind a lawn mower, until finally, the hallucinations began to subside.

I'd caused quite a bit of a commotion by then; the cops had arrived and, along with a crowd of onlookers, they confronted me in my hiding place. I wasn't seeing the Predators anymore, but when I gave the cops my testimony, it involved a detailed re-creation of how they'd chased me all over the resort trying to kill me. I was still high enough that I told the story without a shred of self-consciousness. Everything around me still looked pretty bizarre; even when Steven broke through the crowd and handed me a pair of sweatpants. The cops took me back to my room and found a bag full of syringes, but no drugs; and since I had a prescription for Buprinex, (which did not get you high,) I was allowed to have syringes and nothing seemed amiss.

Still, the Arizona police weren't buying it: at some point they left me in the room to discuss among themselves what to do with me. I was still convinced that everything I told them had happened, which didn't help exonerate me at all. They kept staring at me, like, "okay." They eventually took me in, once they found coke residue in the spoon on the floor. But Doug stepped in; he called Danny Zelisko, this high-powered promoter in Phoenix, who managed to keep me out of jail. Doug and Danny hustled me out of there, minus one shoe, because one of my feet was far too injured to wear one. They got me on a private jet and flew me the fuck out of there. Without Danny's help, I was looking at serious jail time. Thank you again.

WHEN I LANDED IN L.A., I WAS PICKED up and snuck into a suite at the Sunset Marquis. My speedball rally at the golf course had left me exhausted, so I went straight to sleep.

I woke up to Duff standing over the bed. "Hey man . . . you awake?"

"Yeah," I said, trying to figure out exactly where I was.

"Get some clothes on, I'm going to wait for you in the other room," he said. "I have to talk to you about something."

"Okay, cool."

I walked into the living room and every seat in the place was full: my managers, my mom, my bandmates (except for Izzy and Axl)—aside from my drug dealer, almost everyone I knew was there. It was an official intervention. I was still getting my bearings, but I immediately thought that it was ridiculous that Steven was there because he needed rehab as much as I did, if not more. I stared at him, just thinking, *Hypocrite.* Everyone else's attendance meant something to me. I'm not quite sure what, but definitely something. Almost everyone there also had something to say.

My security guard Earl said, "Slash, you were vibrant and alive in Chicago. In Chicago you were so strong. I can't stand to see you like this, in this weak condition."

My mom was stupefied. She sat there in silence for the most part.

Alan Niven was typically bombastic. "Slash, you *have* to go to rehab," he said. "It's all been arranged."

They all said that they loved me, and God bless their hearts, I'm sure they meant it, but being confronted that way was so heavy that it lost something in translation. I was completely cornered, so my usual bullshit lines about being fine were not going to work. I was stuck with no defense, I was guilty without a trial, and there was nothing I could do. Like anyone in that situation, my lying had come into harsh focus.

I never blamed my mom for any of this, I never for a moment thought that this was her idea; she looked as confused as I did that day. The rest of them were scheming motherfuckers as far as I was concerned. Regardless, if I was going to make it right with the band, I'd have to go to some clinic in Tucson called Sierra Tucson, and so I entered rehab for the first time.

The thing about rehab is that you have to want it. When you do, it works wonders—but when you don't, it may clean out your body, but it won't change your mind. That is precisely what happened to me my first time: I went through detox, in a very secure, sterile environment, but there was no way in hell that I intended to take part in any aspect of the clean-living community that is phase two of rehabilitation.

But before I even got there, I did what every dedicated junkie does: I told everyone at my intervention that I agreed with them, that I intended to go along with their plan for me, so long as I could spend one last night in my

own bed before I set off to clean up in the morning. They said okay, because my shenanigans had run their course as far as they were concerned.

I went back to my house, retrieved my stash, did my fix, and hung out with Megan—who was completely unaware of this entire event going down. I told her that I'd be away for a while on band business, and in the morning, I got up bright and early, fixed again, and got into the limo with Doug to go to Tucson. This place was in the middle of the desert in every way: there were no markets, housing developments, strip malls . . . nothing civilized was within miles. It was a little sober oasis.

I was checked in to a two-bed room, but never had a roommate for the duration of my stay, which was *great*. The first three or four days of drying out were typically awful, though they were made less drastic due to the combination of medications I was given. I'd never kicked that way, so it was a welcome relief, but nothing quite so comfortable that I could eat anything or sleep soundly for more than an hour or two at a time.

After a few days, once the sweats and the anxiety and the inescapable discomfort receded, I was comfortable enough in my own skin to get out of bed and walk around a bit. It was all that I could do; I wasn't ready for human interaction at all. But the moment I emerged from my room, the staff was all over me to attend group therapy. It was out of the question—just because I could walk didn't mean that I wanted to talk. I wanted to avoid other people so much that I waited until I was totally famished to seek out food, because doing so meant encountering strangers in the cafeteria.

I learned later that should I have checked in a week earlier; I'd have known one person there: Steve Clark, the original guitarist for Def Leppard. Steve was in there for drugs, but as is customary in places such as those, once you surrender to their methods, they find countless other "afflictions" that are ailing you. In that frame of mind, sex and just about anything else, if you look at it from a certain perspective, can be seen as an addiction that rules your life. In Steve's case, I hear they labeled him as a sex addict and slapped a "No Female Contact" patch on him after he broke the regulations by talking to the same girl more than once in private. He didn't take to that too well and he promptly checked himself out of there. Steve died of a drug overdose two years later.

When I wasn't in my room at Sierra Tucson, I spent most of my time sitting at a massive table with a giant ashtray for a centerpiece. I did my best to avoid conversing with the other residents. When I couldn't avoid it, the conversation generally went like this.

Some stranger would sit down and start smoking nearby.

"Hey, what are you in for?" they'd ask me.

"Heroin."

Usually, at the mention of that word, at least one or more other patients present and within earshot would start visibly twitching and scratching themselves.

"Yeah, cool. That's nothing. Let me tell you *my* story . . ."

Most of the people I met there had multiple addictions and personalities so complex that they defied all of my preconceived notions. They were a strange collection of individuals from all walks of life; it was just like *One Flew over the Cuckoo's Nest*, and like Jack Nicholson's character, I was convinced that I was the least fucked up of all of them. I was operating under the impression that I knew what I was doing when I was doing it, no matter what it was, while these people didn't seem to know what they were doing at any moment ever and had no idea of what they'd done to get here.

After another three or four days, that was it; I decided, *FUCK THIS*. I was sick of rehab on every level, from the staff encouraging me into group sharing and whatever might come from that to the too-fast friends I met while smoking that wanted to meet up on the outside to score drugs together when they got out in a few weeks.

When it came down to it, I wasn't at all prepared to surrender in any way, shape, or form. I was in the middle of the desert, it was fucking hot, and I saw no productive way to spend my next twenty-two days there. I told the head nurse that I needed to check out immediately, and she did everything she could to stop me. The founder of the place even came down to talk me into staying.

He was the type of New Age cowboy that can only exist in the American Southwest: he wore a ten-gallon hat and lots of turquoise jewelry and cowboy boots, and spoke at length about his personal journey to sobriety. He was commanding and insisted that I hadn't yet begun to do the *real*

work. He wasn't wrong, but I didn't give a shit—nor did I care to buy into his road to cleaning up whatsoever.

"*Look,*" I said, just pissed. "You can't keep me here, man. *You can't.* So give me a phone and get me my stuff, because I'm leaving. I'm leaving right now."

"You are making a big mistake," he said. "You are giving in. You are being weak, you need to think about this. Just come to a meeting with me."

"I am not going anywhere with you," I said. "That is not happening. Thank you very much for your help. But fuck that, I am out of here."

I ordered myself a stretch limo to take me to the airport, as the owner continued to try to talk me into staying until the moment I got inside. I lowered the window and looked him in the eye.

"I can't stop you but you are making a big mistake," he said.

"*See ya.*"

A few miles down the road I saw a liquor store.

"Pull over," I told the driver.

I bought a liter of Stoli. I opened it and threw the cap out the window. My anger at what I'd just been through grew as I progressed through the bottle on the way to the airport. I was insulted that my circle had thought that the ridiculous circus they'd sent me to would teach me now to control myself better than I already knew how. It was rude. I can't imagine what my limo driver was thinking that afternoon: he'd picked me up from rehab and watched me down half a liter of vodka in under an hour.

At the airport, while I waited for my plane, I called a high-end heroin dealer who was a friend of Mark Mansfield and Matt Cassel from high school. I made arrangements to meet up with him the moment I landed; I knew that the first hit of heroin after a detox would be the finest, so I intended for it to be of the best quality. After I'd copped, I went home, I got high, and then I called my manager, Doug Goldstein.

"Hello?"

"Hey, Doug, it's Slash," I said. "I'm baaaaaack." And then I hung up.

I've always had to do things my way

again and everything was fine. I also started partying by myself again after she went to bed. She had no idea that I'd just kicked or been to rehab. The thing was, because detox had been forced, I refused to get clean . . . though I knew I had to. I didn't intend to get back into heroin—I just wasn't going to kick it on their terms.

I planned a trip for Megan and me to Hawaii, and I got myself enough dope to allow me to take my use to a certain point, after which I'd kick on *my* terms. She and I checked in to a villa on Kauai, and the moment we got there, I started the detoxing process. I was feverish, sweaty, jittery, and altogether miserable. I told Megan that I had the flu and she believed me; she was happy enough to go shopping and sightsee on her own.

I didn't expect this kick to be as bad as it was, because I thought I'd gotten through the worst of it back in Tucson. Well . . . I hadn't; it wasn't easy at all. I hoped that I could drink it off, but I couldn't: everything tasted bad and everything felt bad. The symptoms were *way* more violent than usual: the dry heaves, the stomach cramps, the profuse sweating, the anxiety, and the creepy-crawling sensations were such horrible unpleasant company. I couldn't watch TV, I couldn't relax, I couldn't eat, I couldn't sleep. I'm sure Megan purposely stayed away most of the time.

Suffice to say, I was miserable. I was in that state for a week or so while Megan and I just chilled in Kauai. The thing is, for as much effort as I'd put into getting drugs to feed my habit, every time I'd kicked, I never invested the necessary time to obtain the appropriate medicine to ease the process. It always seemed like a pain in the ass to get a bunch of prescriptions from my doctor; it always seemed like too much planning before the day that I decided to do it. Besides, I always have to do everything the hard way, so it had always been cold turkey for me.

After a week I got to the point where I could move around and I finally

started feeling better. I could see that I was almost out of the woods; and I started to make plans with Megan to do the usual things tourists do in Hawaii. At the same time, I also got the wise idea to call my dealer and have him FedEx me some smack.

All in all this was a really dumb plan, because at that point I was halfway through the detox process; I would have made it if I'd been able to hold on for a few more days. But I refused to, plain and simple. In any case, my dealer could only send me a finite amount, so it was no more than a short-term solution. Looking back, I must say that it was a particularly stupid decision.

The dealer in question was the most high-end of the guys that sold me heroin; and he convinced me that my yearning could be fulfilled safely, via first-class mail, with very little chance of being caught.

I agreed to it, and the moment after I did, I remembered something: Mark, the guy from Faster Pussycat, the guy we'd duct-taped and sent to the lobby in the elevator, had recently been busted for having someone send him drugs through the mail. What the fuck was I *thinking*?

The next morning I was all jumpy, as junkies will be, anticipating the arrival of drugs. I still worried that I'd be busted picking them up. I weighed the pros and cons back and forth all morning until the phone rang.

"Hello, sir, this is the front desk; you have a package here."

"Huh?" I said. "I have a *package*? I'm not expecting a package."

"Yes, sir, you have a package from the mainland. I believe it was sent from Los Angeles, California."

I decided to take extra precautions; I took the service elevator to the first floor. It let me out in a concealed corner where I could sneak into the lobby maintaining a sniper's perspective. Nobody in the area seemed obviously suspicious, but I wasn't sure whether some of the hangers-about were cops or not.

I was sure, however, that whatever it was that I was wearing was totally unpresentable. I slunk up to the desk, from the alley by the service elevator, and just went for it, keeping one eye peeled, so to speak.

"You know, I got a phone call saying that someone sent me a package," I said, to the entirely innocent-looking-but-maybe-she-knows-about-this-thing girl at the front desk. "It's totally funny because I'm not expecting anything at all." I smiled . . . at least I think I did.

She fetched the package, which turned out to be an envelope full of CDs hiding the dope. When she put it down on the counter in front of me, I froze; I looked at it but didn't touch it.

"Here's your package, sir."

"Is this it?" I asked. "That's so crazy, I wasn't expecting anything." I looked all around the lobby, my eyes prying the corners, searching for cops or feds moving in for the kill. "That's really odd, I'm totally surprised. I did not expect to get a package sent to me here at all."

"Well, this package arrived here for you this morning, sir." She looked at me oddly and held out a pen. "Will you sign here, please?"

I stared at the slip of paper sitting on the counter between us. I realized that if I was being set up, if there was any level of law enforcement watching this transaction, it would be the end of me, and that once I signed this paper, they'd have all that they'd need. I looked up at the girl, I looked down at the paper. I looked all around again, too obviously. I didn't do anything for what became a very pregnant moment. Then I thought, *Fuck it*; I signed for it, I said thank you to her, and I ducked into the service elevator and hurried back to my room.

Megan was still out somewhere at the time, but when she got back I was high, I was happy, and the rest of our trip was *wonderful*. Call me what you will, but that vacation took a one-eighty degree turn for the better once I got my meds. Megan and I started doing stuff, we went shopping, I rented a Jeep, and we toured some of the sights.

From Hawaii, Megan and I flew out to Chicago to spend Thanksgiving with her mother, whom I was meeting for the first time. I finished the last of my smack in the hotel in Hawaii, and by the time we got to Chicago, I was starting to experience the typical junkie itchy twitchy withdrawal. I only knew a few people in Chicago, and I ran into one of them at the Smart Bar our first night there. This guy was one of the engineers who'd set up our rehearsal rig, and though he didn't have a line on heroin, he always had tons of coke, so he hooked me up with a pile of it. When I got back to Megan's mother's house, I started shooting it in an effort to get myself straight.

Megan had no idea, but I could tell that her mom knew that something wasn't quite right with me; I'm just not sure whether she knew exactly what it was. It was tough to keep my whole scene under wraps that holiday sea-

son because she and her mom lived in pretty close quarters. Their bedrooms were divided by a shared closet; so if the sliding doors on both sides were open, you could walk from one room into the other. At night, when I was watching TV and shooting coke after Megan fell asleep, I'd start tripping out, convinced that her mom was watching me from the other side of that weird divider. This went on for a few nights. I don't know what I was thinking; I was shooting coke in her twin bed, between Megan's body and the wall. It was ridiculous.

When Thanksgiving Day arrived, I took a shower and got ready to meet the family and friends; and I noticed as I walked down the stairs that somehow heroin had been cleaned from my system—it defies common logic, but my only explanation is that the coke had inexplicably taken the edge off on a very intrinsic level. I was out of my mind the whole time I was over there, regardless, and that Thanksgiving dinner was one of the most uncomfortable holiday meals I've ever had, but it did have its moments. We had plenty to drink and we had some good times, and then Megan and I flew back to L.A. and at that point I was clean(ish)—or so: no drugs, and very little booze. At least for a while.

Before I knew it Christmas was around the corner and Megan started planning a lavish party: she was *way* into the decorations, she bought a fondue maker, and she invited all of our friends to her winter wonderland. It was the most bizarre thing I had been involved with for a long time, and the fact that I was straight made that feeling pretty hard to ignore. The day before the party, she came home with about $400 worth of useless garbage that she'd bought at the market to decorate the house. That was my breaking point.

I watched her decorate our place, thinking all the while, *I don't even know who the fuck you are.* We had the Christmas party, we had our friends over; and as soon as they'd gone, I set about telling Megan that she had to go as well. It wasn't cool, and it was pretty explicit; I flipped on her for going to the market but that wasn't the real issue: I was done with her, cut-and-dried, and I needed her to vacate the premises as soon as possible. It didn't matter to me how she'd gotten there, it just had to stop. It had to end immediately. It went horribly: I looked her in the eye and said, "Go away." And she went . . . her friend Karen, who hated me anyway, showed up and packed her up.

Looking back, once I was sober, I didn't see Megan the same way at all. She was sweet, she was fine . . . but she was just *there*. Suddenly she was like a piece of furniture that I didn't remember buying and I began to ask myself, each and every day, what we had in common. With nothing to cloud my vision, it felt like she was a stranger. I also didn't have time for the time-consuming responsibilities and distractions of a relationship, so it wasn't her so much as it was me. I was getting back to my old self; I was getting into work mode. All I kept thinking when I looked at her was, *What are you doing here? You've got to go. I've got shit to do. We've got a fucking record to make.* I believe I said as much to her. I treated her harshly, especially for me, because that's not my style. But I just couldn't take it anymore, and that's the last that I ever saw of her. I've always had to do things my way; I've gotten high my way, I've gotten clean my way, I've been in and out of relationships my way. I've taken myself to the edges of life my way. And I'm still here. Whether or not I deserve to be is another story.

10
chapter

When we started this band, our future depended on our uncompromising unity; our attitude fostered a loyal camaraderie among us the likes of which is very rare. Success fragmented that bond by giving us everything we wanted and a lot we didn't need—all at once. We'd made it in the conventional sense; and that meant money and money meant freedom. We were free to splinter off on our own trips. We went so far that we almost forgot what it was like to be in the same room; we almost forgot how we had earned that freedom in the first place.

In the end we found it again, just in time . . . but there were losses and growing pains we could not avoid. To get back to where we started, we had to reintroduce ourselves; we had to trim the fat. We had to rediscover Guns N' Roses. It had only been a few years, but it felt like we'd forgotten how fun it used to be to be us. You'd be surprised how quickly you forget what's important when you've suddenly got everything you'd never thought you'd have.

Once I had dropped the smack again, once Megan was gone, and once I started hanging more with Duff, listening to music, drinking, and doing the occasional line, it all came together. It was all no big deal; I'd transitioned out of smack like I had before and into drinking and I was ready to do some work again. And that was good.

Izzy hadn't come back from Indiana yet—he wasn't ready for the temptation of L.A.—so it was Duff and I who started going back down to Mates to write. We hoped to get the ball rolling by way of our example, by maintaining a regular schedule during which we'd write music. We were feeling out the foundation of a few new songs and doing some work on some preexisting ones. As in Chicago, our goal was to get Izzy and Axl back in the room with us, but we knew that before we could do that, we needed to deal with Steven. Our man Steve had built himself up a pretty pesky drug habit and was in full denial. Steve never grew out of those junior high rock-and-roll fantasies, even when the threat of losing them was staring him in the face, so we had our work cut out for us. Duff and I split our time between jamming at Mates and monitoring Steven, who conveniently lived down the street from Duff, but was as sneaky as could be about his consumption. When we were in Chicago, everyone had started to see signs that he was becoming a little bit neurotic and frail, but back in L.A. in my strung-out haze, I hadn't registered how bad off he was.

At this point I could now see that his mental and physical health had become a bit questionable. Under the circumstances it was forgivable, but I think somewhere along the line we'd forgotten that Steven was the type who needed somebody to look out for him all the time. He was like a curious kid you couldn't leave alone in the house, whereas the rest of us were the kind of people who had a sustainable way of doing things. You could do whatever you wanted to yourself, but you had to carry your own weight; you could make your own mistakes, but you had to deal with the repercussions. That was the way it worked with us.

Until our return from the *Appetite* tour, the years leading up to this had been casual fun drug-wise, more like recreational consumption. None of it

had any real baggage or so we thought, but at this point it had taken its toll. Once I saw how dark it was getting, I pulled myself out. Steve didn't have the wherewithal to see it as clearly or take steps to change it. He was in such denial, but it was tough for any of us to come down on him, even for Duff, who still did coke. Steven just didn't have all his faculties and couldn't maintain a line between his excesses and his productivity.

We did what we had to do to get him back on track, but you couldn't tell Steven anything. He would argue and then throw it back in your face. (In fact, to this day he is still arguing about why he got kicked out of the band.) Sometimes I'd think that I'd gotten him to a place where he could understand . . . then he'd pull a stunt like not showing up for a rehearsal. It was impossible to reason with him—with anyone, I guess, in that state of mind. And, really, emotionally Steven wasn't much older than a third grader, a sixth grader tops.

Now, trying to curtail Steve's abuse was an awkward situation, to say the least: here I was, the pot calling the kettle black, me, Mr. Recently Clean, who still drank, laying down the law to Steven. I was doing nothing more than criticizing my mirror image from the other side of the mirror. I knew there was some hypocrisy involved, but I didn't care—the difference between Steve and me, no matter what our chemical diet consisted of, was that I was aware of my limitations. Unfortunately he wasn't, and Guns N' Roses needed to move forward at all costs.

Like Izzy and myself, Steven had slipped and lost his footing in a pile of cocaine and heroin, but unlike us, he couldn't regain his balance. We'd go over to his place in the afternoon to try to get him to come to rehearsal and his eyes told us all we needed to know: they'd be tiny black pin dots that were way too easy to see against the blue iris of his eyes. He'd sit there insisting that he wasn't on smack, that he was just drinking and doing a bit of cocaine, but we knew differently. It didn't help his cause that Duff and I always found his stash; he generally kept it either behind the toilet or behind his bed. There was no one else keeping tabs on him but us; he'd had a girl-friend but they'd split up, so he was living alone as he went off the deep end. We made a number of attempts at rehab, and we did get him to check in to Exodus more than once. Every time he did, though, we'd get a call that he'd scaled the wall or run off out some back door. Of course whenever he

did that, he'd be predictably irretrievable for the next few days. It must be some kind of record: in total, during this period, Steven escaped rehab twenty-two times. Duff and I stuck by him, but we knew that it was a matter of time before he wore down whatever goodwill the rest of the band had toward him.

Meanwhile, somehow Axl and I had become civil again and were both excited about getting to work on a new record—I guess it was fishing season again. Axl knew I'd succeeded in getting off heroin, and was committed to staying off it. After so many false starts, Axl, Duff, and I started to regain our sense of unity and Izzy wasn't too far behind. We were all glad to see him when he showed up at Mates. He wasn't there every day, maybe two days on one day off, but we worked around all that. Izzy is just so easy to get along with.

He jammed with Duff, Steven, and me on a few new songs, and in those instants the old energy came back and it all became very exciting and electric.

We all gathered at my house, and wrote more than half of both *Illusions* albums on acoustics, literally in two nights. We started off by going through the stuff we had from the old days that we'd never done anything with. We reintroduced "Back Off Bitch" and "Don't Cry"; we had "The Garden," a song that Axl and Izzy wrote with West Arkeen. "Estranged" was a song that Axl had been working out on piano for a long time—he'd been playing the same parts over and over in Chicago and afterward; it was clear that it was working itself out in his head. I had started writing guitar parts for it back in Chicago, so it came together in no time once we focused on it.

"November Rain" had been ready to go on *Appetite for Destruction*, but since we already had "Sweet Child o' Mine," the majority of us agreed that we didn't need another ballad. Besides, the original demo of that song was eighteen minutes long give or take, and none of us cared to conquer it in the studio at that point. It had been a song that Axl had tinkered with for years, whenever there was a piano present; it had been around forever, and it was finally getting its due. Axl had been annoyed when Tom Zutaut suggested that we hold it until the next album, because that song meant a lot to him. He let it go, though he resented that decision for years.

We'd had the rough framework for "Civil War" kicking around since

that first tour of Australia; I wrote the instrumentals, and Axl had written and revised the lyrics for it several times, but everything fell into place when we brought it out again. "You Could Be Mine" was another track that wasn't new: it was written during the *Appetite* sessions and I always felt that it should have been on that album, because it is more reminiscent of that time than anything else on the *Use Your Illusion* albums.

We had spun our wheels for a long time, but over that couple of nights at the Walnut House, the creativity at the base of our band chemistry came back to us: Izzy and I both brought out a few rough ideas, and before we knew it, we'd all contributed to developing them into complete songs. I had a track called "Bad Apples" that was fresh from Chicago, along with "Get in the Ring," which Duff had written the music for. Everyone jumped on those right away, as well as a long, heavy guitar-riff mantra I wrote when living with Izzy that evolved into the song "Coma." The song was eight minutes long; it was just a repeating pattern that got increasingly mathematical and involved in its precision as it progressed. Axl loved it but at first it was the one song that he couldn't come up with the lyrics for. He was very proud of his gift for lyrics, so he was pretty frustrated by it . . . until one night months later when the words just came to him. We finished another epic number I'd begun with Izzy called "Locomotive." And there was "Dead Horse," a tune which Axl had done the guitar and lyrics for years earlier before we'd ever met. Duff brought in "So Fine," complete with music and lyrics. Before long, we realized that we had more than enough songs for an album. In a few sessions, we managed to pull all of that material together quickly and relatively painlessly.

I still had no idea why it had taken us this long, but it was clear that as soon as we took a second, put the bullshit aside, and got together without animosity, we fell naturally right back into the band vibe.

The thing that's funny about the *Illusion* records is that aside from a couple of songs there are no really dramatic arrangements on them at all, because we threw them together real quick. The ones I brought in, like "Locomotive" and "Coma," were fully arranged from the start when Axl wrote lyrics to them. With the exception of the piano epics, the rest of the songs were really simple and didn't need much working out. We didn't spend afternoons debating how many times a bridge was needed in a song or

coming up with tricky chords for a breakdown. Once we got together again, we were in such a good mind frame as a band, just hanging out together for the first time in quite a while. We were all getting along really well, so it was all fun again.

Of course nothing's perfect. The funny thing is that whenever everything was going well, Axl always made it interesting. One of the sticky spots in the re-formation was that once we got into full gear, Axl wanted to add keyboards to our sound. He wanted to hire Dizzy Reed, the keyboardist for the Wild, the generic L.A. band who had practiced next door to us in our dingy storage unit studio at Sunset and Gardner. Dizzy was a nice guy; I just didn't see any reason why we needed a keyboard player in Guns. I was *adamantly* against it and felt that it diluted the sound of what was already a great rock-and-roll band. Piano or electric is cool, but I'm old-school and I was never into phony synthesizer sounds.

Axl, on the other hand, felt passionate about the artistic evolution the band needed to make. Our conversations weren't too heated because we were making an effort . . . so sometimes we'd crack jokes about it, and he knew the rest of us didn't want to do it. All the same, as adamantly as I was against it, he was for it.

So in the spirit of keeping things happy, I finally and reluctantly gave in and so did the other guys. It wasn't worth going backward. Dizzy became a hired gun and we proceeded to pick on him relentlessly. He was like the Ronnie Wood of Guns N' Roses.

That was really the only creative glitch. Writing the songs for *Illusions* felt like the way I'd always pictured an early Stones session to be back in the day; just hanging out up in a house in the Hollywood Hills working out ideas together. It was good to have Izzy, Axl, Duff, and me in the same room again. And more or less sober. I mean, I always had my cocktail, but I wasn't into heavy tipping-the-bottle-style drinking. It was sad, though, that Steven wasn't really there for any of it.

As I feared, he had become the odd man out. At rehearsals, Duff and I had the tedious job of dealing with him. While Axl was aware of the situation, he wasn't obligated to watch over Steven 24/7 like we were. And as for Izzy, he would have nothing to do with it at all. Steven was becoming a heavier burden every day.

I couldn't deny the fact that kicking Steven out of Guns N' Roses for drug abuse was kind of ridiculous and excessively harsh.

WHEN WE STARTED REHEARSING THE material that's when Steven's house of cards came crashing down. He was utterly useless when put to the test: most of the time he'd fade away from the proper time signature somewhere in the middle of a song or just forget where he was altogether. He was just incapable of locking in with Duff or me like he used to do. It was pretty dire; something had to be done. The band finally had momentum; we'd finally written new stuff and we needed to start recording and not stagnate. We couldn't have it be an undertaking just to get through a song at rehearsal.

That's not to say we weren't really patient with Steven. We tried everything we could think of, though we probably should've taken further action . . . though I'm not sure what that could have been. We'd gone so far as to bring in people like Bob Timmons, the rehab specialist who had helped clean up Mötley Crüe, and others who were experienced in dealing with extreme cases. Their efforts were futile.

We got an offer to play Farm Aid in Indiana on April 7, 1990. That gig got us fired up in the same way that those gigs with the Stones had done for us not too long before. These kind of jump starts would kick the band into gear and get it all flowing again because when the band was working, we fired on every cylinder.

We put together a few songs just for the show; we worked up a cover of the U.K. Subs' classic "Down on the Farm" and we fine-tuned "Civil War." I was *really* excited to get out there and play together again, but things went south quickly. The second we walked out onstage, Steven took a run up to the drum riser, which is a pretty big platform that's hard to miss, and took flight. I assume he was planning on landing next to his kit, but his depth perception and reflexes were clearly impaired, so he ended up landing about four feet short. I watched it as if it were happening in slow motion. . . . It was more than embarrassing. Steven hobbled through the show, and our performance was dodgy at best, though well received by the Farm Aid crowd. We all knew why we weren't happy: the timing was all over the place. There's a certain groove and rhythm that Guns and Steven had, and when that went missing the band lost its confidence because we had to use guess-work. That's not what the band was ever about—it was based on a ton of cocksureness.

There couldn't have been a better way for Steven to reveal to us that he'd been lying about being clean—even a full confession wouldn't have come off as honestly as his playing at that show. It was obvious we had a real problem. He was using, and had probably been using in his room up until the minute before leaving for the venue. Afterward, he was still in denial, and as open and social as ever. It was so awkward and uncomfort-able talking to a guy who you know in his mind is thinking the exact opposite of what he's saying. His whole presentation was drowned in bullshit.

At this point the truth was that if his playing had been fine, I don't think anyone would have cared what he was doing to himself—at least I wouldn't have. If you can handle both the music and the drugs, more power to you. We weren't really concerned for Steven's health as much as we were pissed off that his addiction was handicapping his performance, and therefore the rest of us. Since the bass and drums are the foundation of any rock band, the situation was very disconcerting all around.

Farm Aid was the last show we ever played with him. When we got back to L.A., Steven got even worse—I don't know, maybe because he knew the end was near, or maybe because heroin is that shrewd of a devil.

There were a few more rehab stints, but they were short-lived, maybe twenty-four to forty-eight hours at a time. The last straw came when we were asked to donate a track to a charity album called "Nobody's Child," which benefited Romanian children orphaned during the Romanian revolution in 1989. We thought it'd be a great forum for "Civil War." By then we were completely alienated from Steven. In that session, there was us and there was him. After it was finished, before Mike Clink could mix it, he found that he had to cut and paste the whole drum track together. These were the days before digital recording, so Mike was working on tape and it took him hours and hours in the editing bay to get the song to function timingwise.

The writing was on the wall, and things quickly came to a head. Axl's patience as far as Steve went was long gone, so we had the inevitable get-together to discuss the situation; with Alan's support, Axl insisted that we give Steven a written ultimatum. It was a contract that Steve was forced to sign, that at best we hoped would scare him sober and at worst would orchestrate his departure from the band. The paperwork was clear; it said that if Steven showed up high to recording sessions, he'd be fined. If he did this three times, he'd be fired, or something along those lines. Steven signed it, he agreed to all of the terms, and like anyone caught in the throes of smack, he ignored all of the promises he made and continued the way he had been. He made one effort—he tried Buprinex, but he was too weak to kick the smack altogether.

In my eyes, it seemed to me that Axl didn't like Steven. Steven had an unbridled enthusiasm for drums and rock and roll and life in general. He was hyper and totally fun to be around. But he was also blatantly honest and outspoken about his opinions to Axl or anyone else in the band. Oftentimes his opinion was in Axl's face, which wasn't the way that Axl operated. Steven was unfiltered, saying exactly what he felt and he didn't pussyfoot around. Duff and I were used to it and took Steven's comments with a grain of salt, so we could tune him out. But Axl was more sensitive than we were, which Duff and I also understood. With Axl, I didn't want to slow things down at a rehearsal or a studio by confronting him with his lateness or whatever. But Steven would make a comment or get in his face and that *never*

worked. But Steven could never be calculated; whatever he blurted out was always true; it was an innocent side effect of his personality. Unfortunately, up against Axl's hyperemotional sensitivity level, I'm sure Steven offended Axl more often than not without even knowing it. I can see how Steven inadvertently pushed Axl's buttons; but that said, I don't think Axl ever really gave Steven his just credit for what he brought to Guns musically, which was a dynamic that I think hurt Steven. But what do I know? There is probably much more to it than that, none of which I can speak to.

Axl had made his feelings about Steven clear back in preproduction for *Appetite*. When were close to wrapping the album, it came time to discuss writing credits and publishing on the songs. We talked about it standing onstage at Burbank Studios, and someone proposed that as a band we should split the royalties evenly five ways—20 percent each.

Axl scowled. "There's no *way* Steven gets twenty percent, the same as I do. Uh-uh," he said. "I want twenty-five percent and Steven gets fifteen. He's a drummer. He doesn't contribute to the writing as equally as the rest of us." That was the compromise we agreed to: Axl got 25 percent; me, Izzy, and Duff 20 percent; and Steven 15 percent. I think Steven was permanently scarred by that.

I'm not sure of the exact timetable, but it didn't take long for Steven to violate the terms of the sobriety contract we handed him, and once he did, he was done for. It wasn't easy for me to allow, because as I've said, the simple truth is that Steven never had the kind of strength to give that stuff up easily—if he'll ever give it up at all. But at that point, everyone had tried to help him—girlfriends, friends, management experts—nothing resonated with him enough to work on the problem. At this point in particular, Steven was a Catch-22, because as much as I would have hung around long enough to get him together, if the band lost its momentum it might mean the end of us. We were too many variables and complex characters, and now that we were all getting along, the window of opportunity was open— but it probably wouldn't stay that way for long. I couldn't deny the fact that kicking Steven out of Guns N' Roses for drug abuse was kind of ridiculous and excessively harsh. It was also so hypocritical. Think about it, it sounds like a joke: "He got kicked out of Guns N' Roses for *drugs*? Are you *kidding*? How does that happen?"

All I remember is that the next time I saw Steve was in court, because he sued us, which seemed asinine. He was in such bad shape that I knew what he was doing when he headed to the bathroom in the middle of the proceedings. He sued us for a couple million bucks for a glitch in the execution of his sobriety contract. He needed to have an attorney present when he signed it, and he hadn't had one. Of course, thanks to our attorneys, we didn't know this. I was shocked when I found out that Steven won his lawsuit and we had to pay him two million bucks.

As difficult as it was, at least it was over. Now it was time to find a new drummer.

———◆◆◆———

THAT ARDUOUS TASK FELL TO DUFF AND Izzy and me. We set up shop near Alan Niven's office in Redondo Beach, in a little rehearsal studio, where I realized after the very first day of auditions how fucking difficult it was going to be. In the back of my mind I thought, "*Sure, anybody can play drums.*" Right . . . the three of us thought that finding a replacement would be easy considering that our songs were all pretty straight-ahead 4/4 rock rhythms with few fancy time changes—how hard could that be? After all, if we'd pulled it off with Fred Curry when Steven was injured, the prospects looked good. After a few horrible days of trying to play with uselessly inappropriate candidates, though, we realized the depth of our naïveté. The way a drummer plays involves such a personal feel for the rhythm and inflections on the beat that affect the entire vibe of the song—and the entire band for which he keeps time.

We ditched Redondo Beach and returned to Mates to undertake a more thorough search. We tried out Martin Chambers from the Pretenders, who is a great drummer and a great guy, but we should have known that it wasn't going to work out the minute he walked in with that huge octopus drum kit he used with the Pretenders. It was more, for want of a better word, *fantastic* than your average drum kit. That thing had round poles that came over the top of it with cymbals hanging from them—it was just ridiculous. He was setting it all up while Duff tuned up and got ready to play with him for a bit; Duff was the front line. He and the drum-

mer had to click, first of all—if they didn't, there was no point in Izzy or me even picking up a guitar.

I was in the bathroom sitting on the toilet, reading a magazine, when Martin and Duff started playing, and as I listened through the door, I thought, *Oh boy.* I was making something more appealing than what I was hearing at that moment, which just goes to show that putting great players in the same room doesn't mean that they will sound great together. Making great music is much more complicated; it's about chemistry and the commingling of the players' stylistic ticks. It's nowhere near as simple as the sum of the parts; it's more like building Frankenstein's monster: you need ingenuity . . . and lightning.

When I came out of the bathroom, Duff was still playing but he shot me a look that said it all, so needless to say, Martin didn't work out. We were fucked, because at the time, Martin was our best bet at the end of a short list that we'd already exhausted. To Steven's credit, and unbeknownst to most, the feel and energy of *Appetite* was largely due to him. He had an inimitable style of drumming that couldn't really be replaced, an almost adolescent levity that gave the band its spark.

All at once the momentum we'd built over the last few months came to a standstill and although I didn't show it, I was panicked. I thought, *This is it, we're done.* I was convinced that Guns N' Roses would break up because we couldn't find a drummer. And I was worried about what I would do with myself if we did.

<hr/>

DURING THIS TIME DUFF AND I WERE pretty inseparable. He had split up with Mandy, so we'd go out when the band wasn't working—more often than not, to Bordello's, a club owned by former Cathouse founder Riki Rachtman. That place was great, there was a little jam room in the back where a blues band would get up and play, and I would usually end up sitting in on a few songs. That place was so much fun—we'd just go there and drink and jam. But the truth is, even if you're famous and everyone loves you and this and that, after a while that scene or any scene, to me at least, becomes sort of miserable, dull, and monotonous.

After you've done it twice, maybe three times, it is nothing but boring. Even to this day, the Hollywood rock-club scene does nothing for me; it's all there, and as much as times and styles have changed, it's all still the same. If you've just played a gig and you need to blow off some steam, it's great, but if you're just hanging around town, it's like being in some blown-out cliché: from the chicks on down, it's a cliché of what all the kids think life is going to be like if they become rock stars. It's not a mirage that I want to be a part of.

What I'm getting at is that generally I preferred to stay at home, drink all day, listen to records, and play guitar and write music. I wasn't reclusive in the way I'd been on smack, but in my mind, I had switched over to work mode, so going out and socializing was the last thing on my mind—I had committed to being productive and getting our band to the next level. On one of the nights that Duff coaxed me out to this place Peanuts to jam with this great little blues band, we ended up hanging out with this girl, Pilar, that he picked up. Pilar was a sexy Middle Eastern or Latin girl—I'm not sure which. She had a friend with her that I barely spoke to whose name was Renee. And Renee had this too-cool-for-school attitude; she held her head high, with this mightier-than-thou stance. She was really good-looking and she knew it, and that whole vibe locked me in like a tractor beam, because any girl that was going to fucking make my life difficult, any girl that was hard to get, was the girl to go for in my mind. In Lemmy Kilmister's infamous words, "The chase is better than the catch." Renee had *no* interest in what I did or any of the notoriety that came with it; she wasn't a rock chick by any stretch of the imagination.

She was a model and aspiring actress and very independent. Within a couple of weeks I had ditched the Walnut House and was living in her place full-time. She had a great spot that her dad, before he passed away, had bought for her down on Valley Vista—I think there was a dinette set, a bed, and a couch in the whole place. Here's how we spent our time: I'd get up in the morning and fucking lie on the floor and drink vodka and smoke cigarettes until she got up. She'd go do what she had to do that day and I'd do the same and that was our life. I watched a lot of cooking shows; *The Galloping Gourmet, Great Chefs of the East and West,* and The Food Network.

It was the start of a lifelong obsession with cooking shows, though to this day, I don't cook at all. At night we'd order out.

That was my home life. Meanwhile, we still had this quest for a drummer going on.

<center>———◆═◆═◆———</center>

ONCE WE'D EXHAUSTED ALL LOGICAL possibilities, I for one was not going to let the hunt for a drummer end the band. Duff, Izzy, and I racked our brains. We discussed the best drummers we'd seen lately, but nobody appropriate came to mind . . . until one night, I had an epiphany. I recalled seeing The Cult a few months before at the Universal Amphitheater and being mesmerized by their drummer. He was fucking amazing; I was standing at the soundboard and was completely captivated by his playing. I didn't pay attention to the rest of the band at all for the whole gig. His playing was extremely tight and his sound had enormous presence; it was big, bombastic, and delivered with intense authority. The moment I remembered him, I couldn't believe that I'd sat through so many shitty auditions without realizing that I knew just the right guy.

Mike Clink, our producer, had worked with Matt Sorum, the drummer in question, before, so I called him immediately and left him a message. A little later, I was a bit drunk, lying on my back, my head hanging upside down over the edge of Renee's bed, watching the phone on the floor and waiting for it to ring. Finally it did. I picked it up instantly.

"Hello?" Mike said, typically soft-spoken.

"Hey, it's Slash," I said. "So, hey, listen, do you know the drummer from The Cult? We need a drummer, and I saw this guy and he's great, and I'm trying to find out if he's available."

"Well, I don't know," Mike said. "Let me make a phone call."

"Okay, yeah."

The phone rang again in the early evening. "Slash," Mike said. "Here's what I found out. He's possibly available. Do you have a pen? I have his number."

I hadn't moved much that day; I was waiting for this call, focused on it, because I knew this was right. I wrote the number on the sheets, or on the wall or on my hand, I'm not sure which.

I dialed and waited. Matt picked up.

"Hello."

"Hey, Matt, is it? This is Slash," I said. "I'm from Guns N' Roses and we need a drummer. Are you interested?"

Two days later Matt came in to rehearse, and within the course of two or three songs, Duff, Izzy, and I realized that we'd found our man. We'd found ourselves a player with an innate feel all his own, both in step with the rest of us and individually stylized. He had the power, the chops, and the vibe to fill the void—and add to what the band's sound was about to become.

I think Duff and I took Matt out to ask him if he wanted to join—I can't remember where—probably the Rainbow—but we took him out and drank and did some blow, that kind of thing. He fit right in. He was pysched; it was the situation that every touring musician dreams of. There's no easier gig to walk into for a real rock-and-roll player. After hanging out with Duff and me, it was clear that Matt thought Guns was the biggest band on the face of the planet as well as a crew of relentless partiers. The pay was good and there were no rules, except for one: all you had to do was play well.

But Matt had to learn a hell of a lot of stuff pretty fast. We had the demos of thirty-six songs that we planned to record for the albums. Since those tapes weren't really enough to go on, Duff, Izzy, and I had to teach him everything in a reasonably short amount of time, and because of that, the rest of us had to become very professional very quickly. There was a lot of remorse, at least on my part and surely the other guys', about letting Steven go; but when Matt came into it, he brought new life to the proceedings. There was a light at the end of the tunnel when it looked like it might go dark forever.

<hr />

A FEW OTHER THINGS WERE GOING ON during this period as Guns geared up to reemerge—we made a few appearances that are worthy of note. One of them was the night that Duff and I accepted our American Music Award on behalf of the band for Best Rock Album. I had never paid attention to the Grammys or the AMAs or any of that stuff; I never watched those shows on TV or took an active interest in any of it. Duff and I went anyway—mostly for the drinks—and

we really had no concept of the fact that being nominated meant you might actually *win* something, and if you did win you were expected to get onstage and *say* something—to the crowd as well as the TV audience at home.

At this point, I was dating Renee and Duff was with Pilar, and the AMAs were something to take the girls to. All they had to serve was wine, and we had at least eight big cups a piece. The whole thing was pretty boring and stiff. We're sitting there talking when all of a sudden Guns N' Roses was called for *Appetite* winning Best Rock Album. We were dumbfounded. The spotlight shot over our seats and we staggered up there. Once I realized we'd won, I wanted to thank all the different people, so I thanked Zutaut, Niven, all those people at Geffen all the while dropping countless *fucks* caused by the wine and my nervousness. I had no idea what the protocol was at these ceremonies. Anyway, I was a few names in when they cut the mike. I kept talking for a second, until I realized it'd been shut off. We were escorted back to do pictures and have the press conference. I was buzzed, I was having a good time and gave them all the middle finger.

The next day, this AMA thing was all I heard about. I was overwhelmed by the controversy because to this day the incident still doesn't mean that much to me. I was, however, responsible for the seven-second delay being instituted at all future live award ceremonies; plus Dick Clark wouldn't speak to me for eight years. I wasn't allowed at the AMAs until only a year or so ago when I was asked to present some award.

It wasn't intentional but nonetheless it sent a message: the Guns spirit was alive and well.

———⚬✴⚬———

BACK AT THE STUDIO, WE HAD THIRTY-six songs, which was more than enough to fill a double album. I wanted to choose the twelve best of the thirty-six and hone them down to perfection, but I let it go because as long as we were moving forward, I was happy. Axl wanted to record all thirty-six and go the double-album route. He didn't want to sit on these tunes. I understood that: many of them

were old by this point—they'd been held over from our last album, and some were even older. Also, there was a whole bunch of new songs that represented where we were at that moment in time. It might be retrospect talking, but the general consensus was that we were cleaning the slate, getting out everything we had. As a whole, these songs were representative of something important: the band's past and present. It had been such an incredible journey and the only way to express it was all in this body of material.

Matt was great; he was tight with Duff and me; Izzy was around, but not like he used to be. Not only was he 100 percent dead sober, he was also very much anti-alcohol and antidrugs at that point. When Izzy met Matt they got along fine, but it was under the condition that the decision had already been made: it was all okay, but I think Izzy felt dictated to—and he *hated* that. Izzy was pretty fragile from the time he came back to the band until the day he left, and as I look back, this whole shift probably didn't sit entirely well with him. When we had rehearsal we were all there as a band and it was cool, something was off. Izzy wasn't happy . . . but he wasn't saying anything, and Axl had distanced himself from the day-to-day mechanics of the band so much that as long as we had a drummer and everyone was there and playing together, he thought we were cool and ready to move forward.

The first recording with Matt was "Knocking on Heaven's Door," for the *Days of Thunder* soundtrack (which also ended up on the *Illusions* albums). I remember doing the solo for it on my way somewhere and I used a '58 Gibson Explorer. It was an amazing take, I just ran in there with my girlfriend and some friends in tow, picked up the guitar, and really let the solo *sing*: I turned the tone down on the bass pickup, I locked in and let it *scream*. I really love the way that one came out—it was very emotional yet effortless.

"Knocking on Heaven's Door" was also the first song that we could listen to and get an idea of what the band sounded like with our new drummer. It came out great, but there was a definite difference in the overall feel of the new Guns from the old Guns. We had lost a little bit of the mayhem and punk rock, that raw chaotic, seat-of-the-pants feel.

Instead we sounded more epic and solid and huge. That was a good or a bad thing depending on who you asked. In my opinion, I was just happy to be moving ahead.

Next, we went in and Matt learned all thirty-six songs at breakneck speed, basically by playing them with us live because there was no other material to reference. We booked ourselves into A&M in Hollywood and recorded thirty-six songs in thirty-six days. Between takes, we'd go to Crazy Girls, the strip bar across the street, which I'm sorry to say is no longer there. At night we'd go out carousing, then show up the next afternoon and do it all again on a new song. It was a great thirty-six days, during which Duff and I realized that Matt was both an incredible drummer and our brand-new party buddy. Before the drug thing got out of hand and before the incident with Steven, there were some dark periods, but we'd come through that: we were now very functional alcoholics and occasional coke users. Actually, I doubt that it was occasional—Matt and Duff did a lot of blow. I didn't do as much, but it didn't matter because, like them, I'd built up my tolerance of everything to the point that we were all a perfectly productive, chemically driven, and very professional band.

Beverly Hills High should be proud: Slash onstage with Lenny Kravitz.

a lot more, too, by this point. Duff and I ran into Iggy Pop during our down time and he asked us to play on *Brick by Brick*. We went down to meet him at the Rainbow, where we got into his car and listened to the demos, which was very cool. Iggy is Duff's ultimate hero and there was a little bit of history there on my end because of Bowie—he and my mom had gone to visit Iggy at the Cedars psych ward. We showed up in Hollywood and laid down some tracks with him: "Home Boy," "Pussy Power," and a song that Iggy and I cowrote, "My Baby Wants to Rock 'n' Roll." It was one of the most fun sessions I'd ever done. Not long after that, we also did the video with him for "Home Boy."

This was a real honor for us; it was another sign that Guns was getting back out on the scene and that we were being taken seriously as musicians. People wanted to see us plain and simple. At that point in 1990, *Appetite* and *Lies* had become huge commercial successes. This newfound attention also drew the spotlight to me as a guitar player, which took the form of a few calls to our management office. It was flattering to discover that other musicians had started to give me credit for being a fairly good guitar player.

One collaboration I did at the time was with Lenny Kravitz. I already knew him; he and I attended Beverly Hills High at the same time, and although I was in continuation while he was a regular student, we were the only two half-black half-white musicians in the school that I knew of. Duff and I were fans, and our favorite record of the moment was Lenny's debut, *Let Love Rule*. When we were introduced at some awards function, I was ecstatic when he asked me to play on his next record, *Mama Said*, which he was in the midst of writing. Shortly thereafter we met up in a little studio on Robertson in L.A. where I put a solo on "Fields of Joy." As I was warming up in the lounge that day, I played a funky guitar riff that I'd come up with recently but hadn't found a place for in any of the songs I was working on at the time with Guns. It was just another of my exercises at the time.

"Hey man, what is *that?*" Lenny asked

"I don't know . . . Just something," I said. "It's too funky for Guns, but I like it. It's cool."

"Yeah, man. Don't forget it. Bring that into the rehearsal room," he said. "Let's work on it. I'd like to write some lyrics to it."

When it came time to actually write and record the song, Lenny flew me out to New York. He lived in Manhattan but he'd set himself up in a studio across the river in Hoboken, New Jersey. It was where he'd recorded his debut album, and where he was doing the basic tracks for his next album. We took the train there from his apartment, and he played drums while I laid the guitar down for what became "Always on the Run." It was a lot of fun, very raw and stripped down, the way it should be done. There's not a lot going on on that track, but it sounded really good; he put the bass and vocals on later. The studio was like Lenny's castle; every instrument was in place—he could jump from guitar to bass to drums and get it all down as his inspiration dictated.

I had brought Renee with me on that trip and we were staying in midtown at a hotel close to Lenny's apartment and had spent the night before, a Saturday, carousing extensively. It was summertime, it was hot as hell, and once I got to Lenny's place that Sunday morning, I discovered that due to some outdated rule called the "blue law" on New York's books, no bars or liquor stores were open at all.

It wasn't exactly how I pictured this collaboration going down and it was about to be a problem. I remember hanging around Lenny's apartment waiting for him to get ready. The place looked like the world's biggest closet of vintage clothes had vomited all over the room: there were garments everywhere, covering every available surface. It was ten a.m., I was taking this whole scene in, and I was *craving* a drink.

"Hey man, do you have anything to drink?" I asked.

"No, man, I don't think so," Lenny said. "You want to smoke a joint?"

"That's cool. I could really use a drink, though," I said. "Can we stop by a bar or a liquor store on the way?"

"I don't know, man," he said. "I don't think so. That's all closed on Sunday."

"Oh yeah?" I said, getting a little bit nervous. "Do your neighbors have any booze? I need a drink, man."

Lenny did his best; he procured what seemed like a thimbleful of vodka from his neighbor. I downed it but it was like throwing a Band-Aid at a

gunshot wound. As we hopped on the PATH train to Hoboken, which is a trip of about twenty minutes, I began to experience alcohol detox: my hands shook, I was light-headed, irritable, and anxious. It wasn't some big mystery—I just needed a fucking drink, like *now*. My reserve of civility was equally dry.

"Hey Lenny, man, we have to find some vodka right away," I said. "I can't play unless I get a fucking drink."

Lenny could relate to a degree, I suppose: he needed his pot to create and write music—the only difference was that his body didn't malfunction if he didn't have it. Every bar on the way looked like they'd not been open since 1955. When we got to his studio, Lenny sent his people out in search of booze. I'm not sure how they got it, but they returned with some vodka around twelve, and once they did, we settled in. We recorded "Always on the Run" in under an hour; the raw, spontaneous energy of that track is right there in the final product.

<hr>

THE ACTUAL RECORDING OF THE GUITARS and vocals of the *Illusion* albums happened at the Record Plant in Los Angeles. This was a great time for me as a guitar player—we had so many songs and so many possibilities for sounds and techniques in our new material. I was really on top of my game at that point, easily coaxing out the sounds I wanted, all of it came to me so fluidly during those sessions. I had some cool guitars to call upon because, for first time in my life, I had the funds to assemble an arsenal of them.

At the time I had a 1958 Gibson Flying V, I had a 1958 Gibson Explorer, and a few Travis Beans, a few sorted acoustics—Martin, Gibson, Taylor, etc. I had this great Spanish flamenco-style acoustic and a couple of Dobros and a handful of vintage Les Pauls, plus my staple Les Paul replica with its Seymour Duncan pickups. I'd rented a load of guitars, but for most of the tracks I used a Les Paul. There were moments when I needed a Travis Bean, usually when I was doing extensive slides ("The Garden"), or a Dobro ("You Ain't the First"), as well as when I needed to use a tremolo bar ("You Could Be Mine"). It was a gluttonous guitar experience for me (I even took twenty guitars on the road); I was determined

to go to town on all of them, dead set on getting all of those sounds on our new album in some way, shape, or form. I had thirty-six songs to play on—that meant two straight weeks of recording guitar parts. I was in seventh heaven, just absorbed in my guitars, totally in my element. It was great, the room sounded great, and I loved the staff at the Record Plant.

One event that got everyone talking during the recording of *Illusions I* and *II* was the day there was a huge commotion in the alley. It turned out that the cops found a dismembered arm and a head in the Dumpster behind the studio. All I know is that we didn't do it, but Izzy turned the event into a lyric on "Double Talking Jive." And I got to do a great Spanish flamenco thing on that track, which was a gas to do. That song has a really cool electric solo, too, that morphs into an acoustic flamenco groove.

There were a few songs that were very involved guitar-wise on those albums. "Estranged" was a big, long song. I used a Les Paul Gold Top on it; I recorded all of the melodies on the rhythm pickup with the tone turned all the way down. "November Rain" was tough, too, as was another Axl song called "Breakdown." Those were all piano driven and they needed accompaniment; the guitar and bass parts had to be thought out and done precisely. Those songs were all pretty fucking cool, I have to say, but they took some work.

"November Rain" was recorded in one day but we put in long hours ahead of time to get all of the arrangements just right. The funniest thing is that the guitar solo that ended up on the record is the exact same one that I played the first time I heard the song years before. That's a consistent theme throughout Guns N' Roses: pretty much every solo on the record is the same exact one I played the first time I ran through it. It's just the way the song felt to me every time we got to that section. So throughout the band's history, when we were playing the songs live or on record, give or take a few notes here and there, my solos, which have always been more melodies than flat-out busting moves, have always been the same series of notes I heard within the music from the very start. The end result was that there was always a sense of familiarity that I enjoyed when we'd play those songs and get to those sections.

Anyway, "Breakdown" was very complicated as far as getting all of the

drum and guitar parts just right back at A & M, as well as the intricate piano changes. It's a complex song, and as much as it sounds like we partied our way through recording, we were very focused when it came to work. That song was hard on Matt especially—he lost it a few times trying to get the drums perfect. Like I said, we did a song a day—but some days were longer than others.

We had intricate songs, we had complex songs, and I think only bands like Metallica were doing anything similar to what we were doing. They seriously focused on meter changes and all that on *The Black Album*, and I don't know what their process was, but we would get our framework together, then just jam on it. If we made a mistake or did a real train wreck section, we'd go back and do it again, and usually we'd pull it together really quickly. Everyone in the band had a short attention span at that point, and no one wanted to work too long on one thing. We'd spend a few days on the arrangements, but when it came down to recording, we'd do one run-through and then the red light was *on*. It was a given that there would be some guitar overdubs and some vocals done later, but when it came to the basic guitar, bass, and drum tracks, all of those live takes had to be keepers. No one wanted to embarrass himself by causing us to do it over and over while the other guys in the band waited for you to get it right. That's what happens when you have good musicians, good chemistry . . . just the right people, in a good fucking band.

Guns took over the Record Plant. It was definitely indulgent, but we had a lot of work to do, and we had a really, really good time being Guns N' Roses again. I did guitars in one studio and Axl more or less made the other studio into an apartment, because he had decided that he'd get more work done if he lived there. He moved his exercise equipment in, as well as a bed and couches—it became a glorified lounge where he and his entourage might be comfortable. We definitely had a lot of traffic coming through the Record Plant in those days.

In my opinion none of that was conducive to getting our work done any quicker. All the same, while recording the *Illusion* albums we had a very bohemian, 1960s kind of scene going on around the studio; the combination of our friends—musicians and otherwise—plus all the other people we knew made for a very cool backdrop. Any given night I might be laying

down guitars in one studio while Axl was doing vocals in the other while a cast of interesting characters hung around participating in one way or another. Shannon Hoon from Blind Melon came by often because he was an old friend of Axl's from Indiana; he sang backup on "Don't Cry," which made that song all the more soulful.

The biggest change in the band, aside from Matt replacing Steven, was the overwhelming presence of keyboards and synthesizers. Axl had introduced a screaming synth line in "Paradise City," back in the *Appetite* days. That was the start of it, I suppose, and I was opposed to that, too. As I mentioned, on the *Illusion* albums Axl was insistent on a major piano and synth presence. After we'd done the basic tracks, after I'd done my guitar parts, once it was time for Axl to do his vocals, he spent a lot of time adding synthesizer parts. He was like a kid in a candy store with all of these banks of keyboards he'd had installed in the studio. He'd sit there for hours to get the right sound for one section of a song, and remember, this guy was not strung out, he was not wasted, although he was stoned on pot a lot—which probably made him obsess over that stuff even more. Axl was that into the grandiose production thing, which was not so good on the one hand, but all things considered, on the flip side he had so much integrity about it that he'd spend however long it took to ensure that the sonic drama was *perfect*. What he ended up with at the end of the day was fucking brilliant. I don't know if it represented Guns in my head, but it sounded amazing regardless. When we did "Live and Let Die," it was all synths—those horns are not horns. What Axl did there was really complex; he spent *hours* dialing all of that shit in, getting the nuances just right, and I have to give him that. He did the same for "November Rain" with all of those fucking string arrangements—they were all synth. I've heard songs with real strings that sound less authentic. The only time that we brought in outside musicians on those two records were the gospel singers on "Knockin' on Heaven's Door" and the harmonica on "Bad Obsession." The only other effect that wasn't synthesized was the defibrillator at the very beginning of "Coma." Yeah, that was real.

—◆+)◆(+◆—

tracks, I vacated Studio B and Axl took it over and turned the entire Record Plant into a complex where his friends could hang out while he spent a few weeks finishing his vocals and adding the aforementioned synths. The rest of us weren't too happy about that because every day that setup cost us a lot of money. It would have been fine if there was activity all day long, but none of us saw anything getting done on a consistent basis. In the end, Axl finished his work, but *fuck,* those two records cost a *fortune* to make—and I'm talking studio time alone.

This was when Axl started getting obsessive about the details of everything to do with Guns N' Roses, starting with the publishing splits of the songs on *Illusion I* and *II.* The days of band members getting a straight 20 percent were long gone because there were so many outside writers this go-round, especially on the old songs that existed before Guns that were now in the equation, such as "Back Off Bitch." We also had to factor in Matt, who wasn't a full-fledged member: he hadn't been around during the writing of the songs, though he'd played on all of them. In the end, because of contributors like Paul Huge and West Arkeen and Del James, Axl insisted upon splits that were like 22.75 percent or 32.2 percent per song for us core members. It was mathematically worked out according to who wrote what, which made it easy in the sense that we'd never have anything to fight over, but at the same time, it was pored over and complicated things to a corporate degree.

The songs we worked on in Chicago also posed a problem because those months there were so disjointed, and for the most part, Axl wasn't even there, so the splits he devised for songs like "Garden of Eden," "Don't Damn Me," and "Get in the Ring" were totally arbitrary; Duff and I wrote them instrumentally when Axl wasn't even in the room. There were piano-driven songs with complex guitar parts that I'd had to write and arrange that I wasn't even being given a songwriting credit. It was the same with "November Rain" and "Estranged," to be specific. It concerned me, to say the least, but I chose to overlook it.

mixed, we had a decision to make. Thompson and Barbiero, who'd mixed *Appetite*, were no longer a team. The temperament of the band as we now were didn't suit them, or their temperament didn't suit us, I can't remember which. We decided to hire Bob Clearmountain, a guy whose credentials spoke for themselves: he'd mixed everyone from the Kinks to Bowie to the Stones to Springsteen. We had a lot of material ready for him to start on while Axl continued to work on what wasn't finished yet. Clearmountain came in and talked endlessly about Q Sound 5.1, a technology that was still in its formative stages. He was really into it, and I remember that he got Axl pretty excited about it, too. That was all great, but I wasn't having it at all; Q Sound sounded like a wash to me. I didn't care that Bob insisted that it was the future; to hear it properly required five speakers, and especially back then, in the early 1990s, most people had only two. And if you listened to something mixed in Q Sound through two speakers, it sounded like an indistinct mess. It was one of those much-hyped things that time proves to be nothing but a short-term, bridge technology: much like the minidisc, and the Laserdisc, Q Sound was a weak, impermanent version of what was to come.

That said, rather than make a big scene and get the whole band up in arms, which would have resulted in Axl and me arguing the pros and cons of Q Sound until we were blue in the face, I bit my lip and hoped that this would work out. And it did; Clearmountain shot himself in the foot almost immediately: one afternoon we discovered a notepad of his where he'd notated all of the drum samples he planned to mix in over Matt's drum tracks. I'm not a drummer, so I can't explain the technical ins and outs, but he'd brought in samples that would change Matt's sound drastically. We showed it to Matt who had no idea and he wasn't too pleased at all—and that was the excuse we needed to fire Bob Clearmountain.

We ended up hiring Bill Price to mix. We respected Bill's résumé, to say the least: he'd mixed the first Pretenders record, the Sex Pistols' *Never Mind the Bollocks*, and as far as I was concerned, that was all that I needed to know to sign off on him. Bill worked out of a studio in Larchmont, California, and I made it my personal mission to be there every day, watch-

ing him work, contributing where I could, and ensuring that the mixes he did each day were sent out to Axl's house in Malibu immediately.

It was a long, tedious process: I'd show up in the early afternoon and listen to the mix that Bill would have up. Once it was at a place where I was satisfied with it, we'd make a tape of it and send it to Axl. We'd hang around the studio or start working on the next song while the messenger got it there. When he did, I must say, Axl wasted no time in listening to the tape and calling in with his comments, which were usually very helpful. We'd then make whatever adjustments needed to be made, mix it down again, and send another copy out to him. And so on, song by song. It took forever to get them all just right, but it was worth it.

<hr />

DURING THIS PROCESS, THE ANIMOSITY between our manager, Alan Niven, and Axl came to a head. The rest of us had been trying to squash it for a while, but Axl's issues with Alan had been brewing for years—since the moment he found out that Alan also managed and produced *and* cowrote Great White. There was also the fact that Alan was opinionated about a lot of things and Axl didn't always agree with his point of view. So at times Axl felt like he was being forced to do things that he didn't necessarily want to do. Axl thought that Alan had developed an ego, that he'd gone from a Malcolm McClaren to a Peter Grant. And really, Alan's ego was as inflated as ours.

I had been Alan's champion, however, until one incident swayed me against him. One night when Renee and I were at his house with him and his wife, Camilla, Alan said something really inappropriate to Renee. I don't remember what it was exactly, but it was creepy enough that we left immediately. I never forgot it, and I won't repeat it here. As much as I loved Alan for what he'd done to help us, I didn't protest too much when Axl moved to oust him. I knew it was going to happen but I didn't think it would be the tipping point. Looking back, I feel that shift was the moment, the pause at the pinnacle of the band's success . . . and the start of its downfall.

All the same, I saw Doug coming. He had made a place for himself in Axl's life, and once Axl had made his feelings about Alan clear, I don't think it's a coincidence that Doug was right there to pick up the reins. He had

been strategically moving up the ladder from the beginning. He was like an ambush predator. Though at the end of the day no one is more responsible for the demise of Guns N' Roses than Guns N' Roses, Doug Goldstein was a catalyst. His divide-and-conquer techniques were instrumental in achieving our end.

If you run down the history of the demise of great rock bands, more often than not you'll discover that many of them dumped their original manager on their way to grasping the brass ring, and once they did, it all got fucked up. I'm kind of pissed off that we followed that tradition.

As self-destructive as we may or may not have been, and despite the communication barriers between the members, we had the desire to play music and move forward at all costs. That an outside influence completely disrupted the band really is a shame.

It was a dream come true... but as we prepared for our monster tour, the last thing on our minds was being careful what we wished for.

I THINK IT TOOK TWO DAYS FOR DOUG Goldstein to be elected the official new manager of Guns N' Roses. At the time we had not finished mixing the record, but Doug, from the start, wanted to make a name for himself in the industry and make money, and we were the perfect vehicle for that. We booked a series of gigs straight-

away, and on strategic days off, would go into the studio to complete the albums. For a while, our tour schedule delayed the release of the albums indefinitely.

We certainly had our fun, though. Doug took us out of the studio to play Rock in Rio in Brazil in 1991, which would be Matt and Dizzy's first show with Guns. It was incredible; we played two nights in a row to 180,000 fans in Maracanã Stadium. It was a festival that had gone on for weeks, where everyone from Megadeath to Faith No More, to INXS, Run-D.M.C., and Prince, had played. It was something else; I'm not sure that I've ever seen a more insane Guns N' Roses crowd—and that is saying something. When we kicked into the bridge of "Paradise City," people swan-dived from the upper tier of the stadium—seemingly to their death. There aren't words that can do their degree of intensity justice: we had had people stacked outside of our hotel so deep that we couldn't leave. We couldn't even go down to the pool, because when we did, somehow people would launch themselves over the fifteen-foot wall and run up and basically attack us. They didn't want to hurt us, but they definitely wanted to break a piece of us off to keep for themselves. It was bizarre. We couldn't leave our rooms, and our wives, or girlfriends, or any women seen in our company, were taunted and, basically, marked for death by these fans of ours.

We did a bunch more dates. We had three theater dates in L.A., San Francisco, and New York, with various bands opening for us, such as Blind Melon and Faith No More and Raging Slab. At the New York show we shot live footage, which made the basis of the video for *The Terminator 2* soundtrack. That video also featured shots of Arnold Schwarzenegger, the Terminator himself, at the Rainbow. We then started a tour with Skid Row in the United States, including two nights at the Inglewood Forum in L.A. I tell you, being that huge of a band was fucking *killer*. Having Skid Row was my kind of tour: total debauchery.

Way before we finished mixing and mastering the albums, Axl was committed to getting the right image for our cover art. Since he'd been the one who brought that brilliant Robert Williams painting in for *Appetite*, we trusted him to find the art for these two albums as well. Once again he did: the image for the nebulous mix of songs we'd worked up was by Mark

Kostabi. It was a young Dutch-looking figure in a "thinker" pose that had been inspired by a Renaissance painting. At the time, Axl really wanted that image to be the two faces of those albums. In the end we had one in red, one in blue, and the rest of us were just like, "Okay, cool, man." That made the two album concept more palatable.

That was one of what might be considered "big" decisions that, as a band, we were too quick to pass off to our lead singer. But I don't regret it at all: if that was where Axl was going to throw down the gauntlet, it was all good. I was much more concerned that the *Illusion* albums would be released separately so that our fans didn't have to spend thirty or forty bucks to get our new music: they could decide if they wanted one or the other album and buy accordingly. Hopefully they'd want both. In the end, *Use Your Illusion I* sold more than *Use Your Illusion II*.

When the albums went on sale, fans were lined up outside of record stores all around the country. I can vouch for the fact that there was a line down the block at Tower Records on Sunset that night because I drove past there on my way to the airport with Renee. I had the limo pull in and we snuck in the back door and were brought up to the same little office above the sales floor where I'd been detained for shoplifting when I was in junior high; I looked down at all the kids on line to buy the records through the same one-way glass that some manager had watched me through the day I got busted stealing. It was surreal.

The records went to number one and number two the week they were released, which was a record. And then they stayed there. There was fanfare everywhere, and we needed to get organized for our tour. It was going to be bigger than anything we'd done.

The new music was much more complicated, so bringing it to the stage was going to require added musicians. I was elected the unofficial music director, in charge of finding background vocalists and horn players. I had a hard time swallowing the concept of three guys in tuxes blowing brass, so I hired hot chicks instead. Of course, good-looking backup singers were a necessity as well. I sort of did it all tongue in cheek. We also brought in Teddy Zig Zag, this great blues player I'd jammed with countless times, to play additional piano and the harmonica. Actually I relied on Ted to recruit all of the female session players and he did an amazing job.

As we prepared to take off again, I had a lot to do with the stage design as well. I helped design a pretty efficient and good-looking stage that we would live on for the next two and a half years. There were ramps, little stages over the amps for the girls, a keyboard area, and a piano that came from under the floor for Axl. We also had a cool grating for a floor so that lights could shine from beneath us it.

We were hands-on for the whole development of that big-ass stage we ended up with. We had the Guns N' Roses logo on the floor, which was cool, too. It was fucking incredible for us to have the money and the public demand to design our ultimate performance vehicle. It was a dream come true . . . but as we prepared for our monster tour, the last thing on our minds was being careful what we wished for.

Choose Your Illusion

Slash integrates his BMX moves into his guitar playing on the Illusions tour.

11

chapter

I've experienced extreme highs and lows, and rode them all to the end. But when they're so close together that they're virtually interwoven, it is alienating. That is something else altogether; suddenly the once familiar seems strange, and nothing feels stable. As a kid, I'd stared in disbelief from the side of many stages that, to me, were bigger than life itself. Now I was playing on an even bigger one, with my band's logo emblazoned on the floor beneath my feet. We had arenas full of fans waiting to see us everywhere we went, all around the world. We released two albums on the same day that debuted at number one and number two. It couldn't have been going better. And backstage, behind it all, we were splitting apart like the atom in an A-bomb.

When I look back on it now, I can see the roots of the whole thing, but at the time I didn't have that kind of perspective at all. It was always there, but in the post-*Appetite* era, the condition really came into its own: Axl became a Dr. Jekyll and Mr. Hyde. It was one thing during the recording of the *Illusion* records when he was holing up in the recording studio and being excessively overindulgent; none of us liked that much, but we were willing to allow it. We certainly didn't think it could get worse. Those sessions were the times when the rest of us began to let those things happen against our better judgment. It was tedious yet still fun, but we were kidding ourselves thinking that situation was all going to be fine once the album was released. It was really tough for me because I felt very close to Axl for periods of time when we were working together toward a common goal, and then, not much later, I'd feel like we were on opposite sides of a fence. It started a real love/hate situation between us.

Axl and I had a pretty rocky relationship from the very beginning, which continued until the very last time we spoke, for the simple reason that we have such different, different ways of looking at and handling things. I bear him no ill will; I know that his version of events is every bit as viable as mine . . . just different. It took me a long time to even sort of understand Axl—if I ever did at all—let alone predict what made him react the way he did. I wanted to know what made him happy, what pissed him off, what inspired him creatively; all of those things are essential knowledge when you work in such close proximity with someone in a creative endeavor.

Early on, when we first met, what he did would sometimes take me by surprise. We related to each other because both of us were rebellious and anarchistic, but I could never understand why he took rebellion to the point that it made his life difficult for no real reason. I could understand standing up for what you believe in and that conflict often results from that. But Axl took it to a degree of self-sabotage that I just did not comprehend. I spent a lot of time trying to sort that out, to just understand it intellectually in some way, until I realized that there was no rhyme or reason to it whatsoever.

I was drawn to Axl like everyone else is because he is such an amazing singer and performer and has such powerful all-around charisma. I also admired the fact that he always had a point of view that he felt strongly about and was always so sincere about it. He's a brilliant lyricist and such a really tortured artist that he won me over because my mentality has always been to root for the underdog—and that was such a major part of his brilliance.

I learned to take the bad with the good as far as our friendship was concerned because Axl had a lot of stuff going on. We'd have these very in-depth, personal conversations, especially during the period when the band was starting out and we lived together. There were moments there when I loved him to death, when he was just so cool and we had really close, heartfelt talks that he would lead. It was cool to get to know someone like him, because I can go for years without saying anything about how I feel, but Axl is not like that at all; he needed someone to communicate his feelings to. We'd have these great, peaceful one-on-ones about what bothered him and what was on his mind when the static died down. We'd talk about personal stuff from his past, all the things that concerned him, interested him, his goals for himself and for the band, what he wanted to do with his life. It was a great insight into someone that I already admired, and I liked him a lot during those times because he was human and vulnerable and I felt like we really connected.

The flip side to Axl, the Hyde to his Jekyll, was that once you felt that you had a strong bond going with him he'd do something that completely defied what you knew. One of the great things about our band was that we always had one another's back, regardless of the situation, but that became hard to do with Axl eventually. He never did anything directly to me; he did things that jeopardized the entire band and its standing among our peers and our fans. That was something that I could never understand. But that never mattered much because Axl was always there to explain it away and he always had a lot to say about why he did what he did.

The longer this type of behavior continued, though, the I more I harbored mistrust when it came to him, because the guy that I'd have those intimate talks with was not the same guy who would make what I considered inconsiderate decisions. It was a contradiction that became hard for me to handle.

In some instances Axl's reactions to certain things were detrimental only to the band—they weren't huge at first; usually they were worth compromising over to further our collective progress. Izzy was always very calm about dealing with Axl and I'd hang with Izzy a lot during those times. Duff, too, had his way of dealing with Axl, which was also pretty mellow.

Steven, on the other hand, used to get irate, because as far as he was concerned, Axl's behavior made no fucking sense at all. As I've said before, Steven didn't understand him and didn't have the capacity to understand him, so he'd react directly at Axl. But for my part I put a lot of hours into trying to understand Axl and where he was coming from, because for our band to succeed, it had to be *us*, united, against the world. We had to keep our ranks tight. Whenever Axl did stuff that belittled the rest of us, it put distance between us where there should have been none. In my opinion it weakened our foundation.

This situation went back and forth for ages, where we vacillated between being unified and being compromised. During the making of the first record, these incidents with Axl weren't so dramatic. As the band got bigger, though, his demands got bigger. And as time went on, we developed a habit of appeasing him. If it wasn't that big of a deal in the short run, we'd let him have whatever he wanted; we'd tell him what he wanted to hear. But it established a pattern in which he got used to getting what he wanted.

One of the hard things about him back in the day was that when no one else agreed with him, Axl's retaliation wasn't easy: he'd throw something, knock something down, leave the building, or walk away, fuming, down the street and quit the band. In the heat of those moments, you couldn't reason with Axl; he was like a kid having a tantrum. It made me wonder about the dynamics of his upbringing. I'm in no position to give away the details, but from what Axl told me of it, his childhood was very rough.

When we were starting out, his behavior was tolerable because we were all moving in the same direction and we could justify the compromises we had to make. When we got back from the final leg of the *Appetite* tour two years later and all through the business of getting together and eventually working together again in Chicago, I started to see the less sensible side of him come out more and more—that's why I left those writing sessions. Axl never understood why I left Chicago because he thought we were get-

ting so much done, but the truth was that his negative energy was just really hard to work with. I know I'm not the only one to feel that way; almost anyone who ever worked for us would say something similar. The reason that the people working for us hung in there was the same reason that the band hung in there: there were these great, endlessly amazing moments that made all of the negative, really dark, hard moments worth it. Axl was so self-centered at times that everyone was affected by it. I can only assume that the rest of us balanced it out. But what do I know? Well, I do know this: Axl definitely has his version of events that is every bit as valid as mine.

<hr>

WHEN THE BAND HEADED INTO THE STUDIO to record the *Illusion* records, everything going on behind the scenes got much worse very fast: there was so much unnecessary money being spent, and no one addressing the issue, because no one wanted to go there; the mood was that touchy. The truth is, no one in the band graduated high school, let alone had a degree in psychology; none of us knew how to effectively get through to Axl. It could be easy to do sometimes if you hung out with him quietly in his space, on his watch; you could sort some stuff out under those ideal conditions. Actually, it was the only way to discuss anything with him. Any other approach wasn't constructive; usually all it did was double the damage and set him off worse than he'd been before.

The problem that arose for me personally was a deep bitterness at having to deal with this situation at all; I stopped wanting to even try to reason with Axl anymore. I found myself working very hard to accomplish something very simple: I used to have to go and talk to him at length about things I didn't want to talk about just to be able to address one simple band issue. It began to fall on my shoulders to handle these day-to-day decisions that required Axl's input and after a while I just didn't want to do it; I wanted to hand that responsibility off to someone else. I just wanted to play music.

Doug Goldstein took over that role once he spent enough time with us on the road. He watched how we all interacted very carefully, and stepped in to play the part of the guy who "dealt with Axl." Doug played a lot of games to get things done: he'd have the necessary conversations with

Axl . . . but not the way anyone in the band would have done it. The way I see it, Doug was intent on making things happen for the wrong reasons. He was there in the first place to make himself money and to work his way up the industry ladder by establishing his reputation as manager for Guns N' Roses. He'd tell Axl whatever he needed to and do whatever it took to keep Guns together not because he cared about us at all, but because having us as a client was essential to his reputation—but of course that's no more than my opinion.

I saw Doug's true colors pretty quickly, I must say. When he stepped in and replaced Alan Niven in May 1991, just as we were beginning to tour again, I didn't think he'd help mediate for the right reasons—the band's best interests. Nonetheless, I leaned on him to help deal with Axl. He could get us over whatever obstacle was in our way as far as Axl's demands were concerned, but it was a no-win situation, because it was clear that Doug wasn't telling Axl what he needed to hear for our greater good. Axl needed to be talked down, if anything, not appeased. Because that had gone on too long. Doug was never going to do that, though; he was only going to say whatever worked in the short term. Again, that was my opinion, at least.

In two years Guns had become a whirling dervish of miscommunication that spent money like it was water. And every day Doug would tell the rest of us that he was going to stop it all, yet nothing changed. All the rest of us wanted to do was keep moving forward as a band, to have a good time and get things done. To me that never seemed like something that should be that hard to do.

A permanent shift in the mood of the band came at the first mention of the contracts and the ownership of the band name, all of which first happened when Steven was kicked out. Axl insisted that owning the band name was something we needed to litigate, and making our "identity" a "commodity" left us feeling dictated to—which was something that never went over well. That legal arrangement damaged our sense of mutual respect because it made the rest of us apart from Axl feel pretty taken for granted. We could tolerate a lot because we were so easygoing, but an unrecognized tension was building, and the contract issue brought it to a head. Even then, we never talked about it, because we'd gotten well into the habit of blowing

things off, but I know Izzy felt it; I know Duff and I did, too—we'd all look at one another sideways whenever the subject came up.

<hr />

THE EXPANDING GAP BETWEEN AXL and me and between Axl and the rest of us got pretty wide during the process of having the *Illusion* records mixed. As I've said, Axl would be at his house and I'd be down at the studio and I'd have the mix of each song sent out there to him once it was done; then I'd wait to get his input. All things considered, we were on a collective creative high, but there wasn't exactly a spirit of solidarity in that arrangement; it was a one-sided relationship. Still, to me, it was tolerable. Subconsciously, I think I began to see the band as one guy sitting on a throne high above and completely apart from the crowd of people hustling around beneath him.

The first touchy situation I got into with Axl came after I got on the cover of *Rolling Stone* following the release of the *Illusion* records. The impression that I gave the writer, which was also true, was that we were a band who had exploded so quickly that three years later we were still trying to catch up to what we'd become.

Axl got ahold of the interview and he read it, and from what I understand, he was cool with it, or at least didn't see anything wrong with it at first. But apparently, upon further review he found something I said insulting. At least that's what I think . . . actually I don't know what happened there.

The next time I saw Axl was at the Long Beach Arena, where our entire stage setup for the *Illusions* tour was fully assembled and he was not speaking to me at all. If I'd been so deluded as to think that it was just my imagination, he made sure that I knew he was pissed. I had given him this really cool straitjacket for his birthday not too long before and he'd brought it with him that day, just so he could make a point of leaving it on my amp when he left.

We didn't talk to each other at all over the next few days as the band ran through those rehearsals. It was exactly the type of eggshell walking that being in Guns N' Roses had become. The vibe was *bad*; I just tried to do my thing without issue each day. All things considered, I was very

concerned because the truth is that I'm more sensitive than I seem to be. I worried about what was making Axl so angry because I had no idea what I'd done; he wasn't saying anything, and no one else knew either. It eventually came to light as much as it could . . . and it took a *huge* discussion to work it out.

we did amazing things every single night that were godlike.

SO THAT WAS THE STATE OF OUR BAND as we set off on our longest tour with our most intense production to date.

Duff and Slash enjoying the MGM Grand jet.

The touring was fucking *exciting*—it was what kept us together through the increasingly frequent rough spots. After we got our stage show together, backup singers, horn section, and all, and did a week's worth of rehearsals with every element intact, suddenly we found ourselves in South America, before a crowd of 180,000 at Rock in Rio II, on January 20, 1991. We didn't even have a new record out yet; we were there solely on the strength of *Appetite* and *Lies*, which by this point were four and two years old, respectively.

We flew down there on the private 727 owned and leased by the MGM Grand Hotel in Vegas, and that was it—we had to have that thing for the rest of the tour. It was pretty ornate: it had all of these little private lounges and bedrooms; it was a great crash pad. And it was the best way to get from country to country because you took off and landed on your own schedule and you circumvented the standard entry procedure. The paperwork would be handled while you sat on the plane, and I don't think customs officers ever boarded and searched us once in the two years we leased the plane. As much as I was glad to have it, like the rest of the guys in the band, I didn't think we were nearly big enough to warrant that thing—I'm sure Axl told Doug we needed it at all costs, which probably sealed the deal.

That tour was a great time: Duff and I had our new party buddy Matt, and no matter how many days we'd stay up, we could always play the gig. We just felt like we were kings of the world; we had a good time with everything and we always did our job. Izzy, unfortunately, was shell-shocked; he was trying his best to keep far away from our whole partying scene, so that tour from the start wasn't as much fun for him. And Axl . . . well, I don't know where his head was at; I won't pretend to understand what was going on with him then, now, or ever. But I do know that we all came together and enjoyed what we couldn't have without each other: the mutual high of performing onstage every night.

All the same, we began to go on later and later as the tour progressed. That was an Axl thing and it wasn't just one or two occasions, it was *every* night. That hit me, on a personal level, as his biggest betrayal ever. It's not like a band has to cater to their audience or feel as if they are at their mercy,

but it is a band's *job* to play for the people who have *bought* tickets to see them. It became a major issue with me. When I'm asked why I quit Guns N' Roses, I can think of three reasons: the first was the fact that on that tour we almost never took the stage on time; the second was canceling shows for no good reason; and the third is the infamous contract awarding Axl the band's name should we ever break up. That contract was a real slap in the face. We'll get to all that in just a little bit, but at the time I just thought, *Take the fucking name and shove it.*

All of those conditions pointed to a situation where the band and everything around it was arranged to be under Axl's control. Starting with the name issue and moving on to the fact that he wanted every player under a contract that could be terminated for "bad behavior"—this really wasn't a healthy thing. Nor was the inconsiderate treatment of the people who came by the thousands to see us, and the crew and everyone in our entourage who had to work overtime every single night that we went on later and later. It became really humiliating for me to continue because as much as we were always considered a brash rock band, we were always known to take care of our business. It sucked for the band and the crew that we couldn't always do our best because we were handicapped by situations that the rest of us weren't directly responsible for.

There is probably no better way to build up resentment or to make a touring ensemble or any other kind of collective endeavor hate-heavy than by promoting a lack of respect. I'm not one to get angry that easily—you have to really push me—so I remained as elastic as I could going through this tour, but it started to wear on me. There were so many great band opportunities that were shot down left and right because Axl refused to take them—usually those decisions were made between him and Doug and sometimes the rest of us were just informed later. Yet, at the same time, the band was amazing, and anyone who went to one of those magic Guns nights during the two and a half years that we toured was blown away. We were an unreal band with an unreal singer; Axl was just amazing. Despite all of this tension going on behind the scenes, I still had some onstage chemistry with him that was incredible: we did amazing things every single night that were godlike. There were nights when certain moments we would hit gave me goose bumps.

All in all, it was a very tough up-and-down cycle to deal with. That's my side of the story; there's Axl's, of course. I'm sure he'd say that we drank too much and did too many drugs. That's true, of course; I can only vouch for myself when I say, yes, I did, but all things considered, never once in the history of the band was a show ever canceled or started late because of the guys in the band. Regardless of anyone's habits, we back-line musicians were always there. There were a few close calls and a few shows that might have been pretty sloppy, but we are talking about a rock-and-roll band, after all. There were complaints throughout the tour from Axl's camp about what we were doing—"we" being Duff and Matt and me—and Izzy complained about our ways, too. They can say what they like about how we were living; our habits didn't affect the greater machine at all when it came to getting the job done. Of course that's my point of view; I am quite sure that Axl and the other guys have theirs that might differ tremendously from what I have to say.

<div align="center">◆━❈━◆</div>

I'M NOT GOING TO EVEN PRETEND THAT I remember every detail of the two and a half years we spent touring *Use Your Illusion I* and *II*. Even if I did, I don't think recounting every gig, every highlight, every memory, and every milestone would do any of it justice: listing it all would make it seem way more boring than even the dullest day ever was. I'm just going to hit on the shows, the "incidents," the conflicts, and the ultimate highs that stand out among a two-and-a-half-year run that was such a thrill and such a whirlwind of good and bad that I'm daunted by trying to relate the experience at all.

The start of the tour was intense and exciting; we were walking into an amazingly huge limelight and had thousands of people coming to see us. I had never experienced that feeling so directly. We had played to massive crowds at festivals before, which is one thing: usually we were second or third before the headliner, so the energy was high then, but it is quite another thing to go out and play an hour and forty-five minutes to three hours for eighty thousand people who are there just for you.

I used to spend my time after the gigs walking around the venue, checking out the size of the empty arenas and the scale of our stage and

production, and I was never short of amazed. I had plenty of time to do that every night, because usually it took us as long to leave as it did for us to get on—but that's another story. Let's just say we couldn't all go until the "time was right."

In any case, I'd seen enough stage productions on a grand scale since I was a kid that I was rarely impressed, but I'd walk around and check out our setup with stars in my eyes: to be part of that reality was a dream come true. We owe thanks to the great crew, all of the amazing guys who put it all up and took it all down every day. I'd sit and watch them disassemble it; all the union people, loading these massive stage components into a fleet of semi trucks—it was fuckin' bitchin'. We were on a run at that point, on such a high that even the negative stuff was overshadowed by how awesome it was for us every day. Unfortunately, that intense, routine high solidified a pattern: the pissed-off-to-elated yin yang we'd done for so long had gotten us there so hey . . . why change now? All things considered, we kept it up pretty well; it wasn't until way later that it inevitably exploded.

After the Rio gigs, we started off with three warm-up club gigs—with Blind Melon in L.A., Faith No More in San Francisco, and Raging Slab in NYC. Raging Slab were amazing: those guys showed up in a VW bus that they'd driven down all the way from upstate somewhere with all of their gear; and there we were in our limos. I thought it was great that we had bands like that on our bill—one perk of being at that level is that you really can do *whatever the fuck you want.*

From there we set off on the main event—touring arenas with our massive production and stage. That whole tour was stadium after stadium. We had Dizzy Reed, Teddy "Zig Zag," the horn section, and the girl singers. It was such a crazy setup compared to what we'd been used to. First of all there was no set list—we never did the same set on any night. We had our standards, like "November Rain," "You Could Be Mine," "Paradise City," and "Welcome to the Jungle," but the rest was up for grabs.

The girls—the backup singers and the horn players—had to be onstage the entire time, which posed problems that we hadn't thought of, like, what if they had to pee? I'd made Ted Zig Zag the pit boss of that little support band—he'd actually recruited them—and it was funny to watch

him deal with them. Those girls would argue over their outfits, who got to wear what; we'd never experienced crazy shit like that on one of our tours before. When the girls were having their periods, which somehow seemed to be synchronized, I found it was best to just stay out of their way altogether.

Axl was an entity unto himself on the road; after a while we only saw him onstage or on the plane. Izzy was much the same. Traveling between gigs, Duff, Matt, and I hung with the girls: there was Lisa Maxwell, the head horn player, who played tenor sax; Anne, who played trumpet; and this bisexual New York City chick whose name I can't remember who played baritone sax. And there were the two background singers, these cute, racy little chicks who could usually be found arguing over their wigs. There was Roberta, this very pretty skinny black girl, and Tracy, who was this cute little mulatto, and they were very cool.

THE SHOW THAT SET THE PACE FOR WHAT was to ultimately unhinge the tour took place in Uniondale, New York, at the Nassau Coliseum, where we went on late. That night, however, Axl apologized to the fans for being late, which, once it became a regular occurrence, he never bothered to do again.

The first major issue, of course, was in St. Louis, which is well documented in the press. Axl had a beef with a guy in the first few rows who had a video camera. Axl mentioned it to venue security and they did nothing about it. Their attitude and the guy's blatant disregard really set Axl off, so he jumped out into the crowd to take his camera away. When he jumped down, it was great, we kept playing that suspenseful riff that starts off "Rocket Queen," and I thought the whole moment was killer. When Axl got back onstage, everything felt triumphant for a second . . . then he grabbed the mike, said something like, "Because of the bullshit security, we're going home," slammed the mike down, and walked offstage.

The band kept going. We'd gotten good at improvising to fill dead space—drum solos, guitar solos, jams—we had a bag of tricks to keep things moving whenever Axl made a sudden exit. We kept jamming, and I went over to the side of the stage.

"Where is he?" I asked Doug.

He looked at me with a pained expression. "He's not coming back."

"What do you *mean* he's not coming back?" I shouted, still playing the riff.

"There is no way he is coming back," Doug said. "There's nothing I can do."

We were about ninety minutes into our set, which was our minimum, contractually, but the plan was to play a two-hour set and the crowd wasn't close to satisfied. They knew there was a lot more left. I would have done anything to get Axl back onstage at that point.

"Ask him again!" I yelled. "Find out if he's really not going to." I should have known by Doug's expression that there was no use.

Once it was final, we had no choice: the band put down our gear, and it was like pulling the plug on the stereo—the song just ended on a question mark. That entire arena sat there expecting something to happen, but instead we walked offstage without a word. And that set them off. We had no idea how much that set them off.

We all gathered in the dressing room, Axl wasn't there, and the mood was pretty solemn, to say the least. And that's when the racket started. We could hear this pounding; even through the doors, it sounded like mayhem. Axl suddenly came into the dressing room and said, "Let's go back on."

We went down the hallway toward the stage and it was like the scene in the Beatles' *Yellow Submarine* where they're walking through a hall and it's normal but every time they open a door there's a train coming at them or a cat screeching: we'd open a door and there was yelling, we'd open another and see people on stretchers, cops with blood all over them, gurneys everywhere, and pandemonium. At the time we were shooting a documentary, so we have a lot of it on film.

The St. Louis locals weren't having our cancellation—they tore the entire building apart; they did things that I didn't think were possible. It was daunting, if anything—we learned not to fuck around with crowds to that extent. Axl, at least, should have been more wary from that point on not to take an audience to that level of agitation ever again.

We were trapped backstage, not knowing what to do. Doug suddenly appeared and said that he had to get us out immediately and that there was

a police escort in the loading dock. We ducked down in the back of these two vans so that no one would see us and we drove straight on to Chicago. There was no way that we were going to be able to play that gig because every shred of our gear was trashed in St. Louis; that show was a very expensive fluke, to say the least—the crowd did over $200,000 worth of damage to the arena alone.

We crashed in Chicago for a while as the aftermath of St. Louis was added up. It was a major disaster for the people, and for the city, and Guns N' Roses was banned from playing in St. Louis forever.

When I returned to St. Louis with the Snakepit in 1995, the night before my show, I was walking from my hotel down to this row of bars nearby. I wasn't going far, so I didn't bring security because I knew that I was meeting our crew down there, but as I walked up this main drag, I saw five bikers in front of me and no one else around and for a moment I got worried. It was a pretty dark night on a pretty dark street, where tall streetlamps illuminated spots of ground every few yards. I got closer to them and they were looking at me; and I was looking at them. One of them got off of his bike and came at me and I wasn't sure how it was going to go down.

"Hey, man," he said, grinning wide. "I'm the guy who Axl hit." Like I was supposed to pat the guy on the back. He had this attitude like, "Hey, we're both anti-Axl, right?" He seemed to think we had something in common, but I don't work like that; if any of you talk shit about Axl I'm going to get up in your face. Only I can do that; because I have that right, not some punk on the street who doesn't even know him. Things got tense in that moment, but the guy started in with his own story, almost apologetically.

He had just won all of his money in the lawsuit; I think he'd been awarded his damages by the court like two days before. It was a tense situation: it was obvious to me that this was a guy who was riding high on that cash he'd just gotten and he wasn't going to spend it wisely. His "friends" seemed to be enjoying his good fortune with him, that was for sure, because all of them were clearly out on the town. He was the shortest of the bunch, and as all small guys do, he was trying to impress everyone in sight. He had earned his bragging rights—and a decent amount of our cash—but as he

told me in the few minutes I paused to speak with him, in the days after the incident, he couldn't even leave his house. He received death threats by phone, hate mail, all of it. Only after the city won the lawsuit—after which he won as well—did the whole tide turn for him.

I was totally not impressed with this guy. I told him so and that I had to go and that was that. So where was I?

◆━◆×◆━◆

WE TOOK A FEW WEEKS' BREAK AFTER that incident in St. Louis, and put the final touches on the *Illusion* albums. We celebrated with a few shows at the L.A. Forum, which was a highlight of the band's career. When I thought of the Forum, I thought of Bowie, Zeppelin, Aerosmith, and AC/DC; it is an iconic place. In terms of local bragging rights, it was like playing the Long Beach Arena—but better. I don't know how the other guys felt about it, but as the limo came down that ramp all I could think about was seeing Rod Stewart there with my mom; all of those stories were going through my mind. The gigs were all sold out and they were *amazing*. The last one we did there was three and a half hours—in the history of the band, it was the longest one we ever played. That show was July 29, 1991, the very day that the records were finished being mixed. As Axl said from the stage, "The motherfucker is *done!*"

While the records were packaged for release, we went on to do the other shows with Skid Row opening—you can imagine the degree of debauchery Matt, Duff, Sebastian Bach, and I got into. Sebastian was totally enthusiastic and totally green; we'd done it all before but we did it all again with Sebastian. That leg of the tour through the States to Europe was debauched and sick and took hedonism to a new level. It was way too much fun because Skid Row was blowing up at that point and was as young and hungry as we'd been with Mötley.

It's too bad that Sebastian doesn't like Duff and Matt and me much anymore: we tried him out when we were looking for a singer for what would become Velvet Revolver but it just didn't work out. The combination sounded like what I'd call Skid Roses. I must say I'm surprised to hear that Sebastian has been bad-mouthing the rest of us lately.

In any case, when we went to Europe with Skid Row, everything went

along very well, business as usual, until we got to Mannheim, Germany, on August 21, 1991. We had Nine Inch Nails on the bill as well for that date, and we went on late—late even for us—then, pretty early in the set, something happened and Axl walked off for what reason I have no idea. He wasn't getting heckled as far as I could see, no one hit him with a bottle or anything, but he wasn't having it. The stage at that venue was literally about a mile away from the production office and dressing room, so a van was there to shuttle us back and forth. When Axl left the stage, he went to the van and headed off to the dressing room.

The rest of us came offstage and were standing around, waiting to find out if Axl was coming back or if his van had taken off to the hotel. In terms of how he felt and dealt with Axl, Matt Sorum was like Steven—he just didn't understand why Axl couldn't just play his part.

I remember standing there with Duff while Matt was fuming. He'd been in the band long enough that his "new guy" reserve had been earned and dismissed.

"*Fuck* that guy," he said. "I'm gonna go straighten him out."

Matt felt that Duff and Izzy and I had played it too delicate with Axl for too long. Like Steve, he just wanted to get in his face and belt the guy because that would probably have worked with most people. I appreciated the sentiment but it seemed like the wrong answer to a volatile situation. All I wanted was to finish the show.

By this point we'd discovered that Axl's van had not left for the dressing room; he was sitting in it but he refused to come out and return to the stage. Both Duff and I had already gone down there to try to talk him into it, to no avail. So Matt went down to Axl's van to rally him, but as he got down there, he ran into Axl, who had emerged to head back to the stage. Matt was so fired up, though, that he got in Axl's face regardless, to the degree that it almost got physical.

"What the *fuck* are you doing?" Matt yelled. "Get back onstage!"

I ran up and got between them, because it wasn't a good situation. Axl can get completely psycho when he decides to fight and Matt weighs twice as much as I do—and he plays drums—so it wasn't exactly a good place for me to be. Axl went back to his van, and it didn't look like he was coming out again. The clock was ticking.

The promoters saw the drama going on and closed the gates around the venue so that we couldn't leave. They'd heard what had happened in St. Louis, and it's a good thing they did; if they hadn't, I'm positive that the thirty-eight thousand fans there would have rioted, we would have been held liable and arrested, and people might have died. The local police were already there in riot gear, ready to deal with a full-on situation. It was a scary, tense scene, and a very near miss.

We got Axl back onstage once he realized he had no choice, and the rest of the show went as planned. All I could remember thinking as I walked offstage after the encore was *Fuck, that was close.* Well, too close, as it turned out: by the next morning, Izzy sent a message through Alan informing us that he was quitting the band. He would finish the last few dates on the current leg of the tour, but after that he was done.

Seeing that potential for disaster was too much for Izzy, and the truth is, we all should have followed suit. With that many fans out there rabid to see the band perform, I couldn't see any reason why we should let this crap derail us, let alone potentially put people in danger. I'm obsessive-compulsive and dedicated when it comes to my profession, so I couldn't let it go.

Izzy completed the tour, and I tried to talk him out of leaving a few times, but at the same time I couldn't blame him at all.

"Hey, man, I know it's been hard, but I think we can turn it around," I remember telling him. "The shows are really great, man. The audiences are great, we're playing stadiums . . ."

"I know," he said. "But, man, I can't . . . I just can't do it anymore." The way he looked at me at that moment said it all.

Izzy sent out a statement to everyone, and the next day Alan flew out to meet with him. He took Izzy's side and came to us and told us that Izzy wasn't going to rethink the decision. I don't think Izzy even discussed it with Axl.

Once that was decided, once it was set in stone that the second of the founding five members of Guns N' Roses was out of the band, we finished the European tour. Izzy's final show was before seventy-two thousand people at Wembley Stadium, in London, a venue we sold out faster than any artist in its history. But it's more worth mentioning that as far as I re-

member, after Izzy informed us that he was leaving, not one of the remaining European shows started late.

AFTER WEMBLEY, WE GOT BACK TO L.A. and shot the video for "Don't Cry," in which Dizzy Reed is wearing a "Where's Izzy?" T-shirt. Then we took a break, though my break was occupied by finding us a replacement guitarist so that we could get back out on the road. It was every bit of the ordeal that finding a new drummer had been. Axl was convinced that we should hire Dave Navarro, which I didn't think was a good idea at all. I think it was a question of style: whoever was going to fill Izzy's spot needed to play like Izzy, who was a skilled rhythm player that added a unique, subtle texture. Dave Navarro is an amazing guitar player; he's someone better suited for my spot, not Izzy's. I don't think Dave wanted to make the commitment, anyway. Besides, at the time he had a heroin problem and obviously that was a major issue.

Axl had a few long conversations with Dave about joining the band, and he wasn't going to be discouraged, so finally I surrendered and tried to arrange a rehearsal with Dave. We agreed on a time for him to come down to Mates and then he never showed up. He did that three times.

I called Axl after I'd been stood up that third time. "Man, this guy Dave has issues," I said. "I am *not* into this."

"Okay, okay," he said. "I'll talk to him."

Axl convinced me that Dave was really committed and that he'd show up when I called him again. I did call him again, and as I expected, he didn't show up again. That was it, I was furious; that was the last that I was willing to entertain the prospect of Dave Navarro.

I had been thinking about the one guitar player that I'd seen who reminded me of Izzy: he was in a band called Candy that had opened up for Hollywood Rose back at Madame Wong's West before I was ever even in a band with Axl. His name was Gilby Clarke, and as far as I could recall he was the only guy that I knew with an Izzy-like feel, which wasn't easy to come by.

I got in touch with Gilby and he wanted the gig more than anything. He learned sixty songs in two weeks; he came in for an audition and just

nailed it. A couple of weeks later, we rehearsed him with the whole band and we put a set together, and like that, we were back in fighting shape.

It was a strange moment. Izzy's departure happened so quietly, with no fanfare, and no media awareness. It was such a major change within the band, but to the outside world it was a nonevent. Probably because it was overshadowed by the fact that the records came out right before we got back on the road.

On September 17, 1991, *Use Your Illusion II* debuted at number one while *Use Your Illusion I* debuted at number two. We'd broken a record: no other artist of any kind had pulled that off since the Beatles. We were getting all of this major, positive, super news while all of this negative drama was going on simultaneously. By then I'd gotten so used to life being such a rocky road that I dealt with it, and didn't think twice about the possibility that it might not be normal.

<hr />

ONCE GILBY WAS IN AND WE WERE back on tour, we added Soundgarden to the bill for the next leg, which began in December 1991 in Worcester, Massachusetts. They were a favorite band of ours and it was cool to have them, but we didn't have a good rapport with them at all. We had no common vibe with any of the grunge bands, actually, because we were such a big name; we were the Led Zeppelin of the time, so coming from their more underground, indie point of view, they thought of us as "fat, lazy, and self-indulgent." We'd take them on tour and they wouldn't talk to us. It was hypocritical because they didn't really want to be there, but then again, unless I'm mistaken, they didn't say no to the gig. All things considered, Duff and I got along with Chris Cornell and Kim Thayil really well, and I understood their wanting to steer clear of the circus all around them.

We had a much more antagonistic situation on our hands with our other support band, Faith No More, once their front man, Mike Patton, started talking shit about us onstage. We let it go once, twice, but after that, that was it. We had to have a talk with him. Axl came in with me, as did their guitarist Jim Martin, because Jim was as fed up with Mike as we were.

"Listen, man," I said. "If you don't like it here, just fucking leave. It can't be like this. Either let's do this thing and make it great, or forget it, go home."

They ended up finishing the tour and that was the last outburst we heard from Mike during their set.

We did three nights at Madison Square Garden (December 9, 10, 13, 1991), the same arena where Led Zeppelin filmed *The Song Remains the Same*. One of those nights we met one of Axl's heroes, Billy Joel. It isn't obvious until you think about it, but Axl loves all of the great songwriters: the Eagles, Elton John, Billy Joel—he knows his shit. I didn't know anything about Billy Joel aside from the fact that my best friend's mom played his breakout album, *The Stranger*, nonstop back in 1978. But it was great to meet Billy that night because he's such an icon and also because he was very, very drunk—I had no idea that he was such a fuckup, and I loved it. Duff and I could certainly relate to him, and Axl was really fucking happy. Billy was led into the dressing room, where we had all of our booze, and he rummaged around the bar area, making all this noise.

"Where's the Johnnie Walker Black Label?" he said, out loud, as much to himself as to us. "There's no Johnnie Walker Black." Needless to say, we sent someone out and they came back with a bottle for Billy in no time.

<hr />

FEBRUARY 1, 1992, WAS OUR LAST SHOW with Soundgarden, at Compton Terrace, Arizona, and we decided to commemorate it with a little prank. We got ourselves a few inflatable sex dolls and Matt and Duff and I took our clothes off and went onstage with them. Come to think of it, I was the only one of us completely naked. In any case, Soundgarden was touring the *Badmotorfinger* album, and they came from a place where there was no fun to be had while rocking, so they were mortified. They looked around and there we were screwing blowup dolls all around them; I was drunk and I fell. I got separated from my doll, and at that point I was totally naked—it was a scene.

Slash the prankster, naked, embracing a blow-up doll during Soundgarden's show.

WE PLAYED THREE SHOWS AT THE TOKYO Dome in Japan (February 19, 20, 22, 1992), which was something; in fact, I played five shows in a row in the Tokyo Dome—two with Michael Jackson and three with Guns N' Roses. I experienced the biggest contrast you can imagine between those two audiences; I can't think of a more surreal switch than playing one night for Michael Jackson, who was flying around the stage and had kids and toys backstage, to playing with Guns and everything that came with that world two nights later—all in the very same building. To top it off, I spent the day I had off between the two shows at Tokyo Disney.

I flew over early to play with Michael; I had recorded with him back in L.A. between the time that we finished the *Illusion* records and their release. It was while we were home between legs of the tour. I was staying

at the Hyatt on Sunset at the time when I got the call from our office.

"Hey, Slasher, Michael Jackson is trying to get in touch with you," Alan said. "He wants you on his record."

"Oh, wow," I said. "Okay."

The next call that came through was Michael.

"Hello?" I said.

"Hello? Slash?" he said in his typically nervous, timid voice.

Off we went from there. I was flattered and I was intimidated, but it came off great. We did two songs: the first one, the cooler one, was called "Give in to Me," which was kind of like a new take on his song "Dirty Diana." When I went in to record it at the Record Plant Michael was there with Brooke Shields, who he was dating at the time. It was trippy: the studio was as dimly lit and as dark as Guns liked to have it when we recorded.

"Hi," Michael said. "This is Brooke."

"Hi, nice to meet you," I said. I think I put my hand out for a shake.

"I really want to thank you so much for being on my album," he said. "I really can't wait to hear what you come up with."

And then they split—they went off to dinner or something. I recorded my solo and that was it. A few days later I came back and recorded the introduction to "Black and White." They wanted something on the front end, which didn't even make it into the album version of the song. You can hear my part if you watch the video: it's what Macaulay Culkin is playing on guitar before the song starts. That was strange; to say the least, it wasn't quite what I had in mind for that solo.

I think Michael Jackson liked me because of the animated element of my persona. I think he saw me as a caricature. But that's just me. I still don't know if he knows that about me.

<hr />

AS OUR ALBUMS CONTINUED TO CHART worldwide, we toured Mexico in April, and like our South American fans the Mexican crowds were very dedicated. Then we did the Freddie Mercury tribute in London, which was amazing—he was another of Axl's heroes, so although it was a short set, we gave it our all: we did "Paradise City" and "Knockin' on Heaven's Door." Later on I went up and played "Tie Your

I could feel it in my loins that she was having a look.

Mother Down" with Brian May and Roger Taylor of Queen, and Axl sang as well. At the end of the concert we all did "We Are the Champions." It was a monumental gig, but the most memorable part of the evening was when I took my pants off in front of Liz Taylor: I was in the green room changing and she opened the door, her entourage in tow, and caught me in a T-shirt with no pants on at all. She didn't have a look of embarrassment in the least; she was absolutely devilish—I could feel it in my loins that she was having a look.

———————◆◆◆———————

IN MAY OF 1992, WE ANNOUNCED THAT we would coheadline a summer tour with Metallica starting July 7—there could not have been a bigger rock-and-roll bill at the time. It was too cool: they had just released *The Black Album* and we were riding high with *Use Your Illusion I* and *II*. We then headed off to start our headlining arena tour of Europe in Dublin, Ireland, in May 1992.

In my personal life, my girlfriend, Renee, and I broke up during the American leg because someone in our entourage told her how unfaithful I was being on tour. Cheating was the one thing I'd promised I'd never do. It was a weakness on my part that came out of a need to have as much of a good time between shows as possible, which, along with heavy boozing, was my way of self-medicating to get through all of the turbulent emotional activity, the yin-yang psycho-emotional ups and downs. Booze and girls— that was how I dealt. For the most part in our professional career I hadn't taken full advantage of the exorbitant amount of women that were available

to me, so now that I felt unsettled about what we were doing, I took advantage of all of it.

Unfortunately, as is usually the case, it all came out in the wash. We were in Chicago when I got a message on my answering service from Renee's stepbrother, who was a good buddy of mine. I was with a girl at the time, an actress—a real one—that I'd seen in a movie. We were in my hotel room when I called him up.

"Hey, man, it's Slash," I said. "What's going on?"

"*Dude*," he said, deadly serious. "I don't know what you've got going on out there on tour, and that's your business. But I think you should call Renee because she's flipping out about something. She won't tell me what's wrong, but she sounds really pissed."

I called Renee and she told me off very colorfully. Then in no uncertain terms she threatened me, letting me know that she had an uncle in Chicago—not knowing that I was actually in Chicago—who was connected and who would happily "take care of me" if she asked him to.

Slam. She hung up.

I put down the phone. I looked at it for a second. Then I turned to the girl lying in my bed.

"Hey," I said. "You better go."

"Um, *okay*," she said, annoyed. She sat up and started looking for her clothes.

Then I thought about it for a minute. "Well . . . not right *now*," I said, and got back into bed. Needless to say, Renee and I were apart for a while after that.

<p style="text-align:center">———◆•✕•◆———</p>

THE EUROPEAN TOUR WAS AMAZING, AND there were many memorable moments. We did this one show in Paris where Axl got this idea in his head that we should have people come out to play with us to record it for a pay-per-view show on some global TV network. Axl got Aerosmith, Lenny Kravitz, Jeff Beck, and pulled this move that seemed almost gratuitous to me because they were my favorite artists—as you know by now, Aerosmith was my favorite band, Beck my favorite guitarist, and I'd been on Lenny's album.

I felt like this was an effort on his part to keep me satisfied, because he rarely made grand gestures aimed at keeping me happy—he'd have to have been blind not to know how pissed off I was as the tour wore on. He'd dumped all of the band responsibility personally on me, from finding Matt and Gilby to hiring the support musicians. I think in his mind, this pay-per-view concert was throwing me a bone, because when he ever did get around to making a peace offering, Axl never did it with words.

I wish that he did because that concert was very expensive for us, and although it was seen by millions, it didn't seem entirely necessary. But once again, I agreed to it. Truth be told, I was excited to do it, as excessive as it was.

Whenever I get onstage to play with Aerosmith, it's only because we happen to be in the same city at the same time—they usually invite me, but I'm lucky if they even send a car to take me to the venue. We gave every performer on that bill red-carpet treatment: first-class travel and accommodations in Paris—all of it. Everyone got in a day early and we set up rehearsals to go through "Always on the Run" with Lenny and "Train Kept Rolling" with Aerosmith, and Jeff Beck did "Locomotive" with us.

Everyone came out to sound-check . . . except Axl. I remember Steven Tyler coming up to me and asking—again—"Where's your *singer*, man?" As I've mentioned, it's the way he's greeted me ever since our first tour together. This time the joke was too true to laugh at. Steven wasn't the only one asking that question that day—in fact, it seemed to be the comment on everyone's tongue. It wasn't easy to stand there and take it; I never wanted to say anything bad about Axl, but it was pretty hard not to look stressed with Steven Tyler standing in front of me speaking the truth.

I remember doing sound check the day of the show, going through "Locomotive" with Joe Perry and Jeff Beck, and talking through the guitar parts. Jeff was standing there playing while he talked to us . . . it was so cool, he was just laying out these amazing licks nonchalantly.

"So you've been practicing?" Joe Perry asked him. I thought that was a weird thing to say. It was Jeff fucking Beck!

Jeff blew his ears out at sound check however . . . well, actually Matt blew Jeff's ears out: Jeff was standing up near the drum riser playing when Matt slammed on a cymbal and just knocked his head off. It sucked—it was the

day before the gig and Jeff couldn't play; he couldn't hear and do it at all, so he went home. It wasn't cool, he'd sustained some real damage. Years later Matt told me he saw Jeff doing an interview about it and he summed it up like this: "He hit the cymbal and it went *crash* and that was it. Nothing."

He was missed but the show came out really well: Lenny came on and did his thing, and so did Joe and Steve. Unfortunately, their part was at the end of a two-hour set, which was already an hour late going on, so they had to wait backstage all night. I still can't believe that Axl didn't show up for that sound check, let alone go on an hour late. I can count on one hand how many times Axl came to sound check on that tour; he was always careful about his throat, which is fine. But I don't think that's quite why he didn't sound-check for that show. Although, all things considered, I have no idea why Axl didn't sound-check for that show . . . or any of the others on that tour for that matter.

<hr />

BY THE TIME WE GOT TO ENGLAND TO play a few dates, I got lonely and called Renee, and flew her out to meet me. I made that decision on one of those nights when all of the fucking sordid, lunar, promiscuous stuff I'd been doing had caught up to me and left me feeling empty and entirely alone. It's something that musicians do on a regular basis when they're on the road for too long: they get a soft spot in their heart, and in a moment of weakness, against their better judgement, they act on it, usually engaging the wrong person.

So anyway a day or so later, there she was. I waited for her in the hotel bar, and when she showed up I was totally distracted and starstruck because Jonathan Winters was there—he is one of my comedic idols, so we ended up having drinks with him and his wife, which was great.

Renee and I had a very civil time. She travelled through England with me and we discussed getting back together. But she came out there in the same frame of mind that she was in when I first met her—not giving me any. There was no way she was staying on tour very long.

We headed back to Europe after that, and when we got to Germany, a few of us shot a video with Michael Jackson for the song I'd played on his *Dangerous* album, "Give in to Me." It was released as a single in Europe,

though it wasn't in the United States. Gilby, Ted Adriatus, aka Teddy Zig Zag, and I shot the video with Michael: it was a live club gig in Munich, complete with fans. We had the guy from Living Colour on bass, Muzz Skillings, and the concept was "Michael fronting a heavy metal band." Unfortunately, it only aired on MTV Europe.

<hr />

THERE WAS A SPARE-NO-EXPENSE attitude on this tour, which was new for us. If we had days off, yachts were rented. In England, we had a five-hour go-kart rally arranged for us in West London. In Australia, taking a boat out to the Great Barrier Reef seemed to be something the band needed to do. It was all senseless spending. Doug approved one crazy idea after another to fill our free time at our expense. With the exception of Axl, the band wouldn't have cared if none of it ever happened—we were more than capable of entertaining ourselves in any global locale on a shoestring budget.

Our mistake was never giving a thought to the cost of Doug's expenditures, that is for sure. In the back of my mind, I knew that hiring a yacht or closing down a restaurant didn't come free, but at the same time I wasn't going to say anything because at times those events seemed to maintain the status quo. I know that was Doug's motivation: he did everything he could think of to keep everyone happy, but at the same time every time he arranged one of his grand gestures, it was a strike against him in my mind. I resented Doug's influence in that regard, but all the same, I couldn't get too directly pissed at him. Doug was so far up Axl's ass at that point that Doug saw whatever Axl was looking at, crystal clear.

I always found it suspect that Doug was our manager yet he was out on the road *all the time*. He found a million excuses to be there, and aside from the few legitimate ones, the truth is, in my opinion at least, he was there to try to keep Axl under his thumb and so protect his own job. By becoming tight with Axl when he was our road manager, Doug had secured himself his new position as our manager or so it seemed to me. I wanted to keep it all going too much to worry about extravagances, but I thought it was ridiculous that someone who was employed to guide our

career was not only arrogant enough to let these wasteful expenditures happen, but was also arrogant enough to enjoy most of them himself out on the road as if he were earning his keep onstage every night.

AT THE END OF THE EUROPEAN TOUR, we returned to the States and Axl got arrested the moment we landed at JFK in New York on July 12, 1992. He was considered a fugitive, stemming from the warrants out for his arrest by St. Louis authorities in connection with the riot in 1991. Two days later, in court in St. Louis, he pleaded innocent to four counts of misdemeanor assault and one of property damage and a date was set for October. We were allowed to begin our tour with Metallica three days later, as scheduled.

While Axl took care of his business, I had five days off in L.A., and my first night in town I went out to dinner with Renee. After dinner, we had exhausted all the small talk we had in us and the conversation shifted to the subject of seeing each other regularly again.

"No," she said. "I'm not going to do that again."

"Oh no?" I asked, completely into it now. "Why not?"

"I will only be with you if we get married."

"Oh yeah?" I said. "Really?"

She'd handed me the ultimate ultimatum, because marriage was the furthest thing from my mind. I was emotionally needy and I don't know if she sensed that, but under the gun, I folded. I told her I needed to think about it, and then I came back to her with a ring and we set a date.

THE METALLICA TOUR STARTED IN WASHINGTON, D.C., in July 1992. We had a meeting before it began because the Metallica camp was concerned: we were having major problems getting onstage on time, riding that high–low roller coaster. Metallica was not a band to pull that kind of shit at all, so they wisely opted to play first so as to avoid being pulled down by our bullshit.

I have so much respect for James—I think he's one of the most prolific

singer-songwriter-guitarists ever. I had looked up to the band since *Master of Puppets*, which came out just before *Appetite*. When we set out to do that tour, part of me was excited and part of me was worried about how it was all going to work and whether Axl was going to adjust. Metallica was a no-frills, hardworking road band; they did long tours, they never went on late—they were no bullshit. They were macho about their work ethic and dedicated to their fans, which I thought was commendable as well. They represented everything that mattered to me professionally, and I didn't want to see it get fucked up; I didn't want to let them down.

From the start of the tour, Axl was out to impress Metallica and everyone else—in his way. He brought up the idea of having backstage parties every single night—theme parties that would be a lounge for our guests, like the Stones had on their tours. Axl had hired his stepbrother Stuart and his sister Amy to be part of the management team, and they were put in charge of organizing these parties according to Axl's vision. They had no experience doing so, of course. I saw their work in action and it was both uncool and yet another unnecessary extravagance. I never went to one of those parties during the entire tour. The whole idea of it was just too self-indulgent, too self-centered, and too showy for me to even think about participating in good faith anyway.

Actually, I'm wrong, I went into one, one time, to look for someone. As I recall, it was a "Roman Bath" party, with a huge Jacuzzi in the middle of the room. I know they did a casino night, a Mexican fiesta, and a bunch of other things. For each of these parties, Axl's siblings would be hustling every day to get it done. The Metallica guys, off the bat, disassociated themselves from that whole freak show. It was like no one wanted to even say anything about it. The subject of the theme parties and Axl's behavior reminded me of the first *Creepshow* film and the episode about this thing under the stairs in a box that ate people that no one would talk about.

It was always a good time, but all the same, Axl and our inability to get onstage on time was like the big elephant in the room every night. No one would bring it up, but it was obvious that we were all thinking about it. Lars Ulrich never said anything to me, but he did to Matt, and it was humiliating and embarrassing how lame those parties were and how disap-

pointed Metallica was that we couldn't even get onstage on time. I think that the reason Axl went onstage so late, and never understood how offensive, selfish, and inconsiderate it was to everyone involved—from the fans to the band—was that he saw it as something other than what it was. That was why he felt like he was doing something that other people just didn't get. I think somewhere in his mind he thought it was cool to keep people waiting, as if it just served to build anticipation rather than create frustration. I think it was all building up what Guns meant to him in his mind. And in the face of that, he simply could not comprehend how what he was doing didn't make complete sense to us or the rest of the world. And I couldn't do a damn thing about it.

Metallica was earning the exact same paycheck as we were every night, but while they pocketed the whole thing, we were blowing 80 percent both on union dues for all of the overtime we cost ourselves going on late and on these stupid theme parties. It was just bad.

our chemistry onstage was beautiful despite the drama within the band

IT'S TOO BAD, BUT, OUR ROLLER COASTER of dysfunction really peaked on tour with Metallica. When it all went off without a hitch, that double bill was the greatest thing going. When it didn't, it was a nightmare. For us, for the most part, our chemistry onstage was beautiful despite the drama within the band, but there were times when it spilled over. Sitting around for a few hours waiting to go on . . . that really spoiled the music. It was like being an athlete who'd warmed up then cooled down, and then had to run the race: it took a while to get into the groove, but we always got there.

Offstage, however, our chemistry was awful, and it became harder to ignore as the tour went on. The tension was so tangible that Duff and I reached colossal levels of alcohol intake just to get through a day. It was no big deal for us to polish off a half gallon of vodka while sitting around backstage for two hours waiting to play. The disrespect and lack of trust that Axl's behavior inspired was corroding the core of the band. Axl was becoming the quarterback who refused to throw the ball even when we started losing every game.

At the Giants Stadium show at the end of July, Axl barely made it through the set due to the state of his voice. He was advised by his doctor to rest it for a week, so we canceled our next three dates. The tour resumed in Canada, which came to be the infamous coup de grâce of everything that was wrong with our band.

It all went down in Montreal, on August 8, 1992. Metallica went on, and midway through their set, James Hetfield caught on fire when a pyrotechnic malfunctioned. He sustained serious injuries to his arm and shoulder, and the band was forced to end their set immediately. We were still at our hotel when it happened, and we were asked to go on early—it was a nonissue; of course we agreed to do so. The band headed down to the venue right away and discussed what we'd play to fill up the remainder of Metallica's slot and ours as well. We had plenty of time to go over our options but it couldn't happen because Axl did not show up.

Not only did we not go on early enough to fill the void left by Metallica, we went on three hours later than our *own* scheduled stage time. In the end there was something like four hours between the time Metallica were forced to stop the show and the moment we took the stage. And once we did, Axl ended it early, after we'd done just ninety minutes out of a scheduled two hours. I'm sure he had his reasons, but neither I nor the crowd, as far as I know, knew quite what they were.

I can't say that I was surprised when the audience started rioting. Being old pros at this, we sat in our dressing room, which was underneath the hockey rink, basically in the locker rooms. We could hear the stampede overhead, and knew that there was no going back on. The crowd destroyed everything in the outer arena, from the skyboxes to the vending booths. At one point we went upstairs in an elevator and looked out into the hallway

and saw kids throwing rocks at the display cases, when one broke, they'd scrambled to snatch the merchandise.

As we made our escape, we saw overturned cars in the parking lot, we watched kids pulling down the giant light poles, lighting bonfires, breaking everything in sight—the whole deal. It was a fiasco.

Axl did have an excuse for quitting the show early; he did in fact have a reason, and he did go public with it. He had canceled our Boston show and two others because of his throat, and he said that his vocal cords were damaged and that was why he couldn't perform. To us, it was crying wolf, because in Montreal he didn't mention that he was in pain or anything that night before the show. It was a very tense time—a major straw on the camel's back for me and for everybody in our camp. It was actually a huge issue for me because I'd lost face with everyone in Metallica. We didn't keep our promise to them, the fans, or to ourselves to put on the best show possible, come what may. When it had mattered the most it felt like we'd given even less. I felt like an ass. I couldn't look James, Lars, or anyone from their band in the eye for the rest of the tour.

We postponed the remaining dates for nearly a month until James recovered enough to continue. Apparently that was enough time for Axl's vocal cords to recover as well. When we set off again on August 25 in Phoenix, James had one of their techs play guitar for him while he sang; he was right out front with a big cast on his arm. That's how cool they were. It was frustrating to me, because we prided ourselves on being a kick-ass, hard-core rock-and-roll band, but we had a weak spot in the group that was making us vulnerable. We had become larger than life and legendary, so this petty bullshit was *very* trying.

I was pissed off at myself for having died.

WE RESUMED OUR TOUR WITH METALLICA
and made up the dates we'd been forced to cancel. In September, we had
an incident with opening act Faith No More and they opted to leave the
tour earlier than they were supposed to. They broke up shortly afterward.
We replaced them with Ice-T's Body Count, who were about as infamous
as you could be following the release of the single "Cop Killer." We had our
good friends Motörhead out with us as well. I got up and played "Back in
My Car" with them at the Rose Bowl.

When we got to the Bay Area to play the Oakland Stadium on Sep-
tember 24, 1992, I got into a bit of trouble. We were staying in a hotel in
San Francisco, and before I went to the venue that afternoon to sound-check,
I got into a huge argument with Renee over the issue of our prenuptial
agreement. It descended into a screaming match and a fight so abrasive that
I was beside myself pissed. I went to the gig so angry that I was determined
to do what I do when I want to act out: get some smack. I hadn't done any
in so long because, as unhappy as I was with the band, I was not about to
cripple my professionalism. But this gave me a worthwhile excuse as far as
I was concerned.

I got to the show and I ran into an old friend, a porn star we'll call "Lucky,"
who I'd known some years before. She was a friend of an ex-girlfriend of
mine, the porn star Savannah, whom I'd dated for a few months when I had
downtime in L.A. during my time off from Renee. Savannah was intense. I
had no idea that she was a junkie. The clue I should have picked up on was
that she only liked to fuck after she'd fixed; I didn't know it at the time. We
got into a huge fight one night when she spontaneously decided to give me
a blow job in the middle of some bar in New York City.

I first met Lucky when she came over to hang out with us at the Mon-
drian. She and Savannah got stripped down, and when we ordered some
champagne they invited the room service guy into the room to watch them
go at it, and before long the only thing holding this guy's eyes in their sock-
ets were a few little tiny veins.

Anyway, I ran into Lucky at the show and we got to talking. I gave Lucky
passes and about seven hundred bucks in cash to get me as much heroin as
she could find. We did the show—it was great—then I went straight back
to my hotel room and waited. I kept drinking the whole time, maybe did

some blow, but when she showed up at five a.m., I was pretty much ready to pass out.

Lucky and her boyfriend came rolling in with all of this crack and smack and I'm sitting on the floor watching them spread out all of the drugs across the coffee table. They've got rigs, points, shooters, tools, hardware, whatever you choose to call them—they've got brand-new needles. We get it all going, the three of us, and we are all fiending hard. It was intended to be a fun illicit thing—momentary, as far as I was concerned—but this is getting intense. We all do a hit, but the shit isn't strong, so I do a few more. They are sending the crack pipe around.

The hours go by and we are really loaded. Matt calls me sometime in the early morning and he invites me to his room to do some blow.

"Okay . . . yeah . . . I'll be right there."

I get up, weak-kneed, reeling from my last crack hit, and I look over at Lucky and her boyfriend; they are having the time of their lives—they have never had a motherload of drugs like this for free. I make my way across the carpet to the door, dragging my feet, realizing that I'm dizzy and I can't speak. I open the door; I don't have my wits about me at all. I see a maid in the hallway pushing her housekeeping cart and I ask her which way to the elevator. That is what I try to say. I remember it all in slow motion; I remember hearing my voice speak far away.

I collapsed like a rag doll in the hallway . . . I blacked out, and my heart stopped for eight minutes, or so I was told. I don't know who called 911. My security guard, Ronnie, was there and so was Earl, Axl's guy, and they took care of me and got the paramedics. I woke up when the defibrillators sent an electric shock through my chest and stunned my heart into beating again. It was like being slapped in the face hard enough to wake you from a deep sleep. I remember the bright lights in my eyes and a circle of people leaning in over me: Ronnie, Earl, and the paramedics. I had no idea what was going on; it wasn't an easy wake-up call.

I was put in an ambulance and taken to a hospital, where I was given the once-over. I was told to remain overnight for observation, but I wasn't having that. After a couple of hours I signed myself out and went back to the hotel, Ronnie in tow. I had no remorse whatsoever about my overdose— but I was pissed off at myself for having died. The whole hospital excursion

really ate into my day off. I was hoping to make it through without a hitch and was kicking myself for not being able to maintain my balance and just stay awake through the whole thing as planned.

Back at the hotel, the vibe was pretty somber. Apparently, my halfway swan dive didn't look so good. Everyone thought that I was a goner and was acting appropriately serious, which is something that I could never understand. My attitude at the time was, "Hey, everybody, I made it! Let's go!" When I got back, my highest priority was finding Lucky and her boyfriend. From what I was told, Earl had scared them off. I completely understood that because Earl was terrifying: He was a big black guy, over six feet tall, with a football player's build and an oddly sweet face. That feature actually made him more disturbing because when he was pissed, you really knew about it.

I'm sure the mention of prison and me dying was enough to drive Lucky and her man to vacate quickly. It wasn't their fault that I couldn't hold my shit together. I don't know for sure, but Earl probably threw the dope away in the course of kicking them out. At least that's what I told myself because they hadn't left me anything . . . and that bummed me out most of all.

I cooled down in my room for a few hours, with both security guards posted in the hallway outside of my door to ensure that I didn't go anywhere. Eventually Doug Goldstein came in and launched into one of the most pathetic displays of bullshit concern that mankind has ever known. He gave me a long speech at the top of his lungs about what I'd just done, about how people love me and this, that, and the other. It was very aggressive, very dramatic, and *very* fake. To illustrate his "seriousness" he threw a bottle of Jack Daniel's through the television. When he left, I retrieved that bottle, which hadn't broken, and poured myself a stiff drink to get over his intervention.

Shortly afterward, Doug called a band meeting in Axl's room. We all gathered around, and I was still nodding out at this point. Everyone voiced their concern for my well-being, but Axl's comment stood out most of all. It snapped me out of my haze, actually.

"You gave us a scare," he said slowly, looking right at me. "We thought you were dead. . . . I thought I'd have to look for a new guitar player."

The next morning we boarded helicopters and flew to Oakland for the gig, and the whole time Ronnie and Earl monitored me like two hawks

tracking a mouse. From there we did the L.A. Coliseum, then San Diego, which was killer: Motörhead, Body Count, Metallica, and us. We did the Rose Bowl in Pasadena after that, which was just huge, and then we ended the tour in Seattle. And after a few days, everyone realized that what I'd done was a onetime thing.

As great as that tour was, I was relieved the moment it was over. I was thankful that I didn't have to see the Metallica guys every day anymore, considering that I was never sure of what Axl was going to do from gig to gig. That last day I felt as I had felt for the entire tour: I was elated at what we had achieved, yet bummed that it hadn't been as amazingly stupendous as it should have been.

<center>◆━◆✕◆━◆</center>

AT THE END OF OUR YEARLONG TOUR the biggest mistake of all came to light: we'd barely made any money. Between the union dues incurred by Axl taking the stage late night after night and the theme parties that bled us dry night after night, we had next to nothing to show for all of our hard work. Doug finally confronted Axl about the band's spending on the Metallica tour and the fact that our profit margin had been eaten up by our excesses. I think Axl had a few suggestions as to cost cutting that wouldn't have done much, but Doug finally got through to him: he told Axl that if he wanted to keep his nice new multimillion-dollar mansion in Malibu, he needed to earn more money.

And so Doug booked us another year of dates, starting with South America, Europe, Japan, and Australia from October 1992 through January 1993. As hard as it was to endure, Doug got no argument from the rest of us—we wanted to play. What else would I be doing anyway? And at the same time, I thought maybe things would change. I also wondered continually whether the extra tour had been booked out of concern for the band's finances or to land Doug a hefty commission.

Before we headed out again, I got married to Renee in October 1992. We definitely didn't do it small—it was this really big production that I had very little to do with. My only memories of planning it involve Renee showing me an endless number of books full of gifts to pick out. I couldn't relate to any of it and my lack of interest made her very upset. The wedding took

place at the Four Seasons in Marina Del Rey, with Duff as my best man, a couple hundred people, including my bandmates and crew, and a lounge band. As soon as we were married, we headed to Africa, to Tanzania, on safari for two weeks for our honeymoon. For a wildlife fanatic like me, Africa was always on the top of my list for a vacation: there I could see what I'd been reading about in books and seeing on television my whole life. I was obsessed with leopards while we were there; I'd get up at five every morning to go out on safari and get back by six in the evening. It was the greatest place in the world to forget about everything that was weighing on my mind. It's hard to imagine that any of it matters when you're standing in the middle of the Ngorongoro Crater far from any trace of civilization.

Before the wedding, Renee and I had a coed bachelor/bachelorette party at the Troubadour, because Renee didn't want me to get together unsupervised with the guys. And at that little party, I ran into an old friend named Perla.

Perla and I had been introduced in Las Vegas when we were headlining the Thomas & Mack Center during the first leg of the *Illusion* tour. At that point I was sleeping around a lot; it was when Renee and I were still dating very casually. Perla didn't know shit about Guns N' Roses and she didn't care to—she'd come out from L.A. because she'd seen a picture of me and wanted to meet me. Ron Jeremy introduced us before the show, and afterward we met at my hotel and hung out all night long. Let's just say that she left a *major* impression on me that grew into a serious infatuation.

We exchanged numbers and kept in touch when I headed off on tour after that. Eventually she became a tenant of mine; she rented the Walnut House from me for a year and was the best tenant I ever had. It says a lot about the strength of Perla's character that she lived there without losing her mind because that place had a detrimental effect on everyone else who lived there—myself included, I suppose.

My first tenants were two bisexual chicks that I met during one of our four L.A. Forum shows. They were in the front row and they were going at it pretty provocatively during the entire gig. I had them brought to the dressing room afterward for more of the same and we stayed in touch; I'd call them up and have them over and watch them and we'd all have a good time. I rented them the house when I was going off on tour, which seemed

like a good idea, but they completely lost it—they got strung out on meth and one girl killed the other girl's cat and then attacked her. The "victim" moved out, and then the other one moved a meth dealer into the house. I had to go over there and take care of the situation, and when I saw that one girl again I barely recognized her. My second tenant was this guy Jim who worked at a zoo as a snake keeper. I hired him to look after my snakes and eventually took him on as a tenant. Apparently he suffered some kind of meltdown too and completely lost it while living there as well. Perla was the only one who wasn't fazed by the place—and the only one who paid her rent on time and actually enjoyed living there.

Anyway, once I'd gotten back together with Renee, and gotten engaged and all of that, I did my best to avoid Perla because I knew that there was something serious between us that I couldn't deny. After my fight with Renee over the prenup and my OD in San Francisco, I didn't give a fuck, however, and arranged to meet Perla at our San Diego show, just two shows before the end of the tour and just a few weeks before my wedding. We spent the night together there, and the next time I saw her was when she crashed my bachelor party. She was dangerous; there was such an attraction between us that neither of us could deny. At the same time, she was way too ambitious and energetic to get into a relationship with; she was seventeen and I was twenty-five; she was too crazy, so not in a place where I wanted to cancel my wedding to be with her. She was a real firecracker, though, and the connection was strong enough that I spent the night with her once more . . . the night before my wedding, in fact.

IN LATE NOVEMBER, WE SET OFF TO PLAY South America and found ourselves in the middle of sudden political unrest when we did a show in Caracas, Venezuela. Corrupt law enforcement, abundant drugs, and the world's most dedicated and zealous crowds are the status quo across that continent, so I can't say that I was surprised. We were scheduled to play the biggest concert in the history of the country, and since there wasn't a venue large enough to hold the forty-five thousand ticket holders, the promoter created one in a huge parking lot. It was an amazing show, and all went off well . . . until the next night, when the

country experienced a sudden military coup just after we left for Colombia. We made it out, but a few of our crew, and over half our gear, did not—they got held up in the chaos at the airport.

We were supposed to play two nights in Bogotá, Colombia, after that, but without that huge cargo crate of equipment, it wasn't really an option. The promoter decided to roll both nights into one show, to take place the next night, so we had a day off to relax in our hotel. The hotel was pretty huge, it was part of some kind of complex with a big movie theater downstairs, and I remember coming up the escalator and watching a Jurassic Park pinball machine emerge on the horizon as I got to the top. I'd just seen the movie and I *had* to play that thing; it combined two of my favorite interests, dinosaurs and pinball. When I got to my room I arranged to have it brought up and spent the entire day being the ball.

During our stay, word got out to the authorities that we had drugs, so, in another move typical of South America, the authorities got "warrants" to search our rooms, in hopes of finding something that might require us to buy them off, I imagine. The day of the show, the cops barged in on all of us. I had nothing; they came in, guns drawn, and found me, freshly showered, in a towel playing pinball.

"Oh, hey," I said. "Hi!"

They showed me the warrant and started searching my room. I was pretty jovial as they tore through my stuff.

"Señor, is it okay if I keep playing?" I asked.

The show that night—November 29, 1992—was pretty magical; it was one of those moments that you can't believe is happening even as you watch it all unfold, even as you're a part of it. There was a torrential rainstorm the entire day before as our crew set up; the weight of the water buckled the stage roof (which wasn't ours), sending a lighting rig crashing to the ground. Luckily, no one was hurt. The whole stage had to be redesigned. Then the day of the show, a sudden storm damaged some of our equipment. Despite more rain, people filled the arena and were lined up outside, where fights broke out, a few cars were burned, and the police had to use tear gas to calm everyone down.

When we took the stage sometime around eleven p.m., the place went crazy. We were playing really well, and the rain had held off throughout the first hour of our set until we played "November Rain." As we started

that song, literally on cue, the sky opened and it poured once again. It was one of those massive tropical downpours where one drop can fill a coffee cup. It was coming down in a black mist that mixed with the steam rising off of the audience. I could barely see through the clouds that formed in the arena; the people were a sea of silhouettes. It was very dramatic and very beautiful; it felt as if they and the band were one. The audience was as moved as we were—they were into it, truly passionate. It rained so hard that we finished the song then we had to break until the storm passed, and once it did, we came back on and gave it everything we had.

We had every obstacle possible befall us between our show in Venezuela and the shows in Colombia, and considering the band's chemistry in the recent past, you would expect that we'd have fallen apart under such duress. But that was the thing about Guns: we'd self-destruct when everything was *easy*, but in those instances when every single factor seemed to be against us, everyone, Axl included, pulled together to make it happen. The extreme lows might have left me feeling like there was no tomorrow, but when we'd pull off these valiant rock-and-roll productions in the face of adversity, I'd feel like we were invincible; I'd think we were the strongest band around. Those moments renewed our collective faith and boosted morale like nothing else. Rather than be frustrated by what befell us in South America, we let the audiences at all of those gigs sustain us with their passion and drive us to be our best. Our playing was elevated; it was as intense as the fans were—we were carried away along with them. We reached that point that musicians talk about where you are immersed in what you are doing to the degree that you don't even know who you are—you are part of the performance so fully that you aren't thinking anymore. Those moments are magical and that whole tour was like that, every single night. It was the band at its best; it was something that anybody would have given their left arm to be a part of . . . if it occurred consistently. But it wasn't ever that simple: when we weren't being transcendent we specialized in self-inflicted disaster.

<hr />

IN JANUARY 1993, WE SET OFF ON A tour of Japan, Australia, and New Zealand, with an eighty-person crew and entourage in tow. We ran into Ronnie Wood in Japan, which was great.

He and I had been friends for years by then, so he joined us onstage at the Tokyo Dome for "Knockin' on Heaven's Door," and Duff and Matt and I hung out with him after the show. That was a really good night. The rest of that tour was just more of the same—great shows, some drama—plus a lot of expensive go-karting, yachting, and dining. The theme parties might have been eliminated but the wasteful days off were not.

We returned to the States in early February and had a month off before we started the next leg, an American tour we called *Skin and Bones*. This jaunt in particular was aimed at making us money, because the production was stripped back to the bare essentials: we kept Dizzy Reed, but Teddy and the horn section were gone, as were the backup singers. This tour featured an acoustic section in the middle of the set that showcased the hits off of *Lies* as well as a few cover songs, such as "Dead Flowers." I couldn't have been happier: *finally* we were touring as a bare-bones rock-and-roll band again.

This leg, in my mind, was our chance to show the world the *Use Your Illusion* records as I'd always heard them. The day that I'd finished recording my last guitar part for those records I left the studio with a mix of them that was simple and raw, before any synths or horns or backup vocal tracks were layered on. I've never forgotten how cool they sounded in that stripped-down, simple, *powerful* state. I wish that I still had a copy of them; or that they were floating around the Internet somewhere. Believe me, they sounded so cool; they were entirely different beasts altogether from the versions that got released. I'm not going to get into hindsight about what could have been, but all in all they were two wholly different bodies of work. In any case, we got a chance to do the songs scaled back and straight up with the band reduced to its normal size . . . I was *elated*.

The tour started in Austin, Texas, in late February and that first show went fine, but we immediately ran into trouble. Over the first few weeks we had to cancel four shows due to inclement weather. In Sacramento in early April, someone in the audience threw a bottle of Jack and hit Duff square in the head, knocking him unconscious. That was so ridiculous, not to mention dangerous. Anytime people throw shit onstage to get a reaction—I assume because rock bands seem larger than life—is just insane. I'm never sure what they're after when they throw something that can do actual bodily

harm. We'd done about ninety minutes at that point, but that was the end of the show because Duff was really hurt.

I volunteered to be the one to tell the audience that they'd fucked up. They cheered when I came back onstage, but they weren't happy about what I had to say.

"That bottle of piss knocked Duff unconscious and now he's on his way to the hospital," I said. "There is no way that we're coming back out. The show is *over*. Please leave peacefully and don't fuck with anyone. Don't fuck with the building."

We canceled a show in Atlanta both to let Duff recover and because Axl had been arrested there during the *Appetite* tour for kicking in the head a security guard whom he'd supposedly seen roughing up audience members. Doug didn't trust either Axl or the venue's security and he was probably right on both counts.

Then at the end of April, when we were back in L.A., Gilby broke his wrist in a motorcycle accident. We weren't sure how bad it was until he showed up at a band meeting in a very serious-looking cast.

"Wow," I said. "That looks pretty bad."

"How long is that gonna take to heal?" Axl asked him.

Gilby looked truly depressed. "Two or three weeks."

"Aw, fuck!"

"I know, man," Gilby said. "This fucking sucks."

We had a European tour booked, starting with two dates in Russia—our first ever—two weeks later.

"Fuck it," Axl said. "Let's call Izzy."

I was surprised and happy to hear that Izzy went for it . . . though I was completely confused to hear that Izzy didn't want to rehearse at all—not that we had much time to anyway. As it turns out, the political situation in Russia in May 1993 was too unstable for us to play Moscow, so we flew to Tel Aviv, Israel, to rehearse with Izzy before we launched the tour there at the Hayarkon Park Arena. We booked a rehearsal space studio in Tel Aviv and it was a trip: this place was a recording studio as well and I think that the engineers didn't believe the band booked was actually us until we walked through the door. We got together in this cheap old spot that was homey—in a foreign way—and run by these old people who were really cool. It was an

average rehearsal space with midrange recording equipment and they'd clearly never had anyone like us in there, so we totally blew them away and for that reason alone it was worth it. Izzy showed up . . . with dreadlocks . . . and hadn't practiced one song. So we did what we could.

We played to fifty thousand people in Israel for the first time two days later, which was the biggest concert that the country had ever seen. Sadly, it was a pretty loose set, because Izzy wasn't up to speed and hadn't been conscientious about practicing. The press criticized us pretty harshly, saying we had used the opportunity as a warm-up date, which was not true at all; we wanted it to be great, but with a rhythm guitarist who was still unfamiliar with the material, there was only so much we could do. We did the gig, we hung out there for a couple of days; we saw all of the sights.

Izzy, Duff, and I saw where Jesus was born, and we went to eat in the square around the Wailing Wall, and while we were sitting at this outdoor café near the zoo I watched a busload of school kids get off for a field trip. At either end of the bus were parents, or teachers, or adult supervisors of some kind who were armed with rifles. They arranged the kids in a line for their tour of the zoo and one armed adult took the front, one took the back, and one walked in the middle of them, all with their rifles strapped around them. I'd never seen anything like that in my life. I'd had a friend from Israel who'd gone back to do his two years of mandatory military duty and I thought about him just then: he'd come back a completely different guy. He'd gone off as a nerd and returned as a nerd with combat experience.

———◆◆◆———

IZZY STAYED OUT THERE WITH US FOR a while, all through Greece and Turkey—places we'd never played before. I didn't think much of it at the time, but Izzy was doing what he does best; he was checking out the situation, taking stock, observing everything, taking part while committing to nothing. He wanted to see what had changed and what hadn't. He was taking note of how much drinking was going on, what Axl's trip was. He was testing the water to see if he could deal with it. At the time I still thought he'd quit the band because of the riot in St. Louis and the near riot in Germany. I didn't even realize that those incidents were the least of his reasons.

For the entire *Illusion* tour, all two-plus years of it, we had two camera guys with us documenting every single moment. Those guys were close friends, so we really let them in and they really got it all. They captured the kind of history that anyone aside from the members of the band would never see. They were out with us on this leg of the tour, of course, as was Del James, who became a de facto narrator at times, conducting interviews and telling the camera guys what was what. One night Del and the cameras caught Izzy and me jamming on our acoustic guitars, just hitting loose stuff the way we did when no one was around. We fell into the pocket so naturally, and it felt comfortable and so great, that I'd love to see a tape of that. We have two years of footage, in fact, all of which is in a vault that will remain shut forever unless Axl and the rest of us get our differences ironed out. That footage is the Holy Grail of Guns N' Roses: seeing the film that would result from condensing the best moments into two hours would be the be-all and end-all of knowing exactly who we were and who we are.

Izzy remained on board until late May, ending his run with two shows at the National Bowl in Milton Keynes, England. Gilby flew out and hung out and the two of them got along great. There was no drama as the baton was passed, thank God.

From there we continued across Northern Europe; we did our makeup show in Norway, our second try at our first ever. We'd had to cancel it the first time because Axl got "held up" in Paris. Norway was a big one for Matt, since his family is Norwegian; he was pretty into visiting the roots of his Nordic history.

A particularly memorable night took place in Cologne, Germany; the kind of night that I might not remember completely, but one that I am remembered for. We had a day off, which Gilby and I spent sightseeing. Later on we met the band and some friends at this Italian restaurant, where we filled a huge corner banquette. We had tons of food, all of this wine, and at the end of the meal, Gilby and I decided to indulge in a few grappa shots. The first few went down fine and all was well. Then we did one more and suddenly it all went wrong: I puked everywhere. It was an *Exorcist* puke; I was sitting in the deep corner of the booth, so it went all over the table, and inexcusibly all over everyone around me. It flowed across the plates and everything and started dripping on the floor. I don't know what was wrong

with the owners of this place, but they found it charming. They were so honored to have us there that me puking up my meal at the table was A-OK. I commemorated the night by signing their guest book: "Of all the restaurants in the world, this is definitely one of them!" That line, by the way, was definitely stolen from Mike "McBob" Mayhew.

The tour continued through Europe and then returned to South America. We did our last date in Argentina on July 17, 1993. As I recall we played until about two a.m. and then commandeered the hotel bar until about six a.m. And when we returned to L.A. we had the honor of having done the longest tour in rock history. We'd played 192 shows in two and a half years, spanning twenty-seven countries. Over seven million people had seen us perform. I don't really keep track of my achievements, but if I did that is the one I'd point out first and foremost.

I RETURNED TO L.A. EXHAUSTED AND went straight to Renee's stepmom's house for some kind of family gathering. Her stepmom's name was Dee, but everyone called her Ma, because she was a very sweet old lady of about seventy or so. Her house was cozy, with pictures of the family everywhere; it was just nice in every way. And in the middle of this quaint little gathering, a bindle of coke fell out of my pocket.

Before we'd set off on that last South American leg, Matt, Duff, and I spent a lot of our time out on the town doing blow. One of the nights before we left, we'd done as much as we had and I remember thinking that we'd bought more than we were going to do. I'd put that extra bindle in my jacket and forgotten about it. Actually, late that night, I tried to find it and couldn't—I'd rummaged around in my jacket and jeans, and convinced that I'd dropped it somewhere along the way, I just went to sleep with Renee.

The moment I saw it on the floor, Renee saw it, too, and I immediately put my foot over it before Ma or anyone else noticed. Then I casually "checked" my shoe and picked it up. When we got home and started doing it, I realized that this thing had been in my jacket for the whole South American tour—I had actually brought coke *into* South America and back, which is ridiculous, because that is the last place where you need to bring your own coke.

It wasn't my first time averting international disaster: the first time we'd toured South America, I was almost deported back to England: I didn't have my U.S. or British passport and my work visa had expired. The entire band went through customs while I was detained by the authorities at LAX. The only person who stayed with me was my security guard, Ronnie. It didn't look good: I was in the holding room surrounded by armed guards and I was wearing shorts, a leather jacket, a T-shirt, and a top hat. There was this one Asian-American customs officer really putting it to me, while his younger sidekick knew who I was, which only seemed to fuel his boss's contempt for me. In the end we had to pay a hundred-dollar waiver to get me out and I didn't have any money on me. Neither did Ronnie—so he went panhandling in the airport, at the arrivals terminal in LAX, to get it.

———◆◆◆◆———

AMID ALL OF THE HIGH AND LOW POINTS, we did some amazing performances that, thinking back on it, rival all of the bands I looked up to as a kid. We had a very established chemistry and a dynamic that was priceless. We'd made history, but when it was over I was fried, and as hard as it was for me to admit it, I was glad to be home for the first time in my life. The controversy and the struggle to pull the tour off had gotten to me more than anything else: the chaos of that emotional roller coaster, with all of its instability, had worn me out. When I came home, I had to reacclimate, to say the least.

I'd sold the Walnut House and Renee and I had bought a place off of Mulholland Drive, where we tried to stop the wheels for a second, which once again was very hard for me to do. I installed a full-on reptile zoo over there; just a gazillion snakes and all kinds of stuff. I built a small studio over the garage, and when the nagging desire to work started to rear its head again, I began working on demos for songs that I'd written on the road.

I started hanging out with Matt and recording demos of that stuff just for fun, and Mike Inez from Alice in Chains and Gilby started to come around and play with us. The three of us just got into a groove of jamming and recording every night. We didn't know what it was going to be. At some point I played it for Axl, who took a pronounced disinterest in it.

That was fine by me. I was writing for the hell of it, just doing music that was indicative of where I was at that moment. I hadn't grasped the idea of doing a Guns record or what that might be going forward; I was just having a good time with no pressure whatsoever.

We recorded about twelve songs. I had just mixed the last of them the night of the Northridge earthquake in 1994. I'd finished at about four a.m., and I went downstairs to our bedroom. Renee was sleeping, the TV was on, and I put the DAT of the entire twelve demos for what would become *Slash's Snakepit* on the nightstand and got into bed. The second I turned out the light, the earthquake hit. There was a TV in a cabinet that raised and lowered at the foot of the bed. At that moment it was up, and the TV was on, and as it was blasting up the bed between Renee and me it exploded, just as all the power in the house went out. The next five minutes were like Godzilla shaking the place. It took me a few moments to even realize just what was happening.

Renee's cousin was staying with us at the time; it was his first time in L.A., and when we'd had lunch down on Melrose earlier that day, he asked me what earthquakes were like. In the confusion I thought about him. He was asleep down the hall in the office, next to a room full of venomous snakes. I got Renee out of bed, and got her to the doorway of our bedroom. She was so groggy that she opened the door into her head about three times before she thought to move out of the way. After I got her situated, I went down the hall and knocked on the door. There was a giant armoire in that room and Renee's cousin was sleeping at the foot of it on the floor. I panicked and called out for him but there was no answer. I thought that he must be trapped under the armoire until finally he responded. Like his cousin, Greg banged his head a few times on the door getting out of there.

The house continued to shake as the three of us huddled in the doorway to our bedroom. Renee was between us, with no shirt on, and she was pretty well built. Despite what was going on around us, I still found that pretty funny. We rode out wave after wave; each of them felt like something was attacking the house. The noise was deafening: glass was breaking, furniture was being tossed around, our eight cats were howling, and the mountain-lion cub that we had in the bathroom was squealing like crazy.

We waited there for what felt like a few hours until the last aftershock died down. The damage was unbelievable. There were TVs dumped in the

middle of pinball machines, our fridge had flown across the entire kitchen, the huge floor-to-ceiling windows in the front of the house were shattered.

I was most concerned about where my three cobras, Gila monsters, and the other venomous and potentially dangerous reptiles might be. I waited until it was light enough in the house to open the door to the room where they were kept because looking for venomous snakes in the dark isn't a good idea. Somehow none of the tanks were broken and all of the snakes were okay.

The house was completely totaled and too much of a mess for us to handle, so we drove to the Four Seasons in Marina Del Rey and made plans to fly with Greg back to Chicago. We had our mountain lion, Curtis, with us; we snuck him into the Four Seasons in his cage and locked him in our bathroom. Like most of my animals, he was an orphan that I'd adopted and was raising in my home.

We cleaned up a bit and headed to the restaurant, and were waiting for the elevator when I turned around and saw Curtis, who had opened both the bathroom door and the door to the room and was following us to dinner. I realized that we had to deal with him immediately, so I called a friend who is an animal caretaker who picked him up and took him up to canyon country, where a friend of mine had a facility that housed exotic animals.

The next day we took off to Chicago, where we hung out with Renee's uncle Bernie, who turned out to be a very cool guy . . . not someone who would kill me for cheating on his niece.

When we eventually returned to L.A. Renee and I decided to sell that house right away. It had to be torn down and rebuilt, so we leased a place and in the meantime I focused on recording. With Mike Clink producing, and Matt and Mike Inez playing, I properly recorded the demos we'd done. We found ourselves a singer—Eric Dover of Jellyfish—who fit the bill well enough at the time. He and I wrote lyrics for all twelve tracks and I think it's pretty easy to tell which songs he wrote and which ones I wrote: all of my songs are directed at one person . . . though no one picked up on it at the time. I used that record as an opportunity to vent a lot of shit that I needed to get off my chest.

Matt and I got into a bit of a disagreement because I had chosen Eric without getting his express approval. He was really pissed about that, so we had issues for a while. Anyway, Dover finished recording the vocals

and I brought it to Geffen and they got behind it. Everything was in place and we were ready to take the Snakepit on tour, had it not been for the fact that Matt and Mike Inez weren't able to go.

I wasn't going to be discouraged by that, so I enlisted Brian Tishy and James Lamenzo, who are in Zakk Wylde's band, and rounded out the lineup with Gilby Clarke. We booked ourselves a tour across the United States, Europe, Japan, and Australia. We shot two videos and released the single "Beggars and Hangers On." And we had a lot of fun: there was no drama; we just booked gigs, showed up, got up there, and played. We did clubs and theaters and it was great; it really helped me rediscover why I love what I do. That project was the essential soul-searching that I needed, because I felt like I'd forgotten myself over the last two years. It was a shot in the arm for me to rediscover what I always knew: being in a band doesn't have to be so taxing emotionally and psychologically . . . it can just be all about the playing.

DURING THE TIME THAT I RECORDED THE Snakepit demos and put that band together and went on tour, there were a few things going on simultaneously in the Guns universe. We put together *The Spaghetti Incident*, our record of punk covers, and packaged it for release. We'd worked on a lot of those tracks here and there over the previous two years. We'd recorded "Buick McCain," "Ain't It Fun," and most of the others at the Record Plant, but a few, like "Since I Don't Have You," were recorded on days off on the road, probably during the *Skin and Bones* tour, because they feature Dizzy on piano.

That record was released in November 1993, and the single, which wasn't the best idea at all, was "Since I Don't Have You," though it was a stellar version of that song. We did a video for it, too. Around that time I was partying a lot with Gary Oldman, and the day of my shoot, I took him with me to the set. After " November Rain" and "Estranged," I was fed up with the band's high-concept videos, and this promised to be another one—all of them masterminded by Axl. I nearly walked off the set when I was told that I needed to stand in a pool of water and pose while playing my guitar for something like fifteen takes. Gary was the one who intervened.

"No, no," he said. "It will be fine. Just hold on."

He disappeared into the makeup and wardrobe room for quite a while, only to emerge in a completely authentic Victorian costume, made up to look like the Marquis de Sade. He had a few props, too, and he decided that he was going to row me in a boat, across the river Styx, as I played my solo in the pouring rain. By the time we got to shooting, he lost the costume and ended up playing this white-faced demon in tight black shorts . . . he almost did too good a job. After that afternoon, I'm pretty sure that the next time I heard from him, Gary was in rehab.

<hr />

DUFF, AXL, MATT, GILBY, AND I GOT together on and off to try to write new material, which didn't prove inspiring at all. By that point, the support group I'd always enjoyed to help me deal with Axl was gone—Izzy was the last one in the band who'd been able to get through to him creatively. Between Duff and me . . . we just didn't have the proper tools to communicate with him effectively.

After a few months during which everyone did their own thing and we got nothing done when we met, Axl fired Gilby without consulting anyone. His rationale was that Gilby had always been a hired hand and that he couldn't write with him. Axl then insisted on hiring Paul Huge, this guy he knew from Indiana who, for whatever reason, also calls himself Paul Tobias. They had history: the two of them cowrote "Back Off Bitch" among other songs. I was open to the idea . . . until Paul showed up: he had no personality whatsoever and no particular guitar style or sound that I could identify with. He was, without a doubt, the least interesting, most bland guy holding a guitar that I'd ever met. I tried my best to work with him, but it went nowhere. It was even more awkward than it sounds because our stilted interaction took place at rehearsal with everyone else watching us.

I tried to stick with it, but I wasn't alone in feeling like we were being force-fed some guy with no innate qualities who didn't deserve and couldn't handle the gig. But it was hopeless, we couldn't talk Axl out of it at all. I did what I could: I tried several times to have a one-on-one with Huge to see if I was missing some deeper spark in his character that Axl had seen . . . No, it was useless; the guy was irredeemable. It was like talking to a wall,

a wall with a bad attitude. He was totally arrogant and gave off the vibe that he was Axl's boy, that he was in, and that everyone else had to deal with it. In a word, his vibe was "I'm great, fuck you!" And my response was "Yeah? Whatever!"

Duff and I hated him, Matt hated him, and Axl was left grasping for straws, yet determined to ride it out. I didn't know why but I wanted him to be totally sure how we felt, so one day I took him aside.

"Axl, man, listen," I said. "I've tried to work with Huge and I've tried to see what he could bring to the band, but I just don't get it. We have no chemistry as players and he has no chemistry with the other guys. I just don't see how it's going to work with this guy. . . . I can't even have a beer with him."

Axl looked annoyed. "Why do you have to have a *beer* with him?" he said.

"You know what I mean."

"No," he said. "I *don't*."

There really wasn't any arguing with that point of view.

We rehearsed with Huge and I tried to write some new songs at my home studio with him and it only grew more tense in every way. Renee hated the fact that we were there because the negative vibe permeated the entire house. She wasn't even in the studio trying to work: It was so uncomfortable and awkward there that Duff and I actually got into it, which had never happened in the studio ever. And that was the last straw for me: the next morning I told Doug to let everyone know that we'd have to rehearse elsewhere because there would be no more getting together at my studio.

Axl was disappointed and a bit pissed off. The next time I saw him he confronted me. "Why can't we write at your place?" he asked. "What's the problem?"

"I'm at my wit's end, man," I said. "The whole vibe there is so negative and that's my *house*. Everything we are doing right now is just bad energy."

That was the last time that Axl and I spoke for a while. After that, I focused on Snakepit, and I wasn't surprised, when I sent him some demos, that he wasn't interested in the music I was writing at all.

<center>◆◆❉◆◆</center>

sound of a band breaking up sounds like, listen to Guns N' Roses' cover of "Sympathy for the Devil," which was recorded for the *Interview with the Vampire* soundtrack in the fall of 1994. If there is one Guns track I'd like never to hear again, it is that one.

Tom Zutaut arranged the whole thing and it was a great idea: it's an amazing, classic song, the movie was going to be huge, theoretically, it would get us all in the same room working again, and it would give the public "product" to tide them over. We weren't touring *The Spaghetti Incident* and we had no plans to start writing the next album, so Tom was being practical—this might be our only new release for a while. I'm amazed that Axl even agreed to do it, because by then he had stopped talking to Tom Zutaut altogether. All in all, Axl had eliminated and replaced everyone who had helped the band build from the ground up back in the day. He always had a reason: I believe in Tom's case, Axl claimed that he caught him trying to pick up Erin at some point. But don't quote me on that.

Anyway, I was up for the idea of doing this cover because I was very familiar with the Anne Rice books; I thought they were great, which is why I had a hard time imagining Brad Pitt and Tom Cruise playing those roles. Anyway, Axl and I went to screenings of the film separately, and completely disagreed on what we saw. I *hated it*; I thought it was crap.

I called Tom right afterward. "Hey, Tom, it's Slash," I said.

"So what did you think?"

"I thought it *sucked*. I hated it," I said.

"Oh."

"Yeah. It was that bad. Tell the producers to license the Stones' version because we're not doing it."

Axl, on the other hand, loved the movie; he thought it was brilliant and he wanted to do the song. I couldn't have been more disappointed, pissed, frustrated, and confused. The only upside I saw to signing off on it was that it would accomplish what we'd been unable to do to any degree in the past seven months: it would actually get all of us into the studio.

We booked time at Rumbo; we did the basic tracks with Mike Clink over a few days. Duff, Matt, and I showed up together every day, basically going out of our way to do something that only Axl wanted to do, and not

once did he show up to a session. From the basic tracks through to the final overdubs, we never saw or heard from Axl. We were already recording against our will, so his disregard for our time and commitment definitely inspired a *very* uninspired instrumental track. And needless to say, the level of bitterness and resentment reached an all-time high. It added insult to injury that after we'd completed our thoroughly average version of "Sympathy for the Devil," it took him more than a week to even show up to the studio to do his vocals.

Once he got around to listening to the track, he had some constructive criticism. Via a lot of communications between middle people, I was told that I needed to rerecord my guitar solo so that it sounded more note for note like the Keith Richards original. Now that really pissed me off, most of all because the message reached me three times removed like we were playing a game of telephone.

My first reaction, of course, was "no." I stood behind what I'd done, because why would I copy Keith if the song was supposed to be *our* version? The reply, through handlers, was: "If you don't change it, I won't sing." I swallowed my pride—yet again—and went in to record a more Keith-like intro, though it was the last thing I wanted to do: Keith's playing is so awesome on that song that I didn't want to even come near it, but I did. And doing so left me feeling even more pissed off and put out than ever.

A week or so after that I heard that Axl had finally scheduled time to go in and record his vocal tracks, so I went down to see him in person. I waited for three hours. When he finally showed up, he came into the lounge and proceeded to talk to me from behind a magazine, without looking me in the eye, for about fifteen minutes. . . . I couldn't deal with that at all, so I took off.

When I got a DAT of the song with Axl's vocal on it, I noticed that there was another guitar layered on top of mine in the solo. Axl had gotten Paul Huge to double over me. In other words, that guy copied what I was playing on another track and they layered them. It was like really bad plagiarism.

That was it—having another guitar player record over me without telling me was as much disrespect as I was willing to handle. I washed my hands of that song, I washed my hands of Guns for the moment, and I focused my

energy on my own songs and my own project, Slash's Snakepit's debut, *It's Five O'Clock Somewhere.*

ONCE THE SNAKEPIT GOT GOING, I WAS completely content. For the first time in years, touring was easy, my bandmates were loads of fun and low on drama, and every gig was about playing rock and roll—not proving something or putting on a huge spectacle. Everything rolled on: the record sold, the tour was fine; I was on the road with no end in sight. We were in the midst of booking another leg when I was informed by Geffen that they'd sold a million copies of *It's Five O'Clock Somewhere* and had turned a profit so they saw no reason for me to continue our tour. I was to return to L.A. because Axl was ready to begin working on the next Guns N' Roses record. They'd thought it through: in case I objected, they made it clear that the financial tour support for Snakepit was over.

I returned to L.A. dreading what lay in store for me and I had good reason to; what lay in store was the beginning of the end—the conclusion of unfinished, unpleasant business. All things considered, the end had begun long ago; I was just coming home for the funeral. It's funny, when fans ask me, as they do almost every day, whether Guns, in its original form, will ever reunite, it is hard to take them seriously. That question is so asinine to me; if they knew the real story, they'd already know the answer. But my response is always the same: "Take a look at what everyone is doing now. Duff and Matt and I are part of a really successful band. Izzy's content doing his thing; Steven, too. And Axl is touring with the 'new Guns.' No one is making phone calls to see when we can get the band together again."

That's the lowdown of where we're all at. Once you take that into consideration, the answer to the reunion question should be pretty clear, if you ask me. Are we cool?

Breakdown

Sometimes the truth lies in front of your eyes and makes so little sense that you just don't see it; it's like confronting your reflection in a fun-house mirror—it's hard to believe that the twisted figure staring back is you. Guns had become a similar monster; we were such a bizarre version of what we once were that I could barely recognize us. But unlike the fun house, I couldn't escape; when I turned away from the glass, the reflection was still there.

was ordered to come back off the road; I was told to stop something that I was enjoying in every way. I was reluctant to do that. I wanted to keep the tour going beyond Japan; I wanted to take it to Australia, I wanted to finish what I'd set out to do. It might seem inconsistent, because Snakepit was seen as an in-between project and a bit of a party band, but I was ambitious about it. When I set my mind to achieving something, I put blinders on, I put my head down, and drive ahead until I get it. And I hadn't quite gotten what I'd aimed for on that one.

I had been that single-minded and determined when I brought the record to Geffen. I didn't consider and didn't realize what was going on with the label in 1994 when I showed up for my meeting. The entire record business was on the verge of a massive shift; all of the majors would be combined, sold, or dissolved within the next few years. At the time I didn't know or care. I played Snakepit for Zutaut, they agreed to put it out, and that was all I cared to hear. I didn't sense the confusion that was going on up there or in the industry at large and I didn't acknowledge the very obvious anxiety that was circulating about the next Guns N' Roses album. I had no idea that David Geffen was about to sell the company, and that the prospect of a new Guns record might have changed that, but even if I did, there wasn't much I could have done to deliver it "on time."

Looking back, I realize that while they thought I was putting the future of Guns in jeopardy by pursuing Snakepit, they decided that it was more important to humor me, so they went the whole nine yards to let me get it out of my system. They were biting their nails the whole time but if Zutaut or anyone else had voiced their concerns, I would have told them the truth: I had no intention of quitting Guns N' Roses. As pissed off as I was, I always thought that I'd go back, after some time off, when the time was right.

So Geffen released and supported *It's Five O'Clock Somewhere*. They publicized it, and they gave us financial tour support . . . until they didn't. As I mentioned, once Axl informed the label (or so I was told) that he was ready to begin writing sessions for the next Guns record, my leash was

yanked and I was ordered to come home because the way they saw it I'd sold one million records and they'd turned a profit and didn't need me out there supporting it anymore. The funny thing was that even after all these years, I still never looked at touring as album promotion—to me it was still just an excuse to play.

I landed in L.A. and settled into the new home that Renee and I had rented above Sunset Plaza, in West Hollywood. I'd moved all of the snakes over there and we'd been there awhile, just renting month to month indefinitely. I might have been married but I didn't have the married homeowner mentality at that point. I knew that I was "supposed to" own a house, but I really couldn't get my head around the concept. I had leased a place for a decent price right above Sunset that had everything I needed. It was my hang pad: I had my snakes, I had Renee, I had my pinball machines—it was a great bachelor pad . . . for my wife and me.

So I got into town loathing what I had to do because in the back of my mind I knew it was going to be so many things, none of them easy. Doug had set us up at a studio called the Complex, which we later dubbed the Compound. I went down there and Axl had already set up shop. The place had a big rehearsal room and an insane amount of outboard gear—literally a room full of synths—as well as an arsenal of Pro Tools recording rigs that Axl had rented. Axl and I hadn't spoken directly at all since my return, either by phone or face-to-face: I got my working orders from Doug. I showed up at the scheduled time and I found my tech, Adam Day; Duff's tech, McBob; Duff, Dizzy Reed, and Matt and Paul Huge. Axl was nowhere in sight. I got down there that first night around eight p.m.

My immediate thought was that this scene, which was supposed to be our band, reminded me way too much of recording for Michael Jackson on *Dangerous*. When I'd done those sessions for him, I was blown away by how much money was going down the toilet: there was rented equipment everywhere, and I was told that he had multiple studios identically set up around the country, booked, incurring day rates, in case he was inspired to record there at any given moment.

I'm a frugal guy, so that didn't appeal to me at all. I found that kind of recording environment to be a waste and I found Michael's scene to be way

out of control. When I showed up to record, the staff was as hospitable and robotic as a bunch of bellboys at a five-star hotel.

"So what would you like to play on?" I remember some guy asking me.

"What do you mean?"

"We have a wide selection of guitars here," the guy said. "Which would you like to use?"

"I brought my own," I said. "I'd like to play on that."

That whole thing was a disjointed and cold musical scenario. The last place I ever expected to encounter that vibe again was at my band's writing/rehearsing/recording sessions. I can put up with a million and one things, but the one thing I can't stomach is a lack of integrity. At the first whiff of bullshit, I get wary. And what I walked into had me worried.

There were rows and rows of Pro Tools servers and gear. Which was a clear indication that Axl and I had very different ideas of how to do this record. I was open to using Pro Tools, to trying new things—but everyone had to be on the same page and in the same room to explore new ideas. The band managed to do a little bit of jamming and come up with some things. A couple of the ideas I had come up with Axl apparently liked and they were recorded onto Pro Tools and stored for him to work on later.

We'd show up at different times every evening, but by eight p.m. generally everyone in the band would be there. Then we'd wait for Axl, who, when he did come, arrived much, much later. That was the norm; it was a dark, miserable atmosphere that lacked direction of any kind. I hung out for a bit; but after a few days I chose to spend my evenings at the strip bar around the corner, with orders for the engineers to call me if Axl decided to arrive.

———— ◈ ————

A DECADE AFTER WE'D FIRST GOTTEN the band together, every single thing that I knew to be Guns N' Roses had changed. We'd lost Steven, we'd lost Izzy, and while we'd gained Matt, we'd gained and lost Gilby. Duff was the only element of the original back line that remained the same; he was my friend, the only one I could count on. But he was sober now; in May 1994, he suffered a near-fatal episode when

his pancreas almost exploded. Years of heavy drinking had taken their toll, and if Duff didn't get sober, he'd die. We were still tight, and things were basically the same, but we didn't tip bottles together anymore. He was really striving to keep things together in a way, keeping Matt in the loop because, after all, Matt wasn't sure how the process of songwriting to recording worked within GN'R. Duff was the only anchor at that point, while I was fraying at the seams.

Drinking to me was still a fun, recreational activity to be indulged in every day, though I had started to drink to medicate more than just for fun. There wasn't much of a social scene for Guns outside of the studio anyway, so from the moment I reentered the band, I was pretty much on my own. My consumption was excessive, but I still functioned like a normal person—a normal person with a pure internal alcohol level diluted only by their blood. I had worked long and hard to get myself in shape that way. I'd had to, because drinking was the only thing that satisfied me and subdued all of the issues that I would have had to otherwise deal with, in the band and in my life, if I ever let myself get back to normal for a while.

Slash and Axl discussing something backstage on the Illusion *tour. Note the half gallon of vodka stashed in Slash's stomach.*

All the focus was on trying to get things working again. Amid the least creative atmosphere I'd ever experienced in the history of the band, we somehow finally got stuff going. My memories of it are hazy at best because I did everything I could to forget. I do remember going down to the studio and rehearsing without direction. I just had too much animosity blocking my creativity. One of the few times I actually spoke with Axl about how it was going, it was pretty clear that we were coming from *very* different places. I was trying to get through to him once again about how working with Huge was a chore and a creative dead end in my opinion.

"You don't have to be friends to make a record," Axl said.

"Maybe not," I said, "but you do need to have some kind of mutual respect, you know."

We might as well have been talking about the two of us. The negativity was so all-consuming that I couldn't concentrate and I couldn't focus on writing. There was so much bitter stuff nagging at me that remaining calm and tranquil enough to enjoy playing was next to impossible. So I preoccupied myself with being drunk all the time and tried to push through whatever it was that we were doing.

Axl asked Zakk Wylde to come down to rehearse with us as well as Paul Huge. He probably thought I'd like that idea because Zakk was a friend of mine and I respected him as a guitarist, but that really didn't seem like the answer to me. I brought up the option of rehiring Gilby, and that idea was flatly rejected. There were endless messages sent back and forth, through Doug Goldstein, about Axl's wants, needs, and ideas on what we should be doing. The only way that I regularly "talked" to Axl was through Doug at that point. Axl would give Doug a message and Doug would have to massage the words in order to relate it to me. Then I'd give him a message and he'd pass it along to Axl after massaging it appropriately, and so it went, back and forth. At times I'd call Axl but most of the time he wouldn't pick up or ever return my call. And when he did show up at rehearsal, he never sang. My memory of that time is so vague, because so little jamming happened. I must say, though, that the gear was set up *nice*. All things considered, those sessions cost too much for a lot of uneventful, depressing sitting around.

As pissed as I was to have been called home to do nothing, my respon-

sible side kicked in and I was determined to get something out of it despite the fact that my heart was in my boots. I wasn't sure what to expect from Zakk Wylde but I hoped for the best. He's a great guy; I remember that I met him at the Sunset Marquis the night he got hired to be Ozzy's guitar player years before. We hung out in his room celebrating until I left him passed out in the bathtub. Zakk's personality is like Steven Adler's times ten: he doesn't mince words and isn't scared of confrontation. I couldn't see him and Axl lasting more than a week. But aside from that, when we jammed down at the Complex, it didn't make any sense to me. It wasn't the two-guitar-player team that GN'R really was. We were two lead-guitar players going at the songs on opposite sides of the stage and it was overbearing. I was used to working with and playing off of a more low-key rhythm player. If Zakk and I were to do this, it would be a whole new trip . . . more like Judas Priest or something. Even he felt that the concept was wrong.

"That was cool," I told him after jamming for a bit. "It was different."

"Listen, man," he said. "That was all right. We could get this thing together, fuck it, that's cool. But you and Axl have to get the fuckin' *band* going, man. Get yourselves together and fucking get it going again."

It was all about Axl wanting control to the point that the rest of us were strangled.

BY THEN ALL "BAND" DECISIONS WERE being made by Axl and Doug Goldstein. Duff and I and the other members were informed of what they'd decided by phone calls and faxes—Guns N'

Roses had officially become a dictatorship. The reality of what was happening was overwhelming; it was like quicksand. I couldn't get any leverage in any direction to pull myself out of it. What we were supposed to be doing was simple: hire a new guitar player and make a new album. But the whole process was dictated by Axl, and although I know he wanted input from me, I was suffocated by the tension and I couldn't think straight. I think at the end of the day it was a power struggle between him and me, with him wanting to control everything and me wanting to keep it more of a group effort. Oftentimes the public perception centered on Axl and me as the core of Guns N' Roses, and I think Axl agreed, but the success GN'R had garnered up until that point was the result of five guys working together, where nobody was more important than anyone else as far as I was concerned. But that idea was becoming ancient history and it didn't seem like there was anything I could do about it.

Even though I'd seen this coming for so long, when the reality stared me in the face, I still refused to believe that it was true. One of the things that had brought the five of us together in the first place was the fact that we would not be bossed around; based on that alone, we'd always had one another's backs. Axl had always been a part of that team—at least in spirit when he wasn't there in person. In our heart of hearts, even when he was being weird, the rest of us knew that he was part of the collective. Now, all of a sudden, he wasn't. As much as we might have ignored it before this point, he'd made it pretty clear that we were "his" band and that he intended to tweak and torture us as he saw fit, and keep us at his beck and call. It seemed like he believed we'd welcome that opportunity.

For the time being, we all hung around, and in our ample downtime we all talked shit. It was so negative. After a while, I could barely show up because the animosity became crippling. We'd spend each night in the studio maybe writing music or jamming . . . most nights we'd sit around frustrated, waiting to see if Axl would show—which he did, usually after most of us had left for the night—all under the guise that we were writing music for the next Guns record. On top of it all, a new contract issue further disrupted an already volatile situation.

This time it was directed at Duff and me—the only two remaining original members of Guns N' Roses. And it was very strategically presented:

the contract stated that Axl would retain rights to the band name and was allowed to start a new band that he could call Guns N' Roses. Of course Duff and I could be members . . . but only on his terms, which felt to us like we were being defined as hired hands. Axl had hired an attorney to push this through, so Duff and I did as well, and the three of them started haggling, having those attorney fests that do nothing but cost their clients money. Doug Goldstein was also there helping "facilitate" the whole thing.

That situation chipped away at the stone that is me; my patience, my dedication, my determination—all of it finally began to give way. It's been the focus of so much speculation: What actually did Guns N' Roses in? Was it artistic differences? Was it Slash's ego? Was it Axl's attitude? It was all about Axl wanting control to the point that the rest of us were strangled.

I didn't really know what else to do after Axl sent a letter on August 31, 1995, saying that he was leaving the band and taking the name with him under the terms of the contract. After that we tried to put it back together. He pushed this contract issue on us with so much pressure to the point that Duff and I just gave in. We signed some document that we'd agreed to have put in escrow for a certain amount of time to see if we could work things out. But if we didn't agree to put the terms into effect by a certain point, the contract would be null and void, so I signed it and let it go. I just wanted to move forward if we had anywhere left to go together.

Needless to say, my trust in Axl was gone. That entire contract situation was the antithesis of Guns N' Roses in my mind. I was forced into a secondary role, while Axl was now officially at the helm if I officially let the escrowed contract become effective. One time he called me for a private meeting at his favorite Italian restaurant in Brentwood. I showed up and he wasn't there, so I sat at the bar waiting for him. After he arrived, we moved and sat in the back in a dark booth as if we were in the Mafia. As far as I can remember, the meeting was basically an attempt to coerce me into accepting the arrangement he and his lawyers were pushing, but in a lot less heavy-handed manner. Axl treated the situation as if he and I were the two most important factors in this whole thing. He tried to convince me that it was all good, that it was something he and I were doing as partners.

At that point, he was trying to draw me into his world, to show me his version of things in his way, which is a very nice way, but I just didn't go for it. I sat there and listened, not giving too much feedback. There was too much tension and too many unaddressed issues. It became increasingly obvious to me that there was nothing I was going to say that was going to change his mind. And he already knew how I felt. He and I continued this way until it all boiled over later.

It had become no fun. It had become depressing. It was almost amazing to me that this band had taken such a turn; we, the band, had allowed Axl the freedom, over all those years, to transform what we had into some morbid reality that existed only in his head.

There were another couple of meetings like that in Doug Goldstein's office. Then, of course, there were endless meetings with the attorneys going over and over this thing. It was exhausting. I couldn't even understand what the fuck I was doing there. No matter what we might eventually put out as far as a record was concerned, none of this was worth it.

THE STONES WERE IN TOWN DURING this period; they were staying at the Sunset Marquis and recording at Don Was's house, working on *Bridges to Babylon*. I went over and checked out a few sessions, and watching them work, watching them do their thing, made me feel even worse about my situation. They had a chemistry that encompassed all of their very distinct personalities but never lacked respect. Keith would roll in and pick on Ronnie relentlessly but Ronnie is such a nice, amiable guy that it was all okay. It had to be because Keith is pretty sinister and such a profound narcissist that he has to take it out on someone. He can't take it out on Mick or Charlie . . . though he tries. They're so resilient that it doesn't work, so Ronnie gets it all. As Ronnie says, "Keith has these tyrannical moods." But as harsh as it ever gets, it is all within the parameters of mutual respect.

One particular evening, after they were done for the day, I went back to Ronnie's hotel room and hung out for a while. He asked me if I knew Keith. I said I didn't, and had never met him one-on-one, so he took me over to his room, introduced us, and left me there. It was dark, with some old blues

playing on the stereo. The one lamp that was lit dimly illuminated Keith's face with this sort of creepy glow as he sat on the couch. I sat in a chair by the coffee table while he sized me up. He talked for a few minutes, then suddenly pulled out a butterfly knife and flipped it around a few times to show me who's boss. He slammed it down on the table between us.

"Um . . . Okay," I said.

Later that night we went to dinner at Chasen's. Keith and I stood at the bar, talking about dope and jail, and I could tell that he was just putting up with me by that point. I'd been at the studio rehearsing all day, so when the conversation swung around to my band, I let it all out.

Keith took it all in, and then looked me deep in the eye. "*Listen,*" he said. "There's only one thing you never do—you never *leave.*"

I knew where he was coming from; if you never leave, no matter what they say, you were *there.* If you are always the one to show up at rehearsal and stay until the end, even when times are tough and not everyone is getting along, the one thing that your bandmates will never be able to hold over your head is the fact that you walked out. It's true: if you show up early to rehearsal or recording and you're the last one there, you are the guy who can't be fucked with. A perfect example was the great Rolling Stones song "Happy," from their *Exile on Main St.* album. As legend has it, while Keith was waiting for the rest of the band to show up, he wrote the whole song by himself. When they arrived, he presented it to them as if to say "What took you so long?" I definitely wanted to be that guy who could overcome all these obstacles and produce music. When you're always there, you're the one that holds all the cards.

Keith inspired me; I felt like I had to try harder. The next day I tried to refocus my outlook and I showed up at the Complex ready to make it work at all costs. And that's when I got slapped in the face once again: Axl never showed up to rehearse, and the attorneys' negotiation of our "employment contracts" had taken a really insulting turn. God bless Keith for trying, but there was nothing I could do—I had to go.

Our "rehearsals" always went really late; even later by the time Axl showed up. Whenever he did, it was usually around one or two; we'd play for an hour or more and then finally get bored and go home, leaving him in the studio. I didn't hear him sing the whole time we were at the Complex; I'm not sure I'd heard him sing since the last show in 1993, and at this point it

was 1996. So I didn't even know what we were working on. We were supposed to jam and jam until he said, "I like this," or, "I like that." Nobody was having a good time, so nobody was inspired. Generally I'd get home about three a.m. And it was one of those nights that prompted me to get out.

I got in bed and went to sleep. Two hours later, about five a.m., I woke up with cold sweats and in the blackest of moods and felt really suicidal. I wanted to end it; I was so miserable that I wanted it all to disappear. I'd never felt that way before, I'd never wanted to snuff myself—I'd gotten really close a few times but never intentionally. For a half hour, I looked around my bedroom; I had nothing to do it with; I wanted to kill myself quickly; I didn't want to go on. If there had been any dope lying around, I would've done it all in one hit and that would have been that.

For the next hour I stared at the ceiling and thought about my life from start to finish. I was weighing whether or not it was worth living, sorting out how I'd gotten where I was and deciding what I could do about it all. By six a.m. I was exhausted and fell back asleep. Two hours later I woke up with one crystal-clear thought in my head: *That's it.* Other than that, my mind was silent.

Up until that moment, one part of me wanted to push on; the other part saw no future. In the early-morning light, I went over all of the angles once again and every single one of them pointed to the same conclusion. The band wasn't what it had once been and I didn't want to be there anymore. Once I said that to myself, there was nothing else to think about.

I got out of bed and called our management office, BFD, and told Doug that I wouldn't be coming back.

"That's it," I told Doug. "I'm done. I quit."

I hung up before he could say anything.

IN RETROSPECT I WAS NAIVE ABOUT THE whole thing: I didn't protect myself legally because I didn't think I had to. In my mind, what was the name without the players? I didn't think I had given Axl anything, because to me, what could he do with the name and nothing else to show for it?

I didn't have my attorneys get on that situation as well as I should have;

I was so over it and so worn down that I just couldn't be bothered. I didn't want to do a press release, I didn't want to raise a brouhaha or stir up a lot of fanfare. I wanted to go quietly. I didn't want it to be one of those situations where you have two guys bickering at each other through the press. I didn't see any reason why something so simple should turn into a big legal battle either. I thought I'd take my share and go.

In the short run, no one in the Guns corporation actually believed that I was done. Axl contacted those closest to me, telling them that I should change my mind. He called my dad, my security guard, my wife, Renee, and told each of them that I was making the biggest mistake of my life. He said that I was pissing away so much money because of my decision. But none of that mattered to me. I was *done*. The camel's back had been broken and there was no going back.

To tell you the truth, none of the people in Axl's camp believed I was really gone for the next couple years. I was kind of taken aback by their deep sense of denial: I never behaved as if I intended to return, but that didn't matter to them. They just didn't believe that I would rather not be in Guns N' Roses than deal with the reality of being in Guns N' Roses.

❖━◦❈◦━❖

I'D DONE EVERYTHING IN MY POWER from the day we got together to make Guns N' Roses the best band in the world. I'd put my heart and soul into everything we did and I regret none of my contributions in the least. We did things other bands only dream of; in just a few years, we surpassed goals that took bands like the Stones decades to achieve. I don't like to brag, but if you research it at all, you'll see that what we did in the time frame we did it is something unsurpassed in the history of rock and roll.

After working to make that band all that it could be for the better part of my life, saying good-bye to the institution I helped build was as alien as being launched into space. But once I'd done it, a weight was lifted from my shoulders and the lead was out of my shoes. It was like decompressing after a deepwater dive. The day I made my decision, I woke up early and called the powers that be to deliver the news, and went back to sleep. I don't remember anything else of that day aside from the fact that when I woke

up again I was *refreshed*. I felt as if I'd just slept for a week. Later that night I called Duff, Matt, and Adam Day and let them know. Duff accepted my decision without any question, and Matt wasn't surprised either. I was satisfied but it was bittersweet; I had never really given up before in my life.

I enjoyed a period of peace for a while. I started to go out and just jam whenever I had the chance. My attorneys asked me if I wanted to sue for damages and just go after as much stuff as possible, and I said no, in good faith. I can't get into it; aside from saying that they were trying to protect my rights and I probably should have listened, the truth is, I was in denial about just how mercurial and untrustworthy the relationship between the Guns institution and me had become. I didn't see it as such, but when you leave a company you have to protect your interests. At the time I still had a silly amount of trust in what Guns meant to me, so I didn't dwell on it. And to this day there are still issues that remain to be resolved that cause me grief.

All things considered, I stand by my decision, and I stand by the way I did it. Even my dad had told me earlier on, when I was in a state of duress, "Don't go down with the ship." I consider leaving GN'R one of the smartest decisions I've ever made. There's no doubt that if I'd stayed with the band under those circumstances I'd surely be dead by now because of too much unnecessary drama. I definitely would have found junk again or it would have found me. If I knew then what I know now, had I been more experienced and more self-protective and more suspicious of the players involved—and I'm not even talking about Axl so much as the people he hired to guide him through this—it might have been handled differently. He hired people who had nothing but making money off of him in mind. If it had been otherwise, or if he and I had been able to discuss it face-to-face, there might have been a greater degree of preservation in regard to our mutual interests as a band. But I don't believe in "ifs."

It just wasn't meant to be. The road that Axl chose to travel forced me away. And once I left, Duff was next—he split of his own accord less than a year later. Not too long after that, Matt got fired. Apparently, he stood up for me when I was slandered at rehearsal and that was the end of him.

By 1998, Axl was the only one of the original five still in the "band" he'd legally arranged to be able to call Guns N' Roses. By then, Izzy had released a handful of solo albums and toured the world and Gilby had done the

same. Duff had formed a new band and put out two records, and I had, too: my second incarnation of Snakepit was alive and well. Matt, for his part, had rejoined the Cult, recorded a record, and was on tour. Steven was crippled by drug addiction, but Axl didn't have that excuse. I found it morbidly ironic that, out of all of us, the one guy who'd basically browbeat and pressured us into submission into retaining the name had done nothing much with it whatsoever at that point.

<div align="center">◆━◆◆◆◆◆◆━◆</div>

IN 1996 IMMEDIATELY FOLLOWING MY last days win GN'R, I did everything I could to stay inspired by music. It was the best way for me to cure my disillusionment with what had become of my band. I toured the world with players as skilled and diverse as could be and I learned as much as I could from all of them. I went to Japan for two weeks with Nile Rodgers and the original lineup of Chic—and that was one hell of a musical education.

I have all the respect in the world for Nile; we had worked together on the soundtrack for *Beverly Hills Cop III*, so when he called me to go out on tour with Chic, there was no way I was turning him down. He had gathered all of the original players: Omar Akeem, Bernie Worrell, Bernard Edwards, and at least one of the original background singers. They had Stevie Winwood, Simon Le Bon, Sister Sledge, and me out with them for the duration, making cameo appearances during their set.

At rehearsal down at S.I.R. in NYC, during one of the jams I did a dive bomb kind of thing with my Les Paul (this is where that aforementioned crack happened), which is when you push the back of a guitar's head stock forward while pushing the lower part of the neck, where the neck and the body meet, inward instead of using a tremolo bar. I snapped the neck of my guitar, which flew up and hit me square in the face. It felt like I'd been smashed with a baseball bat: when it popped it sounded like an M-80 and it put a huge hole in my top lip. Someone was videotaping the session that day and I'd love to see an instant replay of that. The wound it left behind was the size of a nickel.

The sound alone caused everyone to stop playing and turn my way. And there I was with one half of my guitar in one hand, the other half in the

other, with blood pouring down my chin, neck, and chest. I was dazed; they were all pointing at me and I had no idea what they were talking about. Being that I was in NYC, it was either wait for three hours to be seen by an ER doctor—or not. I opted to go back to the Paramount Hotel, where I sat at the Whiskey Bar with a bag of ice on my face and a bottle of Jack in front of me until I got on the plane with everyone else the next day.

Meanwhile, Adam took my guitar to a repairman to see if it could be fixed, and when I saw him on the way to the gate he told me that his buddy had managed to glue it back together.

"I did my best," he said. He looked pretty tired. "It's kind of a Frankenstein but it looks like it's going to work."

I'd like to take a moment to let Adam Day, my tech for the past nineteen years, know right now just how much I love him. There had been many times before that I'd felt as much, and many times since, but I'd like to give him the credit he deserves for doing what he did in this instance. That thing had broken to the point of no return, at least I thought so, but he stayed up all night getting it fixed, and to his credit, from that point forward, that guitar has sounded better than it ever did before.

<hr>

THAT JAPANESE TOUR WAS JUST GREAT; every show was an event. The band was an amazing group of players, so it was a real learning experience and a lot of fun. I had a fling with one of the backup singers who was really hot. The very last night of the tour I was sitting with her and a few other girls in the balcony of this club celebrating. Bernard Edwards was there with us hanging out, but he was tired and left us a bit early; security escorted him to his room.

The next morning he was found dead on his couch as a result of severe pneumonia. When I got the call it was one of the most surreal moments of my life. "I was just with him a few hours ago!" I said. I really looked up to Bernard as a musician and a person. He was the coolest, smoothest, most gentle guy. He'd been a good friend, taking me under his wing during that tour, which was wild considering that I was a stranger in a strange land, jamming with all of these seasoned session pros, and Bernard didn't even

know that much about me or my music. On that tour he didn't seem like he had any health issues or anything wrong with him at all; he just died peacefully in his sleep. It was a huge shock for Nile because Bernard was his writing partner and closest friend, and they'd just repaired their friendship after a long split. They had just gotten the band back together; they had all of these plans to record and embark on a new phase. Nile was in shock. Everyone was: we left one another in Japan and saw one another again at Bernard's funeral in Connecticut.

I CONTINUED TO FIND INSPIRATION BY pushing myself to do projects outside of my expected range, one of them being the music for the soundtrack to the Quentin Tarantino–produced film *Curdled*. When Miramax asked me asked me to do it, I immediately agreed because I'm such a big fan of his. The movie is great; it's about a cleanup crew that comes in after forensics has finished gathering evidence to clean up crime scenes. They find themselves cleaning up after a serial killer who targets rich women, and one of them—this perfectly nice girl—becomes obsessed with the killer and begins keeping a scrapbook of his murders. It gets a lot more intense from there.

I met Quentin and he told me all about the movie and I started writing music that was inspired by the film's main character, Gabriella, and the actress who played her, Angela Jones. Angela appears to be Latin, but she's a white girl from Pittsburgh and I'd had a crush on her since the moment I saw her in *Pulp Fiction*: she played the cabdriver who drove Bruce Willis to the hotel after the fight. I put hours into working out the music, which is instrumental, all acoustic, eclectic, and flamenco influenced. I recorded the instrumental stuff with Jed Leiber, who is a great engineer I know from L.A.

I flew out to New York, where Nile Rodgers produced the electric version of a few tracks. Then he and I flew out to Spain to have this major Spanish star, Martha Sanchez, do vocals. She is basically the Spanish Madonna, and it was clear to me that Nile had spent all of this money to get her involved just so that he could be with her. It was fine by me; I had a great time hanging out in Madrid. Martha took us to all of these speakeasy-type bars in

these grottoes and ancient wine cellars deep below the city. In every single one of them, there would be the best flamenco guitar players—I learned a lot from jamming with them.

I showed up for the wrap party in Miami and quickly became friends with Quentin, Angela, and a few other people. She and I started seeing each other back in L.A.; that went on for months. Basically it was composed of doing it in her car. We'd meet at a restaurant and we'd do it in her car. We'd talk on the phone and meet up and we'd do it in her car.

<hr />

I CONTINUED JAMMING WHENEVER AN opportunity presented itself, just trying to sort out what to do next. I had my hands full anyway, because while I was out sowing my wild oats, my marriage was falling apart. It was hardly sudden: even when I was in L.A. I was barely living at home. And now that I was done obsessing over Guns N' Roses, I was obsessing over what to do next.

When I traveled I never brought Renee along, and I was never faithful on the road. We did go to Ireland together to visit Ronnie Wood and his family for a while. There were parts of my lifestyle with Renee that I appreciated. She was an aspiring actress and I respected that, yet at the same time she couldn't seem to get a break and her career really wasn't going where she wanted it to. I think she was frustrated because I had already established myself. I'd cemented a foot in the door. None of that really mattered to Renee anyway, or so it seemed, because I wasn't from the kind of band that played the kind of music she was into. Come to think of it, I don't even think she knew the magnitude of what we were doing. She probably thought it was pretty childish.

As our relationship began to erode, Renee started hanging around the lowest echelon of Hollywood actor scumbags, partying a bit too much. At the same time I was doing my thing, completely oblivious to my commitments as a husband.

After I'd been paid by the insurance company for the house that had been totaled in the earthquake, we shopped for a new one and found it in Beverly Hills on Roxbury Drive. It was a big expensive Spanish-style structure built in the 1920s and now in foreclosure. It also had a basement, which

is rare in L.A. The house definitely had an aura; it was run-down, and in the basement there was a big disco ball hanging from the ceiling. I fell in love with it. On the third floor next to the master bedroom, there was this extra room that was stark white that seemed like it had been a darkroom: there were long, thin drawers to store photos and on each was an embossed black-and-white label with girls' names like "Candy," "Monica," and "Michelle."

We bought it immediately. It excited me that it had probably seen a few illicit photo shoots, and I can only imagine what kind of parties had gone down in that basement. All that mattered to me was that it *had* a basement—the perfect place for a recording studio. I got to work on that immediately and it was the first time that I took a "spare no expense" approach to something I wanted—it was the first time I'd really played with my money. I let Renee do whatever she wanted to the house, and we pissed money away on it in every way. The Roxbury house should have been great—it had a recording studio, lots of rooms, Jäger and Guinness on tap, pinball machines and arcade games, a pool table, etc. It was in a nice area of Beverly Hills, but none of that meant anything to me, so I wasn't really happy. The Snakepit II was coming together, yet still I was drinking deadly amounts of alcohol and dabbling with heroin, Ecstasy, and cocaine. I felt sort of empty and lost. Renee loved the house, but I rarely slept at home; instead, I spent an unhealthy amount of time sleeping around.

I spent most of my time hanging out at the Sunset Marquis, running away from everything. I was completely weightless after Guns N' Roses; I entered a phase of just spending my time and money at the hotel pool, chasing girls, drinking at the bar all day, and distancing myself however I could from anything in my life that I considered a nuisance. If John Lennon had his lost weekend, I had my lost year.

My security guard, Ronnie, took care of things at the house. Meanwhile I continued my infidelity tour of L.A. and soon enough I got sloppy. I attended a few high-profile events where I shouldn't have been misbehaving, so people were finding out—and so was Renee. Overall, it was a fun period without any sense of direction, though my desire to play guitar remained the same; I just needed to channel my energy into that.

Slash and Perla during their courtship, on vacation in Palm Springs.

I WAS HANGING OUT IN THE BAR AT THE
Sunset Marquis one night when Perla walked in with a few of her girlfriends,
all of them looking like *trouble*. She was a sight for sore eyes, I must say. She
looked *amazing*. We talked and laughed for a while and I realized at that
moment that I was in it. She gave me her address and the following night I
showed up where she was living over by the Hollywood Bowl. She had a fresh
vodka waiting for me, and that was it: I don't think I left her place for a week,
and after I got up one morning and fed her cats, we were inseparable from
that point on. Perla had a whole set of friends who weren't so much in the
rock-and-roll scene but were every bit as edgy and new to me. It was like a
vacation being with her—new faces, new places. It was like I'd finally gotten
far enough away from my life to relax. I had finally met a girl who could party
as much as I could, if not harder. But she was sharp and very much in control
and I had a lot of respect for her. She was beautiful, intelligent, and classy,
but also very streetwise—and Cuban to boot. Needless to say, I was in love.

Perla and I were in bed on something like our tenth day together when
she fixed me with a serious look. "You're *married*, you know," she said.

"Oh, yeah!" I said, kind of laughing it off. "You're right. I forgot about
that."

The truth was, I had forgotten. I didn't feel married at all, and since I'd hooked up with Perla, marriage seemed like something I'd done in another life. It was almost like leaving Guns N' Roses: I'd essentially checked out long before I officially left.

The next time I saw Renee she confronted me about what I'd been doing and was shocked to hear that I had no desire to work anything out—I just wanted a divorce. The next time I came home one night, I found a guy in bed with her and I told them not to get up; I'd let myself out. Despite her objections, I had insisted that she sign a prenup—maybe my overdose had something to do with forcing the issue. All of it was taken care of pretty quickly, and once it was, we never saw each other again. In retrospect, it's kind of interesting that I suddenly had disconnected with the two most long-term, closest relationships I had had up to that point, just a matter of months apart.

ONCE I WAS DIVORCED, PERLA AND I set off on a crazy, very exciting, and tumultuous relationship. Tumultuous because unlike any of the other girls I'd been around, she was very passionate about the obligations of a relationship and took it very seriously—she was not fucking around. So there was a bit of a clash between my ideals and hers, which made our relationship much spicier. We forged on. Besides, this all made for a very intense sex life, so I really wasn't going anywhere.

When Perla and I started seriously seeing each other, she introduced me to her mom, who is a colorful individual from Cuba. She came to the States the old-fashioned way, on a boat after Castro came to power. I liked her immediately, a sweet but tough lady who, like her daughter, is a very streetwise and observant soul. She liked me from the beginning, mostly because her daughter liked me—she is one of those people whose trust you have to earn. I met Perla's father a couple of years later in Miami. He was in his early seventies, a tall, gaunt fellow who didn't speak much English. We hit it off right away. He was sort of like a tough Cuban cowboy with a checkered past. Perla and I took him to Disney World the day I met him. The morning before we went to the park, at about 8 a.m., he popped us a couple of cold Heinekens from the fridge. He and I sat in comfortable silence watching

TV together, since neither one of us spoke the other's language, until we had to leave for the park. We shared a camaraderie and a silent understanding of each other from that moment on. Unfortunately, he died a year or so later of heart disease. I wish I had been able to have spent more time with him.

She also introduced me to a lot of people with whom I'd become very close friends with, Charlie Sheen and Robert Evans among them, plus a whole slew of other people who may not be as high-profile but are just as cool. We spent most nights going out, socializing, and I was jamming in clubs at least three or four nights a week. I was finally starting to feel a renewed sense of musical inspiration.

I set about putting together a new band; I wanted to do something like Snakepit, but different. Teddy Zig Zag started getting me out on Tuesday nights to jam down at the Baked Potato in Hollywood. I sat in with a lot of blues players and did a lot of classic songs, some of which I'd never played before and I loved every bit of it. Then I got this call from a promoter to do this show, all expenses paid, in Budapest, headlining the jazz festival there. I agreed immediately; it was the kick in the ass that I needed to go out and form a band. I got Johnny Griparic, Alvino Bennett, and Bobby Schneck on rhythm guitar. We put together a cover set that included everything from B.B. King to Steppenwolf to Otis Redding to a few other R&B and blues standards. Then we went off to Budapest to headline and it was *great*. After that, the calls rolled in for us to do more gigs, and before we knew it, we became a touring band, doing whatever gig we were offered as much for the money as for the beer. We became the most extreme gigs-for-beer touring band I'd ever seen and we had a great time doing it. We'd travel with a huge entourage and generally take over wherever it was that we showed up. I was having a really good time playing in clubs with a great bunch of guys who were just in it for the music.

When our tour was done, I approached Johnny Griparic about forming a new version of Snakepit. We put the word out on the street that we were looking for a new singer. At one point I had some guy get in touch with me who said that he was the singer for Jellyfish. Since I'd worked with Eric Dover on the last record, I decided to meet him. What a strange trip that turned out to be.

This guy met me over at Perla's house, and the moment I laid eyes on him I had my doubts. He didn't look the part; he had no rock-and-roll fashion sense at all—he looked more like a construction worker. I invited him in and we sat down in the living room and I pulled out a guitar. Perla was in the bedroom upstairs while this guy started telling me about some song he wrote about this girl. I asked him to sing it while I played the music, and found that the guy couldn't sing particularly well, so I was suspicious of his being in a band that did perfect five-part harmonies. And the lyrics were pretty naff as well. So I tried to be polite and saw him to the door.

After the guy left, Perla told me that everything he claimed to be and said was bullshit—and she knew the girl he was singing about. I was skeptical; I thought she was jumping to conclusions or being paranoid. I wasn't all that interested in working with him but I had him over once again just to see if Perla was right. She confronted the guy and every single thing she said turned out to be true. It was at that moment that I realized that Perla was a lot more astute than I gave her credit for. And, as much as I'd hate to admit it, this was one of many times that she saved me from potential disaster. In any case, the guy was a fraud and had lied to me, so I did the appropriate thing: me and Ronnie went to the guy's houseboat and scared the shit out of him. Ronnie threatened to put a hole in the boat with the guy's head, and told him to never call or contact me again.

Before, I alluded to how Ronnie became the Single White Female in my life; well, it was right about now when that happened. Over time, Ronnie became my shadow, and he seemed almost possessive of me. He did a great job helping move shit into my new house, and he was always loyal, but when Perla and I started hanging out together, it was as if he were listening in on our conversations. The last straw came when I discovered that he'd spun out in my car and totaled it without telling me. I realized that in a weird way he was both living vicariously through me and wanted to be me in a way. It all came to a head, and thankfully, he left quietly. I've since discovered that all the stuff I ever gave him—the gold records, awards, all that shit—he has sold on eBay. Nice.

Anyway, I continued my quest for a singer. When Johnny played me a tape of Rod Jackson, I knew we'd found him. I'd made demos of three or four songs for these different guys to audition with, and Rod did amazing

vocals on a demo track called "All Things Considered." His voice was incredible. It was rock and roll, but it was more like acid R&B delivered at high velocity. So I said, "Let's meet this guy." Rod was a perfect misfit: he was tall, half black and half white, always wore shades, and he had dreads. Being from Virginia, he also had a real southern attitude and accent. And when he sings, he can belt out soul like Otis Redding or hit a higher range like Sly Stone, but he also has a softer blues voice like Teddy Pendergrass or Marvin Gaye. It was a different kind of voice than any I'd ever worked with before, but I had nothing to lose, so I went with my heart on that.

We wrote a bunch of bitchin' stuff over at Mates—Johnny G., Matt Laug, Ryan Roxie—everyone together, then I moved the band into my house in Beverly Hills and we rehearsed and recorded in my brand-new studio. We worked hard and we played hard and we'd written an album's worth of material in no time.

DURING THIS PERIOD I KEPT A CLOSE relationship with Tom Maher, who was the guy who'd been most on my side over at BFD management. When I left Guns, he led me to believe that he'd stopped working over there and would manage me, but I'm not so sure that was really the case. It is possible that he was a mole, letting Doug know my every move. But at this point he was acting as my manager.

At the time, in 1998, the music industry underwent a major change. Black Friday happened, the day that hundreds of music executives were fired; they literally walked down Sunset with their boxes of stuff. Most of the labels were consolidated, one of them being Geffen, which was folded into Interscope. It was the beginning of the end of the music business as I'd known it.

Once Geffen was restructured, I had to make the acquaintance of a handful of people I'd never worked with. I was working on a band that had nothing to do with the grunge sound or whatever you want to call what it was that happened in the mid-nineties: it was a very cool but short-lived moment. And it had been replaced by rap-rock limp crap and boy bands . . . and Interscope was more or less all gangsta rap. I had no interest in any of that, so I was completely unaware about the shifts within the business.

A new breed of executives had become the norm as well; they were much

more bland, much more PC corporate-guy types than any of the characters I'd worked with. My typical loaded charm wasn't going to get me far. The only person that was a familiar face at the label anymore was Lori Earle, who'd worked publicity with me since Guns was signed.

The guy assigned to deal with me was Jordan Schur and I remember coming home from my meeting with him thinking that I did not trust him one bit. He promised me the world and I'd only known him for twenty minutes. His was a kind of whitewashing bullshit: "We're going to sell millions of records, get new cars," all that crap. I knew right away that the guy was not for real. But he was Interscope head Jimmy Iovine's boy, so I had to deal with it. I played him five demos from my next Snakepit record and he told me he loved them and couldn't wait to put it out. I then met with Jimmy Iovine, and he suggested that I have Jack Douglas produce my album, which I thought was a great idea because Jack had produced Aerosmith's *Rocks* and worked with John Lennon and other great artists in the seventies. Jimmy also commented that he had his doubts about my singer because his voice was too soulful, but I stood up for Rod and I told him, "Rod's got an amazing voice. It's just not what you'd expect."

At this point Izzy had been dropped by the label, as had Duff; so I had my doubts, but Jordan appeared to be genuinely excited. Jordan scheduled another meeting, then bailed on it, and then suddenly did an about-face, claiming that Snakepit wasn't the kind of music that his label produced. I wasn't shocked; I felt, "Now, that's more like it"—I could tell from the first time I met him that he was completely two-faced. With that, I decided to leave the label, and having already dumped a lot of money into recording the album myself, I offered to buy it back. In my mind, I had the house, I had the studio, I'd just record it all there and sell it elsewhere. I was very stubborn about the whole thing.

At the same time, Tom Maher hadn't done anything to help me in the situation, so I decided to look for a new manager and I was introduced to Sam Frankel by Jack Douglas, who in turn introduced me to Jerry Heller. The idea was that Heller would manage me while Frankel would be my day-to-day guy. I was meeting a few people, but when I get my mind locked into accomplishing something, I'll do whatever it takes with whoever can do it to get things done—right away. Jerry was *that guy*, but a

very suspicious character, and I'm still unsure of that whole arrangement, Considering that I was a full-blown alcoholic, and not exercising clear judgement anyway, I didn't care—I just wanted to get things moving forward. I had a handshake deal with Jerry and Sam, and Jack Douglas commenced producing my record.

I felt like I was back in the early days of Guns, trying to get a band off the ground while working with subpar players: Jack was great but he hadn't done anything recently, and while Jerry Heller had made his home in the hip-hop world, he hadn't done anything of merit in the rock world; Sam was a nice Jewish attorney from the East Coast who visited his mom regularly and seemed to know nothing about the music business whatsoever. It was the carnival all over again, amid a music industry that was completely alien to me.

As far as the band went, it was no better: the singer, Rod Jackson, turned out to be unmotivated and a junkie, Johnny Griparic was and is a great bass player but didn't have the touring experience he really needed for the long haul, and Ryan Roxie, whom I met from Alice Cooper's band and hired as a second guitarist, was only interested in getting as much of the publishing as possible. The drummer, Matt Laug, was the most experienced and even-keeled of the bunch, and, of course, there was me, playing the role of boss, which wasn't a role I was comfortable with. I split all of the publishing and advance equally with everyone, so it seemed more like a team effort than it really was, so in the end it was just a mess. All I wanted to do was get the record done and get back on the road. I took a deal with Koch Records because they made the most solid offer, which was a huge mistake due to the fact that they dropped the ball soon after the record was released, which did nothing to help the situation at all.

Jerry Heller proved to be a true cannibal manager; he tried to take me for everything given the chance. I've since heard stories to that effect from others in the business as well. The only thing that Jerry did do was get us the opening slot on the AC/DC tour for *Stiff Upper Lip*. And that is how he bought my confidence as a manager.

Meanwhile, Jerry tried to get me to sign a contract that granted him 20 percent of all the money I'd make with Snakepit plus 20 percent of my future earnings from Guns . . . for eternity. Perla didn't trust him and sug-

gested I shouldn't sign it, and when I showed the contract to my new attorney, David Codikow, he told me it was suicidal. He got into it with Jerry and straight up called him an asshole, so Jerry fired him, which was surreal because he had no authority to do so—my manager can't fire my attorney—but not wanting to give him the pleasure regardless, David quit anyway. In hindsight, it's all pretty laughable, but at the time it was traumatic—it was all I could do to keep it together.

I was without an attorney at that point, when one night I was at home with Perla and there was a knock at the door. It was the police, who had a warrant for her arrest for violating probation. She was cuffed and stuffed. Perla had recently gotten a DUI and wasn't supposed to be driving, but she had been. While she did fifty-six days in the county jail, Jerry got me to sign that contract when I wasn't in the right frame of mind. I was drinking insane amounts of vodka from morning to night, and I can't imagine that I was clearheaded enough to make rational business decisions.

It was way back on the Mötley Crüe tour that I first noticed the shakes as a result of having the DT's in the morning. I started drinking early in the day not so much to cure a hangover as to control the DT's. It was a subtle change that would continue and get worse later. When Perla was in jail, I would go to sleep with a cocktail next to my head on the nightstand and would finish it in the morning just to be able to get out of bed to get to the kitchen to make a fresh one to start my day. Often the police wouldn't let me into the county jail to visit her because I had been drinking. I was a real mess: aside from close to a gallon of vodka a day at home, I'd drink shots of whiskey with beer chasers all night when I would go out to clubs. The future didn't look bright for me health-wise but nobody could have told me that back then.

AFTER THE AC/DC TOUR, WE DID A HEAD-lining tour of theaters. It was actually costing me money, personally, but I didn't care. After two months Koch ditched us: they pulled our tour support and didn't promote the thing at all. We'd show up to signings and the record wouldn't be in the stores. I'd have to make a call to get a box of them sent out that day—it was way too *Spinal Tap*.

As the tour wore on, I remember progressively not feeling well. In Pittsburgh, I remember thinking that I should go to the hospital before sound check. My next memory is waking up two weeks later in a hospital bed with Perla sitting there, looking very worried. I had suffered cardiac myopathy. Years of overdrinking had swollen my heart to the point of rupture, to the point where it was barely strong enough to circulate my blood properly. I couldn't get it through my head that I was out of commission, but I was. The doctors gave me six days to six weeks to live but not much more. Once I was well enough to fly back to L.A., I was on bed rest and forbidden from drinking or any kind of strenuous physical activity.

The doctors installed a defibrillator to keep my heart from stopping and to keep my heart rate steady. After a time I began therapy, starting with very minimal exercise and working my way up. Miraculously, my heart started to heal, and the doctors could not believe that my condition was improving. Eventually I was able to play again and I was determined to finish up our club tour. I had been out of circulation for about four months and I was totally sober. When I saw the band again, this time through clear eyes, I realized how dysfunctional it was.

Between the junkie singer who was on the verge of withdrawal at any moment and the bass player, they seemed like they wanted nothing but to live the whole lifestyle that I had a reputation for. But in my new, clear-minded state, it appeared to me that the whole thing was very unprofessional and all over the place. A couple of the guys seemed less committed than guys in my high school bands had been: they were treating this whole thing like a free ride, and no one was carrying their weight. I spent the rest of those dates when I wasn't onstage in my bunk. When we got back to L.A. after the last gig, I stayed up there until everyone was gone, and that was the last I spoke to any of them for quite some time. I am good friends with Johnny and Matt again, now that enough time has passed.

———•◦✕◦•———

SOBRIETY ALSO CONFIRMED THE FEELING that Jerry Heller was draining my life and needed to go . . . but I had signed that contract and was bound by it. I finally got a break when Jerry made a mistake that Perla and I discovered after some thorough investigating. Early

in our partnership, Jerry got me to record a guitar part for Rod Stewart on the song "Human" from the album of the same name. He had booked that recording gig for me, which was a material breach of our contract—a manager can't book something like that and take a commission, which he had. In the end, his own actions gave me the legal out I needed to be rid of him. I felt lucky.

This particular period, from 1999 to 2001, was easily the darkest period of my existence on this planet. Recreational drinking had morphed into *severe* alcoholism. I allowed myself to be thrown to the wolves . . . all these people were taking advantage of me when all I really wanted to do was play and not deal with it all. It was a huge reality check.

I figure I paid my dues after Guns. It was tough going, but I guess it was something I had to go through to be able to focus and see how tenacious and resilient I really am. And to rediscover how badly I still wanted it.

<hr />

BY NOW PERLA AND I HAD MOVED INTO a new house up in Nichols Canyon, determined to relax and make a new start. We settled into a nice pseudo-domestic life together, as best we could, as I continued to jam wherever I chose to and waited for inspiration to lead me to my next band situation. In 2001, I agreed to play at Michael Jackson's fortieth birthday celebration at Madison Square Garden and Perla and I flew out for it. This was my first gig since my operation, so I was looking forward to it, and it turned out to be memorable . . . to say the least.

I did a couple of days of rehearsal to prepare to perform on September 8 and 10. It promised to be a huge event; Michael had everyone from Jamie Foxx to Liza Minnelli to Marlon Brando, the Jackson Five, and Gloria Estefan on the bill, among others. It was a great show, and everyone in the Michael Jackson entourage was rocking out, though I was doing the best I could to stay away from alcohol. After all, I now had a pacemaker, which made things interesting.

When the doctors put in the defibrillator, it was for maintaining a normal heart rate. For most people, this isn't a problem, but I neglected to tell the specialists that once I get up onstage my heart rate skyrockets. When I took the stage with Michael and got into it, I was suddenly hit in the chest

by a shock, and my vision was flooded with electric blue light. This happened about four times during each song and I had no idea what was going on—I thought I had a short in my guitar cable or a photographer's flash had popped in my eyes. And each time it happened, I had to stand there and make it look like everything was status quo. I saw it later on TV and you couldn't tell, so I guess I pulled it off. It was all extremely disconcerting, however, until I finally figured out what was what.

On the morning of 9/11, we were woken up at 8:15 by David Williams, Michael's house guitar player.

"Slash, turn on the TV," he told me.

"It's already on," I said.

"Is it on the news?" he asked, looking at me kind of oddly.

"No, it's on the E! channel," I told him.

"Well, put on the news!" I saw that a plane had hit the Twin Towers, and moments later the second one hit while I was actually watching. The windows were open in my room, so I could see what was going on in the distance. That was probably one of the most unnerving events I'd ever experienced. As you can imagine, the whole hotel was in pandemonium. There were people running around the hallway as if it were the end of the civilized world. And Perla was still asleep. I had to wake her up and try to explain what was happening. I think it took a few minutes before it sank in. Michael and his immediate entourage had left the building and were safely on a plane out of the country, I believe. But we were stuck there in a city turned upside down.

I thought the safest place to be was where we were, but Perla thought differently. She wanted out of there. She was convinced that the air was filled with toxins, but we couldn't get a ride out. And for some reason, a lot of Michael's dancers and background singers had convened in our room, because everyone was trapped in Manhattan with no way out. Perla really wanted to get home, so she was in an intense state trying to figure out a way to get us across the country.

Eventually we found a limo that took us across the only bridge that was open at that point, the George Washington Bridge. We continued across New Jersey to the Poconos, which is a resort area in Pennsylvania. Perla found us a room in the Pocono Palace, this love-theme hotel that she knew about—I didn't ask how. When we finally got there, it was like something

I'd only seen in magazines. This place had a champagne glass for a bathtub, satin sheets and velvet blankets on a rotating bed, tacky red carpets, and mirrors on the ceiling. By the time we got there, we were dead tired.

We collected our dinner tickets from the front desk—because that's the kind of place this was—and headed to the smorgasbord-style dinner. Like every other couple there, we were assigned a number and had designated seats at a big round table filled with other couples. We were sitting there with old folks from New Jersey who had renewed their vows, nerdy people who'd just gotten married, and a few couples who should have known better. There was nothing beautiful or romantic about that place at all. Everyone we interacted with was clearly scared of us, but what scared us most about them was that no one was aware of the tragedy that had just occurred a hundred miles away.

There was a shitty band and a stand-up comic booked as dinner entertainment, there was miniature golf, horseback riding, couples riding, and every clichéd romantic activity imaginable. Love was the Pied Piper for all of those fucking misfits. When we got to talking to any of them who knew about the attack, they didn't seem to care. They were there wallowing in love, and were so into it that 9/11 wasn't an issue worth discussing. We were stuck there, strangers in a strange land, for three days. Then we bunny-hopped, flight by flight, back to L.A.

<hr />

I HAD ONE RUN-IN WITH HEROIN DURING this period of my life. I'd stayed away and lost interest in it for so long that I actually believed my own bullshit when I told myself I'd never touch it again. Even as I began to hang around where it might be or as I made plans to hook up with people who probably had it, I still believed myself. I assured myself and I assured Perla that I was done with it, but I should have known—or at least admitted it to myself—where it was going.

One night I got some and went back to the Hyatt on Sunset and got so high that I nodded out and fell asleep with all of my weight on one leg. When I woke up I couldn't feel it at all. I couldn't bend it, I couldn't stand up, and it didn't seem to get any better once I stretched it out. Junkies do that all the time; some of them cut off their circulation so badly that gangrene sets in.

I had to call 911 and I was taken to Cedars-Sinai, which was completely full at the time. So they put me in a holding room until they could find me a permanent room. As I lay there smoking cigarettes, which they weren't too happy about, they got in touch with Perla and she came down and I told her what had happened. The whole episode scared her and she threatened to leave me if I continued down this road. I was in there for a week and it was a great chance to get some peace and quiet . . . and watch the History Channel.

Seeing her there only confirmed for me that she was the one. I asked her to get married and luckily she agreed. We had a beautiful little ceremony

Slash and Ray Charles recording at Ray's legendary studio in Los Angeles.

in Maui, and spent a week together, enjoying each other. Things were definitely looking up.

Before the honeymoon, I carried my guitar around and constantly set up sessions, though everything around me remained chaotic. With my black book and cell phone, I tried to keep things going musically. I lacked focus, but I was committed, and sometimes my efforts lead to a lucky break. One was working with the legendary Ray Charles. The day after Perla and I returned from our honeymoon, I went to South Central L.A. to record "God Bless America Again" with him. I used my '54 Telly and it was one of the more amazing sessions I've ever participated in: it was, a huge honor and a humbling experience. I didn't think Ray had even heard of me, but there we were playing together.

Ray was involved with a benefit for underpriviledged kids with an interest in music—he'd let them record in his studio and use his equipment, and sometimes Ray even played with them. They'd work on songs, techniques, and arrangements while he coached them. I'd go down there at times to play some tracks with the kids. Helping them out was an incredible feeling.

I also contributed to certain parts of the *Ray* movie tracks; I played with guys *way* out of my league, big-band old-time blues jazz players. I played guitar on "Sorry Seems to Be the Hardest Word" on his *Genius Loves Company* album, but after Ray died, the executive producer used a friend of his instead and took my part off, even though Ray thought I was more bluesy.

My period of rootlessness in the musical sense was about to come to an end. I had wandered and I had learned. I was ready to come back to my center and make a new start. It was time. I got together with Pete Angelus, who had managed the Black Crowes and had wanted to manage me. He got me together with Steve Gorman, the Crowes' drummer, and Alan Niven turned me on to a bass player. We started to write and came up with the music for what became "Fall to Pieces." All we needed was a singer—again. But then my good friend Randy Castillo passed away and I went to his funeral, and out of his death came a rebirth I could have never imagined.

Coming Up
for Air

Velvet Revolver and some of their biggest fans on the Santa Monica Pier in July 2004 during the making of the "Fall to Pieces" music video.

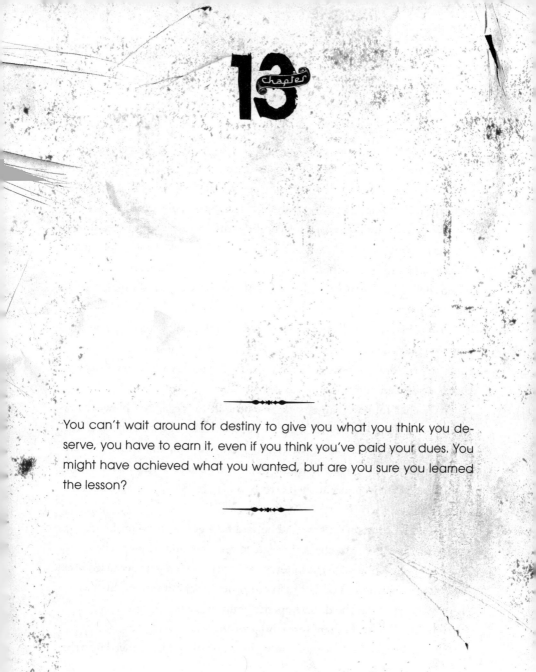

13

chapter

You can't wait around for destiny to give you what you think you deserve, you have to earn it, even if you think you've paid your dues. You might have achieved what you wanted, but are you sure you learned the lesson?

In 2001, I went to Ireland and hooked up with Ronnie Wood to be part of the tour for his solo record. He called it the *Not for Beginners* tour. Perla came with me and we hung out with Ronnie and his wife, Jo, and had a great time. We'd rehearse in Ronnie's bar: he has a building apart from the house that is a proper pub with a snooker table and Guinness on tap. We ran through great stuff: Woodie's stuff, Stones stuff, Faces songs, a Guns N' Roses song, and a Snakepit song. We had sixty songs rehearsed and a great band to play them made up of Ronnie's son Jessie, two of Jessie's friends on bass and drums, and a couple of other guys; plus Ronnie's daughter Leah singing background. It was a really cool thing because we toured all of these little clubs all over the U.K. We had the Corrs come up and sing and we'd play the Faces' classic "Ooh La La" every night. There was a lot of fun and a lot of Guinness to be had. As Perla and I would later discover, that is where our son London was conceived.

After that tour we came back and headed to Vegas for New Year's. Before we'd gone to the U.K., we'd spent a weekend down there at the opening of this resort called the Green Valley Ranch, and while we were there, in the *Vegas* magazine in our room we noticed an ad for Guns N' Roses live on New Year's at the Hard Rock Hotel & Casino. We decided that we had to check it out.

I called a promoter I knew and he said he'd get us in no problem. We got to the Hard Rock to check into our room a few hours before the show, and as we walked through the lobby, people were noticing us because Guns fans were everywhere. We'd been in our room for about ten minutes when there was a knock at the door. I opened it up to see hotel security.

"Oh, hi!" I said. "Is there something wrong?"

"Sir, we have come to let you know that you will not be allowed into the Guns N' Roses show tonight."

"Oh yeah? Why is that?"

"We have strict orders from Guns N' Roses management not to allow you admittance under any circumstances. I'm sorry."

"C'mon, man, that's ridiculous," I said. "Just sneak me in. I'm not here to cause trouble, I just want to see the show. I'm sure you can understand why."

"I'm sorry, sir, there is nothing we can do about it."

I got in touch with my promoter friend and there was nothing he could do either. He said that the word was that I'd been spotted with my guitar and top hat as if I was going to get onstage. That was preposterous—I didn't even have a guitar with me! It was no use; the entire staff was instructed to keep me out at all costs. We decided that it wasn't worth it; I'm not the type to cause a scene.

Perla and I checked out and got a room over at the Green Valley Ranch and went to the grand opening of Whiskey Blue at the resort and had a blast at the huge New Year's Eve party they were having. That night, I ran into a guy whom I'd met before but didn't know very well, though he knew me. He took me into the bathroom and laid out a line of what looked like blow for me to snort.

I love to be deviant and do what I'm not supposed to do, which includes doing whatever drugs are given to me without really asking what they are or wondering where they came from. I snorted this stuff up, and within five minutes a very familiar euphoria came over me. I knew that feeling well; it wasn't coke, it was an opiate . . . this was some form of heroin. A very good form indeed, because suddenly everything in the world was wonderful as far as I was concerned.

I asked him for more and he gave me a handful of pills. "What is this?" I asked. "This is what I just did?"

"It's OxyContin," he said. "It's basically synthetic heroin. You smash it up and snort it. I've got a great connection." He sure did: he'd just beaten cancer and had a bottomless prescription.

"Wow," I said, barely concealing my enthusiasm. "I'll keep that in mind."

Now Perla and I had spent the first years of our marriage and our relationship being pretty wild. She was the most awesome, coolest girl: no matter how many parties we went to, no matter how much shit she'd done or I'd done or what was going on around us, Perla was always in control. She could remain grounded in insane circumstances and was always the one to take care of anyone who needed help. During that phase, we drank

a lot, we did a lot of Ecstasy and coke, but the one thing she would not tolerate was dope. She threatened to leave me after my episode at the Hyatt and there was no way that she was going to allow this high-grade shit—which made it all the more appealing.

I told myself I'd tell her as I crushed another OxyContin and snorted it and entered a blissful state. I brought that habit back to L.A. with me and snuck this stuff in secret for a while. I started calling my new friend to get more . . . he'd run back and forth from L.A. to Vegas to keep me supplied. Pretty soon I had a new type of monkey on my back.

if there is one thing I am, it's "the eternal teenager."

IT WAS NOW 2002 AND AEROSMITH WAS playing the L.A. Forum with Cheap Trick opening up. I was all set up to go and my Vegas friend was in town with a big batch of OxyContin and we were armed to the teeth and ready to have a *great* night. Perla and I got into a huge fight about something insignificant shortly before I had to leave. It was bad enough that she didn't want me to go—she wanted closure before I did.

I was stoned and stubborn; I didn't want to hear it, I was going to the show whether we worked it out or not. My friend was waiting in the car and I was trying to get out of the house. I walked to the door as Perla stood at the bottom of the stairs, still talking to me despite my unresponsiveness.

"*Slash!*" she yelled. I turned around. "I'm *pregnant.*"

High as I was, that cut straight through it. I stared at her for a long moment. It felt like time stopped.

"Okay," I said. "Let's talk when I get back."

I got high as a kite that night, so deliberately and obviously that the Aerosmith guys, the Cheap Trick guys, and everyone I ran into were aware of it. Under the circumstances, I did the only thing that made sense: I hung out with David Lee Roth all night. But, in the back of my mind, I couldn't get what Perla had said to me out of my head.

When I got home we talked about everything. We'd been married only four months, but together for five years. Up until then, nothing had happened and we'd never used protection. It didn't take us long to decide that we would have the baby. We surmised that my Guinness consumption in Ireland must have had something to do with my sudden potency. The running joke was that we'd name the kid Guinness, but we decided against it since that was Ronnie Wood's dog's name.

More than any other incentive I've ever had, Perla's pregnancy straightened me out: I got off the Oxy, still without telling Perla what I was up to. I just kicked as I had in the past—cold turkey, with no one the wiser. I kicked standing up, and told Perla that I had the flu. But it was no use: I'd forgotten about a stash I'd hidden in our guest room, and when she found it she knew exactly what I was up to.

We'd been hopping from rental to rental and finally decided that we needed to buy a house. I'd had the house where I'd recorded Snakepit on the market for a while and it had finally sold, so it was like a new start. I remember starting our house hunt while I was getting clean and just sweating profusely as we looked at these places. I think I was still clinging to the flu excuse at that point.

We looked at this one house that was straight out of "Hansel and Gretel": it was a medieval cottage that the owner had decorated ridiculously. It turned out to be Spencer Proffer's house, the guy who produced *Live! Like a Suicide*. We had a quick hello and good-bye, just a drive-by catching up. I was surprised to find out recently that he has nothing nice to say about us at all. He said that during those sessions I peed on the floor and that Axl shot up in the studio and threw up on the control board and tried to get Spencer to shoot up, too. You can read these lies and more in the extensive library of unauthorized Guns N' Roses stories available at bookstores and online. None of that is true; he must have a case of ill will because we didn't hire him to produce the whole record.

So I got clean, and I was inspired by Perla: from the second she knew she was pregnant to the day she had the baby, she didn't touch a drink and quit smoking on the spot. She underwent such a huge, abrupt switch; the maternal instinct took over immediately and it was amazing.

Perla had some complications with the pregnancy; London was a breech baby, which means that he was sitting in such a way that it was very uncomfortable and painful for her for most of the nine months. She had to remain on bed rest for most of her term.

During those months I started looking to put a new band together. Pete Angelus, who had managed Van Halen, David Lee Roth, and the Black Crowes, had taken an interest in managing me, so he hooked me up with Steve Gorman, the then former drummer for the Black Crowes, who was available because at that point they'd broken up. My old buddy Alan Niven gave me the number of a bass player that he thought I should hear, so we brought him in, and I can't remember his name but the three of us started rehearsing, just jamming with no real agenda. I was on the straight and narrow, not really even drinking. It was the first time since before the final months of Snakepit that I had gotten myself back into gear: I was in a better head space than ever, I'd started to think about a band again, and I'd started writing material. During that time I came up with the music that evolved into the song "Fall to Pieces." We jammed for a very short period of time, but I came up with a lot of ideas, the most complete one being that song. Those were the first signs of me taking any kind of a responsible, adult role in my life, because if there is one thing I am, it's "the eternal teenager."

IT WAS AROUND THIS TIME THAT I HEARD Randy Castillo had died. I'd known Randy for years; we'd met in the metal touring circuit of the eighties. He was one of the most in-demand session and touring drummers around; he'd played with Ozzy, Lita Ford, and everyone else you can think of. But Randy was as far from the typical L.A. metal musician as could be: he was one of the most genuine, down-to-earth, and easygoing people I met during that entire period. He was always fun to hang out with and just no bullshit: he was totally self-abusive with booze and coke, but was always a great drummer with a heart of gold. I don't

remember exactly how we met, but we had mutual friends, and in my mind it felt like I'd always known Randy. What set him apart from everyone else in L.A. was that he was always happy and never judgmental of anybody. Unlike most of the other characters around back then, he was never preoccupied with talking shit about other people, or spending the night critiquing how other people looked or acted. That kind of conversation is such an L.A. staple; Randy didn't care—maybe because he was from New Mexico originally.

I played New Mexico with Snakepit, and by then I'd heard that Randy had cancer and that it was very serious. When we came through, he came down to the show and hung out on the bus with us. At the time he was undergoing chemotherapy and he didn't look good at all. He was very thin and weak but I was just so happy that he'd even come down.

A short while later I heard that his cancer had all but disappeared and that he was doing much better. And not long after that I saw him and he was a different guy altogether—he looked *great*. When I got the call, maybe five months after that, that Randy had died, I was shocked. I hadn't even known that he'd taken a major downturn.

The funeral was at Forest Lawn Cemetery and everyone Randy had ever known was there, all his old musician friends from all of the bands he'd been in, including Ozzy, Randy's extended family, and all of his friends who loved him—it was a huge gathering. At the reception I ran into Matt Sorum, who told me that he and some others were setting up a fund-raiser for Randy's family and organizing a benefit gig to raise money and commemorate him. Matt asked me if I wanted to play at the gig and I thought it was a great idea; any excuse to play guitar onstage is all I need. Besides, I wanted to do it for Randy.

Matt and I decided that we'd do a set together and we agreed to call Duff, who'd moved back to Seattle, to ask him if he was interested. He'd formed a band called Neurotic Outsiders with Steve Jones from the Sex Pistols and they had put out a record and done a tour. Then they disbanded; Duff had put another band together with some friends from Seattle called Loaded. I'd run into him a few times in the past year: he'd come down for my birthday, and we'd jammed with Izzy in a studio one time, so we were definitely on speaking terms and in contact.

We needed a singer (as usual) and we needed a rhythm guitar player. I had my eye on Josh Todd and Keith Nelson from Buckcherry. I'd heard that their band had broken up, so that was an option. I liked Josh's voice on some of the stuff of theirs that I'd heard and this seemed like a good opportunity to try him out.

We wanted to make this thing something special, so Matt called B-Real and Sen Dog from Cypress Hill to see if they'd be willing to come down and do a song or something with us. They were in, so we all showed up to rehearse and it was really a landmark afternoon. When we walked in over at Mates there was a tangible vibe: being in a room again with Matt and Duff instantly took me back to the chemistry we'd shared onstage every night with Guns. We got up together while the other guys watched, and the moment we hit the first chord, there was a confidence and a musical camaraderie that spoke for itself. And it said, *"This* is how it's done, boys."

We rehearsed "Paradise City," "It's So Easy," "Mama Kin," Thin Lizzy's "Jailbreak," "Rock-'n'-Roll Superstar," and the Sex Pistols' "Bodies." B-Real and Sen Dog came up and rapped the verses of "Paradise City." It was fucking great. For the first time since the first Snakepit, I felt fulfilled musically. I was surrounded by musicians who really knew how to hold down a mean groove and put forth an even meaner delivery. The core of Matt, Duff, and I was undeniable. When we started jamming, people who were rehearsing or working at Mates that day began wandering in to watch and listen. Soon we had a small audience and we plastered them to the wall.

Randy's tribute was at the Key Club on April 29, 2002. It was the first time that that many members of Guns had played together in years. We went on last and we just slammed the place. Steven Tyler came up and did "Mama Kin" with us. All in all it was a momentous evening. I was elated.

I was home with Perla the next day when Duff called.

"Hey, man," he said. "That was great last night. Like *really* great."

"Yeah, it was," I said. "I've been thinking about it all morning."

What I'd been thinking was that I'd been wasting time. I'd been tinkering around with other musicians; talented guys, sure, but none of them were right for me. I'd been looking for something when what I was after had been right in front of me the whole time.

"Duff, we should do something with this," I said. "We would be stupid not to. Fuck all of the obvious Guns N' Roses connotations."

"All right . . . okay," he said. "Let's do it."

Duff and I had never said it, but the two of us had been consciously avoiding working with each other. We didn't want to be pigeonholed, we didn't want to be labeled: we didn't want to resign ourselves to the compartment we'd be relegated to—an ex-Guns side project. At this point enough time had gone by, and even if it hadn't, we'd experienced enough energy playing together again to know that we could get beyond any bullshit expectation that might be dumped on us.

Matt was in, too, and since Josh and Keith were interested in going for it, we started getting together a few days a week at their rehearsal space in North Hollywood. I wasn't sure about them because I didn't know them, but I was willing to give it a shot.

Keith and Josh brought in a couple of good songs that we worked on and Duff and I started making things up on the spot, just as naturally as we always did. The one thing I didn't like about the space was that I couldn't hear Josh singing at all. It started to worry me that after a few weeks, as we got more and more involved, I still had no idea what the whole band sounded like. I started making board tapes, and boy, was I surprised. When I played them back, I was shocked: Josh's voice was just too linear and grating; it was a distraction from the music, not to mention just a tad off-key.

I am embarrassed to admit that I was willing to quit the band prematurely because of that. I assumed that Duff and Matt had been listening to the same tapes of our sessions that I had; and it's my fault that I presumed that since no one was objecting to what we were doing, they were all fine with it.

"I can't do this anymore," I told Duff and Matt after rehearsal one day. "I'm done."

"Hey! What are you talking about?" Duff asked.

"What's wrong?" Matt asked.

"Have you listened to these sessions we've been doing?"

"No," they both said.

"Well, you should."

That night they did and the next day we were all on the same page. Josh's voice is perfect for Buckcherry, but it wasn't musical enough for

what we had in mind. I am happy to say that Buckcherry has gotten back together and their big single in 2006, "Crazy Bitch," was one of the tracks we worked on during that period.

We let Josh know that we didn't want to continue with him and it was all very amicable, but we weren't quite sure how to handle it when Keith told us that he intended to keep working with us. Those two were writing partners, they were friends, and they were bandmates; we'd always thought of them as a package deal and assumed that Keith would split when Josh did.

"Fuck that," he said. "I like what we're doing here. I'm staying."

There was only one problem: generally Keith just played whatever I played at the same time. There was no interplay and he had no sense of complementing what I played. So the sound we got with Keith was basically two Les Pauls playing identical licks. He hung around for two more weeks, we thought he might get the hint . . . but he didn't, so we had to let him go. Again, I was happy to hear it when those guys re-formed Buckcherry.

<hr>

MATT AND DUFF AND I STARTED REHEARSING and writing like crazy. I had my eyes and ears open for another guitar player and a singer. I had gone with Josh Todd to see Duff play with Loaded one night as part of Metal Shop, this weekly glam metal revue, at the Viper Room. I went in through the back door and it was as if I'd stepped into 1984. I saw people I hadn't seen since then, and they looked exactly the same. I saw girls and guys from the different spots—the Troubadour, the Whiskey, the Rainbow—looking the way they did twenty years ago. There were a few guys from Faster Pussycat, L.A. Guns, and all the same chicks I knew from back then, all there as if they'd been caught in a time warp; everyone with the same clothes on, the same makeup on, seemingly doing the same shit. And of course, Gene Simmons was there having his picture taken with a crowd of girls. To top it all off, Ron Jeremy was there with a few porn chicks.

Duff had told me about the show earlier that day.

"Hey, man," he said. "So the guy playing guitar in my band has alleged that he is like one of your best friends from junior high."

"Oh yeah?" I had no idea who he might mean.

"Yeah, really," he said. "His name is Dave Kushner. He swears up and down that you were buds, I just wanted to let you know, he's in my band."

It was true, Dave and I were buddies in junior high and high school; he used to come to my Tidas Sloan shows before he even picked up a guitar. Dave is a supercool guy and I'd always thought the best of him all these years. The last time I saw him he was working at Tower Video when Guns N' Roses was just taking off, at the time he had a pretty serious drinking habit going. He worked in the basement between the music and video shops, boxing and unloading the product, just drinking hard down there apparently. He'd gotten it together, however, and by that time he was fifteen years sober. I was kind of curious to see him again.

The overwhelming eighties vibe at Metal Shop got to me pretty quick that night, but I got the chance to say hello to Dave before I left. It was really good to see him. After Keith left, Duff suggested that Dave come down to jam, and I was all for it. We clicked instantly; Dave brought a cool vibe to what we were doing. There was no deliberation; that was it, it was a perfect fit. He brought a new dimension to the sound of the band as it was and an interesting guitar style that complemented mine as mine did his. The lineup was now Duff, Matt, Dave, and me, and the music was coming very naturally. We just had that age-old nagging problem: no singer. It is the story of my life, isn't it?

For a group of seasoned, professional musicians you'd think that we'd have a clue of how to find a singer. No chance. We looked at one another with no idea of the proper process for a group like ours to find one.

"Should we put an ad in *The Recycler?*" I asked at rehearsal one day.

"Man, I don't know," Duff said. "I *guess* so. We don't know any singers."

"This feels like the time that we first hooked up," I said. "When Steven and I first met you and we had a band. We wrote some great shit but finding a singer was just impossible."

"You're right. We're at square one," Duff said. "That's pretty sad, man. What the fuck? I guess we should put an ad in the paper."

Before we did that, we thought it would be a good idea to make a list of every good living rock singer, regardless of whether they were in a band or not. Our list was pretty short: among others, there was Sebastian Bach,

Ian Astbury, and Steve Jones. There was one other name that everyone in the band seemed keen on: Scott Weiland . . . but as far as we knew he was still in Stone Temple Pilots.

After we made our list and realized that almost everyone on it was otherwise accounted for, we did put an ad in *The Recycler* as well as the *Music Connection*. We even went so far as to place an ad in the *Hollywood Reporter*. But the most significant thing we did was put a blurb on MTV.com. We could never have done that in the old days and perhaps I was naive about the impact that it would have. I soon learned my lesson: that one blurb set off a barrage of CD and cassette-tape demos sent our way. They arrived on a daily basis, as our little beginning of a band became public knowledge.

Our "project" started being reported on the radio, blogged about on the Internet; all of a sudden we'd generated a lot of attention just by trying to find ourselves a singer relatively on the down-low. We began receiving two hundred submissions a week from around the world, all of them pouring into my P.O. box. I'd show up to collect these huge boxes of shit, and the guys at the mailbox place, who've watched this band from that phase on out, have given me the knowing wink ever since.

<hr />

I GOT A RANDOM CALL ONE DAY.
"Hello?"

"Hey, what are you doin'? It's Izzy."

"Hey, man, I'm good," I said. "I'm actually going to rehearsal. I've been working with Duff and Matt and this guy Dave. We've got something really good going."

"Hey, cool. I'll come down."

It was classic Izzy; he's so elusive, he'll pop up somewhere out of the blue, hang out intensely, then disappear for a couple of months. He came down to the studio with his guitar and amp and he brought a couple of demos. We jammed with him for two weeks and it was great: we wrote about twelve songs that would have been the best Guns N' Roses record, hands down. We talked about the old days, we shared war stories; we laughed a lot and we had a really good time.

At the same time we continued the quest for a singer, which didn't interest Izzy one bit. Whenever we brought it up, he wanted nothing to do with the conversation in any way; he wanted to distance himself as much as possible. He didn't actually want to be in the band, if that's what we intended; he just wanted to hang out. Discussing where to find a lead singer was too much for him. He was, in general, very anti–lead singer. I can't imagine why.

The singer thing had been a problem for me in every band I'd ever joined, and I couldn't believe that after all of this time, it plagued me still.

"I got an idea," Izzy said at rehearsal one day. "Know what we should do? Duff and I will sing and we will just do a club tour in a van."

He said it in Izzy's way, which means that it was hard to tell if he was serious or kidding.

I was dead set on finding a solid front man regardless, because I was taking this project very seriously. I was getting sick of the fact that we weren't getting out there and playing. I wasn't going to let this situation go until it came to fruition. But I have to admit, I contemplated that idea . . . for a minute.

We called legendary A&R man John Kalodner to ask for his advice as far as singers went. John came down to see us rehearse and he thought that we were the best thing since sliced bread . . . but he told us that he didn't know any good singers who were available.

Izzy suggested that we go track a few of the songs we had worked out at Rumbo, which we did. At the time I wondered what Izzy was thinking: in my mind, what we were doing with him was just fucking around and having a good time, with no expectation of where it was going. At the same time I was intent on pursuing this, as was Duff and Matt, so I wasn't sure why Izzy would want to take it to the next level by suggesting the studio.

In any case, the songs we did together were great, and I wasn't going to put an end to that. The three of us had also been listening to the demos that were trailing in. We'd found one that we were curious about: this guy named Kelly from Florida. We flew him out to try a vocal on a track or two, and as soon as he showed up in the studio, Izzy ducked out. There weren't any hard feelings or anything, he just had to go and said his good-byes.

but he was a step in the right direction. Still, months went by without us getting any closer to finding the right match. I hoped to find a diamond in the rough, some unknown talent out there. I told Gilby, who at the time was hanging at Mates every day because he was producing a band called the Bronx. He thought we were crazy.

"You're *never* gonna find a singer," he said, smirking. "With the level you're at, you just can't do that. You can't just look for raw talent; that's nowhere near your level. There are only so many singers around who are even worth considering—and we know all of them!"

I wasn't going to be discouraged; I persevered. We had endless tapes coming in and there had to be something of value in there—or so I thought. We rehearsed five days a week: three hours were spent writing and the last two every day were spent listening to the mountain of tapes that came in. We listened to *all of them*. It was grueling. More than that, it was discouraging. I am amazed that we actually stuck it out as a band at all: we held it together for ten months doing that. I'm not sure that I can explain how bleak it got. That is, after all, why we listened to those tapes *after* we rehearsed. Usually they were so bad that we'd need to sleep it off just to be able to start fresh again the next day.

Most of them were so bad that we assumed that they were taking the piss . . . but we were never quite sure. Too many were like some guy in Wyoming who lived in a garage sending us his very best imitation of Guns. There were too many tapes by singers who just loved Guns to an unhealthy degree. I wanted to ask a lot of them if they'd actually listened to what they had sent us or at least played it for someone else before they sent it, and if they had what that person thought of it.

There were endless examples of guys doing really bad versions of "Welcome to the Jungle"; there were too many people who considered themselves poets submitting dramatic lyrics on a variety of subjects. We got folksingers, we got thrash-metal singers, we got people who sent us recordings that were so poor that I swear to God they must have recorded them on the mike in their boom box.

I was driving through North Hollywood one day thinking about how strange this process was. At the same time I thought that it should be

documented, because I knew that it was going somewhere. I thought that I should talk to my friend Eric Luftglass, a producer at VH1 about it, but literally before that thought got more mature, he called me.

"Hey Slash, Eric Luftglass. I hear that you and Duff and Matt are putting together a band and looking for a singer," he said.

"Yeah, do you know anyone?" I said.

"That's funny! No, but I wanted to know if you'd be interested in having us document your search for a VH1 special. It would be a great launchpad for the band. Hey, do you guys have a name?"

"No, we haven't gotten there yet. We're still stuck on the singer part. But wait, I swear, I was just thinking that I should call you to let you know about all of this."

Eric sent a pair of camera guys down to Mates and we weren't sure about how it would work. We decided to reserve judgment until we met them. They were both named Alex and they'd recently shot the Aerosmith episode of *Behind the Music*, which I'd enjoyed. We started hanging out with them and it was cool; they started to get casual behind-the-scenes footage of us. We had gotten some interesting demos that were pretty good; most of them were done with talented singers who were just not the right style for what we were looking for but they were good nonetheless. I estimate that one out of every two hundred demos we listened to was someone that intrigued us enough to have them come in to the studio. One of those was this guy named Steve from England who was pretty good. He was in a band called Little Hell, but I might be wrong about that. His band was almost punk rock with lots of attitude and sarcasm in the lyrics. We had him come out and he ended up on our VH1 special but nothing happened as far as his joining the band.

By this time about eight months had gone by since we decided to do this thing and we were starting to get weathered. It didn't help much when some bigwig at VH1 who had seen the footage of our show came down to the studio to tell us to "turn up the drama." The reality of us behind the scenes apparently wasn't cutting it, so we fought with the producers from that point on. In the end, the footage they captured of a few of the singers was made to look way more dramatic than it actually was. Unfortunately, our time with Sebastian Bach became the main theme of that program.

Among the professional singers we knew, Ian Astbury of the Cult came down to check out what we were doing (off camera); Sebastian Bach was also a contender, but that was never really considered as a possibility. We rehearsed with Sebastian for a while and even had him come into the studio to put vocals on a few tracks. At the time he was singing in a production of *Jesus Christ Superstar* and it was great to see this whole new professional side of Sebastian. Nonetheless, it didn't work out; it sounded too much like the sum of our parts, not like anything new—it was Skid Roses.

And throughout it all, Scott Weiland's name kept coming up. Everyone in the band knew him one way or another, except for me. Dave had been in a band called Electric Love Hog that had opened for STP, and Matt had been in rehab with Scott. Duff's wife, Susan, was friends with Scott's wife, Mary. I just thought he was a great singer, and he'd always been on my mind for this band. He was the one vocalist that I knew had the kind of voice that would serve what we were going to do: he had a John Lennon-ish quality, a little bit of Jim Morrison, and a touch of almost David Bowie. He was the best singer to come out in a long time in my opinion.

Since everyone else knew him, I told Duff to call him up. He did and he asked Scott if he'd like to hear some of our demos. Scott was into it, so we got four tracks together, got them recorded, and I brought them down personally to his apartment. At the time he was living on Blackburn, ironically, just a few doors down from where I'd lived with my dad for a while when I was a kid. That night he was doing a show with STP, so I left the CD on his doorstep and the rest of us waited eagerly for his call.

A week later he called us, and as positive as he was about the music and what he thought we were doing, he was honest about the fact that STP was still together. They were having their problems, but Scott was straightforward about the fact that he intended to stick it out and see where it was going.

"Listen," I said. "I don't want to try to drive a wedge between you and your band."

We left it at that. And Duff, Matt, Dave, and I went back to the tape pile . . .

WE ENLISTED THE ASSISTANCE OF MY old attorney, turned manager, Dave Codikow in our quest. It's a good thing we did, because as it continued to go nowhere, a few months later, David let us know that Stone Temple Pilots had broken up. I was happy to hear it—for entirely selfish reasons. I didn't really care about being polite; I asked Duff to call Scott right away to ask him if he was interested in coming down and checking us out.

We had just written the music to "Set Me Free," and we gave Scott the demo, asked him to listen to it and, if he liked it, to come by and see us rehearse—no pressure. He kept the track for a week, in which time he took it into his own studio and put a vocal track on it. At the time we were very much seeking him out, while Scott was trying to map out a plan for himself. He was unsure if what we had going on was right for him, but when we heard his vocal for that track, we knew that it was *exactly* what we'd been looking for: what he did was far beyond anything I'd imagined for that song. He took it to another level; it sounded different and better than anything we'd done up to that point. I've never asked Scott how he felt after he'd recorded those lyrics . . . all I know is that the rest of us were excited as hell. And I got the feeling he was, too.

Scott delivered the track himself that day; he came walking into Mates wearing one of those fisherman's hats pulled way down over his eyes and one of those surfer sweaters with a hood and two-sided pocket in the front. The door of our rehearsal room was about two hundred feet from the stage we were on, but even at that distance, as low profile as he was, he had an amazing presence that struck me immediately. When he came up onstage to say hello, it felt like I'd known him for a very long time. We got to talking, we listened to the demo he'd made, and it seemed like we were reconvening more than starting anew.

SCOTT'S VOCAL SOLD US. WE WERE TOTALLY committed; it brought together all of the elements that we'd been working on. The only problem was that he wasn't sure he wanted to join our band. He was thinking about recording another solo record and he also had some personal issues that he was trying to sort out.

Slash and Scott belting it out at the Avalon Ballroom in Hollywood in May 2007.

David Codikow, who with Dana DuFine had gone to work at Immortal as a management team, took an active interest in us and set up a showcase for the industry down at Mates. We performed just one song: "Set Me Free." Our audience was made up of music producers, musical directors,

and music coordinators from the big movie studios. Tom Zutaut was there, too—it was sort of like old times.

It was the first time the band had ever performed together for an audience. And that was interesting because Scott didn't show up until moments before we had to go on. We were scurrying to find him and he got there in the nick of time. We hadn't established the kind of bond with him to know what he'd done with his previous twenty-four hours so we were a bit on edge.

It didn't matter because when he got there we ripped into it, and from the first note all was fine. It was one of those situations where you're nervous before you play, but as you're standing there in front of those industry executives, and from the first note on, you know exactly who you are and you don't give a shit. There is nothing cornier than a showcase like that, but we were so into the song that we didn't care. We just did our thing and that was that.

It felt like a band. It felt like us against them again. We made a good impression on our own terms that day. That was first gear, but I knew that we were just getting going and wouldn't be stopped. The open road lay ahead.

WE TALKED ABOUT SCOTT GETTING CLEAN a lot, because it was definitely an issue. We let him know that basically all of us had been there and that we'd rally for him if he needed our support should he decide that he really wanted to get clean. We weren't pressuring him, we were showing him that we understood, firsthand (to say the least), and I think in the end that is what made him feel more comfortable. Once it seemed that Scott was in, we started taking it to the next level.

I THINK THE GREATEST THING ABOUT this band is that we never behaved like a new band; from the start we acted like we'd been together for years. I suppose in some ways we have. We found an appropriate vehicle to use as a first run for a band that had been together a while: David and Dana reached out to a few movie studios to see what films were coming out that needed an original song. We were

presented with a handful but we decided on *The Hulk* and *The Italian Job*, which were offered to us by Kathy Nelson from Universal, mostly because they seemed perfect and because we liked Kathy.

We went into the studio with Nick Raskulinecz, and did a cover of Pink Floyd's "Money" for *The Italian Job*. Scott nailed it and the whole thing came together very quickly. We rehearsed it at Mates in one afternoon, then took it to Chalis Studios in Hollywood and got it down. Then, for *The Hulk*, we went into Oceanway to do a proper version of "Set Me Free." We knew that track would be the one to establish our sound and we'd seen a rough cut of the film and liked it. Plus we were excited that Ang Lee was directing. We had Nick produce that track as well, but it wasn't smooth sailing: we had a hard time getting it mixed because we couldn't get it right. We ended up going through a series of mixes and eventually got it together the morning of the deadline.

That wasn't the most awkward aspect of that session: on the way down to Oceanway Studios to record the track I got a call (from Duff) telling me that Robert and Dean DeLeo from Stone Temple Pilots were producing Alien Ant Farm in the studio right next door to ours. I was very concerned about how Scott might react to that. I got down there before him to make sure nothing happened and I ran into Robert at the Sparkletts machine in the lounge. He was leaning over me as I filled my Solo cup with water, and I had no idea who he was.

"Uh, Slash?" he said.

"Uh, yeah. Hi."

"Hi, I'm Robert DeLeo. Nice to meet you . . . Much respect."

He seemed nice enough, but I was still worried about Scott. He came in through a back entrance so they didn't have to cross paths for the duration of that session.

Those soundtrack jobs were a test; we were putting ourselves out there in a controlled, limited way. We were a solid rock-and-roll band, but we hadn't made the final leap: Dave still had a day job as a construction worker at that point and Scott had been through a long and arduous decline in his last band, so he was still wary and fragile. Duff and Matt and I were one hundred percent committed: we'd dropped everything else at this point to focus on this band. So we persevered and moved forward.

Choosing a name was a recurring theme at rehearsal and we'd not really gotten anywhere on that front. One night Perla and I went to the movies and I can't remember what we saw, but once the lights went down and the credits came up, I was struck by the name "Revolution Studios." Perla mentioned something about it as well. There was something there . . . I liked the beginning of the word. And so I thought of Revolver. It seemed an appropriate name to me because of its multiple meanings: not only did it evoke a gun, but there was also the subtext of a revolving door, which, considering how many members of other bands this band was composed of, seemed entirely right. Plus of course it's the name of one of the Beatles' best albums.

The next day I met the band at Universal Studios, where we were going to see a screening of *The Hulk* to decide if we wanted to lend our song to the soundtrack. On the walk from Kathy Nelson's office to the screening room, I brought up my idea of the name Revolver as a possibility.

"That's cool, I like that," Duff said.

"I do, too," Matt said.

Scott was quiet for a minute. "How about Black Velvet Revolver," he said. "I like the idea of something intimate like velvet juxtaposed with something deadly like a gun."

I thought about that for a minute. I totally agreed with where he was going, but it seemed like a mouthful.

"Hey," I said. "How about just Velvet Revolver."

"That's cool," Scott said.

Everybody else agreed.

We were all on the same page and I was inspired; I sat down and started sketching logos right away. I came up with the VR that we are still using and everybody seemed to like that as well.

We were on a roll: we booked a small press conference and performance showcase at the El Rey Theater. It was primarily for industry people, but the public was admitted as well: we wanted to announce that we were officially a band, with a singer and a name, and we would be recording an album very soon. We had just written "Slither," so we did that; we did "Set Me Free," "It's So Easy," "Negative Creep" by Nirvana, and the Pistols' "Pretty Vacant." It wasn't so much a question of song selection; at the time those were the only songs we knew.

It didn't matter; the energy level was so high that it was just in-your-face. The chemistry of the band live was powerful stuff and as organic as it gets. That was the defining moment for us: we were finally a group. We had worked together in every capacity except for the most essential one—live performance. That El Rey show was the moment of truth. In the dressing room afterward, we were so inspired by our chemistry onstage that we didn't know what to do—should we make a record or should we just go on tour—right now?

<center>◆━━◆</center>

WE OPTED TO MAKE A RECORD BECAUSE that was the more practical thing to do. Besides, at the time we were in a writing zone and new material was coming to us very quickly. Before we'd gotten together with Scott, we'd been writing for over ten months, so to say that we overloaded him with potential songs to write lyrics for is an understatement. We gave him more than anyone could expect anyone to listen to.

He came through, though: he chose a few and turned them into things that we'd never have expected and loved all the same. Scott has a small studio and rehearsal space in Toluca Lake called Lavish, where he works with his engineer, Doug Grean. They took those demos and rearranged the music to accommodate the vocal parts that Scott came up with. Out of that huge body of material, we got "Big Machine" and "Dirty Little Thing," while we continued to come up with new stuff, like "You Got No Right," "Slither," and "Sucker Train Blues," which we all worked out, as well as a song called "Do It for the Kids," among others. Everything came together really cool.

It all seemed to be going great until Scott got arrested in the parking lot at Lavish one night: he was caught sitting there with some girl and they had drugs in the car. He was already on probation, and that was his last strike. It was a real turning point for him: when he was released from jail, he didn't go home, he went back to his studio. He cued up a piece of music we'd given him a while before. And he wrote the lyrics to the song that became "Fall to Pieces." Scott let it all out in that song: it's a more honest portrait of where he was and what he was dealing with at that particular time than anyone could ever hope to see. It really paints a picture of what was really going on with him, and consequently with us as well.

WE WEREN'T SURE WHO SHOULD PRODUCE
our record, so we tried out a few people; we threw around a few different
names: Rick Rubin, Brendan O'Brien, and a few more. I'm not exactly
sure who suggested Bob Ezrin, but we went into the studio and recorded
"Slither" with him at Henson Studios. He'd just done the latest Jane's Ad-
diction record, but aside from that, his past work with everyone from Al-
ice Cooper to Pink Floyd spoke for itself. It didn't go as well as I'd hoped
it would; Bob's creative input for the song was too produced. He had too
many things going on at once, using up too many tracks; the end result
sounded too congested and too complex for what we saw as a simple song
from a fairly simple rock-and-roll band.

We then decided to record a track with Josh Abraham, whom all of us
knew. He was relatively new on the scene; his big claim to fame was pro-
ducing the Staind record, which was a big hit. At least I was familiar with
it and at the time he was working on the new Courtney Love record. We
did a test track of a new song called "Headspace" with him at NRG Stu-
dios in North Hollywood. The track sounded good, the drums and gui-
tars and vocals sounded good. It was enough for us to decide to do the rest
of the album with him.

At that point the word was out about Velvet Revolver and we were
getting a lot of interest from all of the major labels, although there weren't
that many left at that particular time. There was Chrysalis, Elektra, RCA,
and Warner's, and they were all interested. In the end we went with
RCA.

But first we did the whole wine-and-dine free-lunch shuffle out in New
York for a week or so. It wasn't hard to decide who we'd go with once Clive
Davis got on a plane with his A&R guy, Ashley Newton, to come see us re-
hearse in Toluca Lake. It was a great show of integrity and solidarity consid-
ering the setting. They sat in a room that was about twenty feet deep, with a
pool table separating them from us and all of our amps right in their face.
They sat through five songs like that. They wanted to get past the hype that
now surrounded the band and see us play in our natural habitat.

"That was great, really great," Clive said when we were done. "Thank you."

They loved "Slither" and "Fall to Pieces," and pretty much after that, our mind was made up. We went with RCA.

After preproduction with Josh at Lavish, we moved over to NRG to do the basic tracks. Coincidentally in the studio next door, Dean and Robert from STP were working on some new stuff, once again, right next door to us. This time they were unavoidable; they were literally in the next room and we shared a lounge. It was only a matter of time before Scott ran into them no matter what we did, but it was cool. They'd gotten over it; Dean sat down with Scott and I don't know what they talked about, but afterward there were no hard feelings. Scott even played him our demos, all of us hung out, and it was all okay. That was the first time I met Dean, and I've seen both of those guys around since then and it's been nothing but fine—both of them are really good guys.

WHEN IT CAME TO RECORDING MY guitar parts for the album, I wanted to go into a smaller studio to save the band some money, so Josh suggested that we do them at his studio on the south corner of Highland and Sunset boulevards; it is where Jimi Hendrix recorded *Axis: Bold as Love*. I walked in and the place was just a bit funky: bad shag carpet, an old paint job, cockroaches . . . stuff like that. I got into the studio with Josh and there was a really nice mixing board, but I looked up and noticed that there were just two small Yamaha AS-10 studio monitors for speakers, which are great for listening to stuff back, but I record my guitar in the studio by placing my amps in the main room, where the microphones are, and playing in the control room, where the producer and the mixing board are. I do this mostly because I can't stand headphones. This setup was not going to work at all for my purposes. Up until then, as a rule, I'd recorded the basic tracks live as scratch-guitar tracks and redone them in the control room at megadecibel levels so that it felt like an actual concert when I truly laid them down. The monitor speakers are my reference points as to what I am recording, so they need to be big and they need to be *loud*. The pair in front of me weren't going to cut it.

"So is this how you record guitars?" I asked Josh.

"Well . . . yeah, usually these studio monitors are enough."

"I've never played that way and I can tell you right now that they're not going to be loud enough."

At that moment I thought of what my wife, Perla, had told me over and over again: I like to do things the hard way. I could see that I was throwing Josh and his whole studio setup into a tailspin. I wanted to work on that tendency of mine, so rather than make a fuss and insist that we book a new studio and perhaps a new producer, I chose to adapt.

"Listen, just call in some bigger speakers and we'll make it work," I said. Josh looked genuinely relieved.

I can't say that it was a pleasant experience. The studio engineers kept renting us new speakers but none of them did an acceptable job. That's not true—they got exactly the right set on the very last day of recording. In the end, I was satisfied with my work on our debut record, but when I look back on it now, it was a very uncomfortable, confining session for me. All in all, my playing is pretty reserved on that record, which is why there aren't as many solos as there could have been. I felt too restricted to improvise the way I usually do.

I think Dave got a lot more out of the digital studio setup than I did when he came in to do his parts. He did great; he added all of these sound textures that really made the guitars complete.

At the time Scott had been court-ordered to stay in a halfway house, a sentence that resulted from his arrest. He'd come in and do his vocals and then go right back. He was only allowed to work for three hours a day.

———◆×◆———

DUFF AND I WENT TO NEW YORK CITY to sit in on the mixing sessions with George Marino engineering and then *Contraband* was finished. I had my first drink in over a year that night. I remained pretty quiet about my feelings on the GN'R/Axl situation up until Duff and I did a promo tour supporting the release of Velvet Revolver's first CD. At that point, I hadn't gone public about what had transpired between Axl and me, and I hadn't planned on going there. But the media wanted to know my thoughts on the subject and I couldn't help it. I had nothing pleasant to say. It was as if they had touched a raw nerve, and suddenly everything that came out of my mouth was bitter and spiteful—the

complete antithesis of how I really wanted to react. When GN'R and I parted ways, I had honestly wanted to stay low-key and never bicker in the press, mostly because so many artists before me had gone that route and I thought it distasteful. But here I was, put in a corner with press in every direction, hungrily looking for controversy and prodding that raw nerve. I couldn't control my responses. Everything I said about Axl was negative; it was almost emotional. This, of course, pissed off Axl and was definitely the catalyst for rant against me in his 2005 press release, not to mention complicating the GN'R lawsuit even further.

While the CD was being packaged, Duff and I went on a press tour to promote it in Europe and Japan for a few weeks. The band went on the road before it even came out. Our first gig was in Kansas, and from there we hit every city in just about every state. We managed to generate enough buzz that when the album was released in June 2004, it went to number one in its second week. We were in Vegas for a show when Clive called us to let us know that we'd hit the top of the charts, and I have to say that after all I'd seen and all I'd done, getting a call from the legendary Clive Davis with news like that gave me goose bumps: it was an *arrival*, in my book. That was the start of a tour that seemed to keep going and going, building momentum the longer it went on. All in all we remained on the road for nineteen months, playing everything from clubs to festivals to stadiums.

The band played to crowds of thousands around the world and our record sold three million copies worldwide. We worked hard on that tour; we'd often play five nights a week, a different city every night. We did it all on a bus, in close quarters. We did Live 8, we did the Donington Festival, we put out three videos on that record. It was pretty successful; suddenly we were once again in a major band.

Our last gig was in Orlando, then everyone went home and resumed their lives. And once we did, we got into all kinds of shit. There were rumors that we were breaking up, there were rumors that all of us were back on drugs and on the verge of self-destruction, and too many more rumors to name.

◆━◈◈◈━◆

I, FOR ONE, YET AGAIN, DID HAVE A very hard time readjusting to being home. When we were writing *Contra-*

band, way before we went in and recorded all of it, my son London was born in August 2002. I had gone with Perla to get her ultrasound and at the time I was still getting my head around the fact that I had a child on the way—obviously this was going to be a new experience for me. That said, once I knew one was coming, I thought I wanted a little girl, figuring she'd be just like her mom and they would be inseparable, a notion that further fed my denial about my inescapable new responsibilities.

That was my little idyllic vision of fatherhood until I realized something I'd been ignoring: I have a hard enough time with grown women, forget about little ones. A daughter would probably be my undoing. I breathed a sigh of relief when Perla delivered a beautiful, healthy nine-pound baby boy. We named him London not only because he was conceived in the U.K. but because I'd had a friend with that name in grade school and never forgot how cool I thought it was.

I didn't have any experience raising children, obviously, but I did get some training. Perla felt an overwhelming rush of the maternal instinct when she first got pregnant, and one day she brought home a Pomeranian puppy from the pet store. The dog immediately became my responsibility, especially once Perla was ordered to a few months of bed rest. I was forced to raise this dog and that was my preparation for fatherhood. It was the only experience I'd had raising anything, because one thing is for sure—having cats and snakes doesn't really count. All things considered, I must have done something right because our dog was very well behaved by the time London was born.

Having a child forced me to be present; it insisted that I honor my sobriety. When I wasn't with Velvet Revolver, I was home with my wife, raising our son. I was the dad, assembling the nursery, shopping for toys, putting together the electric mobile sets. And then Perla got pregnant again. We found out that it was another boy, and I breathed another sigh of relief. Our new baby was a breech as well, though the complications didn't develop until later on in her term. It was rough on Perla once again.

I was on tour when my second son was delivered. I managed to fly home regularly to visit Perla in the hospital, but the day that my second son was to be delivered I had a show the night before. I had to fly from the hospital to Atlantic City on a red-eye then fly home on a red-eye to be there in time

for his birth the next morning. I missed my flight back to L.A. and was lucky enough to get another one. They had to hold up Perla's C-section until I got there. I went right to the hospital and arrived just before he was born. I spent that night and the next morning with Perla and my perfect new little eight-pound baby boy, then I flew back out and met the band at the next gig. Such is the life my two sons have been born into.

We didn't know what to name our second son until we remembered what our good friend movie mogul Robert Evans told us we should name our first son. As usual, he had a strong opinion that I couldn't deny.

"Give him the coolest name that a man could ever have," he told us in that signature baritone. "Name him Cash."

"Robert, it's too late," I said. "We've already named him London."

"All right. But if you get a second chance," he said, "do the right thing."

The family Hudson: Slash, London, Perla, and Cash on a Disney cruise in 2006 where they were undoubtedly the local outcasts.

After a very short period of deliberation, we decided that he was right. And so our second son is named Cash.

AFTER TWO YEARS AT THE FEVER PITCH

that is nonstop touring, I was once again dropped into the real world, and as familiar as I was with the condition, it hadn't gotten any easier to bear—if anything, it had become a harder adjustment to make. When all you care about is the grind of going from gig to gig, when the next show is the only thing you're looking forward to for an extended period of time, when room service and your hotel room are your reward, you exist in a very stylized mode of living.

Home, no matter who you are, is nothing like that. When you are home you have to get off of your ass and do things yourself; when you are home you become as normal as you'll ever be because you have to rely on your own faculties. In the past, I'd relied on booze and drugs to offset that transition and make it a bit easier to take in the short run. Once you have kids, if you intend to be a dependable parent at all, that option goes out the window: when you come off the road and you're a parent, you get home and you have to deal. You go from a situation where you're taken care of to one where you're taking care of.

It wasn't easy on either Perla or me when I got home. I had started drinking wine—a lot of wine—on tour, and she'd been watching me slip into my old ways once again. For whatever reason, when she came to visit me on tour, I chose that day to sit at the bar drinking, under the guise of waiting there for her. All that I accomplished was getting myself smashed to the point that I was useless when she finally arrived. I'd say hello and go pass out. So we had some issues to deal with.

WHEN VELVET REVOLVER GOT SIGNED,

got our album together, and set about preparing to tour, we underwent a change in management that I didn't agree with at all. This eventually led me to find my own manager separate from the band. In theory that sounded like a logical solution to me, but all that it did in reality was alienate me from the other guys and cause a great degree of animosity among us and among the management teams whenever a business arrangement came up. This situation added an extra level of stress that two years on the road did nothing but escalate. The tension never affected our chemistry onstage or creatively, but on a day-to-day interpersonal level, things were touchy, and by

the end of the tour, everyone was at one another's throats. I stand by my decision, but I understand now that it made me the pain in the ass of the band in the other guys' eyes. I get why I drove them nuts.

It was around this time that Axl chose to send out a press release that did nothing but add fuel to the fire. It's been widely documented, so I won't do it justice by going into it all, but in short, Axl released a statement claiming that I'd come by his house, extremely coherent, early one morning to ask him to please settle the lawsuit between us that had been ongoing for years at this point. It also claimed that he and I talked for a while and that I had nothing but disparaging comments to make about Scott Weiland and everyone else in my band.

The truth is, I haven't spoken a word to Axl personally since I left the band in 1996. It's sad but true. I did go by his house one night but I was drunk—Perla wasn't and she was driving. I walked up to the door and delivered a note that read something like "Let's work this out. Call me. —Slash." But I didn't give it to Axl, I gave it to his assistant.

In any case, Axl released his statement, and it was a big deal in the press because it was the first time Axl had gone public with his opinion about me, the lawsuit, or anything like that.

As I've said, this incident was widely reported in the press and on the Internet and anyone who is interested can go read all about it if they so choose.

The fact of the matter is, this incident and the resulting negative effect it had on Velvet Revolver was very unsettling to me; I can barely even talk about it still, let alone re-create it in detail here. I thought I was going to see everything I'd just finally gotten together fall apart.

First things first; the lawsuit was a nightmare that had gone on too long. For fear of further litigation, the easiest way to explain it is to say that since 2001 we were involved in a lawsuit over the rights and profits stemming from licensing and merchandise. It was a typical broken-up-bands litigation where one party complains of underpayment by another party. The road of rock and roll is littered with that kind of shit.

But what hurt the most was that I had to defend myself to my band. I showed up and insisted that what was alleged wasn't true, but the way that Axl had written this thing made it sound so matter-of-fact that everyone seemed to think it was.

The guys were very dubious about accepting my story. At the same time I was very sincere about telling them the truth. At first I thought I should respond publically, and told my band I would, but later decided it would only complicate the issue and prolong it.

I wasn't sure what to do; I still wanted to proceed—my credibility was riding on it. We had a band meeting a few days later and Scott didn't show; it was obvious to me that since I hadn't made a move, I'd let him down.

Then Scott released his own rebuttal. He attacked Axl on every level. And my instinctual reaction wasn't "you're right," it was "you can't talk shit about Axl!" I can talk shit about Axl, I can talk shit about Axl all day if I want to—that's because I've had to deal with him for years. But neither Scott nor anyone else has that right.

Tensions in the band escalated as a result and I got my gear out of Matt Sorum's home studio, where we'd been writing and rehearsing.

Word on the street was that I'd quit Velvet Revolver to rejoin Guns N' Roses. I don't know who started that rumor but it had legs long enough that it caused an exhausting internal battle. The media took a particular liking to that story: that Slash had ditched his former Guns bandmates to rejoin Axl in whatever his idea of Guns N' Roses was going to be. At that point I think *Chinese Democracy* was still thought to be on the way any year now.

It looked like what I was doing was a fact, but for the fact that I wasn't doing it. If you picked up any music paper around that time or listened to the radio or checked out blogs on the Internet, there was no avoiding it. It was etched in stone: I'd left Velvet Revolver, I was going back to Guns. The reality was that neither happened: during those few months I was just at home, recording musical ideas on my digital sixteen-track.

It literally was a waiting game: it took all of us a while to get past all of that bullshit. Finally, when it all went away, we got back to work. I just went over to Matt's house one day like nothing had ever happened.

"Listen, man," I said. "All of that was ridiculous and all of this is ridiculous. Can I tell you what really happened?"

"Yeah, man."

I said my piece, relating the story once again as it had gone down. Clearly, time had proven that I had had no reunion with Axl and that I

wasn't rejoining Guns N' Roses—because nothing had happened! That fact seemed to convince the guys that my version of events was the truth. I never felt that I'd needed to explain myself to those guys, but I had, which always pissed me off. But I got over it and so did they. After I had a one-on-one with Matt, I had one with Kirschner and then Duff and Scott. All in all, it was completely unnecessary drama, whether it was unsaid or not. I just didn't have the time for it. But we got through it. And we're all better for it today.

⬦

THE BAND FINALLY GOT TOGETHER AND started rehearsing at Matt's house, in his recording studio in his garage. Everybody was getting along again and we started to work on new material for our next record. It was at this time that I tore my rotator cuff working out in the gym and went to see a doctor. He prescribed a few therapeutic exercises and gave me a bottle of Vicodin. I knew damn well what Vicodin was and what effect it has on me, but in the form of a prescription from my doctor, it all seemed okay and actually necessary. I took the Vicodin as instructed, one every four hours. It soon became two every four hours, then one every hour, then one every fifteen minutes—that's just the way it works with me.

Not only was my band situation in jeopardy, Perla and I were at odds like never before. I was heading one way with the Vicodin and she was heading another way: after the birth of our second son, Perla wanted to lose all the weight she'd gained having children, and in doing so got addicted to prescription diet pills. Diet pills are basically a gourmet form of speed and she'd been taking them long enough indiscriminately that it had altered her personality. She was already a superattentive, superassertive person who was always a few steps ahead of me. Adding speed of any kind to that equation accentuated those traits to the point that she became too intense for me to deal with.

Our interactions were getting increasingly agitated, so I went to Las Vegas to take part in VH1's Rock Honors in 2006, where, along with my buddy Tommy Lee, we did a set of Kiss songs. While I was there I met up with my Oxy-connected friend and got more pills than I could handle. My

friend had beaten cancer but in the interim he'd allegedly gotten into a near-lethal car accident and had a newly unending prescription for them. When someone tells you they have a prescription like that, you don't ask questions.

By then I'd gotten familiar enough with the drug that I wondered what would happen if I crushed them up, liquefied them, and melted them down to inject. I was quite pleased to discover that it worked. I had a great time in Vegas; it was the perfect place to face the fact that that's where I was heading. I stayed there for a few days more than I needed to. I just got high. I was just chipping; I didn't have a habit. (Chipping is a here and there relationship with smack.)

I came back to my home and as my relationship went further downhill, I was self-medicating; I had a stash of Vicodin and OxyContin. Perla and I split up abruptly; we were apart for a day: I went to a hotel out near the airport. I packed up our Hummer with my clothes and my cat and in my mind I wasn't ever coming back. I wasn't at all a saint, but I couldn't handle where she was at. I told her that she needed to go to rehab.

She agreed. "If I'm going in, take care of the kids" was the last thing she said to me.

◆→◆

WHILE PERLA WAS IN REHAB IT GOT bad—our nanny took care of the kids while I maintained a healthy Oxy habit. I found an L.A. connection and bought about a three-month supply. And while I didn't do it every day, eventually I did it every night. I kept it from the band like I kept it from my family. But then eventually it crept in: I'd do a shot before rehearsal. I'd pursued the creative vibe with the band in a clear mental state, but eventually there I was again . . . foggy. It was so out of hand that I was shooting up in Matt's bathroom, and it was obvious to everyone that I was high. All the same, no one said a word, at least for a while, and it says a lot about our collective tolerance. I wasn't even trying to hide my habit from a band of guys who'd had their share of problems and a singer who still had his. I was so obnoxious about it that Matt even found blood on the wall. If my nodding out at rehearsal didn't give it away, that surely did.

We kept on keeping on, not really going forward, just kind of writing

Slash and his boys.

and creatively treading water. I accompanied Matt to a Camp Freddy gig in Vegas, not so much to see the show as to hook up with my Oxy connection and stock up. I thought I knew what I was doing but I don't think I'd realized how quickly I'd become the dark horse. I remember being backstage at that show: everyone would get quiet when I walked into the room. It was starting to be like that wherever I went.

My manager at that time and now is Carl Stubner, and while I was in Vegas he called me. We talked about a few things, and though I didn't realize it in the moment, he was listening carefully, trying to gauge where I was at. I don't remember what I was talking about but suddenly he interrupted me.

"Hey," he said. "Be honest with me. Are you okay?"

"Yeah, yeah, man," I said, lying. "I'm fine. Why?"

"Listen to me . . . I'm not going to tell you how to live your life and I'm not here to be a cop. I just want to know if you're okay. Because if you're not, I am here for you. But you have to be *honest* with me."

"I'm fine, really . . . Yeah, I'm fine."

I did the gig, I met my drug buddy, I came home to L.A. and knew I was too fucked up to be around Perla, who had come home entirely clean and sober, let alone be around our children. I did the only thing that made sense to me: I checked myself in to a West Hollywood hotel, and I scheduled the day that I would check myself in to rehab. Until that morning I intended to finish up the drugs I'd bought right there in my room or wherever they might lead me. Perla and everyone else was worried about me. But she was patient and tolerant and that is why we love each other the way we do.

I wasn't fine. But I was almost ready to admit it. I knew that my debauchery needed to end. I had planned to get some space from my wife and from my band after I'd allowed myself those predetermined four months to let it all hang out; I knew I was in need of some solace and quiet. And I got it. This time rehab turned out to be really good for me, because this time I surrendered. First I kicked the drugs, then I cleared my head and did some work on figuring out why I liked to put myself in the same position over and over again. Early in the morning of July 3, 2006, I checked into rehab. I did a full thirty days, I fully surrendered . . . I learned more about myself than I had ever thought was possible. And as of this writing, I've been sober ever since.

got back on track and we got down to recording and writing our second record, *Libertad*. It was a different experience; we were different people exploring new ideas, united by our camaraderie. There was a freedom to the whole thing that was refreshing; it was as if we'd truly grown, or maybe just grown comfortable with who we are as a band.

We'd started working with Rick Rubin back before I got sober; actually I believe it was before and after my Oxy binge. We were excited to do so for obvious reasons—Rick's track record is legendary. But it didn't really work out: Rick has his methods; he has his crew there to do the producing and engineering and every few days he pops in to see how it's going. Usually he's got a few bands set up like that around town.

That really didn't work for us. Rick would listen to a bit of what we were doing and tell us to take one part of a song and combine it with something else that he'd heard that he liked. We also got jealous of the fact that he was spreading his focus around, doing four albums at once. It felt like he was always leaving us to see another one of his concubines, and when he was there we didn't really connect—he sat back and let us go. Under those conditions it felt like this record would take us a year or more to complete.

We broke it off with Rick and moved our operation to Scott's studio, Lavish. Scott suggested that we give it a go with Brendan O'Brien, who had done most of STP's records. I'd only known him in that capacity. I liked him well enough when I talked to him on the phone and so we had him come in and everything just seemed to fall into place. Brendan liked working fast and hard and he insisted that every member of the band be present for every session. I think that is one of the best pieces of advice I could ever give to any band.

If one of us didn't show up on time, Brendan refused to work until everyone was present, which both whipped us into shape pretty good and motivated us to be there. But he brought more than just discipline to the equation, he brought a musicality that stems from the fact that he plays guitar, bass, and drums. At any given moment he could play along with us and it really helped the process. With someone that informed, we progressed very quickly.

OUR SESSIONS W.ERE CONSISTENT; EVERYONE was there, everyone contributed, and everyone appreciated what each player was doing. I didn't think it was possible, but the chemistry that came out of that mutual participation surpassed the first Guns sessions. Everyone was so inspired and everything we did, every experiment even, was very musical. We were playing great, Scott was singing great, and what we ended up using as the final tracks on the album were, for the most part, the first or second live takes of each song. That record is what happens when you pair a really good rock-and-roll band who loves what they're doing with a producer who really understands them and knows exactly what he's doing.

every day I'm glad I found the strength to take the high road.

PERLA AND I ARE BOTH ALL CLEANED up now and we're really happy. July 2007 will be my one-year anniversary, and I've gotten more done this past year than in the two years before that combined. You only get so many karmic "Get Out of Jail Free" passes; you're bound to run out eventually. So far I've been extremely lucky, so I'm not taking any more chances. A junkie has only two options, and I've got a long list of friends on both sides of the fence. They can get clean or they can get dead, and every day I'm glad I found the strength to take the high road.

If Memory Serves

I've been asked more than a few times why I decided to do this book at all and here's why: A few people who know me well kept telling me that I should do it—and finally I agreed with them. I was very reluctant to share my life in any way, particularly in a medium open to public consumption, most of all because I regarded a memoir as something you do when you've got no career left to speak of. That isn't the case for me, and even if it were, I wouldn't have much interest in that. It's not natural to regard your life objectively, but once I did, I realized that my story up until now made for something pretty entertaining. I also realized that if I didn't get it all down now, there was a very good chance that I'd forget it all. In the end I realized that this book would serve another purpose: it would put one era of my career to rest and signify the start of the rest of it.

I'd like to make one more thing pretty clear, because this is another question that haunts me almost every day, usually because it's asked by people who don't know me at all. I'd like to state, very simply once more why I chose not to continue on with Guns N' Roses so that no one feels the need to ask me this ever again when they see me on the street. Here it goes: 1) the constant disrespect for all involved by going on late for no good reason night after night after night, 2) the legal manipulation that Axl forced on us, from demanding ownership of the name to downgrading us, contractually, to hired hands, and 3) losing Izzy and Steven, who were such an integral part of the band's sound and personality . . . without them, the band no longer had its original chemistry.

My departure had nothing to do with artistic differences, as many people claim to know. It was not as simple as "Axl wanted synths and Slash was old-school." It had nothing to do with Axl wanting to go digital and Slash staying analog. To think that dissolving the kind of band and the kind of musical chemistry we had over something so trivial is just asinine. It's true, I am old-school, and I do like keeping it simple—but I've never been close-minded. If anything, I was more than flexible and willing to try any kind of recording technique or explore any new sound, so long as I was doing so on an equal playing field with musicians that

worked together toward a common goal. I would have hung in there with Axl through an industrial record or whatever else he wanted to try if the creative vibe between us was positive. My flexibility is the only thing that kept me in the band as long as it did—that's how a team works. Unfortunately, we stopped being a team somewhere along the way.

As for the rest of how it all played out, I learned, looking back on it all, that the people Axl hired to "represent his interests" through all of the band's undoing could have been a bit smarter than they were. Maybe intelligence has nothing to do with it: had they cared enough about him and about Guns N' Roses as a band to have advised him to pursue any other path than the one he did this story may have had a different ending. Anyone could have foreseen the lack of positive outcome that lay ahead on the road Axl chose to go down. But then again, maybe that is how he wanted it

MY BEST FRIEND MARC CANTER IS putting out a book that is the visual accompaniment to all that you read here. Here's a guy who way back when I was living at my mom's house, before junior high, always had an Instamatic in his hand and was snapping pictures. Marc came to as many of my gigs in high school, in Hollywood, and once I was in Guns as he could possibly get to. His ever-present camera was just part of Marc. I never thought anything of it and never thought that any of those pictures would ever be seen again. I never thought that a side effect of that hobby of his would be a pretty extensive and intimate chronology of everything Guns N' Roses did prior to 1988. All of it was just sitting around Marc's house all these years—until now. It is now a book of pictures called *Reckless Road*. I never would have expected my childhood buddy to be capable of such shots.

BEFORE I WRAP THIS THING UP I HAVE something important to say about my parents. In the retelling of my childhood, I emphasized the negative over the positive, because the negative aspects of how my family evolved ended up informing my decisions as a kid more than any of the positive ones did. The negative is what explains where

I turned in my youth. But what was lost in my re-creation was how my parents' positive influences taught me to be the person I am.

My parents were such a prominent, encouraging influence on me as a child during the years when I strove to find out who I was going to be. I couldn't have asked for better guides because they are, truly, two of the most creative people that I've ever met—and at this point I've met many. Both of them are amazingly talented, and though they didn't ultimately prove to be the right match for each other, they did see beyond their differences to raise their children in a unique and informed fashion. The way they brought my brother and me up was unconventional but infused with love and discipline that never veered into being overly domineering.

<hr />

I LIVE SO MUCH IN THE MOMENT THAT I've never daydreamed about the future beyond tomorrow. I've never related to those people who plan their lives five years down the line. As much as those types think they have control of their reality, I beg to disagree, because how much can anyone really "plan" what is going to happen to them beyond the next twenty-four hours? It's not that I don't care what happens five years from now, it's just that the next twenty-four hours is the stepping-stone to getting there.

I've found that just *being*, day to day, just waiting to see what comes, and going from there is the only way to grow. It's informed how I've dealt with Velvet Revolver in nothing but the best respect: we have come so far in so short a time. Whenever we're onstage, it's at once so familiar and exciting that it seems like our first show even though it's our thousandth. I'm consumed with what we're doing, I'm proud of the record we made in *Libertad*, and I feel that we're in a place where we are just now capable of tapping into what this band is really capable of.

At the time of this writing, our second record is just a few weeks old, but I can't wait to see where our next record is going to go. We're lucky; we stumbled upon something that is just beginning to evolve and it's doing so in such a positive way. As this book comes to a close, Velvet Revolver is about to embark on our first headlining tour of arenas and sheds. We got to that level by the end of our two-year promotion of *Contraband*, but this

is different: we're starting where we ended, and from there we can only build a bigger beast.

I'm happier than I've ever been musically. This band writes creative, earnest, complex rock and roll. It's not quite ironic, but as far as I'm concerned, it sure is funny that I found my future by revisiting my past. After looking around and ignoring the obvious so as to avoid anything that seemed like a revisitation, I ended up locking in with the guys I'd spent the better part of my career and my life with. And once we did, the past became an afterthought. And the present has been better than it has ever been.

As for the future, aside from playing in Velvet Revolver, at some point I want to do a record with all the players I've played with and admired over the years. I have a list of them, which is long. At this point, all that I know is that I plan to call it "Slash and Friends." I'm actually looking at my wish list of collaborators right now and no, I'm not going to tell you who is on it.

<hr />

I'M HAPPY TO SAY THAT I KNOW FOR A fact that as of summer 2007, Steven Adler is doing better. I've been helping him help himself to get off of crack, smack, and Jägermeister, which has been a compound addiction that has been ruining his life for the past quarter century. Counting from before he was ousted from GN'R, this is the longest that he's ever been clean. He has some pretty good people around him now and I'm happy to report that he seems genuinely happy.

Ron Schneider, my bass player in Tidas Sloan, is working with Steven as a tech/moral supporter. It's funny how things come full circle, even when you think your circle has expanded infinitesimally. At the same time, hearing about Ron's situation, I couldn't help but realize that almost everybody that hung around a lot with Guns N' Roses ended up becoming a junkie at one time or another.

<hr />

WHEN YOU REVIEW YOUR LIFE LIKE THIS, it's strange; there have been parts that I've looked at as if I wasn't there—I've read a few of these stories as if for the first time. But more than anything

you gain perspective; this kind of exercise isn't easy, but in the long run it's a really good idea.

It's a good thing to truly understand how and why I'm the same yet different than I've always been. It's as if my personality remains but my wisdom has grown. If there's one thing that made my bullshit recede, it's fatherhood. The reality that I was going to be someone's dad didn't kick in until I found myself staring at the assembly instructions for a crib. We'd just finished painting our guest room and there I was having to assemble this thing. There was no going back. And as much as I freaked out at that moment, after that I didn't *want* to go back. If anything I ran toward it, not away: I let myself be consumed with baby stuff, which is great, because I enjoy it.

All things considered, it came very naturally. Once I'd gotten the crib together, I knew it was real; I knew that we were going *in*. By the time that Perla and London and I were photographed for the cover of some baby magazine whose name I can't remember, I was totally into it. That photo shoot wasn't the cover of *Creem* or *Rolling Stone*, but I was pretty excited— we'd hit the big time on the baby circuit. And I was just as proud.

Being a parent has its moments where you find yourself doing what you are doing, but with this new little person who has integrated themselves into your life who's just . . . *there*. Kids become a part of your everyday existence so instinctually and so naturally that before you know it they're there . . . and you can't remember what life was like when they weren't.

My boys are three and five and I've started catching myself, at least once or twice a day, realizing how fast they are changing and growing. It's a constant reality check. How can it not be? When your four-year-old stands in front of you defiantly and argues like you're both equals, how can you not ask yourself "Is this *happening*? Am I negotiating with a four-year-old?" I wouldn't have it any other way: Perla and I made beautiful kids, and our personalities are so strong in them that it's entertaining to us. They are definitely a product of their parents. . . . In fact they're a mirror of their parents: they are both defiant yet sweet.

Slash and Velvet Revolver in Santa Barbara, September 2007.

Photography Credits

Interior

Photographs by Gene Kirkland appear on pages:

ix, 136, 192, 219, 223, 232, 234, 242, 266, 294, 312, 334. 348, 382, 387, 434

Photographs by Marc Canter appear on pages:

28, 48, 58, 66, 72, 89, 93, 134, 155, 174

Photographs by Ola Hudson appear on pages:

xii, 2, 6, 8, 12, 19, 22, 326

Photographs by Karl Larsen appear on pages:

416, 459

Photographs courtesy of Perla Hudson appear on pages:

402, 414, 444

Photograph by J.Nez appears on page

450

Photograph by Jack Lue (recklessroad.com) appears on page

110

Insert